BRETONS &
BRITONS

BRETONS & BRITONS

The Fight for Identity

BARRY CUNLIFFE

OXFORD
UNIVERSITY PRESS

OXFORD
UNIVERSITY PRESS

Great Clarendon Street, Oxford, OX2 6DP
United Kingdom

Oxford University Press is a department of the University of Oxford.
It furthers the University's objective of excellence in research, scholarship,
and education by publishing worldwide. Oxford is a registered trade mark of
Oxford University Press in the UK and in certain other countries

First Edition published in 2021

Impression: 1

Published in the United States of America by Oxford University Press
198 Madison Avenue, New York, NY 10016, United States of America

British Library Cataloguing in Publication Data
Data available

Library of Congress Control Number: 2020945333

ISBN 978-0-19-885162-2

Typeset by Sparks—www.sparkspublishing.com

Printed in Great Britain by
Bell & Bain Ltd., Glasgow

In memory of Pierre-Roland Giot
and for Patrick Galliou

PREFACE

A T one level this book is a simple narrative: a history of Brittany from early prehistoric times to the beginning of the twentieth century. Its real purpose, however, is to explore the fascinating subject of identity: how a people living in a remote peninsula of Europe, to distinguish themselves from their neighbours, created and fought to maintain a distinctive culture. The sea played an important role in protecting them, but it also enabled a close relationship to be built up between the Bretons and the Britons, forming a bond that has developed over the years. Today increasingly large numbers of people travel on Brittany Ferries between the ports of Plymouth and Roscoff and Saint-Malo and Portsmouth to spend time in each other's countries, their journeys echoing those that began in prehistoric times and have continued ever since.

While Breton identity and the relationship between Bretons and Britons are the main themes of this narrative, underlying it all is a desire to pay homage to a country and a people I have come to know and admire over the last sixty years. In 1960, when an undergraduate at Cambridge, I attended a lecture given by Pierre-Roland Giot, doyen of Breton archaeology, and later sent him a photograph of a Bronze Age arm-ring of Breton type that had recently been found in west Sussex. It began a correspondence that continued over the years, accompanied by a deluge of offprints of scientific papers that he and his colleagues had published. A few years later, after I took up a post at Southampton University, we became neighbours separated only by the sea, and contact was more frequent. Giot was a generous colleague who loved sharing his country with his friends. In doing so he ensured that Brittany featured large in the European narrative.

Patrick Galliou is another Breton scholar who has always seen Brittany as part of the wider world. We shared interests in the Roman period and it was when we were discussing late Roman coastal defences that he suggested we might co-direct an excavation at the site of Le Yaudet, a fortified promontory at the mouth of the river Léguer occupied in the Late Iron Age and throughout the Roman period. It was evidently a key site in understanding cross-Channel interactions. Excavations began in 1991 and were to last for twelve happy seasons, involving Breton, British, and Spanish students. During this time we were made welcome by the local community, enjoying both their hospitality and their enthusiasm. Those friendships have continued and have grown. Returning now, several times a year, to the little settlement of Pont Roux in the shadow of Le Yaudet is like coming home.

This book, then, is a labour of love written to celebrate the forces that have bound our two countries, and in profound appreciation of the ever-fascinating Breton countryside. Above all, it is a tribute to the remarkable resilience of the Breton people.

B.C.
Oxford and Pont Roux
August 2020

CONTENTS

PROLOGUE

THIS book is about the people who have lived on the peninsula we now call Brittany, a slab of land on the edge of Europe jutting into the fierce Atlantic. To the land-bound French the western extremity of the continent has long been known as Finistère, 'the end of the earth'. But to the inhabitants their peninsula was the centre of the world: it was the rest of Europe that was peripheral.

Remote places like peninsulas and islands have a particular fascination because, to distinguish themselves from outsiders, their communities spend much effort in defining and protecting their cultural identity. Islanders find it easier because they are surrounded by the sea, which gives them a degree of control over the acceptance or rejection of external influences, but those who inhabit peninsulas are less fortunate. While the sea offers welcome protection on many approaches, there is always a land border making the territory vulnerable to intrusion. They may try to fortify it, creating a marcher zone, but more often the border is vague and porous, allowing easy access to outsiders. This is why peninsular people have to work hard, not only to safeguard their culture but to intensify their differences with their land neighbours, the better to distinguish themselves from the alien 'other'. As one social anthropologist put it, remote places are 'the very crucibles of the creation of identity'.

The sea is all-important. It provides a barrier to unwanted outside interference while at the same time it allows maritime networks to develop, offering connectivity. By embracing overseas neighbours and becoming part of a broader maritime community peninsula dwellers can further enhance the distinctiveness of their culture in contrast to their continental neighbours. The sea also binds maritime people together.

The narrowing strip of the Atlantic which we call the English Channel or La Manche separates the Breton peninsula from the parallel coast of southern Britain, itself ending in a peninsula comprising Devon and Cornwall. The narrowness of the Channel seaway has allowed close contact to develop between communities living along confronting coastlines. These links began to be forged seven thousand years ago and have continued to develop ever since. Many generations of Bretons have looked to their British neighbours as compatriots whose values they shared, while the neighbouring French were considered to be a threat to their culture and their being.

Remote places are, by definition, on the edge of the familiar world. When viewed from the centre, they are distant and peripheral: irrational places where reality fades into fantasy. In the popular imagination Brittany has been seen as a land where ranks of warriors were turned into rows of stone. It was a place of enchanted forests with magic fountains providing a haunt for Druids and later the magician Merlin of the Arthurian romances: it was a twilight zone where anything was possible. Remote islands, too, were steeped in mystery. The Greek writer Strabo described several islands off the coast of Brittany where strange rites were enacted, and when some Roman soldiers were shipwrecked on the British shore sometime before the Roman occupation of the island, they reported monsters, half-man and half-beast, lurking in the persistent mists. These far-western fragments of land, washed by the ocean, were in the thrall of irrational powers and their magic.

0.1 Ernest Renan (1823–92) was born in Tréguier in Brittany. His father and grandfather were fishermen. He was educated in the local seminary until the age of 15 and went on to become a scholar of international reputation: historian, philologist, philosopher, and critic. The statue, erected in Tréguier in 1903, caused much controversy. It shows Athena, pagan goddess of wisdom, applauding the seated Renan, who stares critically across the square at the cathedral.

In the minds of the romantic, remoteness takes with it a wistful nostalgia. In such places live primitive people untouched by the corrupting grasp of civilization. These are 'noble savages' whose simplicity is to be envied. They are the product of their landscape and their isolation. In the mid-nineteenth century this romantic ideal was at its height, especially in writing dealing with the Celtic-speaking people of the west. It is nowhere more clearly expressed than by the Breton priest and scholar Ernest Renan (1823–92). In an emotive and somewhat over-indulgent passage, he introduces his beloved Breton countrymen, beginning by detailing the change in landscape experienced by a traveller passing from Normandy into the Breton peninsula:

> A cold wind arises full of a vague sadness, and carries the soul to other thoughts; the tree-tops are bare and twisted; the heath with its monotony of tint stretches away into the distance; at every step the granite protrudes from a soil too scanty to cover it; a sea that is almost always sombre girdles the horizon with eternal moaning. The same contrast is manifest in the people: to Norman vulgarity, to a plump and prosperous population, happy to live, full of its own interests, egoistical as are all those who make a habit of enjoyment, succeeds a timid and reserved race living altogether within itself, heavy in appearance but capable of profound feeling, and of an adorable delicacy in its religious instincts.
>
> *The Poetry of the Celtic Races* (1854; translation by W. G. Hutchinson)

Here, then, the stern purity of the Bretons, moulded by the harsh landscape, is contrasted with the lush life of the self-indulgent Normans. In this striking antithesis the Bretons are given their identity. Renan was writing at a time when Brittany was desperately trying to hold onto its own distinctive language and culture in the face of intrusion from outside: crushing French bureaucracy and an increasing flood of tourists. But thus it has always been. Remote peoples suffer from two opposed forces: attempts to incorporate them in the wider world and the corrosive effects of those who come to be amused by the exotic. By actively resisting such forces through the ages the inhabitants of Brittany have forged a distinctive otherness. This book attempts to trace their remarkable story.

1

THE LAND
AND THE SEA

MANY writers who have tried to explain the distinctiveness of the Bretons and their culture have seen the harshness of the Breton landscape as one of the determining forces. The point is most strikingly made by Ernest Renan, writing in 1854 (above, pp. 2–3), but it was already apparent earlier in the writing of the folklorist Émile Souvestre (1806–54), in particular in his *Les Derniers Bretons*, published between 1835 and 1837, and recurs as echoes in the work of novelists like Gustave Flaubert and Guy de Maupassant, who both made extensive tours of Brittany (below, pp. 374–5). Geographical determinism can be taken too far, but landscape does affect people and their culture. A glance at any map, particularly a geological map, shows that the Armorican peninsula has a dominant east–west grain caused by its geological formation. Communication from north to south is difficult, except where the rivers Rance and Vilaine and the Blavet and Trieux create routes across the peninsula. This tends to separate the interior from the coastal regions and to give a much greater prominence to the sea as a means of communication. But while coastal traffic along the north and south coasts was not difficult, to sail from one to the other around the dangerous Pointe du Raz and past Ouessant, particularly in the face of westerlies, was a journey needing particular skills, not to be embarked upon without a pressing reason. Geography, then, tended to affect both perception and reality. The communities living on the north and south coasts formed two separate groups, the sea giving each a degree of cohesion, while the interior, always more sparsely populated, remained largely isolated.

There was also the east–west gradient. The distance across the neck of the peninsula where, as it were, peninsular Brittany joined the mainland of France is about 140

1.1 The sea-girt promontory of Armorica (Brittany), thrusting far into the Atlantic, provides a focus for the maritime networks connecting the peoples of the Atlantic façade. Occupying this extremity of Europe, the Armoricans were able to play a significant part in trade while maintaining a distinctive identity.

kilometres measured between the Baie du Mont-Saint-Michel and the Loire estuary. It provided a broad interface across which cultural influences and invading forces could pass with comparative ease. The two principal towns, Nantes and Rennes, both in existence by Roman times, became centres where the culture of the east and west met, but once across the rivers Vilaine, Ille, and Couesnon, eastern influences decreased and the peninsular culture became increasingly strong. In more recent times it has become conventional to divide Brittany into two broad regions: Basse-Bretagne (Lower Brittany) in the west and Haute-Bretagne (Upper Brittany) in the east, Basse-Bretagne being the region in which the culture of the Breton people has retained its distinctive quality and where the language is still spoken.

In the Beginning

The westernmost peninsulas of Europe that now thrust into the Atlantic Ocean are, for the most part, composed of old hard rocks: heavily folded and metamorphosed sediments with periodic intrusions of crystalline granites and volcanic rocks. The Breton peninsula is the western extremity of such a region. Known as the Armorican Massif, it extends eastwards into Basse-Normandie as far as the valleys of the Sarthe and Orne and south into the Vendée to the northern edge of the Sèvre valley. The Armorican Massif is part of a sinuous zone, zigzagging across Europe, comprising the Ardennes, Vosges, Morvan, and Massif Central to the east and north and the Atlantic zone of the Iberian Peninsula to the south-west. It owes its origin to plate tectonics: the movement of parts of the earth's crust on the surface of its viscous core. When two of the earth's plates collided, a zone of metamorphosed rocks was created, further compressions causing the edges to ruck up, forming mountain ridges. Along this zone of instability volcanoes spread ash and lava, and molten rocks welled up, creating the granite masses so evident in Brittany and south-western Britain.

There were two main phases of intense mountain building. The first, known as the Cadomian orogeny, took place between 650 and 550 million years ago. During this time the mudstones, siltstones, and sandstone of the region that was to become Brittany were forced up into mountain ranges, metamorphosed by the extreme pressure and heat, and penetrated by intrusive masses of granite. Then followed a long period of erosion and the deposition of more sedimentary rocks before the second phase of mountain building, known as the Hercynian (or Variscan) orogeny, created new mountain ranges about 380–280 million years ago, accompanied by further granite intrusions and volcanic activity. Since then the mountains have been gradually eroded until now they have been reduced to an undulating peneplain mostly between 100 and 300 metres above present-day sea-level. These episodes of mountain building and erosion have given rise to the very distinct east–west grain so evident in the Breton landscape, the harder rocks created by the compression, standing out as narrow ridges.

Thus the big story, but recent detailed geological work has added some intriguing details. About thirty million years ago what is now north-western France and Britain comprised three different plates, Armorica, Avalonia (England and Wales), and Laurentia (Scotland), all moving in relation to each other and colliding. The Armorican plate first pushed up against the Avalonian plate and then the two pulled apart, shearing along the line later to become the English Channel, leaving a small sliver of the Armorican plate—now Cornwall and south Devon—stuck to the Avalonian

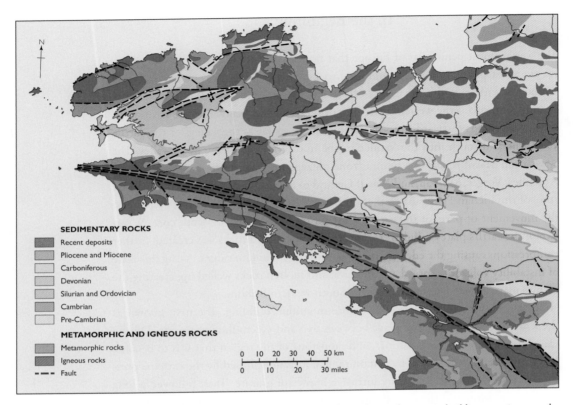

1.2 The complex geology of Brittany was the result of two phases of mountain building, one 650–550, the other 380–250 million years ago, each followed by a period of intensive erosion. The mountain-building episodes, when the land was forced up by lateral pressures, created the ridges and faults which give the peninsula its predominantly east–west grain. At various stages molten masses intruded into the crust from below, cooling to become igneous rocks like granite.

plate. This explains why the southern part of the south-western peninsula of Britain is so similar to Brittany.

In more recent geological times, during the Ice Ages (470,000–12,000 years ago), Brittany escaped glaciation, though for long periods of time, together with southern Britain, the region became a cold, bleak tundra. During the last phase of the glaciation, bitterly cold winds blowing across the tundra from the north carried very fine particles of dust, which were deposited over parts of southern Britain, the Channel Islands, and northern Brittany, creating a blanket of fine clayey soil called loëss (*limon* in French), which covered the eroded surface of the old hard rocks to a depth of up to a metre. Today's highly productive vegetable-growing region along the north coast owes its fertility to the loëss.

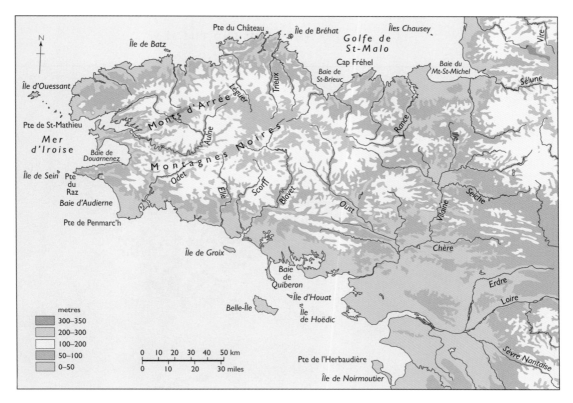

1.3 Intensive erosion following the last mountain-building episode has left Brittany as a fairly level peneplain mostly between 50 and 300 metres above sea-level. The highest point, in the Monts d'Arrée, is only 384 metres. The river system has cut through the east–west ridges, creating routes from north to south.

1.4 Brittany is part of the Armorican Massif, one of the earth's plates which, in the distant past, collided with each other. When Armorica bumped up against Avalonia, the two plates stuck together. Later, they pulled away from each other, leaving part of Armorica, now south Devon and Cornwall, attached to Avalonia.

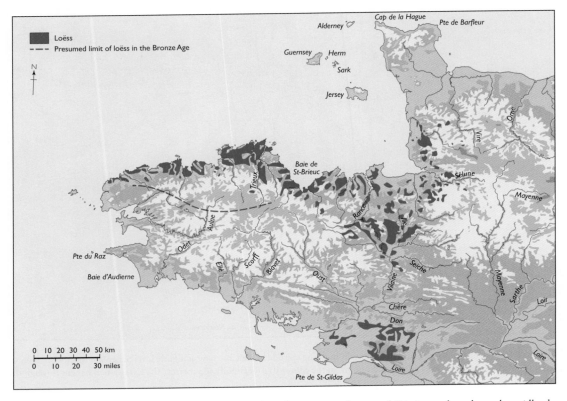

1.5 During the Last Glaciation, when the ice covered most of Britain southwards to the midlands, southern Britain and Brittany were tundra. Wind blowing from the ice cap carried fine sediment, which was deposited over parts of southern Britain and Brittany as a loamy clay known as loëss. The loëss deposits remaining in northern Brittany have created a highly fertile soil.

At the end of the last Ice Age, about 12,000 years ago, the water locked up in the ice caps began to melt, causing the sea-levels to rise. Before this, at the height of the last glaciation, when the sea was 100 metres below its present level, the English Channel was an area of lowland crossed by innumerable rivers flowing into one main channel, which gradually widened into an estuary as it reached the sea somewhere between western Cornwall and the north-west corner of Brittany. The rising sea inundated this lowland zone. At first the rise was rapid. Between about 9000 and 7000 BC the sea rose from −50 metres to −16 metres. Thereafter the rate slowed so that by 4500 BC it had reached about −3 metres, since when the rise has been even more gradual.

By 9000 BC the sea had reached nearly to the cliffs of northern Brittany westwards of the Trégor, but further to the east the gulf of Saint-Malo, including the Channel

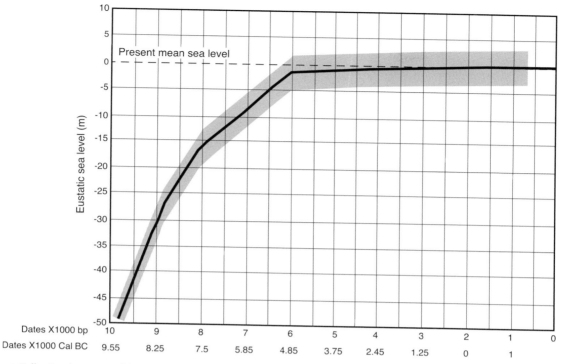

1.6 Following the retreat of the ice sheet at the end of the last glacial period, the sea-level began to rise, rapidly at first and then more slowly. Many attempts have been made to plot the change. The Lambeck curve, shown here, calculated in 1997, shows the main trend. The shaded area on either side of the line represents the range of variation assuming a 3-metre tidal range.

Islands, was still land. It was not until 5500 BC that the sea was high enough to isolate the Channel Islands, though there were still large expanses of low-lying land off the western coast of the department of Manche. But by this time the Breton peninsula had taken on its familiar shape.

The Land

The Gaulish word Aremorica, after which geologists have named the Armorican Massif, means 'the land facing the sea' and, like the geological term, was used to include much of north-western Gaul between the Loire and the Seine. The peninsula, therefore, is part of a more extensive geological region. The Bretons have tradition-ally distinguished between the ocean-facing Armor and the forested inland regions, the Argoat. This is far more than just nomenclature: it goes deep into the soul of the people, reflecting very different values and ways of life. The point is well made by the Breton writer Pierre-Jakez Hélias, who, in his description of early twentieth-century life, stressed the stark divide between those who looked to the sea for their livelihood and those living only a few kilometres inland, who relied on the land to sustain them and firmly turned their backs on the sea.

The coastal regions of Brittany, the Armor, were favoured environments. Those who worked the land along the northern coasts had the advantage of the fertile, well-drained loëss soils, which they could enrich with seaweed collected from the extensive intertidal zones, while the more acid soils could be treated with the shell sands readily available around the heads of the bays. The littoral zone itself was rich in resources: molluscs, crustaceans, fish, seabirds' eggs, and edible seaweeds. All could be harvested for much of the year, with little effort, to supplement the diet of cereals, milk, and occasional meat. Cropping the coastal resources has left many physical traces: engineered trackways across the intertidal zones for the carts collecting seaweed, stone-built fish traps in the estuaries to capture fish on the falling tide, and barriers across narrow inlets which could trap the sea to power tidal mills, at the same time making it easy to net fish as the seawater flowed out through sluices. Those living close to the littoral were indeed fortunate. In contrast, those who lived inland had little to fall back on in times of crop failure or when their livestock suffered from disease or decreased fertility.

Given the richness of the maritime resource, it is no surprise that through time people favoured the coastal region for settlement. This is evident by looking at the distribution of Neolithic settlements, passage graves, and artefacts, all of which cluster along the coast with particular emphasis on the southern coastal region, encouraged perhaps by a more favourable, warmer climate. In later prehistoric periods, as the population increased, the inland regions were more widely colonized, but the draw of the sea is still evident in the Roman period, when, apart from two towns, Vorgium (Carhaix) and Condate (Rennes), most of the rest of the nucleated settlements were within 40 kilometres of the coast. The Armor–Argoat divide was even more evident in the medieval period. Records of tax returns in the period 1426–43 allow the population densities of each commune to be plotted. The entire north coast and selected enclaves along the south coast had densities of more than six households per square kilometre, while in much of the inland region, except around Rennes, there were fewer than four households. This disparity has continued, and indeed has been intensified since then by internal migration. Statistics for the period 1831 to 1954 show a steady flow of population from the inland areas to the major towns, which, with the exception of Rennes and Carhaix, all lie in the coastal zone.

1.7 The coasts of Brittany, because of the large tidal variation, are productive of a wide range of seafood—molluscs, fish, crustaceans—as well as seaweed and shell sand collected and spread on the land as a fertilizer. The image shows the estuary of the river Léguer, from the promontory of Le Yaudet, at low tide. The estuary has been a rich food resource for the local inhabitants from the prehistoric period to the present day.

The interior of the Breton peninsula is altogether different, for long dominated by the *landes*: uncultivated tracts including moorland, heath, marsh, and other waste, and great expanses of forest. Surveys undertaken in 1733 showed that about 46 per cent of the land area of Brittany was uncultivated. By the time of the Napoleonic survey in 1807, the departments of Finistère and the Morbihan in the west and south were still 40 per cent wasteland, though in the northern departments of Côtes-d'Armor and Ille-et-Vilaine the waste had been reduced to 20 per cent. A vivid, if perhaps somewhat jaundiced, view of Brittany is given by the English agronomist Arthur Young, who travelled around the peninsula on his second journey to France in 1788 (below, pp. 347–8). He was not impressed by 'all the wastes, the deserts, the heath, ling, firz, broom and bog' he had crossed on his three-hundred-mile journey. At Montauban he wrote, 'One third of what I have seen of this province seems uncultivated, and nearly all of it in misery.' At Châteaulin, which is more hilly, he found the soil to be good, though 'one-third waste . . . no exertions, nor any marks of intelligence'. Young's lively observations confirm the extent of the *landes* given in the surveys of 1733 and 1807. That so much land was uncultivated he was content to assign to the indolence and ignorance of the people rather than to the poverty of the soil.

The most extreme tracts of *lande* now surviving lie towards the western end of the peninsula where the land rises to two ranges of hills, the Monts d'Arrée and the Montagnes Noires, separated by the Châteaulin basin. Neither range includes a true mountain, the highest point being Roc'h Trevezel in the Monts d'Arrée, which rises to a mere 384 metres, but their dominance is accentuated by the general flatness of the land about. It is from the Montagne Saint-Michel in the Monts d'Arrée that the barren moorland and the lakes and marshes are seen at their most impressive.

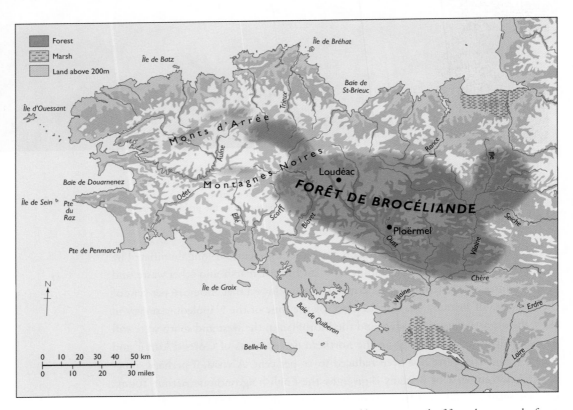

1.8 In the past much of the centre of Brittany was covered by a great swath of forest known as the forest of Brocéliande, which gave way in the west to the heathlands of the Monts d'Arrée and the Montagnes Noires. The eastern edge of the dense forest together with the marshes of Dol in the north and La Grande Brière in the south presented a significant barrier to those approaching the peninsula from the east.

1.9 The Monts d'Arrée (Menezioù Are, in Breton), once a great mountain range belonging to the Armorican Massif, have been eroded over millions of years to form an upland plateau below 400 metres. It offers a barren landscape of moors and crags lying at the heart of Basse-Bretagne.

The Argoat is, by definition, a forested area (Breton: *ar*, 'next to'; *koad*, 'forest') and there can be little doubt that much of the interior of Brittany was once extensively wooded, the density of the tree cover varying with the underlying soils. The most famous woodland in the early Middle Ages was the forest of Brocéliande, in tales current at the time, home to Arthur, Merlin, and the other personalities peopling the Arthurian romances. Originally the great forest extended west of Rennes for a distance of 140 kilometres. All that now remains is the forest of Paimpont, reduced to some 7,000 hectares. To the west of Brocéliande is another forest remnant: the forest of Loudéac north-east of Pontivy. Further west again lies the forest of Quénécan. The forests were a major resource not only for the deer and wild boar hunted by the elite but also to provide pannage (the right to pasture pigs) and leaf fodder for cattle. In 1419 pannage was paid on 1,497 pigs and 1,409 cattle fattened in Brocéliande, and

1.10 The forest of Brocéliande once occupied a vast region in the centre of the Armorican peninsula, presenting a significant barrier between the communities of the north and south coasts. It was a place of mystery and legends where the stories of King Arthur are set. Though now much reduced in extent, areas of the forest still survive, of which the largest is the forest of Paimpont.

in the thirteenth century the viscounts of Rohan raised wild horses in the forest of Quénécan. For all its remoteness and lack of easy communication, the Argoat could provide a good living for those prepared to make use of its varied resources.

The Sea

For the communities living in the coastal regions the sea was central to their well-being. The coastal waters provided access to fish and allowed local journeys to be made in inshore waters, keeping land in sight. Longer journeys could be made across the open sea, northwards across the Channel to Britain and southwards crossing the Bay of Biscay to the coast of northern and western Iberia. Sailors from these distant lands could also make the crossing to Brittany. There is ample evidence, as we will see later, that long-distance journeys were being undertaken across the open sea at least as early as the Mesolithic period. The implication is that serviceable boats were available from early prehistoric times and that among the coastal communities there were men with highly developed navigational skills.

Of boats before the first century BC we know little. Log boats carved from a solid tree trunk were in use from the early Mesolithic period. Such vessels would have functioned well in rivers and estuaries and, fitted with outriggers or joined together in pairs, would have been serviceable in coastal waters and even the open sea in the right conditions. For longer journeys at sea the skin boats made of hides sewn to a light wooden framework would have been more suitable. Several classical writers refer to such vessels in Atlantic waters in the later centuries of the first millennium BC, and a gold model of the first century BC, found at Broughter in Northern Ireland, gives a brilliant evocation of such a craft. It had eight seats for rowers, a stern steering oar, and a mast cross-rigged for a sail. In a favourable wind a light but sturdy vessel of this kind would have sped across the waves, its oarsmen coming into their own as land was approached and the pilot began to guide the craft to a safe landing. The suitability of such vessels to Atlantic conditions is shown by the continued use of the currach in western regions of Ireland to the present day, the only significant differences being that tarred canvas is now used in place of hides.

The technique of building boats from planks was certainly under way by the middle of the second millennium BC, facilitated by the production of sharp bronze axes and adzes. Several plank-built vessels have been found in British estuaries, the earliest being the Dover boat, dating to about 1500 BC. Though substantial constructions, they had a low freeboard and would have taken water in high seas, but under favourable

1.11 An early first-century AD coin issued by the British king Cunobelinus shows a ship, cross-rigged and with high bow and stern, just like the vessels of the Veneti described by Julius Caesar.

conditions they could have made open-sea journeys and it is possible that some may have been fitted with removable masts and sails.

It was from these comparatively simple craft that vessels with deeper plank-built hulls were developed requiring transverse ribs to keep the structure rigid. The first glimpse we have of these in Breton waters comes from Julius Caesar's description of a sea battle between the Romans and the native Veneti in the Baie de Quiberon, off the south coast of the Morbihan, in the summer of 56 BC. Caesar was impressed by the Venetic ships. They were high-sided and solidly built with their timbers nailed together with massive iron spikes, and were provided with sails of raw hide and iron anchors attached by iron chains (below, p. 162). Here were vessels honed to face the ocean. Ships of this kind continued to be used in Atlantic waters throughout the centuries of the Roman occupation.

The skills of the shipwright developed over the millennia; so, too, did those of the navigator. For those who kept to coastal waters local knowledge of the landmarks, the shoals, reefs, and the tides was essential. The massive tidal range—some 16 metres in the Baie du Mont-Saint-Michel—required the pilot to carry with him a detailed mental map of the constantly changing coastal environment in his sphere of activity. Those engaged in coastal trade would have chosen to stay as far out to sea as possible, well away from the hazards of the inland waters. Since the Breton peninsula is generally quite high, the pilot could have steered his course 15–20 nautical miles out to sea and still kept the land in sight sufficiently to be able to recognize the landmarks that gave him his position. Only when he approached his landing would he need to call up his knowledge of the coastal hazards he was about to face.

Those who made cross-Channel voyages required an additional set of skills: knowledge of the changing tidal flows through the Channel, the ability to navigate out of sight of land using the stars and the sun, experience in judging speed, and the all-important skill of distinguishing the underlying swell (mother wave), generated by a strong prominent wind, long after the wind has died down. Armed with this knowledge, and with an understanding of many other signs, like the clouds which formed above the distant land and the flights of birds at dawn or in the evening, the practised navigator would have been able to guide his craft across the Channel or on the rather more hazardous journey across the Bay of Biscay to Galicia.

Where and when these navigational skills were first developed it is impossible to say. Hunter-gatherer communities in the Palaeolithic and Mesolithic periods would have used celestial phenomena to guide them back to their home bases after long hunting expeditions, and evidence for deep-sea fishing suggests that people were taking to the open sea in the Mesolithic period. Certainly, by Neolithic times long-distance journeys were being made along the Atlantic face of Europe. Sea lore accumulated, to be passed from one generation to another, always committed to memory. Each navigator carried with him a mass of detailed information which he could recall, aided by rhythmic recitations, enabling him to create a mental map of his voyage, but once at sea he had to be alive to a constantly changing environment in order to maintain his course and come safely to land. To take to the sea was to enter a liminal space governed by unknown forces. The point was well made by a classical thinker, possibly the poet Anacharsis, who said, 'There are three kinds of men: the living, the dead, and those who go to sea.'

Networks of Communication

Although any route could have been taken across the Channel, it seems likely that, over time, favoured ports of departure and entry will have emerged. The most desirable would have been those providing a safe, sheltered anchorage with good onward routes, usually by river, leading to the interior. An added advantage would have been ease of approach with clear landmarks to guide the incoming vessel and a safe channel free of hazards like shoals, sandbanks, and reefs. The coast of Brittany and of south-western Britain has many such places, rias, created when the sea-level rose, flooding the lower reaches of the river valleys. All will have played a part in maritime activity but some, by virtue of their special qualities, became particularly favoured and have produced abundant archaeological evidence of trade over a long period of time: places like Alet (near Saint-Malo) and Le Yaudet on the north Breton coast, Nacqueville near Cherbourg, Mount Batten near Plymouth, and Poole Harbour and Hengistbury Head on the coast of Wessex. All were in use in the first century BC, but several show evidence of earlier maritime activity.

What routes linked the favoured ports we can only speculate, but in the first century BC Alet and possibly a port in the Baie de Saint-Brieuc were in direct communication with Hengistbury, the voyage probably taking in Guernsey en route, while Nacqueville was trading with either Hengistbury or Poole Harbour or both. At the western end of the Channel there is some evidence to suggest that Le Yaudet was in contact with Mount Batten. Thus, there may have been two main communication axes: an eastern axis linking north-eastern Brittany and the department of Manche to central southern Britain and a western axis between north-western Brittany and the south-west peninsula of Devon and Cornwall. Those plying the eastern route would have had to deal with stronger tidal streams than those in the western Channel, but they would have had the advantage of being out of sight of land for a much shorter time. In addition to these two cross-Channel axes there would have been lively east–west networks along both coastlines providing connections between the two systems.

The southern shore of Armorica was part of a separate maritime system linking the peninsula to the western coast of France as far south as the Gironde estuary and incorporating the Loire estuary. The two major rivers, the Loire and the Gironde–Garonne, offered easy access into central and southern Gaul. The maritime route along the south coast of Armorica to the Gironde posed few navigational problems, a chain of offshore islands, Groix, Belle-Île, Noirmoutier, Île d'Yeu, Île de Ré, and Île d'Oléron, offering sea-marks and convenient landfalls if required. South of the Gironde the coast is far less congenial, with long sandbars backed by marshes as far as the Pyrenees. The Cantabrian mountains along the north side of the Iberian Peninsula presented an inhospitable face to anyone approaching by sea until Galicia was reached at the north-west extremity of Iberia, where the deeply incised ria coastline offers ample safe havens.

Sailors wanting to make the journey from Galicia to Brittany had several options. They could choose to make the direct journey on a bearing east of north across the Bay of Biscay. An alternative route would have been along the north coast of Iberia to somewhere in the vicinity of Gijón, then taking to the open sea to make for the Gironde before following the coast northwards. Since the summer currents favoured the direct, cross-Biscay route and the winter currents were better suited to the longer route via Gijón and the Gironde, it is quite possible that people travelling between Galicia and Brittany set out in winter, keeping in sight of land for much of the way, and returned across the Bay of Biscay in late summer. In all, the round journey itself would have taken in the order of fifty days.

The western extremity of Brittany with its three great promontories, les Abers, Crozon, and Cornouaille, and its scattering of islands including the much-feared Ouessant, swept by treacherous fast-flowing currents and frequently batted by storms coming in off the Atlantic, was an uncongenial place for sailors. While ship's masters were prepared to face these perils and to round the peninsula, the need to do so was reduced by developing overland routes using the main river valleys. The harbours which commanded these river mouths gained added importance as places of transhipment.

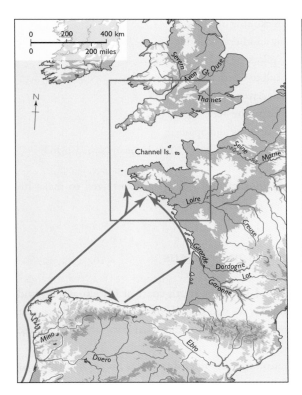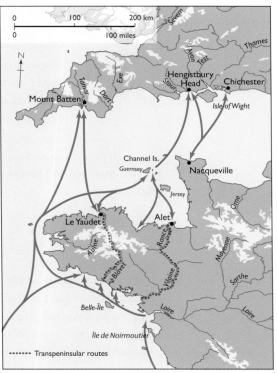

1.12 The sea-routes linking Brittany to other parts of western Europe were many. Those shown here are all attested by archaeological evidence and have been in use from at least 4000 BC to the present. While some may have chosen to sail round the peninsula, transpeninsular routes via the major river valleys also formed an important component of the communication network.

From the earliest development of sea-going boats, ship's masters would have learned the vicissitudes of the waters in which they chose to sail and the character of the individual harbours and havens that gave them safe shelter. This accumulated wisdom, passed on from generation to generation, was essential for survival. One such man was the skipper of the *Maudelayne*, a character encountered in the General Prologue to Chaucer's *Canterbury Tales*. This thirteenth-century sailor from Dartmouth, tanned brown by the sun and riding a farm horse with evident difficulty, was something of a rogue: 'few were the rules his tender conscience kept'. He stole wine at Bordeaux, captured ships, and made his prisoners walk the plank. But, that aside, he was an experienced seaman. 'Hardy he was, prudent in undertaking, his beard in many a tempest had its shaking.'

As for his skill in reckoning his tides,
Currents and many another risk besides,
Moons, harbours, pilots, he had such dispatch
That none from Hull to Carthage was his match. . . .
And he knew all the havens as they were
From Gotland to Cape Finistère,
And every creek in Brittany and Spain.

(translation by Nevill Coghill)

He had mastered the knowledge of the Atlantic seaways and survived to make his pilgrimage.

Harbours and Havens

Of the many harbours and havens used along the south coast of Britain and around Brittany over the last ten thousand years we will select a few, from among those that have produced evidence of prehistoric activity, to illustrate what it was that made these places so attractive to mariners.

Saint-Malo–Saint-Servan at the mouth of the river Rance was not, at first sight, an obvious choice since its approach was strewn with reefs and sandbanks, but the river offered a wide channel and access to a rich hinterland, and the topography of the land on either side of the estuary was distinctive, allowing the pilot to recognize where he was and position his vessel for a safe approach. The rock upon which the fortified town of Saint-Malo was built in the twelfth century lay to port; to starboard was the Pointe du Moulinet, while dead ahead was the rocky peninsula of Saint-Servan. Once in the estuary the boat could be guided around the southern side of the Saint-Malo rock into the large tidal basin protected from the sea by a long shingle bar which joins the rock to the mainland. Alternative landings were to be had in the Anse des Sablons on the north side of the Saint-Servan peninsula or the smaller Port Solidor on the south side.

In the first century BC, the topography of the estuary was slightly different. A long shingle bar ran north-westwards from the Saint-Malo rock and another bar ran south-eastwards from the southerly tip of the Saint-Servan peninsula, creating a freshwater lagoon between it and the land. At this time the Saint-Servan peninsula was a fortified settlement with trading links with the Channel Islands and Britain. Settlement continued throughout the Roman period (it was now called Alet) and in the late third century a defensive wall was built around the edge of the peninsula. A rise in sea-level eventually broke the southern bar, allowing Port Solidor to be used by shipping. It was probably at this time in the fourth century that a small offshore rock, the Bastion de Solidor, was fortified as a command post. Alet continued in use into the early Middle Ages. Its first cathedral was built at the beginning of the ninth century and rebuilt on a grander scale at the end of the tenth. But in the twelfth century a new settlement, Saint-Malo, was established on the better-protected northern rock and thereafter became the foremost port of the region, but it was only in the late nineteenth century that the mouth of the lagoon was barred and provided with a lock so that a series of permanent sea-water basins could be created.

A second favoured port on the north coast of Brittany was Le Yaudet in the estuary of the river Léguer. The river flows into a wide bay, the Baie de Lannion, its northern and southern limits marked by headlands, Pointe de Bihit and Pointe de Séhar. Once inside the estuary, the promontory of Le Yaudet confronts the sailor, guarding the point at which the river valley narrows. Le Yaudet was occupied in the Bronze Age, and by the Iron Age had become a substantial settlement protected by an enclosing rampart. Occupation continued in the Roman period, and in the third century AD a defensive wall was built. Thereafter occupation has been continuous until the present day. The attractiveness of the site was its protected position with three safe anchorages on the west, north, and east sides, but Viking raids in the tenth century showed it to be vulnerable to attack from the sea. It was because of this that the focus of settlement moved 6 kilometres upriver to a convenient crossing point where the town of Lannion developed.

There were many other ports along the north coast of Brittany that could have been used in prehistoric and Roman times and had developed into significant settlements by the medieval period, but archaeological evidence is lacking or sparse. Of these Cesson on the Baie de Saint-Brieuc and Morlaix further to the west have produced Roman finds, and both could well have been Roman ports or even fortified naval bases in the later Roman period. On the west coast, Brest, situated on the well-protected Rade de Brest, was a fortified naval base from the late Roman period, and further south on the Baie de Douarnenez a major fishing port was operating in Roman times. On the south coast, Quimper on the river Odet was a centre of occupation in the Iron Age and went on to become a Roman town, while another major Roman town, Darioritum (Vannes), developed on the north side of the almost landlocked gulf of Morbihan. Nor should we forget Nantes, situated at the first bridging port of the Loire. Somewhere hereabouts was the famous Iron Age trading port of Corbilo. Later, the Roman town of Condevicnum was established, which grew to become the medieval city of Nantes.

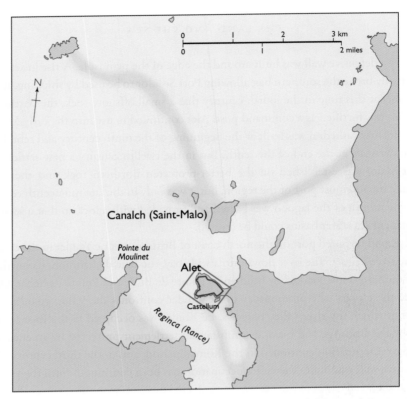

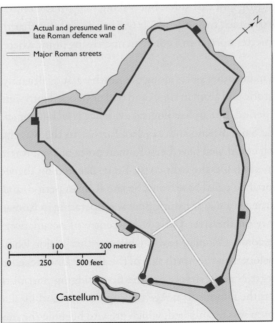

1.13 The estuary of the river Rance was a significant point of entry. The first major settlement, dating to the early first century BC, was at Alet. The site continued to be used in the Roman period and was provided with a defensive wall in the late third century. It was still a thriving settlement in the late tenth century, when the cathedral was rebuilt on a grand scale. In the twelfth century the settlement moved to the rocky island of Canalch, where Saint-Malo was founded and still thrives.

1.14 The medieval walled town of Saint-Malo commands the entrance to the estuary of the river Rance. It was originally a rocky island joined to the mainland by a sand-bar. Nearby (*near top, slightly left of centre*) is the promontory of Saint-Servan, which also controls the approach to the Rance. Known as Alet, it was fortified in the Iron Age and the Roman period.

The entire coastline of Armorica with its many rias offered hundreds of places where sailors could seek shelter and offload their cargoes.

On the British side of the Channel one of the principal points of entry in the pre-historic period was Christchurch Harbour, dominated by Hengistbury Head, which projects from the mainland and partially encloses a large sheltered harbour. Its attrac-tions were many. Approaching by sea from the south, the pilot would first have seen the land-mass of Purbeck to port and the Isle of Wight to starboard. If he positioned his vessel midway between Durlston Head and the Needles, the distinctive shape of Hengistbury Head would appear on the bow. Keeping the headland on the port side, he would reach the wide entrance to the harbour. Now the entrance is closed by a spit of land, leaving only a narrow, fast-running channel, but the spit is a compara-tively recent phenomenon. In the prehistoric period the entrance would have been at

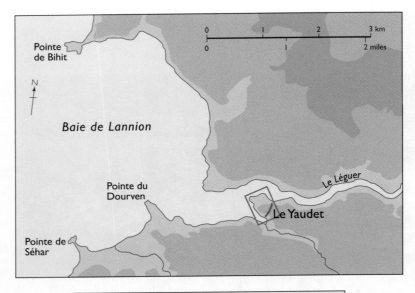

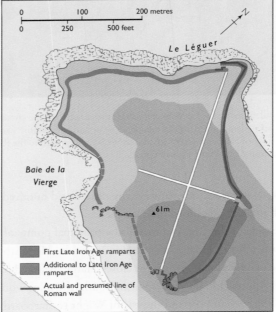

1.15 The estuary of the river Léguer is dominated by the promontory of Le Yaudet, occupied from at least the Bronze Age. In the first century BC a massive earthwork was built across the neck of the promontory and lesser earthworks protected the outer edge of the headland. Later, in the late third century AD, a masonry defensive wall was built. The site has been in continuous occupation since the Late Iron Age.

1.16 Le Yaudet from the air. The promontory has landing places on all three sides where ships can be beached in safety.

least half a kilometre wide. Once in the safety of the harbour the ship's masters would have sought shelter along the northern side of the headland, where there were gravel beaches suitable for hauling up the vessels. The other great attraction of Christchurch Harbour was that it lay at the confluence of two major rivers, the Stour and the Avon, giving access to much of Wessex, one of the most densely occupied and fertile parts of Britain.

There is ample archaeological evidence of the use of the headland from the Upper Palaeolithic period until the end of the Iron Age. In the Roman period the port was abandoned in favour of Poole Harbour to the west, but in the seventh century AD a new settlement called Twynham was founded on the gravel promontory at the confluence of the two rivers. In the early Middle Ages, now called Christchurch, it became a flourishing port, but with the silting of the harbour and the development

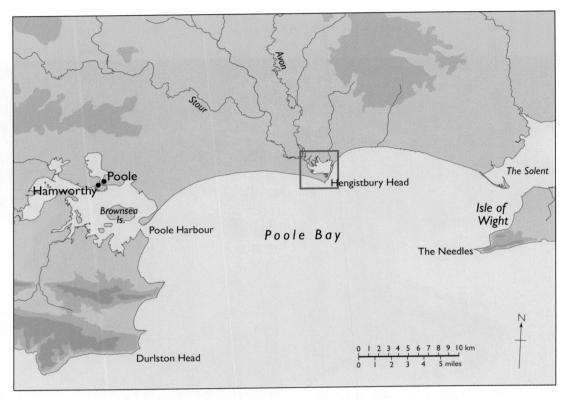

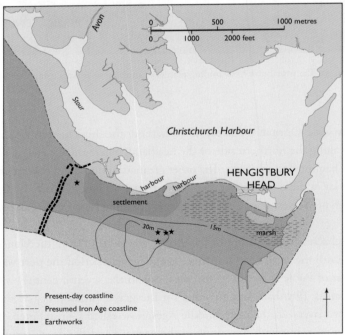

1.17 Hengistbury Head protects Christchurch Harbour, a large enclosed stretch of water into which the rivers Avon and Stour flow. The headland was occupied from Upper Palaeolithic times and was a major port of entry in the Neolithic and the Bronze Age. In the Late Iron Age it became a port of trade visited seasonally by Armorican traders. It seems to have been little used in the Roman period, and in Saxon times the focus of settlement moved to the site that is now Christchurch, at the confluence of the two rivers.

1.18 The promontory of Hengistbury Head, now much eroded by the sea, was, in the Iron Age, twice its present width and was defended by a massive earthwork across the landward approach (*far left*). The Iron Age settlement lay on the sheltered north side of the headland. The rivers flowing into the harbour provided access to the Wessex hinterland.

of the sandbar across the entrance its prosperity waned as nearby ports at Poole and Southampton grew in importance.

The second British port to consider is Mount Batten in Plymouth Harbour, where the rivers Tamar, Tavy, and Plym come together. It is a classic example of a ria, where the lower reaches of the river valleys have been flooded by rising sea-levels, creating a maze of sheltered deep-water channels. The rivers flow into the sound, a bay about 5 kilometres wide and of equivalent length enclosed by a wall of cliffs on three sides, at the head of which is the modern town of Plymouth. Mount Batten is a small rocky island, now joined to the mainland by a narrow neck of shingle, sited where the estuary of the river Plym enters the sound. It was in regular use throughout most of the first millennium BC into the Roman period by communities actively involved in cross-Channel trade. The site was well chosen. It was easy to defend and commanded two excellent anchorages, Cattewater and Hooe Lake, but it was of limited extent and it was probably this that eventually encouraged the growing community of fishermen and traders to move just across the water to the promontory where Plymouth was established at the edge of the small but well-protected Sutton Harbour. The particular attraction of Mount Batten in the late prehistoric and Roman period was its access to metals, particularly tin and copper, which could be found on the edge of the Dartmoor massif just to the north. Little is known about the extraction of the ore at this time, but it is likely that the tin was now streamed from the alluvial gravels fringing the moor. The discovery, in a first-century BC context at Hengistbury Head, of a lump of copper ore with a high silver content, identified as coming from Callington on the western edge of Dartmoor, is a tantalizing hint of the coastal trade there must once have been along the southern shores of Britain.

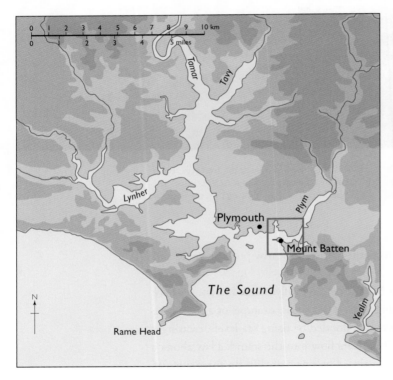

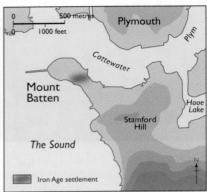

1.19 Four rivers flowing from Dartmoor converge into a single large estuary, Plymouth Sound. A rocky promontory, perhaps once an island, now known as Mount Batten, served as a port of trade during much of the first millennium BC. Through the port metals, copper, tin, and some silver, all obtained from Dartmoor, will have passed. From medieval times the nearby town of Plymouth became a flourishing port and a major naval base.

In addition to the two main ports of trade on the south coast of Britain, there were many other convenient points of entry on navigable waterways. Southampton Water, leading to the rivers Test and Itchen, provided access deep into Hampshire. In the late Roman period a naval base was established at Clausentum, and in the early Middle Ages the nearby port at Hamwic served as the port of the royal town of Winchester upriver. Hamwic was short-lived, to be replaced by the growing port of Southampton. Further west, the Isle of Portland, guarding Weymouth Bay, was used by traders in the Late Iron Age. The southern coast of Devon had many ports. Of these, Exeter on the river Exe, probably used in the Iron Age, became a Roman town. There is also evidence of prehistoric shipwrecks (or at least detritus from ships) in the Erme estuary and Salcombe Bay. Finally, in Cornwall, St Austell Bay, Falmouth Bay, and Mount's Bay, dominated by St Michael's Mount, all offered convenient landing places for maritime traders.

The four ports chosen for detailed discussion here give some idea of what it was that attracted sailors to particular places. As the more congenial landfalls became known among the maritime community, and more frequently used, so their commercial importance will have increased. But maritime environments are ever-changing. Sandbars can form as coastal currents shift, and the silting of channels can be triggered by many events, not least sea-level rise and fall. Even minor variations can render favoured havens unusable. Changes in boat construction, too, can have their effect, larger vessels requiring deeper-water approaches. Nor should we forget the dislocating impact of the outbreak of hostilities. So it is that the patterns of maritime connectivity are kept constantly in flux.

Armorica

Armorica, the land girt by the sea, is, and always has been, a huddle of different regions (*pays*) each with distinctive characteristics and each, until recent times, speaking its own dialect of the Breton language. It is a patchwork born of geography. The wide coastal zone encircling the hilly, forested interior is cut into blocks by deep river valleys, each block given character by the quality of its soil and the subtleties of climate. Brittany, then, is not a single entity but a clustering of different microenvironments within which communities have developed their own character. What gives these disparate groups coherence and their sense of being a people is their peninsular location, sharing the sea and confronting alien influences threatening to arrive landwards from the east. But the sea gives more than a degree of protection and an easy

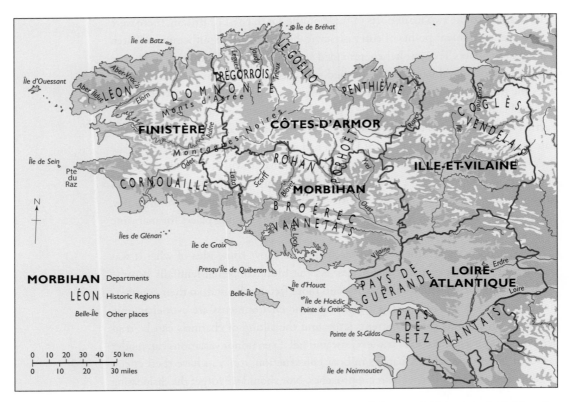

1.20 The Armorican peninsula is made up of many *pays* (sub-regions). Today it is divided into five departments created in 1790, Finistère, Côtes d'Armor, the Morbihan, Ille-et-Vilaine, and Loire-Atlantique, the first four constituting the region of Brittany as it is now defined. Its many *pays*, determined largely by their distinctive geography, have their origins far back in time.

means of communication. It creates a resilience built of expectation and a sense of unboundedness. With the sea as a partner, albeit a fickle one, anything is possible. Renan is surely right: it is the bleak landscape and the ever-mournful sea that have created the Breton.

2

CLAIMING THE LAND
6000–2700 BC

T OWARDS the end of the Last Glacial Maximum, between twenty thousand and eighteen thousand years ago, an ice sheet covered Scandinavia and the British Isles as far south as the midlands. At this time the sea was about 100 metres below its present level and Britain was joined to the continent. Between the ice front and the Alps and Pyrenees lay a bitterly cold tundra. The warming of the climate and the thawing of the ice, which heralded the period known as the Holocene, saw the relationship of the land and sea begin a long period of readjustment. It was a complex process driven by two forces. Most dramatic was the release of huge quantities of water from the melting ice caps, causing a rapid eustatic rise in world sea-levels, but in some areas this was countered by an isostatic rise in the land as the weight of the ice sheet was lifted. Areas like Scandinavia and Scotland, once depressed by the thickness of the ice, rose rapidly, but beyond the limits of the ice cap the rise was much slower. The eustatic rise in sea-level and the isostatic rise of the land were in competition. The adjustment continues today in Britain about an axis roughly from Anglesey to the river Tees, with Scotland rising in relation to the sea by about 2 millimetres a year while south-eastern Britain is sinking by about the same amount.

In the area of the English Channel and around the Armorican peninsula, overall sea-level rise was at first rapid and then gradually slowed. By 9000 BC the sea was at about −52 metres, at 8000 BC −40 metres; by 7300 BC it had reached about −30 metres, and by 5500 BC it was in the order of −4 metres. In this last period, with the sea-level rising about 1.4 metres in a century, the encroachment of the sea upon the land would have been noticeable—a fearsome fact of nature wondered at, remembered, and passed on from one generation to the next. Where cliffs were sheer and land rose rapidly from the sea, such a rise in sea-level would have had comparatively little effect on lifestyles, but in other areas, like the Baie du Mont-Saint-Michel and the southern Morbihan, where the land was shelving, slight rises inundated large areas, turning them first into intertidal zones and then into open sea. Since a lifetime would have seen major changes, the inexorable power of the sea cannot have failed to make a deep impact on the minds and beliefs of the people. It is tempting to think that the Breton legend of the drowning of the city of Ker Is may have had its roots in these long-distant memories.

Hunter-Gatherers in All their Variety

Climatic improvement following the end of the Last Glacial Maximum turned the once barren tundra of the Armorican peninsula into a highly congenial environment for hunters and gatherers of the Epipalaeolithic and Mesolithic periods (c.12,000–4800 BC). The wooded inland regions provided a variety of game like red deer, wild boar, roe deer, and aurochs as well as a wealth of smaller creatures—beaver, fox, marten, and wild cat—useful for their fur, while the coastal regions abounded in food such as fish, shellfish, crustaceans, and a wide range of seabirds living on the cliffs and in the marshes. Even a few grey seals were caught and the occasional stranded whale made a welcome addition to the food stock. Nor should we forget the rich plant life available for the gathering in the inland forests, the river valleys, and the shores and estuaries.

By the Late Mesolithic, about 6000 BC, it is possible to distinguish two cultural groups, named after archaeological sites: the Retzien, occupying the Vendée and Loire-Atlantique, and the Téviecien, in the central and western parts of the Armorican peninsula. Téviecien communities were the more conservative, but Retzien groups, influenced by Neolithic communities living to the south in the Mediterranean zone, developed new types of arrowhead. It is in this difference that we can see for the first time the isolating effect of remoteness on communities living in the western parts of the peninsula.

The Téviecien are named after a Neolithic shell midden site found on what is now the tiny island of Téviec off the coast of the southern Morbihan. It is one of four Mesolithic shell middens known on the south coast of the Armorican peninsula, the others being on Île de Hoëdic, off the coast of the Morbihan, Beg-er-Vil at the end of the Quiberon peninsula, and Beg-an-Dorchenn on the Penmarc'h peninsula further to the west in

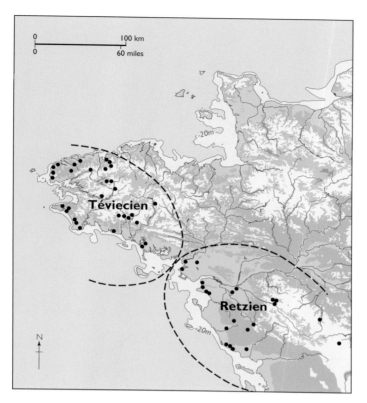

2.1 In the Late Mesolithic period two broad social groups can be recognized based on their techniques of making flint tools. The Retzien were more innovative and were receiving new influences from south-western France, while the Téviecien were more conservative, adhering to traditional methods.

Finistère. All four sites are midden accumulations of marine molluscs representing the food detritus of Mesolithic foraging groups who used the same bases over a long period of time. At Téviec the accumulation was up to a metre thick, while at Hoëdic it varied from 0.3 to 0.5 metres. The importance of such deposits to archaeologists is that the intense concentration of shells counteracts the natural acidity of the Breton soil, preserving bones of animals, including humans, thus providing a detailed insight into the fauna collected by the hunter-gatherers.

Téviec and Hoëdic differ from the other two sites in that they had both been used as cemeteries as well as for habitation. At Téviec ten graves were found holding the remains of twenty-three individuals. They had been cut through the midden and into the beach deposits below, while at Hoëdic nine graves were found containing fourteen individuals. These were placed in depressions in the bedrock at the base of the midden. Since the sites had been partly eroded by the sea, and only a sample had been

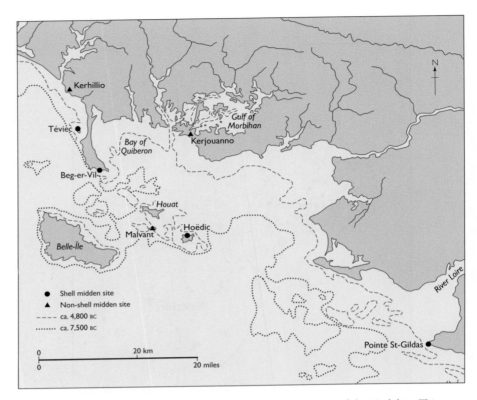

Kerhillio

Téviec

Bay of
Quiberon

Beg-er-Vil

Gulf of
Morbihan

Kerjouanno

Houat

Malvant

Hoëdic

Belle-Île

River Loire

Pointe St-Gildas

● Shell midden site
▲ Non-shell midden site
--- ca. 4,800 BC
..... ca. 7,500 BC

0   20 km
0   20 miles

N

2.2 A number of Late Mesolithic sites are known in the coastal regions of the Morbihan. This was a time of rapidly rising sea-levels, when coastal zones were being inundated and islands formed. It was an environment rich in varied food resources, especially shellfish, crustaceans, and fish.

excavated, the original number of burials is likely to have been significantly higher. At Téviec seven of the ten graves contained multiple burials, while at Hoëdic three of the graves contained more than one skeleton. In all cases the latest skeleton was found to be intact and articulated, while the bones of the earlier burials had been disturbed and moved aside. Various grave goods accompanied the dead including flint implements, utilized stones, bone pins, awls, fish gouges, antler picks, boars' tusks, red-deer teeth made into necklaces, and headdresses made of perforated shells. Many of the bodies had had red ochre placed on them, usually in the area of the chest. Some of the graves had been lined with stone slabs, and on the covering slabs of some, fires had been lit, probably as part of the ritual associated with death. In other cases feasting hearths were found nearby. The detail derived from these two small cemeteries gives a vivid impression of the richness and complexity of the belief systems of those late hunter-gatherers.

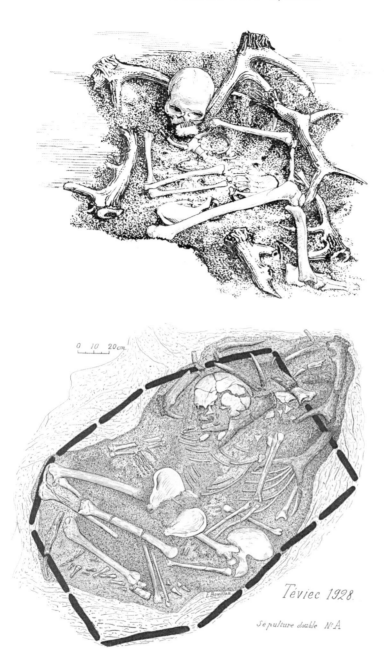

2.3 Some of the sites used by Late Mesolithic communities accumulated large middens composed of the discarded shells of marine molluscs that had been collected for food. Human burials, accompanied by deer antlers and other items, were found within with the middens at Hoëdic (*top*) and Téviec (*bottom*).

But there is more to be learned of the human bones from stable isotope analyses, since the different percentages of isotopes indicate from what sources the individuals may have obtained their protein intake. Not surprisingly, between 60 and 80 per cent was shown to have come from seafood, the rest deriving from animals like red deer, wild boar, and aurochs obtained from the forested interior either by hunting expeditions or through exchanges with inland neighbours. A small but significant difference was found between the isotope percentages of the Hoëdic and Téviec skeletons, suggesting that the two communities remained separate and adopted slightly different food-gathering strategies. A further point of particular interest is that the women were found to have consumed a lower proportion of marine food than the men. This can be explained by supposing that they had grown up in inland communities and had come to the coast to become wives in exogamous marriage exchanges. This was a not uncommon arrangement among hunter-gatherer groups and served to provide bonds between communities who might otherwise be in competition for resources. That relations were not always harmonious, however, is suggested by injuries suffered by a number of the individuals buried at Téviec and by one of the burials from Hoëdic who had a fractured jaw and had probably been killed by two arrows, the tips of which were found embedded in his backbone.

The coastal hunter-gatherers had access to a variety of resources from different ecozones, between the open coastal waters and the inland wooded zone, ranging from cliffs and rocky shores to sheltered coasts with sandy and muddy shores and the woodland fringes. Each ecozone produced a distinctive array of food. A detailed study of the food detritus contained within the middens, particularly those of Beg-an-Dorchenn and Beg-er-Vil, where the excavation techniques were more refined, showed that the sites must have been occupied all year round, though this does not preclude that segments of the population may have been away for short periods.

These sedentary communities were privileged through their access to copious food resources and the ready availability of pebble flint, found on the beaches, so essential for making tools and weapons. Those living in the wooded interior are likely to have maintained a more mobile lifestyle, moving with the seasons to follow migrating birds and animals and the changing plant resources and possibly making trips to the nearest coast to replenish stocks of flint. The archaeological evidence for Mesolithic groups in the interior is sparse, but at one of the better-studied sites, La Presqu'île in the Monts d'Arrée, over half the assemblages of stone tools and detritus was made of flint, which must have come from more than 35 kilometres away. Whether this was acquired by the foragers going directly to the coast to collect it for themselves or arrived through gift exchange it is difficult to say. In any event a degree of social mobility is implied.

Ideal though the location of the coastal settlements was, the people lived in an ever-changing environment. At the time when Téviec and Hoëdic were in use, between 5300 and 4800 BC, the sea-level was lower. Téviec would have been a peninsula and Hoëdic part of a much larger island incorporating the island of Houat, but the rise in sea-level, at the rate of more than a centimetre a year, would have had a dramatic effect on the coastal environment over a generation or two, changing the configuration of the resource patterns and forcing adaptations. If this was not enough to contend with, people reliant on new economic practices involving animal domestication and plant cultivation were beginning to infiltrate the approaches to Armorica.

The Arrival of the First Farmers

Communities bringing with them domesticated cattle, sheep, goats, and pigs and cultivated grain, mainly wheat and barley, began to arrive in Greece from Asia Minor in the late eighth and early seventh millennia BC and soon developed a distinctive cultural package which included pottery and ground stone tools. Neolithic farming communities spread quickly throughout Europe in two broad waves, one through middle Europe, making use of the river valleys and arriving in the Seine basin by about 5400 BC; the other moved via the Mediterranean, setting up farming enclaves in coastal areas as far west as the Atlantic coasts of Portugal by 5500–5300 BC. It was an astonishingly rapid spread and, as ancient DNA analysis has shown, involved the movement of people whose ancestors originated in the Near East. The middle European Early Neolithic cultures are generally referred to as Linearbandkeramik, while the Mediterranean groups are called the Cardial or Impressed Ware culture, the designations of both referring to the dominant style of pottery decoration.

In France the Linearbandkeramik groups established themselves in the Seine valley extending as far south as the Loire. The Impressed Ware groups extended around the whole of the north coast of the western Mediterranean, those in southern France expanding inland in two directions, one along the Rhône–Sâone corridor, the other through the Carcassonne gap and along the Garonne valley to the Atlantic coast south of the Loire, where the first incomers arrived about 5300 BC.

In the last centuries of the sixth millennium, then, the hunter-gatherer communities of the Armorican peninsula were being approached by waves of farmers advancing from the south and from the east. Those coming from the Seine valley were essentially land-based peoples whose familiarity lay within the European river valleys, while those from the south came from a tradition in which the sea had featured large in both their economy and their mobility. The impact of these two forces on the indigenous hunter-gatherers of the peninsula gave rise to a spectacular and highly original culture.

Farmers from the South

Neolithic enclaves using Impressed Ware pottery had spread to the coastal regions of the Vendée by the second half of the sixth millennium and, as we have already seen, types of arrowhead using the technology of the farmers were being adopted by later hunter-gatherer groups in Loire-Atlantique. These are known as Châtelet arrowheads and examples of them have been found further west along the south coast of Brittany as far as southern Finistère, implying that exploratory sea journeys were probably being made by people from south of the Loire. Claims have also been made for the presence of the bones of domesticated animals in the shell middens of Beg-an-Dorchenn, Téviec, and Hoëdic, but the validity of the evidence has been questioned. More reliable is the discovery of carcasses of two domesticated bovines buried in pits beneath the long mound of Er Grah at Locmariaquer in a context dated to 5300–4800 BC. If the Impressed Ware farmers south of the Loire were in contact with hunter-gatherer communities along the south coast of Brittany, there would be nothing surprising in them bringing joints of meat or even whole live animals as gifts.

The implication that Impressed Ware farmers were making exploratory voyages along the south coast of Brittany raises the intriguing possibility that they may also have been embarking upon even more adventurous voyages. Bones of domesticated cattle have been found in Late Mesolithic contexts at two sites on the Irish coast, at Sutton on the east coast, dating to 5500 BC, and Ferriter's Cove on the south-west coast, about 4350 BC, both well before Neolithic farmers had moved into Britain and Ireland to settle. The simplest explanation is that joints of meat, salted or smoked, were being carried by maritime explorers from the south to be used as gifts to establish friendly relations with the indigenous population. If adventurers from the Impressed Ware Neolithic settlements south of the Loire were exploring the southern shores of Armorica, it needed only one bold and imaginative ship's captain to open up the route further to the seaways around Ireland.

The cultural impact of such voyages need not have been great, but there is some tantalizing evidence from the Morbihan to suggest that contact may have introduced more than casual gifts. The evidence came from an area of ancient coastal marshland at Kerpenhir near Locmariaquer. It was sampled to produce a pollen sequence to study changes in the local vegetation over time. The results showed that mixed oak forests tended to dominate throughout, but at two stages it was possible to define episodes representing some woodland clearance and the opening up of land for cereal cultivation. The first episode (zone b) was dated by radiocarbon to somewhere between 7243 and 5817 BC, the second (zone d) to 5265–4866 BC. There is nothing surprising about the later episode. It coincides with the occupation of the Late Mesolithic sites at Téviec and Hoëdic and could represent the appearance of groups of farmers coming from the Neolithic communities south of the Loire or from the Seine basin. The earlier episode is much more difficult to explain since it comes well before farming communities are believed to have reached north-western France. It may be that the cereal pollen has been misidentified and that what was represented was a clearing made by hunter-gatherers to encourage wild animals to congregate to eat the grasses and new shoots, the easier to capture them. That said, it is not impossible that pioneer farmers were exploring the area much earlier than we at present credit. The debate illustrates the fragility of the currently available archaeological evidence.

Farmers from the East

In dealing with the impact of farmers spreading west from the Linearbandkeramik communities of the Seine valley region we are on much firmer ground. The culture is defined by its characteristic pottery style, polished stone adzes and axes, stone rings, and impressive timber longhouses, as well as burial practices and evidence of its food-producing economy. Settlers had reached the Paris basin by 5400 BC. The later stages of the culture covering the period about 5000 to 4700 BC are named after the site of Villeneuve-Saint-Germain. It was during this phase that farmers spread westwards into the Armorican peninsula and across the sea to the Channel Islands.

Several settlements of Villeneuve-Saint-Germain date have been found in Armorica. At the eastern end of the peninsula the sites of Le Haut-Mée and Pluvignon have both produced evidence of buildings. At Le Haut-Mée the plan of an impressive timber-built longhouse nearly 23 metres long surrounded by pits was totally uncovered, while at Pluvignon the location of six longhouses was identified associated with pits and postholes. Other settlements of the same period have been discovered at Le Dillien and Bellevue in the valley of the river Blavet in the heart of the peninsula, while three large longhouses were identified at Kervouric overlooking the river Léguer. By the end of the Villeneuve-Saint-Germain period, settlements were being established as far south as the southern Morbihan. Although the dating is still in need of refinement, we can say that the first three centuries of the fifth millennium saw farming communities spread rapidly throughout Brittany. The imperative seems to have been for each new

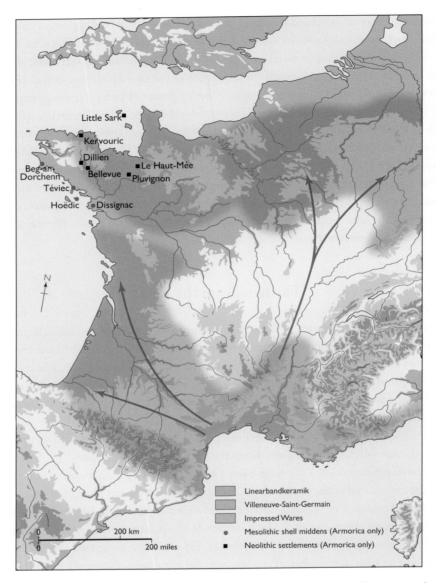

2.4 Knowledge of farming spread into Armorica from two directions in the sixth millennium BC, from the east, as part of the westerly extension of Linearbandkeramik groups, and from the south, as the result of the coastal expansion of the Cardial Ware cultures. Neolithic settlements of the Villeneuve-Saint-Germain group (a variant of the Linearbandkeramik) are known across Armorica.

generation to move on to find new land to colonize. Once the network of pioneer settlements had been set up, the land in between could begin to be filled.

Some of the farmers occupying the Cotentin peninsula of western Normandy will have been aware of offshore islands lying in the western ocean: the Îles Anglo-Normandes, or Channel Islands as we now know them. They were already occupied by hunter-gatherer bands who exploited the seas around and were no doubt competent sailors. It was not long before farming communities set out from the mainland to establish pioneer settlements. Two are known on Guernsey, two on Jersey, and one on Sark. The settlement on Sark, Little Sark site A, was dated to the period 4800–4700 BC. The inhabitants used mud-bricks to build their houses and cultivated barley. The enterprise of colonization would not have been easy. The pioneers had to transport their seed grain and livestock across 40 kilometres of open sea and haul it all up cliffs 100 metres high before the farm could be set up. Given that these land-based farmers had little experience of the sea, the probability is that they enlisted the help of the resident hunter-gatherers, whose maritime skills would have been essential to the success of their venture.

After the phase of pioneer settlements, the farming communities began to multiply, the habitation sites becoming more complex and long-lived. One such, sited on a low

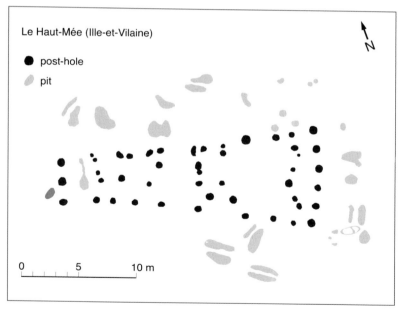

Le Haut-Mée (Ille-et-Vilaine)

● post-hole

🌢 pit

N

0   5   10 m

2.5 The houses of the Villeneuve-Saint-Germain period were long, either rectangular or trapezoidal in shape, like this example excavated at Le Haut-Mée, represented now by the postholes for the wall timbers and pits from which the clay to daub the walls was dug.

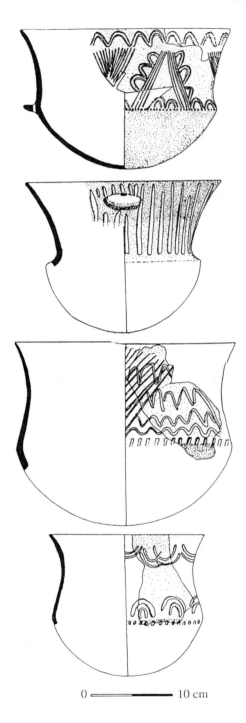

0 ▭▭▭▭ 10 cm

hill at Lillemer, near Mont-Dol, on the edge of a marsh flanking the Baie du Mont-Saint-Michel, grew to over 30 hectares and occupation spanned the second half of the fifth millennium. In an early phase, dating to about 4400 BC, rectangular houses of mud-brick were built terraced into the hill slope. Later, between 4200 and 4000 BC, the entire hill was surrounded by a ditch and bank strengthened by a wooden fence. To build such an earthwork, over 1.5 kilometres in length, was a massive undertaking reflecting the coercive power of the community's leaders.

The initial spread of farming communities into Brittany introduced the art of pottery making. As a plastic product manufactured within the household, pottery provided a ready medium for self-expression. While the basic shapes were dictated largely by function, the decoration was a matter of personal choice. It reflected group identity and could change over time. Thus, for the archaeologist, pottery—an artefact that tends to survive well and is often plentiful—provides a way of identifying different cultural groups and tracing the way in which they developed. The original pioneer settlers of the Villeneuve-Saint-Germain phase (5000–4700 BC) introduced a distinctive ceramic assemblage. Thereafter regional changes led to what has been called the Cerny style, which is divided into the Ancient sub-phase (4700–4600 BC) and, later, the Middle Neolithic, including the Castellic style (4600–4300 BC), represented by highly decorated forms found mainly in southern Armorica. These rather esoteric studies help to provide a framework of reference, but they also contribute to our understanding of the way in which distinct communities were beginning to crystallize out as people began to take control of the landscape and to form stable communities.

2.6 Pottery making was a skill introduced by the immigrant farmers. Regional styles soon developed. These vessels belong to the Middle Neolithic Castellic style found in southern Armorica.

Marking the Land: Great Stones

Humans share with other animals the desire to mark their territory and to impose themselves in some way upon the natural world. It could be argued that the creation of the Late Mesolithic shell middens was just such a deliberate act of marking. An extensive mound of gleaming white shells up to a metre high would have been a notable feature. It represented a place where the social group had come together to feast and perhaps to live over a period of time. The association of some of the middens, like Téviec and Hoëdic, with the burials of revered ancestors gave enhanced significance to the mound's monumentality.

The introduction of farming provided added impetus for monument building. Large blocks of stone were detached and set upright as menhirs (standing stones) either singly or in rows, and long mounds were erected covering burials and areas of ritual activity. Such monuments concentrate in the southern Morbihan region but menhirs are ubiquitous throughout much of the Armorica peninsula.

Let us begin by considering a comparatively modest example. At Porh Fetan, in what is now the intertidal zone on the coast of the Quiberon peninsula, an alignment of more than thirty stones was set up extending for a length of 15–20 metres. Now covered by normal tides, the area had originally been a marshy environment protected behind a sand-dune. The contemporary peaty soils showed evidence of cross-plough-ing and the hoof-marks of cattle. Nearby were found two deposits each of a pair of pol-ished jadeitite axes from the Alps placed in the ground face to face with their cutting edges uppermost. A fine fibrolite axe from a local source was also found set upright against one of the standing stones. What is to be made of this remarkable find? Clearly it was the result of a series of acts requiring a group to expend a considerable amount of energy and to commit items of great value to the spirits of the place. What motivated the people and what they hoped to achieve by their act we can only guess. Perhaps by marking the territory in this way and making such a valuable offering they may have been hoping to persuade the gods to avert the inexorable rise of the sea that was now beginning to inundate their cultivated land.

A second stone row of particular interest was found at Le Douet on the island of Hoëdic less than a kilometre from the shell midden. It consisted of a row of eight standing stones, split from the local rock and set at right angles to the cliff face. One of the blocks, the so-called Dame du Douet, was anthropomorphic in form with two large natural bosses resembling breasts. Limited shaping had attempted to define legs. Charcoal from a hearth at the base of the stone gave a date between 4700 and 4500 BC comparable to the date suggested from the Porh Fetan stone alignment.

2.7 At Le Douet on the island of Hoëdic a row of six standing stones was discovered. One, illustrated here, known as the Dame du Douet, had two natural protuberances and was enhanced by carving to resemble more closely the female human form.

These two comparatively modest examples of stone alignments are probably fairly typical of many that were being put up in the landscape the early farmers were beginning to bring under control. Whether they represent statements of ownership or engagements with the gods, they are a clear reminder of the cohesiveness of society and of a desire to express identity. Estimates suggest that there are probably between eleven hundred and twelve hundred menhirs in Armorica, the greatest concentration being in the western part of the peninsula. The most impressive of all the Breton

2.8 The focus of the megalithic complex at Locmariaquer, now much sanitized for presentation to the public, incorporates three visible Neolithic monuments: the long mound of Er Grah, the Grand Menhir Brisé, and the Table des Marchands passage grave. Compare with 2.9.

menhirs is the Grand Menhir Brisé at Locmariaquer, which once stood at the end of a row of eighteen standing stones represented now by the sockets dug for the bases of the stones. The Grand Menhir now lies fallen, broken into four segments, but originally it was 21 metres in length and would have stood 18–19 metres above ground. The stone weighs between 270 and 330 metric tons and had been dragged for a distance of at least 8 kilometres from the outcrop from which it had been quarried. Its transportation, shaping, and erection were astonishing feats by any standards. Carved high up on one face of the stone is a motif known as an *hache-charrue* (axe plough) but more recently, and more convincingly, interpreted as a sperm whale. Of the rest of the alignment we know very little except that the stones appear to have been smaller: only the broken base of one remained in position, the rest having been removed in their entirety.

The Grand Menhir and its alignment were erected in the middle centuries of the fifth millennium BC and there is evidence to suggest that the great stone fell sometime around 4300 BC. The cause is unknown, but one plausible suggestion is that it may have been the result of an earth tremor. While the Grand Menhir was left where it had fallen, the remaining stones, fallen or still standing, were carted away. One stone carved with a sperm whale and two horned quadrupeds, possibly the stone standing next to the Grand Menhir, was broken into three parts. One slab was used as a capstone in the nearby passage grave of the Table des Marchands, another fragment was transported across the estuary of the river d'Auray—a distance of 4 kilometres—and used as a capstone in the passage grave of Gavr'inis, while the whereabouts of the third fragment have yet to be identified. Broken decorated menhirs, possibly from the Grand Menhir alignment, were also reused in the nearby tombs of Mané er Hroëck and Mané Rutual and it may be that the back stone in the Table des Marchands also came from the alignment.

The reuse of menhirs in later megalithic tombs is evident elsewhere in Brittany. While it could reflect an act of iconoclasm, with a new order deliberately destroying the visible evidence of an earlier belief system, it could equally be that later generations were showing reverence for their ancestral roots by incorporating parts of earlier monuments into their own tombs. Archaeologists can identify behaviour, but it is not always easy to explain it.

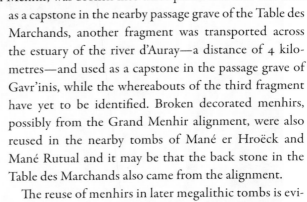

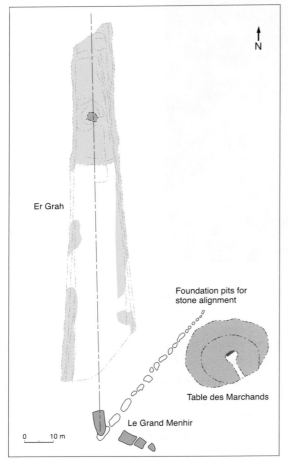

2.9 The Grand Menhir was the largest and most southerly menhir in a row of standing stones. The Er Grah long mound was aligned with the fallen base of the Grand Menhir and incorporated in its structure a fragment of one of the menhirs that once formed part of the row. Another carved menhir from the alignment was used as an orthostat in the Table des Marchands, while a fragment of another was used as a capstone.

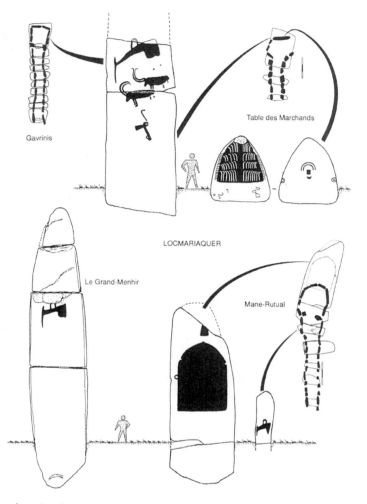

Gavrinis

Table des Marchands

LOCMARIAQUER

Le Grand-Menhir

Mane-Rutual

2.10 Carved menhirs from the row, of which the Grand Menhir was the largest, were incorporated into a number of megalithic graves in the vicinity.

Marking the Land: Long Mounds

Another way chosen by the earliest agricultural communities to mark their landscape was by the construction of long mounds. The term covers monuments varying considerably in size and complexity, but what all shared in common was that they began as a defined elongated area, sometimes outlined by stones or ditches, within which a range of ritual activities was carried out, including human burial. When the cycle of rituals

2.11 A part of a menhir from the Grand Menhir alignment, carved with a representation of a long-horned bull, was used as a capstone to cover the end chamber of the passage grave built on the island of Gavr'inis.

was over, the sacred arena and the structures contained within it were sealed with a mound. Some were quite small, barely 20 metres long and a metre or so high. These are usually called *tertres tumulaires*, but a few are much larger, up to 125 metres in length and 15 metres high. These are referred to as Carnac mounds. It is probably best to regard the two types as part of the same tradition, the differences being created by the degree of communal effort invested in them. More than a hundred long mounds are known in Armorica, the great majority being concentrated in the southern Morbihan coastal region. It is here that the six or seven Carnac mounds are also found. A few of the smaller type are known in the centre of the country and two examples have been identified on the Channel Islands, one on Guernsey and one on Sark.

What activities were carried out in the ritual area we can only guess, but they involved the construction of small megalithic chambers with capstones, small cists covered by cairns of stone, the digging of pits, the placing of stones and menhirs, and the use of hearths. The likelihood is that the rituals were funerary in nature, but human bones are seldom preserved in acid soils.

In the small mounds little cultural material was deposited other than pottery and occasional stone axes, but in the Carnac mounds the deposits were much richer, including polished stone axes, stone rings, and beads and pendants of variscite (from Iberia) often found in large numbers. The cist found in the centre of the Tumulus de Saint-Michel produced thirty-nine polished stone axes, of which eleven were of jadeitite from the Alps, nine pendants and 101 beads of variscite, a number of smaller beads of bone or ivory, and two flint flakes. Clearly, the individual whose grave this was must have been a person of considerable status in society. The long mounds, then, in their size and the elaboration of the deposits buried with them, represent differences in the status of the groups responsible for their creation. If both types were of broadly the same period, this would denote a highly stratified society, but it is not impossible that the Carnac mounds came late in the sequence, suggesting that the power of the social elites grew over time. At present the dating evidence is not precise but is sufficient to indicate that the long-mound tradition belonged to the middle and later fifth millennium BC.

What all these monuments share in common is the fact that the ritual activities enacted on the site, probably associated with the burial of a significant individual, were brought to closure by the construction of a covering mound, which, in the case of the larger examples, involved a very considerable effort. The existence of these mounds in the landscape would have been a constant reminder of the social cohesion, power, and history of the community. Several of the large mounds, including the Tumulus de Saint-Michel, incorporated a thick layer of silt brought from a nearby lake or estuary. This deliberate choice of material is interesting, suggesting perhaps a desire to associate the site in some way with water, or more specifically, the sea. A small long mound found at Gaudinerie Field on the island of Sark adds some support for this, for here the mound, nearly a metre high, contained a large number of sea-worn boulders up to half a metre in length, all of which would have to have been hauled up a 100-metre cliff from the nearby shore. The mound builders must have felt an imperative to create a connection between the sea and the act of burial.

Fitting the Pieces Together

The relationship of the menhirs to the long mounds is complex. At the long mound of Le Manio 2 in Carnac, the mound can be shown to have been built around an existing menhir decorated with serpent-like carvings at its base. The precedence of menhirs is also implied at Locmariaquer, where the long mound of Er Grah is aligned with the Grand Menhir Brisé. The significance of the Grand Menhir to the mound may explain why it alone was allowed to remain even in its fallen state while the others of its alignment were removed. That part of one of the other menhirs was used as a capstone for the cist in the long mound implies that the alignment was in ruins when the long mound was built. The use of fragments of standing stones in the nearby long mound of Mané er Hroëck again demonstrates that menhirs preceded the construction of at least some of the Carnac mounds.

While the evidence of monument building is rich on the ground, it is difficult to know what to make of it in terms of the aspirations and beliefs of the populations at the time when agriculture was beginning to be established in the first half of the fifth millennium. Some observers argue that the early menhirs and long mounds were concepts introduced by the pioneering farmers coming from the Seine valley and the Atlantic coastal region south of the Loire. Others would stress the influence of the Late Mesolithic hunters and gatherers, comparing the shell middens and their burials with the smaller long mounds. Both may in part be right. The early monuments of the Carnac region may well be the result of the cultural fusion of incoming farmers with indigenous hunter-gatherers, each contributing to the new belief system which demanded that people expressed their power over the land and reverence for the gods and ancestors by erecting great stones and building long mounds. It resulted in a remarkably vibrant and energetic society which was soon to find itself at the centre of an interregional network of exchange perhaps brought about by the growing fame of the spectacular monuments and their attraction to pilgrims.

Responding to New Ideas: The Passage Graves

Sometime during the fifth millennium the practice of collective burial in megalithic tombs designed to be reused over a period of time became widespread in Armorica and the Channel Islands. Whether this was the resurgence of the beliefs redolent in the multiple burials typical of Late Mesolithic shell middens or the introduction of a new idea from outside is a matter for debate (below, pp. 59–60) but the practice was very different from that implied by the long mounds, in which all access to the original grave was prevented by the construction of the mound erected over the ritual arena.

A typical passage grave, like the Table des Marchands, consists of a megalithic chamber with a passage giving access from the outside of the mound. Both chamber and passage were usually roofed with capstones, but corbelling was sometimes used to create the chamber roof, the whole of the built structure being embedded in a mound of earth or rubble usually circular in plan. In the case of the Table des Marchands, as we have seen, the capstone was one of the broken menhirs from the nearby alignment, while its back stone may have come from the row as well. The nearby passage grave of Mané Rutual was similarly roofed, showing that in the Carnac area the passage graves were built after the destruction of some, at least, of the alignments. Another good example of the relative sequence of building in the Carnac region is the tomb of Le Petit Mont, sited on a headland close to the entrance of the gulf of Morbihan. The monument began life as a small long mound 50 metres long and 1.6 metres high with a standing stone set up at its seaward end. At the end of the fifth millennium a series of changes was initiated. First a cairn (Cairn I) was built on part of the mound and this was later extended (Cairn II), the new part containing a typical passage grave chamber. At a later stage, in the first century of the fourth millennium, the cairn was further extended (Cairn III) to accommodate two new passage graves. Another example of a long mound apparently being modified by the addition of a passage grave is Mané Lud, but here the chronological relationship has not been demonstrated archaeologically. Even so, the evidence is sufficient to show that in the southern Morbihan the construction of passage graves follows the floruit of the decorated menhirs and the long mounds, the first ones appearing in the century or two before the end of the fifth millennium.

Passage graves are widely distributed in Brittany, with a particular concentration in the southern Morbihan. The distribution is strictly coastal, with many of the monuments located within sight of the sea. While this pattern echoes the distribution of Early and Middle Neolithic settlement, which is conditioned to a large extent by the availability of fertile, easily worked soils, it also suggests an intimate relationship between the graves and the sea. In many cases the monuments were sited so that they would have been visible to those approaching from the sea: the ancestors, perhaps, welcoming returning sailors.

One of the most impressive of the passage graves found on the north coast of Brittany is the great cairn of Barnenez, 10 kilometres north of Morlaix, sited at the end of a promontory overlooking the estuary. It is a composite structure of two phases. In the first phase a rectangular cairn 35 metres long by up to 20 metres wide, reveted by two drystone walls, was constructed to protect five individual passage graves, each comprising a burial chamber reached from the outside by a long narrow passage. The middle chamber was built of upright slabs roofed by a massive capstone. The others had corbelled roofs. At a later stage the cairn was more than doubled in size, with a western extension built to accommodate six more passage graves, some of megalithic construction, others corbelled. The radiocarbon dates from Barnenez suggest that construction may have begun in the middle of the fifth millennium, but doubts have been

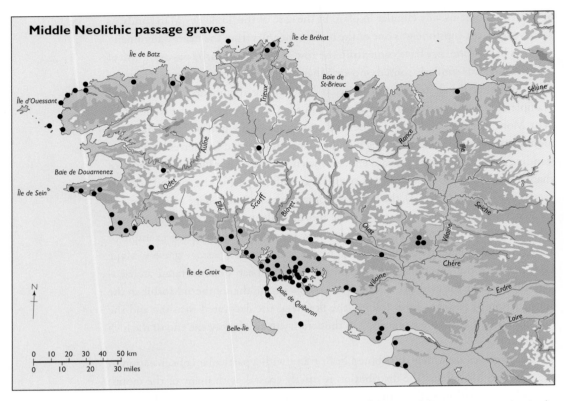

Middle Neolithic passage graves

2.12 The distribution of passage graves of the Middle Neolithic period shows a concentration in the coastal regions, particularly in the southern Morbihan.

expressed about their reliability. However, the passage grave cemetery on Île Carn, on the north-west coast of Finistère, produced a series of dates ranging between 4500 and 4000 BC, while human bone from the passage grave at Ty-Floc'h, in the west of Finistère, was dated to 4300–3920 BC. Taken together the radiocarbon dating suggests that the passage tombs of the north and west coasts were being built in the second half of the fifth millennium, possibly a little earlier than those in the Morbihan region.

The most spectacular of the Breton passage graves is the tomb of Gavr'inis, sited on a small island at the entrance to the gulf of Morbihan. The burial chamber, with its long passage built of standing slabs and roofed with large capstones, was buried in a roughly circular cairn about 60 metres in diameter with stepped sides rising to a height of 8 metres. What is remarkable about the monument is that twenty-three of the orthostats (upright stones) comprising the passage and chamber walls were covered by a profusion of carving, mostly in the form of concentric arcs and chevrons

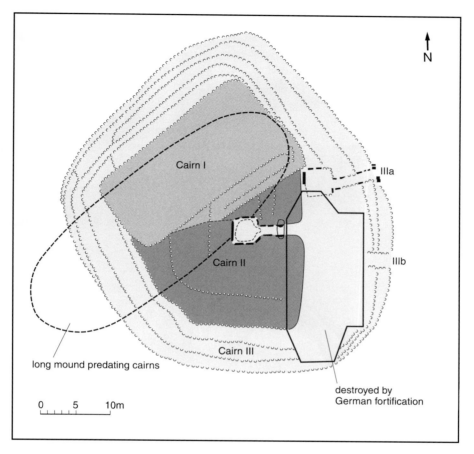

Cairn I

IIIa

Cairn II

IIIb

Cairn III

long mound predating cairns

destroyed by
German fortification

0   5   10m

N

2.13 The monument of Le Petit Mont, Arzon, was a multi-period structure beginning as a long mound. Cairn I was built over part of it and was later extended with an addition containing a passage grave (Cairn II). A final extension (Cairn III) contained two passage graves, one completely destroyed by a Second World War bunker.

but incorporating clear representations of stone axe blades often arranged in pairs: a reminder of the pair of real axes deposited near the stone alignment at Porh Fetan. There were also serpentine motifs. The overall impact is overwhelming; the stones reverberate with energy. In flickering lamplight the strobe-like effect would have been deeply unsettling. Gavr'inis is an exception in the quantity and exuberance of its carvings. A few of the other passage graves incorporate stones bearing carved motifs, but it is often not possible to tell whether they were taken from earlier monuments.

Standing back from the detail, it is clear that the appearance of passage graves by the second half of the fifth millennium marked a significant and widespread change in

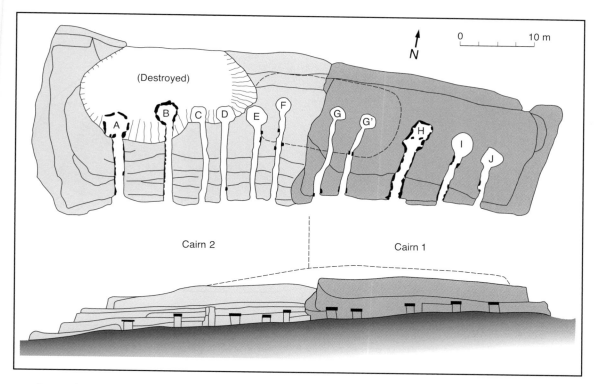

2.14 (*Opposite*) The passage grave of Barnenez was built on a low hill overlooking the Baie de Térénez, part of the estuary of Morlaix. The mound was discovered when a quarry was opened in its side. After excavations the monument was restored to its present form.

2.15 (*Above*) The long burial mound of Barnenez was built in two phases. The first phase contained five passage graves, the second, six.

burial practice, from rituals that required chambers to be closed and made inaccessible on completion, to beliefs that demanded continued access to the chambers so that people could re-enter them at will to introduce new bodies and enact further rituals. There is no reason why such changes should not have evolved in the highly innovative culture of the southern Morbihan and to have spread quickly to other parts of Brittany and to the Channel Islands, but the alternative—that passage grave architecture and the belief system associated with it was introduced from outside the region—is also a possibility that has long been entertained by archaeologists.

A recent detailed reconsideration of the albeit limited radiocarbon data from western Europe has suggested that the earliest Breton passage graves are earlier than those found in western Iberia, the implication being that the concept of the accessible grave, reflected in the construction of passage graves, may indeed have developed first

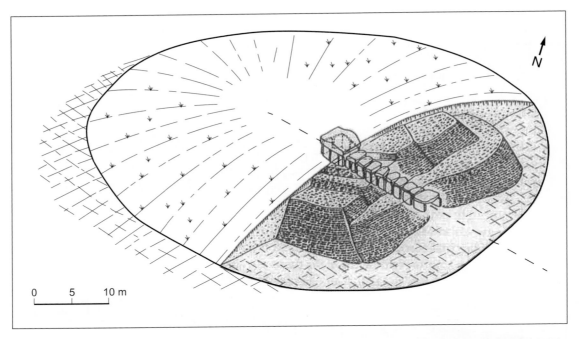

0   5   10 m

2.16 The passage grave of Gavr'inis is situated on what is now an island in the gulf of Morbihan. The drawing shows the main façade reconstructed.

in Brittany, most likely in the southern Morbihan. That there were, however, maritime links with western Iberia is shown by the quantity of the attractive blue-green stone variscite, derived from western Iberian sources, which was used to make the necklaces and pendants so frequently found accompanying burials beneath the Carnac mounds. This would imply the existence of a maritime exchange system linking Galicia with Brittany. If the tradition of building accessible grave chambers originated in the Morbihan, which now seems probable, then it may have been by this route that the idea spread to western Iberia.

Once it had developed, the form of the passage grave and the beliefs associated with it spread fast among the coastal communities of the peninsula. Most of those that have been dated belong to the second half of the fifth millennium, with a few still in use in the first centuries of the fourth millennium. By this time the Neolithic way of life was well established and the population was beginning to grow. The favoured coastal zone was now at capacity and it was time for new land to be opened up in the interior. It is tempting to see the few passage graves found in the more inland areas, the Saint-Just region, the upper valley of the Blavet, and the middle valley of the Aulne, as those of the pioneers whose successors were to create large new enclaves of settlement.

2.17 The orthostats used to create the passage walls of the megalithic tomb of Gavr'inis were elaborately carved. This example incorporates representations of a pair of polished stone axes and two serpent-like motifs seen towards the bottom.

The Alignments March On

The tradition of constructing alignments of standing stones, which began in a modest way with simple stone rows like those of Porh Fetan and Le Douet (above, pp. 47–8) and soon evolved into remarkable structures incorporating huge shaped and carved menhirs like the alignment of Locmariaquer, is found in several parts of Brittany, in particular in the Bas-Léon region of western Finistère and the area around the Rance estuary and Saint-Malo, but nowhere did it reach the extremes of elaboration as in the Carnac region of the southern Morbihan. Here multiple rows of standing stones strode across the landscape, often making for hill-top enclosures, oval or rectangular in shape, built of stones set upright edge to edge. The serried ranks of stones of different shapes and sizes were, and indeed still are, inspiring. They reminded early observers of petrified armies on the march. Eleven multiple stone rows are known within 8 kilometres of Carnac. Of these the three largest are Kerzerho with ten rows 2,105 metres long, Kermario with up to ten rows 1,151 metres long, and Le Ménec with twelve rows 943 metres long.

The hill-top enclosures seem to have been the focuses from which many of the alignments were built. At Le Ménec it would seem that the monument began with an oval hill-top enclosure, to which ran an avenue defined by two parallel stone rows. It was only later that the other ten rows were added parallel to the avenue. A similar situation is apparent at Kerlescan, also at Carnac, where the original avenues made for the gap between a rectangular enclosure and a long mound against which the enclosure had been built. Thereafter additional rows were added on both sides. The rows were also sometimes lengthened by subsequent additions. This is nicely shown by the Le Ménec alignments. They began as two separate complexes, each focused on an oval hill-top enclosure, the stone lines extending eastwards from the West Enclosure, eventually being made to join those extending westwards from the East Enclosure.

What these vast constructions meant to the people who built them we can only guess. Suggestions that they were sophisticated lunar and solar observatories lack conviction, but the very form is redolent of processions and assembly, encouraging the passage of people along the avenues leading to the enclosures where communal rituals and feasting were carried out. The very act of building them proclaimed the power of the community and the ability to work together. They symbolized the cohesion of society reaffirmed at intervals by the addition of new stone rows and the lengthening of existing ones.

Stone-built enclosures of the type to which the alignments ran are found widely in the Carnac region and around the gulf of Morbihan and clearly played a significant

2.18 (*Opposite*) The stone alignments of La Ménec, Carnac.

2.19 The small island of Er Lannic in the gulf of Morbihan is the remnant of a larger land-mass reduced by sea-level rise after the Neolithic period. It is the site of two conjoined enclosures defined by standing stones, one now wholly below high-tide level, the other partially on the dry land of the island.

part in the life of the community, most likely as centres for gatherings when, on special occasions, social bonds could be reaffirmed and the gods propitiated. Two conjoined enclosures on the island of Er Lannic in the mouth of the gulf of Morbihan throw some light on these activities. One entire enclosure and much of the other have now been submerged by the rising sea-level, but originally they would both have been on dry land at the end of the peninsula. Excavation here exposed numerous small hearths, associated polished stone axes, and fragments of more than 520 ceramic 'incense burners': specially constructed vessels with a domed upper surface upon which birch resin was burnt. Twenty-seven complete fibrolite axes and forty-seven fragments were recovered together with eleven polished axes and 152 fragments of other stone types. Clearly axe production was a major preoccupation. Roughouts of fibrolite axes were brought to the site for finishing, probably from a source in the Port-Navalo area 2 kilometres away, along with roughout dolerite axes from other sources. The finely polished fibrolite axes would have been items of considerable value, a value which may have been enhanced by the knowledge that the axe was created on a sacred site. The

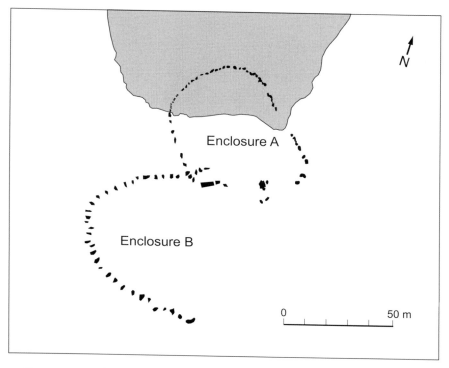

2.20 The two conjoined enclosures at Er Lannic planned at low tide.

manufacture of prestige goods and the burning of aromatic resins were no doubt only two of the many activities carried out in the stone enclosures.

Colonizing the Interior

Simple passage graves were being built throughout the entire coastal region of Brittany by about 4000 BC. This distribution reflects the most densely occupied zone, but farming communities had already begun to colonize inland areas. Their settlements are known in the Rennes basin and the upper valley of the river Blavet from as early as the early fifth millennium, and a few passage graves were being built in these interior regions by the second half of the millennium. It was, however, in the fourth millennium that the settlement of the interior really got under way. This much is implied by the distribution of the gallery graves (allées couvertes), which became the principal tomb type in the fourth and early third millennia. Besides the coastal distribution

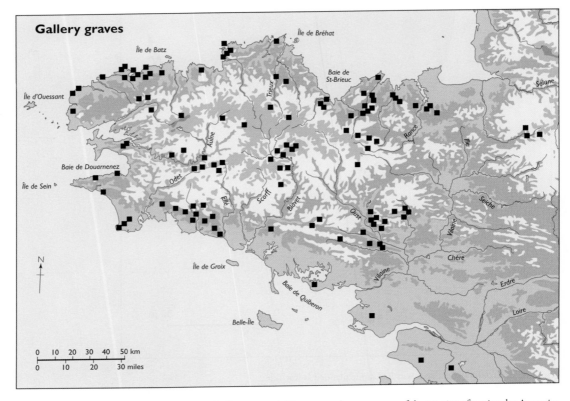

2.21 The distribution of gallery graves (*allées couvertes*) covers more of the interior of peninsular Armorica than did the earlier passage graves (Figure 2.12, shown on p. 56). There is a marked absence in the southern Morbihan, where the passage graves were at their densest and probably continued in use.

there are significant concentrations in the upper Aulne valley, the upper Blavet valley, and the valley of the Oust.

Gallery graves took a variety of forms, but they were essentially corridor-like megalithic chambers, sometimes with terminal cells, entered from the side or from one end. In all probability they developed in Armorica from the earlier passage graves. One particularly well-preserved example is the gallery grave at Crec'h Quillé near the north coast, 4 kilometres north-east of Lannion. It was set in a long rectangular mound, 28 by 8 metres, edged with curbstones. The chamber, 16 by 1.8 metres, was reached from the south side by way of a short passage. In the wall of the chamber, facing the passage, is a large stone, anthropomorphic in shape. The head has been slightly dished by pecking, possibly to remove facial features, and on the body, in relief, is a pair of breasts with a looping necklace hanging below. Carvings are rare in gallery graves, but pairs of breasts, often with necklaces, are a recurring motif in tombs along the north coast,

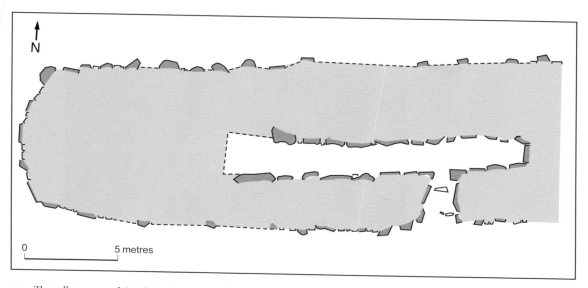

2.22 The gallery grave of Crec'h-Quillé, north of Lannion, was entered from its side. In the wall of the elongated chamber facing the entrance passage is a large stone slab, roughly anthropomorphically shaped and carved in relief with two breasts and a necklace below.

2.23 The gallery grave of Crec'h-Quillé after excavation as it is now presented to the public.

2.24 The statue menhir from Le Trévoux, with breasts and wearing what appears to be a necklace, is comparable to that found incorporated in the Crec'h-Quillé gallery grave.

occurring at Prajou-Menhir and Kergüntuil within a few kilometres of Crec'h Quillé and at Tressé to the east, in the Rance valley. Similar features are shown on statue menhirs from Le Trévoux near Laniscat in Finistère and on two statue menhirs found on Guernsey at Le Catel and Saint-Martin. This distribution, embracing the north Breton coast and Guernsey, might suggest that we are seeing here a broad cultural region with the sea connecting two societies sharing similar beliefs.

Dating of the gallery graves is not precise, but most are likely to have been built and to have remained in use during the period about 3800–2500 BC. It was during this time that distinct regional groupings began to crystallize out as communities, bounded by ties of kindred and tribal allegiance, developed their own cultural

2.25 The statue menhir now standing in the churchyard at Le Catel in Guernsey is in the same tradition as those from Le Trévoux, Crec'h-Quillé, and other sites on the north coast of Armorica.

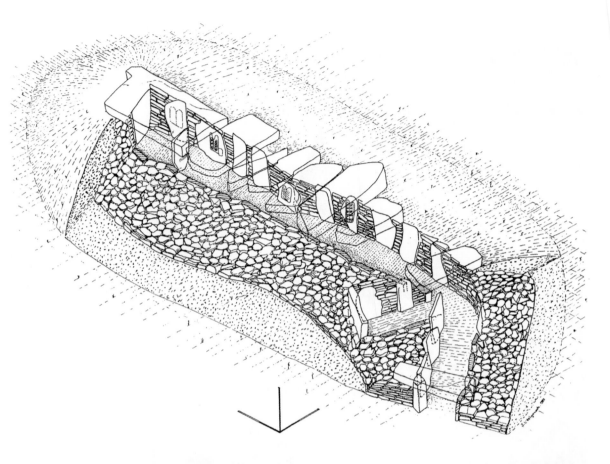

2.26 Les Pierres Plates at Locmariaquer is classified as an angled gallery grave (*sépulture coudée*). Many of the orthostats were decorated with distinctive carvings which some observers referred to as 'buckler' designs, believing them to resemble shields.

preferences. Throughout, the Carnac region of the southern Morbihan remained pre-eminent. Here later tomb development did not favour the classic *allée couverte* type of grave but rather a variant known as the *sépulture coudée* (angled graves), in which the gallery chamber was entered at one end by a corridor at right angles to it. There tombs have produced distinct assemblages of pottery and fine blades of Grand-Pressigny flint from the Loire valley (below, p. 75). From one, at Luffang, came ten variscite beads. Another characteristic of the *sépulture coudée* is the highly distinctive style of engraving found on the upright slabs of which the gallery was built. The recurring composition is referred to as 'buckler' design, a term suggested by its shield-like outline, but really they defy interpretation. To some observers the images represent cephalopods, while

2.27 There has been much discussion about the interpretation of the 'buckler' motifs engraved on the orthostats at Les Pierres Plates. One suggestion is that they are anthropomorphic, perhaps human torsos in various states of decay.

others see them as human torsos in the process of becoming de-fleshed. All we can be sure about is that they must have held a deep meaning for those who carved them. They reflect a specific thread in the belief system that helped to give cohesion to the Carnac community in the late fourth and early third millennia.

Connectivity

Across Brittany the farming polities that emerged strove to maintain their own identities, but at the same time it was essential for the general well-being that peaceful relations be established between the different groups. Celebrations and feasting held at neutral places at agreed times would have been one mechanism; so too would intertribal visits during which valuable gifts were exchanged. In all probability stability, both within a particular society and between rival polities, was ensured by cycles of exchange involving the structured redistribution of prestige goods. The most valuable of those surviving in the archaeological record are items of stone including polished axes, rings, and beads, as well as raw materials in the form of flakes of high-quality flint. But we must not forget furs, feathers, aromatic resins, relishes, and a host of other exotic materials that do not normally survive in archaeological contexts.

Gifts will have been valued according to rarity. At the lower end of the scale would have been items produced from locally available materials like axes made from the distinctive dolerite (dolerite type A) found at Sélédin near Plussulien in the middle of Armorica. The quarries where the axes were made have been extensively explored. They stretch across a square kilometre and were in use, producing finely polished axes, over a period of some twelve hundred years. The excavators estimate that during this time about six million axes were made: some five thousand a year. This is consistent with the very large numbers of axes of Plussulien dolerite found across north-western France, accounting for more than 40 per cent of all the axes found in Brittany and up to 20 per cent of the axes from the region between the Somme and the Gironde. The distribution patterns show the particular importance of the Loire valley as a corridor of distribution, but some axes were getting as far south as the Pyrenees and travelling north across the Channel into southern Britain. It is clear that the axes were perceived to have a special quality that gave them a value as gifts well outside the confines of Armorica. How the system of production and distribution worked it is difficult to say. One possibility is that the quarries were under the ownership of a particular resident group who controlled the initial stages of the distribution. Another is that the outcrops were regarded as sacred ground to which people from all parts could make a pilgrimage and where they could extract the rock to manufacture their own axes. Something of the complexity of the processes involved is shown by the manufacture of axes of fibrolite occurring in the gulf of Morbihan and in the extreme north-west of Brittany. As we have seen (p. 64), fibrolite from Port-Navalo was taken to the enclosures at Er Lannic to be worked into finished axes. This may suggest that the sanctity of the place of completion added value or gave legitimacy to the finished product.

Items made of exotic materials are likely to have had enhanced value. This is particularly true of the axes made of jadeitite from the Italian Alps that were distributed throughout western Europe. They are found across Armorica, but with a particular concentration in the southern Morbihan. Many were deposited in the Carnac mounds. At Mané er Hroëck, for example, in the layer below the stone floor of the chamber, eleven jadeitite axes were found together with ninety of fibrolite. But they are also found in other ritual contexts, like the two pairs stuck upright into the peat near the stone alignment at Porh Fetan. What is particularly remarkable about the jadeitite axes found in Armorica is that many of them were reworked into the rather thinner, very highly polished versions preferred locally, remastered to suit local tastes. The southern Morbihan was particularly well sited to receive axes arriving along the Garonne corridor or by way of the Loire valley, but some seem to have arrived by more circuitous routes having been first reworked in the Paris basin before arriving in the Morbihan to be reshaped yet again.

Another exotic material used for making the beads and pendants found in the Carnac mounds was variscite, a fine blue-green stone that takes a high polish (above, p. 53). Variscite occurs naturally in Iberia and the finished items from Brittany can be matched with sources in Catalonia, north-west Castile close to the Portuguese

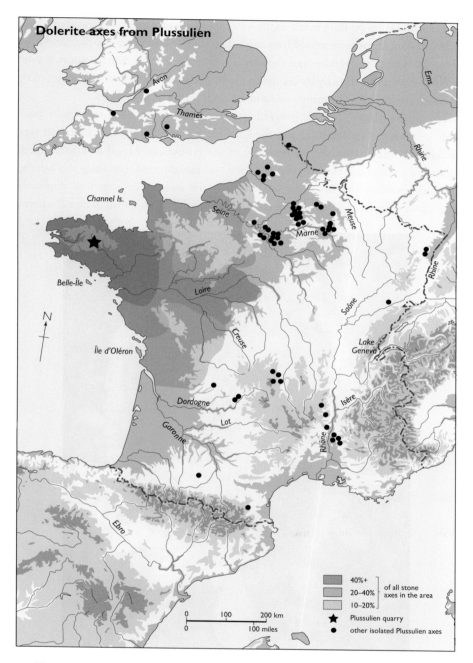

Dolerite axes from Plussulien

Avon
Thames
Ems
Rhine
Channel Is.
Seine
Meuse
Marne
Rhine
Belle-Île
Loire
Saône
Rhine
Creuse
Lake Geneva
Île d'Oléron
Isère
Dordogne
Lot
Rhône
Garonne
Ebro

N

40%+	of all stone
20–40%	axes in the area
10–20%	
★	Plussulien quarry
●	other isolated Plussulien axes

0   100   200 km
0   100 miles

2.28 The quarry site at Plussulien in central Armorica produced tens of thousands of polished stone axes during the Neolithic period. These were distributed widely throughout the peninsula and along the Loire valley to the Paris basin. A few reached Britain.

frontier, and from a quarry in the south-west, in Huelva province. While it seems likely that Catalonian variscite would have arrived in the Morbihan via the overland route along the Garonne corridor and then by sea, that from the western sources is more likely to have come directly by sea across the Bay of Biscay. It may be that some of the fibrolite axes found in Brittany also came by sea from Iberian sources.

From the earliest Neolithic period large rings made of polished stone were being widely exchanged in Armorica and the Channel Islands. Two main production areas are known. One lay on the eastern edge of the Armorican Massif at L'Ermitage in Normandy, where a grey schist was quarried and transformed into rings at a number of nearby workshops. The other source lay at the western extremity of Armorica, where two separate quarries, Lanhuel near Brest and Ty-Lan on the Baie d'Audierne,

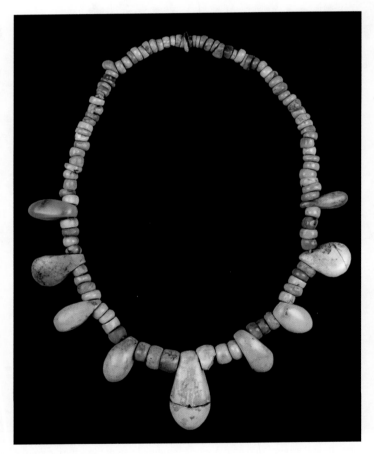

2.29 A necklace made of variscite, probably from an Iberian source, was found with a burial in the Carnac mound at Tumiac, Arzon, in the Morbihan.

produced a fine dark-green chloritite manufactured into flat, highly polished rings. One workshop is known at Kermont, close to Ty-Lan. Rings of both types are distributed throughout Armorica. On the Channel Islands stone rings are particularly numerous: twelve are known from Guernsey, six from Jersey, four from Sark, and one from Herm. While these high numbers could be the result of the intensity of archaeological activity, they may reflect the particular suitability of rings as lightweight, low-bulk goods for use in seaborne exchange cycles.

The other stone to feature in exchanges was flint. The only flint available in Armorica was pebble flint washed up by the sea, which is of inferior quality. The nearest supplies of high-quality flint were in Normandy, from where came grey-brown Chingis flint and a fine black variety, and from Grand-Pressigny in the Touraine south of the Loire valley, which produced a distinctive honey-coloured flint. Axes of Normandy flint from the fifth millennium are widely distributed in Brittany and the Channel Islands,

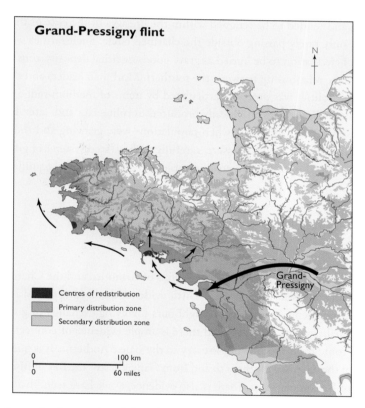

Grand-Pressigny flint

Grand-Pressigny

■ Centres of redistribution
▨ Primary distribution zone
▨ Secondary distribution zone

0 — 100 km
0 — 60 miles

2.30 The fine-quality honey-coloured flint from Grand-Pressigny was widely distributed in north-western France. It was transported down the Loire and then by ship to the various ports along the south coast of Armorica, most particularly to the Carnac region and Penmarc'h, for onward distribution inland.

and blades of the fine black flint are known on two sites in the Channel Islands of late fifth-millennium date. Grand-Pressigny flint arrived later, most of it in the first half of the third millennium though earlier finds are known (below, pp. 83–5). It occurs usually in the form of daggers or long blades. Concentrations around the Loire estuary and in the southern Morbihan, and the fact that 90 per cent of the finds came from sites less than 10 kilometres from the sea, show that it was along the southern coastal route that the flint was distributed to the peninsula.

The range and quality of the elite stone artefacts found throughout Armorica in the Neolithic period reflect many levels of social exchange. At the lower end of the scale, axes made of local stone like Plussulien A dolerite and the more readily accessible flint axes from Normandy, together with the schist and chloritite stone rings, would probably have served in gift exchange cycles between regional elites. The use and dispersal of more exotic materials like the jadeitite and fibrolite axes and the variscite beads and pendants—rare and spectacular items brought from abroad—had a far more limited circulation and tended to be retained within the lineages of the elite of the southern Morbihan, only rarely passing outside the charmed circle. Such rarities were usually taken out of circulation to be buried as grave goods or ritual deposits, thus enhancing their value. The relationship between the southern Morbihan leaders and those of the other nearby polities was probably articulated by items of medium-range value such as the smaller jadeitite axes and locally produced fibrolite axes and, later, by items of Grand-Pressigny flint. At a time when populations were growing and the landscape was beginning to come under pressure, carefully orchestrated systems of gift exchange were of increasing importance in enabling at least a degree of social equilibrium to be maintained.

Crossing the Channel

The Neolithic inhabitants of the coastal regions of Armorica and the Channel Islands were well used to the sea. Though there is little evidence that fishing played a significant part in life, social engagement with neighbours involving exchange of goods would have been facilitated by sea travel and there is ample evidence of connectivity along the coastal route from the Gironde estuary to the Baie d'Audierne. It is quite possible that some of the open-sea journeys to and from Galicia across the Bay of Biscay were in the hands of Breton mariners. There is also evidence, as we have seen, that occasional journeys were being made northwards to the seas around Ireland, perhaps as early as the sixth millennium (p. 42).

Towards the end of the fifth millennium Britain and Ireland began to receive waves of colonizing farmers from the adjacent continent. The most prolific inflow came from north-eastern areas of France and Belgium, introducing not only domesticated animals and cultivated cereals but also the technology for making pottery and polished stone tools, sophisticated timber longhouses, and flint mining. The movement was at its most intense between 4100 and 3900 BC and the new lifestyle spread quickly throughout much of England and Scotland and from Scotland across to Ireland, the rapidity of the advance facilitated by sea passages along the shores of southern Britain and northwards following the long eastern coastline to the Firth of Tay.

But the western sea-routes also had a part to play. In the period 4300–3900 BC there is some suggestion that migrants from Armorica were moving northwards to settle in the west of Wales and Scotland, in the north and west of Ireland, and possibly in south-western Britain. The evidence put forward for this is comparatively slight and is based largely on the appearance in these areas of burial monuments consisting of closed polygonal megalithic chambers or small simple passage graves set in low circular cairns. Such structures are well known in Armorica, particularly in the Morbihan. A typical example was excavated at Achnacreebeag, on the west coast of Scotland. Here, in a single cairn, a closed chamber was later replaced by a small passage grave. The excavation produced a pot decorated with arc motifs closely comparable in style to pottery of late Castellic type found in simple passage tombs in the Morbihan dating to the period 4200–3800 BC. Radiocarbon dates for simple passage graves excavated in the cemetery of Carrowmore, County Sligo, on the north-west coast of Ireland indicate construction within precisely this period.

If adventurers from the south of Armorica were exploring the Irish Sea and establishing enclaves of settlers, it is quite probable that people from northern Brittany and Normandy were making Channel crossings to the coasts of south-western Britain. Here again the evidence is very slight, but simple passage graves like the one excavated at Broadsands on the Devon coast may well have been inspired by cross-Channel contacts, and it has been suggested that the closed burial chambers beneath circular cists, known as rotundas, which are sometimes found embedded in megalithic tombs of the Severn–Cotswold group, may be a reflection of similar structures found within the long mounds of the Morbihan. While it must be admitted that evidence for contact between Armorica and the western seaways around Britain and Ireland is limited, it does satisfactorily explain the introduction of the megalithic burial tradition and the concept of the passage grave to western parts of the British Isles and Ireland. Movements of people can never have been large in comparison with the immigrants from north-eastern France and Belgium whose culture soon came to dominate the

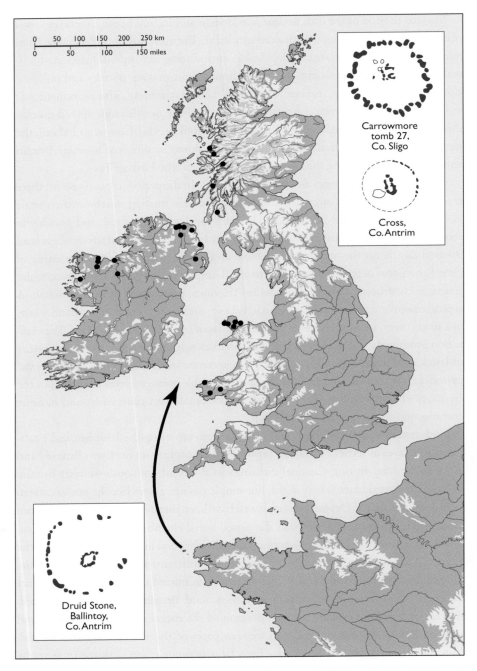

2.31 Tombs with closed chambers and simple passage tombs were probably introduced into Britain and Ireland from Brittany along the Atlantic seaways as their distribution suggests.

islands, but, that said, these early Atlantic travellers established a connectivity which persisted and in times to come was to grow in strength.

So the Scene Was Set

In the thousand years or so following the arrival of the first farming communities around 5300 BC, Armorica was transformed, with the southern Morbihan becoming the centre of a powerful polity whose elite exerted considerable coercive power and were able to maintain themselves by manipulating the distribution of luxury goods imported from afar. Why the region should so quickly have risen to dominance is an intriguing question. One factor may have been the stability of the indigenous hunter-gatherer bands already occupying the region, but location must also have played a significant part. The southern Morbihan lay on a major maritime corridor stretching from the Gironde estuary to the Penmarc'h peninsula, a zone of islands, bays, and estuaries linked to the great river corridors of the Garonne and the Loire. With the spread of Neolithic communities from the south and east, introducing new technologies and a greatly increased demand for raw materials, movements along the maritime corridor intensified and new connectivities developed. But why, along this 400 kilometres or so of coast, should the Morbihan rise to such prominence? There are no easy answers. It is not unusually endowed with resources but could offer furs from the inland forests, salt from the coastal marshes, and attractive stone, like fibrolite. Was it the vigour and density of the hunter-gatherer population or perhaps the mystery of the landscape and its battle with the inexorable encroachment of the sea so evident to every generation that drew the attention of visitors? Certainly knowledge of the rows of carved menhirs would have spread: the Grand Menhir Brisé must have been one of the wonders of the ancient world. Whatever the reasons for the cultural vitality of the southern Morbihan, it is a remarkable fact that it retained its pre-eminence for three millennia into the beginning of the Bronze Age.

Sometime in the middle of the fifth millennium maritime contacts developed with western Iberia, introducing a new range of exotic items like the variscite necklaces. It was at this time that the idea of the accessible burial chamber, manifested in the form of the passage graves, began to spread along the Atlantic seaways. There is a strong possibility that the concept developed in the precocious culture of the southern Morbihan, spreading south to the Atlantic coast of Iberia, north to the northern coastal region of Armorica, and later to the communities surrounding the Irish Sea. Atlantic maritime connectivity, once established, was to remain a persistent dynamic for the next millennium.

The farming communities of the rest of Armorica shared many of the cultural characteristics of their south-coast neighbours but without apparently developing the complex social hierarchies that distinguished the southern complex. That said, their passage graves were substantial, and later in the fourth millennium they developed a distinctive culture reflected in the gallery graves, with lateral entrances and with breasts and necklace motifs carved on the tomb walls. These communities of the north coast inevitably looked north and developed maritime networks encompassing the Channel Islands and the coasts of Normandy and Britain. It was through these connections that the idea of the passage grave reached the coasts of Devon and Somerset and a few exotic items of exchange—axes of Plussulien dolerite and Alpine jadeitite—began to find their way into the archaeological record of south-western Britain. So it was, in the centuries around 4000 BC, that the Bretons and Britons began their long and continuing interaction.

3

THE METAL-RICH WEST
2700–600 BC

B Y 3000 BC the inhabitants of the Armorican peninsula had established contacts with neighbours, by land and by sea, which were to continue to influence their cultural development for centuries to come. Across the long land frontier had arrived the pioneer Villeneuve-Saint-Germain farmers advancing from the Paris basin at the end of the sixth millennium. Not long after, the valley of the river Loire became the prime corridor of communication with the east, with links extending northwards to the Paris basin and eventually reaching the lower Rhine valley. The distribution of dolerite axes made in the Plussulien quarries during the fourth millennium echoes the importance of the route, with very large numbers of axes distributed along a wide corridor as far east as Orléans. Beyond that the more distant networks are reflected by concentrations of axes in the Paris basin, along the Seine, the Oise, and the Aisne. It is no coincidence that it was in just these areas that gallery graves, very similar to those found in Armorica, cluster. The two groups appear to be broadly contemporary. Another link between the two areas is suggested by preferences for similar pottery types. The style of pottery known as the Seine–Oise–Marne type, so common in the Paris basin, was copied by the users of the Armorican gallery graves. The importance of the Loire–Paris basin–Rhine axis is also reflected by the distribution of Grand-Pressigny flint, an iron-rich, honey-coloured flint dug out of the clays in the valley of the Claise and Creuse near Poitiers. The flint was exported in the form of finely worked narrow blades and long daggers or lance-heads as well as large blade

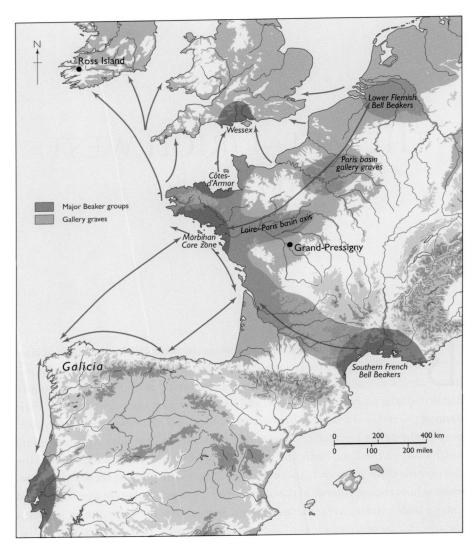

3.1 By the middle of the third millennium the land and sea-routes linking the innovative region of Atlantic Europe were in active use, creating a network of connectivity. The central position of Armorica ensured that the communities of the peninsula played an active part in maritime exchanges, which intensified as metals (tin, gold, and copper) began to be exploited on an increasing scale.

cores known as *livres de beurre*. Grand-Pressigny flint was found in quantity along the south coast of Armorica, but it is also found in third-millennium graves in the Paris basin and in the lower Rhine. This network of connectivity, extending in an arc across northern France from the Loire mouth to the Rhine, became a highly innovative zone through which not only materials but also belief systems and people were to flow (below, p. 93).

The second land route that contributed to the cultural development of Armorica was the Garonne corridor leading from the Mediterranean. We have already seen that in the late sixth and early fifth millennia there were contacts with the farming communities occupying this area (above, pp. 42–3). That interactions continued is suggested by similarities in gallery graves found in Armorica and western France and along the Garonne corridor. Finally, there were the sea-routes linking Armorica to the wider Atlantic world. To the south journeys were made to and from Atlantic-facing Iberia, while to the north more tenuous links were beginning to develop with south-western Britain and the Irish Sea beyond. Over the next two millennia the inhabitants of peninsular Armorica were to benefit from this web of connectivities, and in doing so they would enhance their distinctive identity.

The Beaker Phenomenon

The middle centuries of the third millennium, about 2700–2200 BC, saw much of western Europe and parts of central Europe adopt a series of new belief and behaviour systems which created the appearance of widespread cultural unity. It was once called the Beaker culture and now, less didactically, the Beaker package. There has, inevitably, been much debate about what the cultural similarities mean, and opinions have changed as new evidence has emerged and new ways of modelling the phenomena have been attempted. For a long time it was believed that people, sometimes referred to as the Beaker folk, migrated throughout western and central Europe on a large scale. Fashions then changed, migrationist views were rejected, and new explanations sought. But more recently the study of stable isotopes in human teeth and of DNA recovered from human bones has shown that movement did, indeed, take place. The outstanding question is, on what scale? The stable-isotope work has suggested that it was comparatively limited, with most people usually moving only short distances, though some longer journeys are implied. The initial ancient DNA results have, however, generated startling headlines claiming large-scale movements leading to population replacement. More detailed regional studies need to be made before these intriguing issues can be fully resolved.

Bringing the scientific and archaeological evidence together and taking a Europe-wide view, it would seem that the Beaker phenomenon resulted from the impact of two cultural processes, one eastern and land-based, the other western and dependent on the sea. Sometime around 3000 BC there developed on the North European Plain, stretching from Germany to Ukraine, a cultural complex known as the Corded Ware, or Corded Ware–Battle-Axe, culture. The group is characterized by single burials often under round barrows arranged in cemeteries. The bodies, usually male, were accompanied by stone battle-axes and handleless beakers decorated by wrapping a cord around the body of the vessel to impress the surface before firing. Recent studies of the genetic structure of the population have shown that a significant percentage of its DNA was derived from incomers from the Pontic–Caspian steppe. The latest of these people, known as the Yamnaya culture, had travelled from the steppe to settle in the Great Hungarian Plain about 2800 BC. By the middle of the millennium the Corded Ware culture had spread into Denmark, the Netherlands, and Switzerland and it was in the lower Rhine valley that it came into contact with influences emanating from the Atlantic zone.

The earliest beakers in the west are found along the Atlantic coast of Iberia, especially in the Lisbon region, in contexts dating from 2800 to 2700 BC. The classic type, known as the Maritime Bell Beaker, is decorated with thin, evenly spaced bands of decoration covering the outside of the vessel, each band infilled with oblique lines created by impressing a comb or the edge of a shell into the clay before firing. The vessels were usually finely made and fired in an oxidizing atmosphere to a bright red colour. In some examples there is evidence that a white paste had been rubbed into the impressed decoration to make the design stand out. When found in burials, the beakers were often accompanied by archers' equipment, notably flint arrowheads and stone wrist guards, together with small tanged blades of copper known as Palmella points.

Classic Maritime Bell Beakers originated in the Tagus region, from where the concept spread northwards along the Iberian Atlantic coast to Galicia and across the Bay of Biscay to the south coast of Armorica, where beakers are found in some number. A detailed analysis of the group has shown that while the Armorican beakers were very closely similar to those from western Iberia in details of their technology, the clay used to make them was obtained locally. In other words, it was not the beakers themselves that travelled but the people with the technical skill to make them, bringing with them other aspects of the culture and beliefs. Besides the pottery, two Palmella points are known in Armorica, one in the lower Loire valley, the other in the southern Morbihan. We will look in some detail at the beakers in Armorica (below, pp. 91–5) but first we must complete the big picture.

It was very likely from Armorica that the idea of the Maritime Bell Beaker spread inland along the Loire corridor, using the long-established networks, reaching the lower Rhine valley and interacting there with the Corded Ware tradition in the period 2700–2500 BC. At the same time the practice of single burial accompanied by a stone battle-axe spread from northern Europe westwards along the network reaching

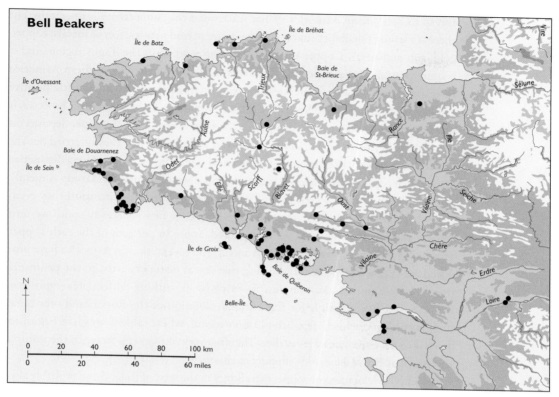

3.2 A distinctive type of pottery known as the Maritime Bell Beaker was found extensively in the southern coastal regions of Armorica. Though locally made, they were inspired by ideas and values brought in from western Iberia, quite possibly carried by people searching for copper sources.

the Atlantic coastal region. The Loire–Rhine corridor soon became a highly innovative zone—a fusion corridor—where peoples mixed and ideas and beliefs were shared, creating new cultural configurations. It was from this region that people crossed the Channel, apparently in some numbers, in the period 2500–2250 BC, to settle in the British Isles.

The Search for Metals

The Atlantic route across the Bay of Biscay, by which Maritime Bell Beakers reached southern Armorica ultimately from the Tagus region, followed the long-established networks along which variscite beads and pendants had been introduced into Armorica in the fifth and fourth millennia and the passage grave concept may have spread to Iberia from Armorica. What reactivated the connectivity is uncertain, but there is a strong possibility that it was the desire to find new sources of metals: copper, gold, tin, and silver. Copper was already being worked in the Tagus region, and it is quite possible that prospectors from here made the journey to southern Armorica in search of ores. While there are copper lodes in Armorica, there is little positive evidence that they were exploited at the time. What we can be sure about, however, is that sometime about 2400 BC prospectors had discovered the rich copper deposits on Ross Island in Lough Leane, in the south-west of Ireland. Here they quarried out the fahlerz and chalcopyrite–arsenopyrite ores and smelted them to produce a distinctive arsenic-rich copper with traces of antimony and silver (designated as Group A metal). The Ross Island mines served Ireland's need for five hundred years until they eventually became flooded about 1900 BC, by which time new sources in south-western Ireland and north Wales were being exploited. Some 80 per cent of the early copper axes found in Britain were of Group A metal, and several sites in Armorica have produced axe-ingots of this metal, showing that it was being exported to the peninsula from the Irish mines. The complexities involved in working fahlerz ores imply that the prospectors responsible for the initial exploration of the Ross Island ores came from abroad, most likely from the Lisbon region, where fahlerz ores had begun to be worked for some centuries earlier. The discovery of Beaker pottery in the mining settlement as Ross Island adds support to this view.

The early development of copper metallurgy in the west of Ireland and probably also in Armorica was quickly followed by the exploitation of other metals in the region: gold soon after 2400 BC and tin by 2200 BC. Gold is found in workable quantities in north-west Iberia, Armorica, Cornwall, south Wales, and Ireland, while tin is restricted to north-west Iberia, Armorica, and Cornwall. Both metals occur as ores formed around the edges of intruded masses of igneous rocks, but it is likely that, in the early stages at least, the tin ores and native gold were extracted from alluvial deposits derived from the erosion of the ore bodies. In Armorica tin-rich sands are found along the south coast, particularly around Quimperlé and south of Quimper, and there are extensive deposits in the north-west of the peninsula in the Léon region, particularly around Saint-Renan, where evidence has been found of the smelting of tin ore in the late second millennium BC. Alluvial gold deposits are to be found around Mûr-de-Bretagne in the centre of the peninsula and in the Montagnes Noires. In south-western Britain

3.3 (*Opposite*) The old hard rocks of Armorica, and the igneous intrusions that penetrated them, created mineralized zones rich in metals. The maps show the location of deposits rich enough to warrant exploitation in the Bronze Age. At this stage the tin and gold extracted probably came from alluvial deposits resulting from the erosion of the ore bodies.

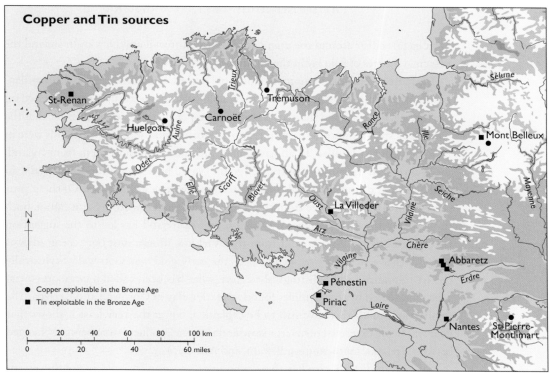

Copper and Tin sources

● Copper exploitable in the Bronze Age
■ Tin exploitable in the Bronze Age

St-Renan
Huelgoat
Carnoët
Trémuson
Mont Belleux
La Villeder
Abbaretz
Pénestin
Piriac
Nantes
St-Pierre-Montlimart

Sélune
Trieux
Rance
Ille
Aulne
Odet
Mayenne
Elle
Scorff
Blavet
Oust
Seiche
Vilaine
Arz
Chère
Erdre
Vilaine
Loire

N

| 0 | 20 | 40 | 60 | 80 | 100 km |
| 0 | | 20 | | 40 | 60 miles |

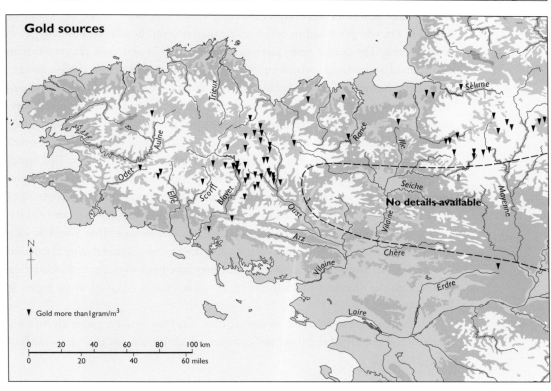

Gold sources

▼ Gold more than 1 gram/m³

No details available

Sélune
Trieux
Rance
Ille
Aulne
Odet
Elle
Scorff
Blavet
Oust
Arz
Seiche
Vilaine
Mayenne
Chère
Vilaine
Erdre
Loire

N

| 0 | 20 | 40 | 60 | 80 | 100 km |
| 0 | | 20 | | 40 | 60 miles |

both metals occur around the granite massifs of Cornwall and Devon. In Ireland the principal sources of gold lay in the mountains of Wicklow.

The most spectacular items made from gold in the last centuries of the third millennium were lunulae, large crescents of sheet gold with geometric decoration incised on the surface, worn around the neck to cover the upper chest. It is quite possible that the 'necklaces' shown on statue menhirs from Armorica and the Channel Islands were in fact depictions of lunulae. In all, 115 lunulae are known, most of them from Ireland, representing an astonishing output of gold. Twelve have been found in Britain, in Wales, Scotland, and Cornwall, and eighteen in north-western France. Of these, four came from Armorica, three from the cist at Kerivoa and one from Saint-Pôtan, both in Côtes-d'Armor. That eighty-five were found in Ireland has led to the suggestion that they were made using gold from the Wicklow Mountains, but recent analysis suggests that a major source of much of the early gold was Cornwall. Stylistically the Irish lunulae can be distinguished from what has been called a more provincial type represented by the examples found at Harlyn Bay in Cornwall and Kerivoa. The implications of all this have still to be explained, but at the very least it shows that gold was being extracted on a large scale and that the products were being exchanged between Ireland, south-western Britain, and Armorica.

It is not at all unlikely that those who were panning for gold in south-western Britain and Armorica were also extracting cassiterite, from which tin could be smelted. Tin was produced in considerable quantities to be alloyed with copper to make bronze. The change from arsenical copper to tin bronze took place in Britain and Ireland and possibly Armorica over a very short period before 2200–2000 BC. Thereafter the metal of choice was bronze with about 8–10 per cent tin. This produced an alloy that was tough and malleable and could easily be cast. Clearly the metalworkers had been experimenting to discover the optimal ratios. What is surprising is that in the rest of Europe, including Iberia, where there were ample sources of tin, the new metal, bronze, was not adopted for another three or four hundred years. This brings with it interesting implications. Although it was prospectors from Atlantic Iberia who introduced copper working to Armorica, Britain, and Ireland, it was the successors of these pioneers who experimented to develop the new alloy. Only much later did the knowledge reach Iberia, flowing back along the Atlantic seaways. That it took so long might suggest that maritime contacts with Iberia were interrupted during the period 2200–1700 BC. The only evidence that there may have been some limited interaction comes from the discovery of an Iberian gold collar known as a *gargantilla* found at Rondossec in the Morbihan.

Standing back from the detail we can see that after the initial contact with Atlantic Iberia in the middle of the third millennium, which introduced the Maritime Bell

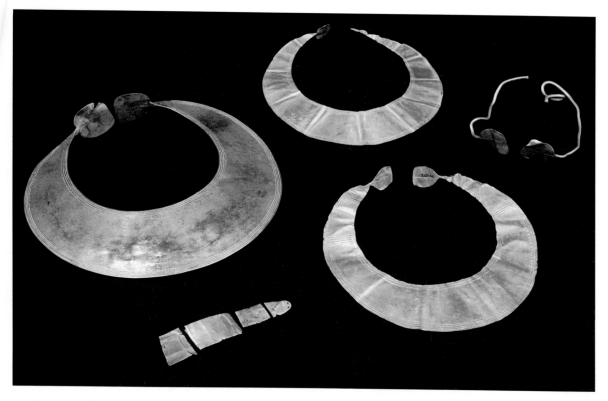

3.4 The three gold lunulae and other items of gold found in a hoard at Kerivoa, Bourbriac, in Côtes-d'Armor date to the late third millennium BC. The lunulae may have been made in south-western Britain.

Beaker to Armorica together with the skills of the coppersmith and gold panner, the communities of Armorica, south-western Britain, and Ireland rapidly developed their metallurgical skills, creating a sphere of interaction in which knowledge as well as artefacts were widely exchanged.

Beakers in Armorica

Beaker pottery arrived in Armorica around the middle of the third millennium. In all some 230 vessels are known, the great majority of them coming from the south coast, with only a few from the coast of the Côtes-d'Armor and from the interior. Most of the Beaker material comes from megalithic tombs; indeed some 20 per cent of the Armorican tombs have produced Beaker finds. In other words, people using beakers seem to have continued to be involved with the collective burial rites of their predecessors, making use of existing structures. But, that said, there is a mismatch between the distribution of beakers and gallery graves. While the gallery graves are found across much of the peninsula, it is only those close to the coast that have yielded Beaker material.

Quite often the Beaker finds placed in megalithic tombs are found scattered or are so ill-recorded that there is little to say about the burial ritual, a problem exacerbated by the fact that human bones rarely survive in the acid soils of Armorica. But individual tombs often produce a number of beakers, suggesting that collective burial was still being practised. In the gallery grave of Men-ar-Rompet, Kerbors, on the coast of Côtes-d'Armor, forty-one beaker vessels were found, some stacked inside others. Some were so similar in form and technique that they were probably made by the same potter. The implication would seem to be that here the pots were deposited at one time either for an individual of some eminence or perhaps as the debris of a funerary feast held at the tomb in honour of the ancestors.

While the majority of the beakers from Armorica belong to the classic Maritime Bell Beaker tradition and are closely similar to those in use in Galicia and the Lisbon region, implying Atlantic inspiration, other types similar to those developing in the lower

3.5 Beaker pottery is often found in gallery graves representing the late reuse of existing megalithic structures. The large collection of beakers and associated pots found in the tomb of Men-Ar-Rompet, Kerbors, on the coast of Côtes-d'Armor were similar in style and technique and may well have been made by the same potter.

Rhine valley have also been found. The tomb at Goërem, Gâvres, in the Morbihan, produced an All-Over Cord Beaker (AOC), flint arrowheads, a copper awl, and four thin plaques of gold, while at nearby Kerouaren, Plouhinec, a burial cist was found containing an All-Over Ornamental Beaker (AOO) together with several gold items including a diadem and a stone wrist guard. It could well be that we are seeing here people who had migrated westwards from the Netherlands along the Loire–Paris basin–lower Rhine corridor. The discovery of a large number of All-Over Ornamental Beakers during the dredging of operations in the Loire at Ancenis, between Nantes and Angers, is further evidence of the use of the Loire route at this time.

Besides the beakers themselves, other items of the Beaker packages have been found in Armorica. Flat tanged copper daggers are known, though not in any number. One, found in one of the passage graves at Barnenez, was made from copper with a high arsenic content not unlike the metal from Ross Island. Flat copper axes have been found in greater numbers west of the river Vilaine. Normally they occur as single finds or in hoards and rarely in tombs. Eight hoards are known; that from Ploudaniel in Finistère comprised seventy axes but the rest were much smaller, with fewer than ten axes. Where analyses have been carried out, they were all of arsenical copper. Other finds include copper awls, stone archer's wrist guards, bone buttons with V-perforations, and a number of gold objects, including bracelets, a diadem, globular and tubular beads, and a variety of plaques. Most of the gold items were found in the southern coastal zone, their distribution echoing that of the Beaker pottery.

While the objects mentioned above are of the kind found in Beaker contexts throughout western Europe, Armorica has produced two exceptional items: cast copper battle-axes with copper shafts, found at Kersoufflet, Le Faouët, in the Morbihan, and Bon Amour, Trévé, in Côtes-d'Armor. These remarkable weapons very probably originated in northern Europe, perhaps the Nordic region, and somehow found their way to Armorica, carried by migrating warriors or exchanged as gifts passing hand to hand along the lower Rhine–Paris basin–Loire valley network.

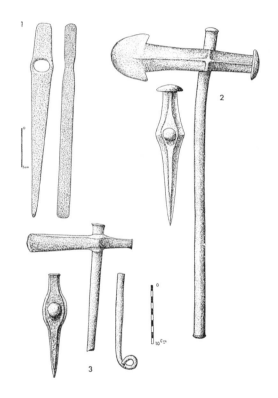

3.6 Three battle-axes cast in copper alloy, found in Armorica, may have been imported from northern Europe, where the type was in regular use. (1) Fougères, Ille-et-Vilaine; (2) Kersoufflet, Le Faouët, Morbihan; (3) Bon Amour, Trévé, Cotes-d'Armor. They may have inspired the manufacture of stone copies.

It was these two high-status items or others like them that inspired Armorican craftsmen to make their own versions of battle-axes out of stone. The stone chosen was hornblendite quarried at Pleuven near Quimper. These battle-axes are found extensively in Penmarc'h near the quarry, and along the south coast, particularly in the Morbihan, extending further south to the Gironde estuary. They were also exchanged

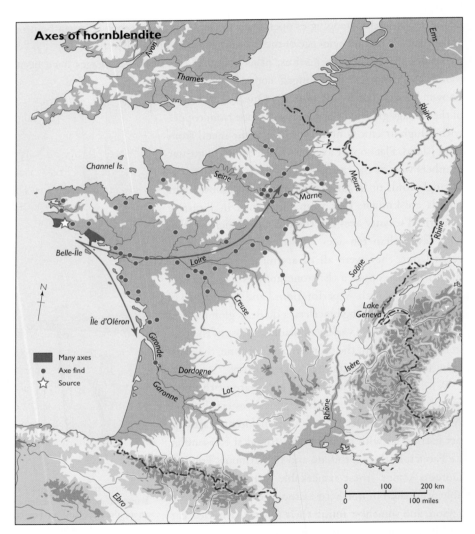

3.7 Battle-axes made of hornblendite were found in some number along the south coast of Armorica and some passed, in processes of gift exchange, along the Loire to the Paris Basin and along the coast of western France to the Gironde estuary.

along the Loire corridor to the Paris basin and beyond, with one reaching the lower Rhine region—another manifestation of this important axis of communication.

The Beaker phenomenon in Armorica, though clearly evident in the archaeological record, is not easy to understand. The simplest explanation would be to suppose that in the first half of the third millennium migrants settled on the south shore in an already densely populated region, some eventually moving on to the north coast. They brought with them knowledge of metalworking and seem to have lived in harmony with the local population. As part of the same movement some of the migrants travelled east along the Loire valley to settle in the Paris basin and the lower Rhine valley, where again they merged with indigenous peoples. A little later, in the period about 2400–2200 BC, there was a movement in the reverse direction, with people from the Rhine valley introducing their distinctive styles of cord-decorated beakers and their preference for battle-axes. Some of these people turned north to cross the Channel to Britain; others carried on into the Armorican peninsula. These latter do not seem to have been invasions or mass migration; rather, movements of small groups establishing friendly relations with the natives among whom they settled, contributing aspects of their own culture to the general mix. By about 2200 BC change was in the air. The production of metals—copper, tin, and gold—was inspiring a new sense of mobility, and the old social order was beginning to come to an end.

Closing the Tombs

Passage graves, and the gallery graves that developed later, were constructed in such a way that they could be entered at any time to allow new burials to be added or for rituals for the dead to be performed. They were accessible tombs: places where successive ancestors could rest and be revered. The blocking of a tomb or the placement of a final deposit therefore signifies the end of collective burial at that particular place. There could be many reasons for closing a tomb. The lineage may have come to an end, superstitions may have developed, making the place taboo, or the belief system may simply have changed. That evidence for the blocking of tombs in Armorica and the Channel Islands spans the period from about 3400 to 2200 BC implies that there was no single cause.

The earliest evidence for tomb blocking comes from three passage graves: Île Carn, Ty-Floc'h, and Gavr'inis. Île Carn consisted of three passage graves, a central grave to which two others had subsequently been added. The first tomb closure saw the passage of the central grave walled across at both ends. This might have happened when one or both of the other passage graves were added. The latest radiocarbon data for the use of

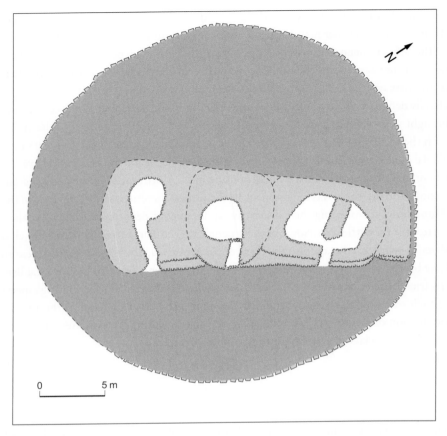

3.8 The agglomeration of three megalithic tombs on Île Carn shows two stages in their decommissioning. First the entrance to the central tomb was blocked with stone walls, and later the complex was buried in a single large mound blocking all access.

the north chamber lies in the first half of the third millennium. Thereafter the entire monument was buried within a large circular mound blocking all the tomb entrances. At Ty-Floc'h and Gavr'inis the entrances to the passages were blocked with deposits of rubble in the second half of the fourth millennium. In all the cases the early closure is likely to have resulted from reasons specific to the actual monument, such as the demise of the lineage to whom it belonged. Many of the passage graves continued in use much longer since thirty-eight of them are known to have contained Beaker material.

A number of the gallery graves have also yielded finds of the Beaker period, and in some the way in which the items had been laid out and the state of preservation suggest that the act of deposition represented the final stage in the use of the chamber. Examples include the gallery graves of Penker, Plozevet, and Kerandrège, Moëlan, both in Finistère, and Men-ar-Rompet, Kerbors, in Côtes-d'Armor, which, as we have seen (p. 92), contained forty-one beakers, all complete or nearly so. The fact that no earlier material was found suggests that the chamber had been cleared out before the final deposit was placed. The practice also extends to the Channel Islands. At Ville-ès-Nouaux on Jersey intact vessels including bell beakers and locally made wares were arranged in groups of three, protected by stone slabs, along the north side of the gallery.

Some gallery graves were also deliberately sealed. At Crec'h-Quillé, in Côtes-d'Armor, a fire had been lit in the entrance passage, after which a wall was built across it. Radiocarbon dates from the hearth show that the blocking took place between 2400 and 2000 BC. A similar date was obtained for the blocking of the tomb at Champ-Grosset, Côtes-d'Armor, and it is possible that the passage of the tomb of Goërem in the Morbihan was also deliberately blocked with rubble after Beaker use.

Standing back from the detail one can see that, while tombs could be blocked at any time, there is clear evidence at many of a cessation of use after Beaker material had been placed in them. This suggests that in the years around 2200 BC the old rite of collective burial was coming to an end after more than two millennia. It is tempting to link this to the new ideas introduced with the Beakers, but the situation was probably more complicated. Clearly those who adopted the Beaker package were content to use existing megalithic tombs in Armorica just as they were in Iberia and Ireland: it was part of the Atlantic tradition. What may have brought about the changes was increasing contact with practices and values arriving from the east, ultimately from the Rhine valley region, in the latter part of the third millennium. We have already seen evidence of this in the appearance of beakers decorated with cord impressions and of the growing popularity of battle-axes (above, p. 93). One of the characteristics of the area was that individuals were buried singly in sealed graves. In all probability it was these new practices that brought about a radical change in the burial rites of the Armoricans after about 2200 BC.

New Expressions of Power

The period from about 2200 to 1500 BC, traditionally known as the Early Bronze Age, saw the emergence of a new style of elite burial: the placing of the deceased in a chamber of stone or timber buried beneath a tumulus (round barrow). The tumuli were often arranged in cemeteries of up to twenty individual structures. Some 250 examples have been identified, with the vast majority lying west of the rivers Blavet and Trieux, with concentrations in the Blavet valley and the Monts d'Arrée. That only five were found in the southern Morbihan shows that power had now shifted, the old Carnac centre becoming a backwater. Why the Monts d'Arrée should have become such a focus is a matter of speculation. The region was reasonably metal-rich but there could be other reasons. It may be that animal rearing had become increasingly important, with animals being taken to the upland pastures in the summer, and it was here that the ancestors were buried.

It has long been recognized that the Early Bronze Age tumuli could be divided into two broad groups: a First Series, in which large numbers of flint arrowheads were buried with the deceased, and a Second Series, all of which contained pottery vessels. The First Series were fewer in number and were concentrated in the Penmarc'h peninsula and in the Léon and Trégor regions, while the Second Series, considerably more numerous, account for the concentration in the Monts d'Arrée and the valley of the Blavet. More recently a finer chronology has been proposed based largely on the changing styles of the daggers found in most of the graves. Four types of dagger were defined, which, when considered together with the other finds from the graves, allowed three broad phases to be identified, named after individual burials: the Prat phase (2200–1900 BC), the Kernonen-Kerodou phase (c.1900–1700 BC), and the Guerveur phase (1700–1500 BC). Since it is only in this last phase that pottery has been found, it means that the comparatively few burials of the First Series (with arrowheads) cover some five hundred years while the many more burials of the Second Series (with pottery) have to fit into only two hundred years. The implications are that significant social changes must have taken place about 1700 BC associated, perhaps, with a sudden rise in population and a reorientation of the subsistence economy.

In the First Series, the tomb structure varies. The covering barrows are circular, averaging 20–30 metres in diameter, though some are up to 50 metres across. The maximum height is about 5 metres, but most are lower, reduced by ploughing and erosion. They were usually built of clay or earth, but some had central cairns of rubble. The burial chambers were variously constructed: some were entirely of timber, some were of megalithic structure, and some were built with dry-stone walling covered by a capstone. One is known that was built wholly of corbelling. There are also interesting differences in the distribution of these various styles of building. The timber-built tombs concentrate in the north, in the Trégor, while the dry-stone-built tombs with capstones are found predominantly in the west of Finistère. These patterns would suggest that we are dealing with different social groups, each with their own stylistic

3.9 (*Opposite*) A simple chronological division of the Armorican grave series can be made between those burials accompanied by flint arrowheads and those containing pottery. Those with arrowheads date to the period about 2200–1630 BC; those with pottery were in use for a much shorter period, about 1630–1500 BC, but the number of burials had dramatically increased.

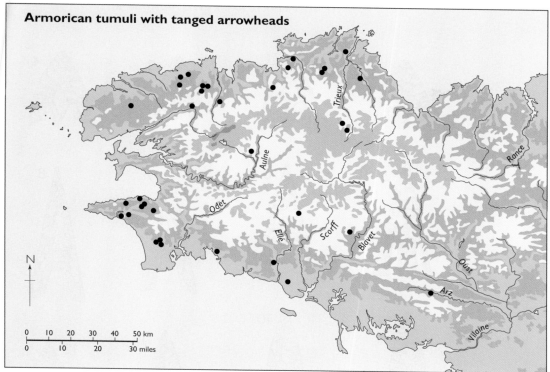

Armorican tumuli with tanged arrowheads

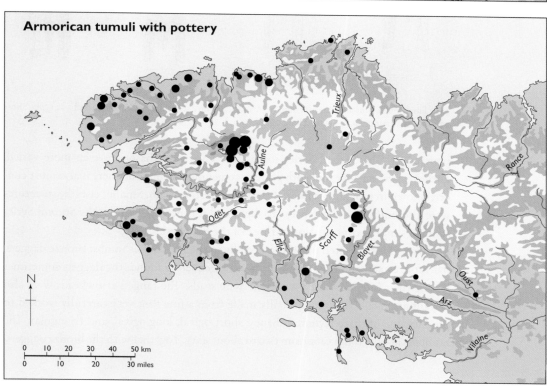

Armorican tumuli with pottery

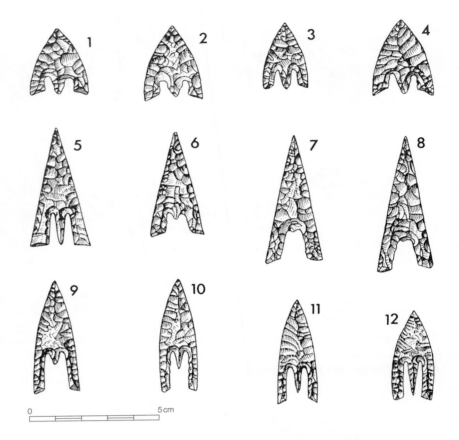

3.10 Finely made flint arrowheads from the Armorican grave series illustrating the three basic types: short ogival (1–4), triangular (5–8), and long ogival (9–12).

preferences. The Second Series tombs (the Guerveur phase) are even more varied. Earlier types continue, but corbelling becomes more common. There is also more concern shown in providing a floor of timber or of stone slabs. Smaller cist-like structures were also built. The differences are slight and it is best to consider the Second Series styles as simply a continuation of those of the First Series.

Grave goods are often prolific, especially in the First Series tombs. Bronze daggers, flat bronze axes, and flint arrowheads were frequently found, the daggers sometimes having their hilts decorated with gold wire studs. The tanged arrowheads were also elegant artefacts. They were usually made from a fine flint very carefully worked to produce one of three favoured shapes: short ogival, long ogival, and triangular. The numbers in each tomb vary from two to about sixty. Together with the bronze daggers, the bow-and-arrow set was clearly a mark of elite status for the duration of the First Series tombs (2200–1700 BC). Second Series tombs were usually provided with pottery vessels, often accompanied by daggers, but occasionally there are richer deposits.

A few burials stand out as being those of people of exceptional status. The First Series burial of Kernonen, Plouvorn, in Finistère is notable for the massive size of its covering barrow, 6 metres high and 50 metres in diameter. Underneath, the rectangular burial chamber was built of stone and floored with wood. Most of the grave goods were placed in three wooden boxes. They included a dagger with bone pommel, two daggers and a short-sword with hilts inset with gold pins, four bronze axes, sixty flint arrowheads, and twelve pendants of amber. Clearly the lineage of the deceased was able to command great wealth as well as a significant labour force to build the tomb. The amber is a reminder that contact with northern Europe, probably Denmark, was maintained either along the Loire–Paris basin–lower Rhine corridor or indirectly through southern Britain.

The First Series tomb of Saint-Adrien in Côtes-d'Armor produced a similar range of grave goods, two short-swords, two daggers, one with a pommel decorated with gold pins, a bronze axe, and forty-five flint arrowheads, but in addition the deceased was provided with a silver cup. A similar silver cup was found at Saint-Fiacre in the Morbihan and the top part of a gold cup is recorded from Ploumilliau in Côtes-d'Armor. Cups made in precious materials—gold, amber, and shale—are known in southern Britain and clearly played a part in elite behaviour, but the two Armorican silver cups are similar in form to a series of pottery cups, evidently copying metal forms, found in south-eastern Iberia at the time, a region in which silver was plentiful. It is not impossible, therefore, that the precious metal cups enjoyed by the Armorican aristocracy were imported from the south.

It would be wrong to give the impression that all the Early Bronze Age tumulus burials in western Armorica were accompanied by grave goods. Of the 250 or so recorded, only about a hundred produced artefacts characteristic of the First or Second Series tombs. The rest were the graves of people of lower rank. Some of the richer burials were associated with much smaller mounds covering simple burial cists, perhaps for the servants or retainers of the elite. The rich offerings found in a few graves should not distort our view of Early Bronze Age life: we are clearly dealing with a highly stratified society and there must have been a large subservient population whose labours supported the conspicuous consumption of the rich.

The elite tumulus burials of Armorica are comparable to the chieftains' burials of Wessex which had their floruit between 1900 and 1700 BC. The similarities have led some observers to suggest a direct relationship between the two regions, even to the extent of Wessex having received an influx of warriors from Armorica. There are,

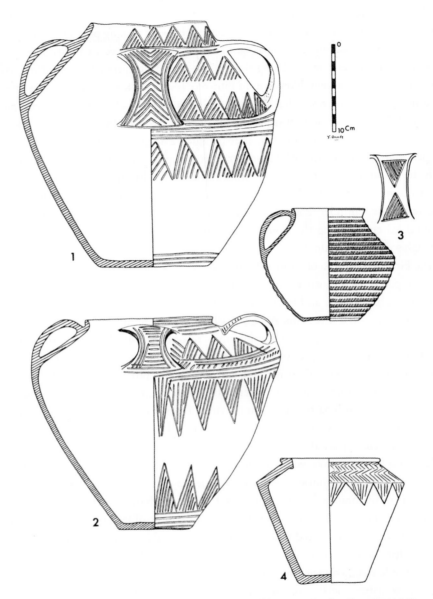

3.11 A selection of pottery from the Armorican grave series: (1) Berven, Guiclan, Finistère; (2) Kerouaré, Guimiliau, Finistère; (3) Gouer-Ven, Lesneven, Finistère; (4) Parc-ar-Vouden, Guidel, Morbihan.

3.12 (*Opposite*) A large settlement enclosure defined by a ditch was excavated at Bel Air, Lannion, Côtes-d'Armor. It dates to between 2000 and 1600 BC. Two contemporary funerary structures lie just outside the enclosure.

however, significant differences between burial practices in the two regions. The over-riding importance of the bow-and-arrow set and the frequent appearance of bronze axes and short-swords in the Armorican tombs distinguish them from those in Wessex.

That said, there are signs that the elites on the two sides of the Channel maintained contact, leading to the exchange of high-status goods such as bronze daggers with hilts ornamented with inset gold pins. These were probably made by Armorican craftsmen. Twelve are known from Armorica and two found their way to Wessex, one to be buried in the famous tomb of Bush Barrow near Stonehenge. A much less valu-able import was a decorated handled pot found in a burial called Gallibury Hump on Brighstone Down on the Isle of Wight. The minerals in the clay from which the vessel was made show it to have originated in Armorica. Several other handled pots very similar to Armorican types are known from coastal districts of Wessex, witnessing to the arrival of visitors from across the sea. A few luxury items found in the Armorican tombs probably came from Wessex. The tomb of La Motta near Lannion in Côtes-d'Armor produced a small box made of gold, decorated with zigzag lines. The style is highly reminiscent of British goldwork but is hardly known across the Channel. Another item likely to have come from Britain is a spacer plate from a jet necklace found at Kerguévarec near Plouyé in Finistère. The amber ornaments from Kernonen mentioned above may also have reached Armorica from the Wessex region, where amber circulated widely among the elite.

There is sufficient evidence, then, to suggest that cross-Channel journeys were being made linking the Armorican elites and their counterparts in Wessex. Who were involved in the journeys, how many there were, and with what frequency they set out, we can only guess. While it could have been the occasional entrepreneur hoping to make a good deal, it is likely that regular visits were being made by members of the elite to maintain social relationships. On such occasions gifts would have been exchanged and marriage alliances made. It is tempting to suggest that the great reli-gious monuments of Wessex, not least Stonehenge, would have been an attraction, striking awe into the soul of the visitor and encouraging pilgrimages.

The Early Bronze Age tumulus-building society of western Armorica, forged from the indigenous Neolithic population and reinforced by incomers from western Iberia and from the Rhineland, created a highly distinctive culture with a unique series of burial customs reflecting their belief systems. This cultural group occupied the west-ern extremity of the Armorican peninsula west of the rivers Blavet and Trieux, and was able to maintain its identity because of its comparative isolation and its use of the sea to build alliances. Thus the pattern was set for what was to come over the next three millennia. The communities of western Armorica (Basse-Bretagne), pro-tected by their remoteness, were able to develop their own culture, while those in the eastern parts (Haute-Bretagne) remained more open to influences from the European approaches. It is a divide recognizable through time, apparent even today.

The English Channel Comes Alive

The production of copper and later bronze had a transformative effect on many aspects of life. This is particularly true of seafaring. Before metal tools became available, the boat builders' creativity was limited. The toolkits were adequate for making simple dug-out canoes from a single log, suitable for river transport. For sea travel these craft could be modified by the addition of stakes to give them greater freeboard and outriggers to provide improved stability, but they had their limitations on the open sea. Hide boats, that is, vessels made of a small wooden framework over which leather hides were stitched, would have been far more able to face ocean conditions. The technology needed in their construction was simple, and suitable tools of stone and bone were to hand. The revolution which the availability of tools of copper alloy brought about meant that planks could far more easily be made and complex carpentry undertaken to enable them to be rigidly attached to each other. In the middle of the second millennium, sophisticated plank-built vessels were in use around the British Isles, as witnessed by a number of wrecks preserved in the mud of estuaries. Although no similar examples have yet been found around the coasts of north-western France, it is likely that vessels of this kind were now widely in use.

Hide boats and plank-built vessels would have been used both in coastal trade and in cross-Channel sailing, greatly facilitating the connectivity which developed between western Armorica and Wessex in the early second millennium. It may even be that the sea now became an arena in which young men could display their competitive abilities. It has even been suggested that the cups made of precious materials—gold, silver, amber, and shale—were in some way associated with engagements of this type. Seven have been found in Britain all along the south coast from Cornwall to Kent, and three are known in Brittany: the two silver cups from Saint-Adrien and Saint-Fiacre and part of a gold cup from Ploumilliau (above, p. 101).

The cross-Channel networks which linked the chiefdoms of Wessex and Armorica in the first half of the second millennium intensified after 1500 BC, creating a remarkable convergence of culture on both sides of the eastern Channel–southern North Sea region as far west as Normandy and Wessex. Not only was metalwork shared, but pottery styles on both sides of the Channel developed close similarities. Even settlements began to look alike, with clusters of circular houses set among regularly laid-out field systems and occasional ring-works (circular entrenchments) where the elite resided. The simplest way to explain this convergence of culture is in terms of heightened interaction between the communities on either side of the Channel. This was no longer sporadic contact but sustained social intercourse on a much more intensive scale. There would have continued to be visiting elites, but now trading missions became more frequent and we can reasonably suppose there to have been intermarriages and fosterage arrangements designed to create lasting bonds between the communities. While there would, inevitably, have been a flow of people to and fro, there is nothing to suggest large-scale movements intent on invasion and domination.

That organized trade had now begun to play a significant part in social interaction across the Channel is evident from shipwreck sites found along the south coast of Britain. Perhaps the most dramatic was discovered by divers in Langdon Bay, below the chalk cliffs at Dover. A vessel had foundered here sometime between 1300 and 1150 BC carrying a cargo of scrap bronze composed of implements and weapons assembled from the continental coastal region between the Seine and the Rhine. In all, some 360 items were recorded. Much further west, in the Salcombe estuary in south Devon, evidence suggestive of several wreck sites (or losses overboard) has been found together, yielding a range of scrap bronze that had been collected from Britain and northwestern Europe. The two sites date to the last centuries of the second millennium, but they reflect a kind of international trade that must have been well under way centuries before. They are representative of perhaps many hundreds of failed trading ventures: a glimpse of the very considerable scale on which metal was now being moved.

In the western part of the Channel zone there is less evidence of close social relations between the inhabitants of south-western Britain and Armorica, but the sea-lanes were still busy and it may well be that the ship's masters who used the Salcombe estuary made journeys between the two peninsulas, providing a network for goods to be exchanged. That said, this seems to have been a time when the Armoricans continued to develop their own culture in relative isolation.

Armorica after the Tumuli

The fashion for burying the elite beneath tumuli accompanied with grave goods came to an end around 1500 BC. Thereafter the dead were disposed of in less ostentatious ways, leaving little or no archaeological trace. It may be that excarnation—the exposure of the body above ground—became the normal mode of disposure, but this is difficult to demonstrate.

Much of the evidence for the Middle Bronze Age (*c.*1500–1200 BC) comes from the many hoards of bronze implements found throughout Armorica. What motivated people to consign metal to the ground is a matter of debate. Many of the deposits were no doubt votive offerings made to the gods. By placing items of value in the ground the donor was giving a tithe of his or her wealth to the chthonic deities either in payment of a debt or in anticipation of support in some pending enterprise. Once placed, the hoard was intended to remain there. That this practice goes back to Early Neolithic times, if not before, is witnessed by the pair of jadeitite axes buried in the mud close to the Porh Fetan alignment (above, p. 47). The growing number of hoards deposited throughout the second and early first millennia may be a reflection of the increasing dependence of humans on the productivity of the land, perceived to be in the gift of the gods presiding in the underworld. A more prosaic explanation for the hoards is that some, at least, were buried by itinerant bronze-smiths who hid their stock-in-trade in caches to be recovered when required. Another possibility is that some of the hoards were personal possessions buried for safety. Whatever the reason—fear of the gods, forgetfulness, or death—it ensured that many of the deposits remained in the earth, donated to posterity.

As the bronze technology developed, tools and weapons evolved in form. One notable achievement of the Middle Bronze Age bronze-smiths was the production of a short-sword with a hollow metallic hilt attached to the blade with rivets. These are known as the Tréboul type after a hoard found near Douarnenez in Finistère. Swords of this kind developed in Armorica out of the Early Bronze Age dagger types accompanying tumulus burials. They have been found extensively in the peninsula, but mainly from coastal regions. Some were exported, a number reaching the Paris basin, with a few travelling further afield to eastern and southern France.

Another item developed in Armorica at this time is the Bignan type bracelet—a heavy penannular bracelet of bronze with its exterior face covered with incised geometric decoration. Concentrations of these bracelets are found in the valley of the Vilaine in the east of Armorica, where they were probably made, with a few scattered in the north and west. They also reached the Paris basin and eastern France, with a few

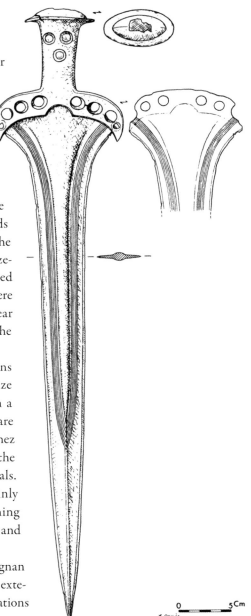

3.13 Sword of Tréboul type from Plourivo, Côtes-d'Armor.

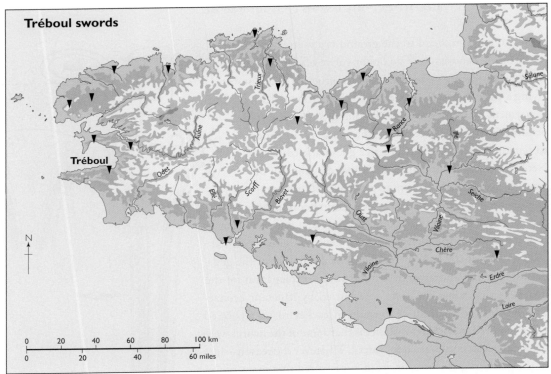

Tréboul swords

Tréboul

Séiune
Trieux
Auine
Odet
Elie
Scorff
Blavet
Rance
Ine
Oust
Seiche
Vilaine
Chère
Vilaine
Erdre
Loire

N

| 0 | 20 | 40 | 60 | 80 | 100 km |
| 0 | 20 | | 40 | | 60 miles |

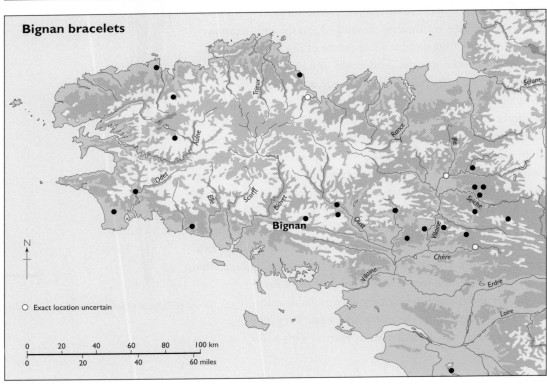

Bignan bracelets

Bignan

Séiune
Trieux
Auine
Odet
Elie
Scorff
Blavet
Rance
Ine
Oust
Seiche
Vilaine
Chère
Vilaine
Erdre
Loire

N

○ Exact location uncertain

| 0 | 20 | 40 | 60 | 80 | 100 km |
| 0 | 20 | | 40 | | 60 miles |

3.14 The distribution of Tréboul swords (*opposite, top*) and the distribution of Bignan bracelets (*opposite, bottom*). The swords were found in hoards, often together with flat bronze axes and socketed spearheads.

3.15 (*Above*) Massive decorated bronze bracelets from the hoard found at Kéran, Bignan, Morbihan. The hoard gives its name to this kind of bracelet. Collection musées de Vannes, ancien fonds SPM.

crossing the Channel to Britain to be found mainly in the southern coastal region. Some of the British bracelets may be local copies inspired by Armorican originals.

It is difficult to characterize Armorican society in the Middle Bronze Age (1500–1200 BC), but the general impression given by the rather sparse archaeological record is of a community maintaining its traditional contacts, east along the Loire corridor and north to the ports of the Solent and the Dorset coast, but otherwise enjoying a degree of isolation.

The Atlantic Seaways

The intensification of connectivity which became so apparent in the eastern English Channel region as the second millennium progressed is also to be seen along the entire Atlantic face of Europe, particularly from 1200 to 800 BC. The period is usually referred to as the Atlantic Bronze Age to stress the degree of cultural unity which developed along the maritime façade at this time, but what we are really seeing is a series of different superimposed exchange networks, regional in their extent, which emerge and decline over time. The best way to try to understand the processes at work is to look at the distribution of a few individual objects.

Let us take three types of artefact originating from Ireland. The first is the Ballintober sword—a slashing sword, slightly leaf-shaped with a flat rectangular hilt plate. Common in Ireland, this type of sword is found across southern Britain, with a considerable concentration in the Thames valley, a focus for sword making and depositions at this time. The continental distribution shows that the two principal points of entry were the Seine and Loire valleys. While it is likely that the swords found in the Seine valley were carried along an eastern Channel route from the Thames, the Loire valley concentration and the single example from the Morbihan would almost certainly have arrived by an Atlantic route direct from Ireland, the single find in Cornwall perhaps reflecting a stopping point along the way. Another Irish product, the basal-looped spearhead found extensively in Ireland and Britain, shows a similar pattern, with some entering the continent between the Seine and the Rhine from south-eastern Britain and others being transported from Ireland along the Atlantic sea-routes to the Loire mouth, the Gironde, and to Galicia and beyond. The discovery in the Charente of a stone mould for making a basal-looped spearhead suggests that it was the technology that was being transmitted and not simply the finished spears. The third item of exchange is the neck ring, or torc, made from a twisted bar of gold. Some thirty-eight have been found in Ireland, where they were almost certainly manufactured, with about fifty in Britain, but unlike the swords and spearheads the continental distribution favours the Atlantic route, with examples found in western Normandy, Jersey, Armorica, and the Gironde region. Clearly the system by which the gold torcs were distributed differed from that controlling the dispersion of the bronze weapon types. The weapons seem to have been marketed to specific redistribution points in the Seine and Loire valleys, while the gold torcs may have travelled as individual gifts exchanged between elites.

The crucial position of north-western France in the Atlantic networks is apparent in the distribution of items associated with feasting: cauldrons, flesh-hooks (for lifting meat from the cauldron), and roasting spits. Two types of cauldron have been

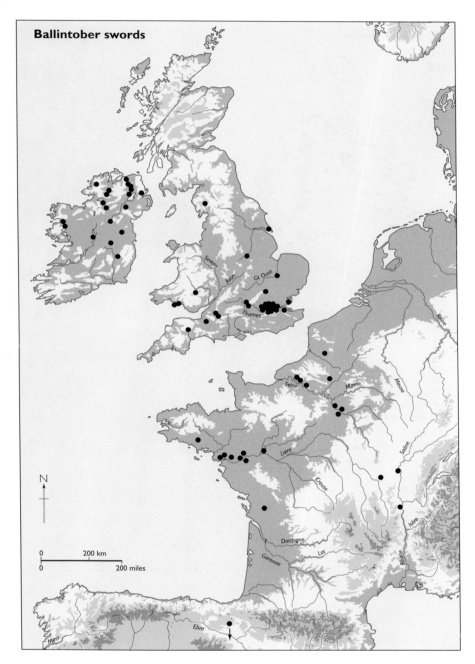

Ballintober swords

3.16 Distinctive long swords known as Ballintober swords were probably made in Ireland and distributed to Britain and France. The known distribution suggests that the rivers Seine and Loire were the main points of entry to the continent.

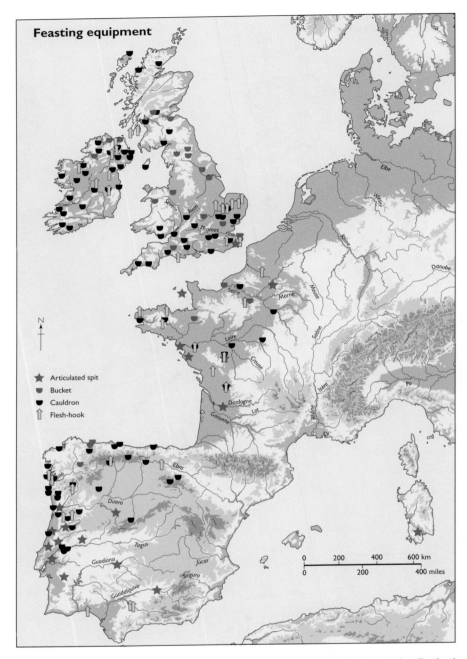

Feasting equipment

Articulated spit
Bucket
Cauldron
Flesh-hook

3.17 During the Atlantic Bronze Age specialized feasting equipment, including situlae (buckets), cauldrons, flesh-hooks, and articulated roasting spits, was widely used by the elite. Its distribution along the Atlantic seaways reflects a zone of connectivity where similar social customs were practised.

recognized: type 1, with a predominantly British and Irish distribution, and type 2, found mainly in Iberia. Examples of type 1 are also known from western Armorica, the Loire valley, and northern Iberia, while type 2 cauldrons are found in western France as far north as the Loire. The flesh-hooks and roasting spits echo the dual pattern. The flesh-hooks are found predominantly in Britain and Ireland but spread to Armorica, to western France south of the Loire, and to western Iberia, while roasting spits are mainly found in western Iberia but extend north to western France and the Channel Islands, with one found in Kent. Amid all this detail, western France from Armorica to the Gironde stands out as the region where the northern and southern distribution systems overlap: it is the pivotal region that linked them.

One final example will demonstrate the importance of the Armorican region. In the early tenth century BC, craftsmen in south-western Iberia developed a specific

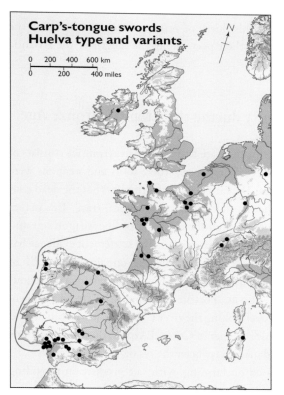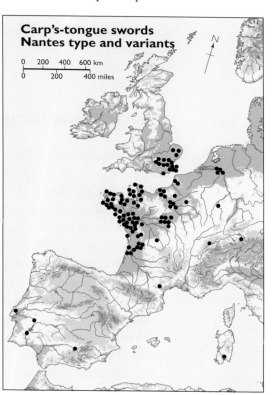

3.18 Carp's-tongue swords first developed in the period 950–875 BC in the Huelva region of south-western Iberia, and the type spread along the Atlantic seaways to western France, with one reaching as far as Ireland. Later in the ninth century a variant, the Nantes type, developed in the Loire valley and was widely distributed in western France and south-eastern Britain. The distributions demonstrate the extent of the trading networks then in operation.

type of sword which combined the qualities of the Atlantic slashing sword and the Mediterranean thrusting rapier. The resulting hybrid is known as a carp's-tongue sword (referring to its long, narrow tip) of the Huelva variety, Huelva, in south-western Spain, being its probable site of production. These swords were distributed in Iberia and western France with a concentration in the Loire valley, at least one reaching as far as Ireland. A little later, somewhere in north-western France, perhaps in the Loire estuary, a new type was developed, named the Nantes variant. For a brief period (c.950–875 BC) it was distributed throughout north-western France and south-eastern Britain, a few travelling south on the Atlantic route to southern Iberia.

What all these different distributions show is that during the period 1200–900 BC the maritime systems of Atlantic Europe had developed to such an extent that communities from Scotland to Iberia were linked in networks of connectivity that allowed people, ideas, and value systems, as well as artefacts, to move and to be moved. Armorica was intimately engaged in this flurry of activity, its elites embracing the weapon sets and the feasting habits of their peers along the length of the Atlantic façade.

The Armorican Community during the Atlantic Bronze Age

Most of the archaeological evidence for the Late Bronze Age in Armorica consists of metalwork, usually found in hoards, or from rivers, where tools and weapons were also deposited to influence the deities. The rarity of burials implies that the dead continued to be disposed of in a way that has left little archaeological trace. This makes it difficult to talk of social hierarchies, though the existence of fine weapon sets and occasional items of gold shows that warrior elites existed. The settlement evidence has little to offer. A number of farmsteads have been identified. At one site, Lenn Sec'h in the Morbihan, some circular timber houses have been found, suggesting continuous occupation during the period 1000–800 BC. Fortified promontories are also known, like those excavated at La Rochette, overlooking the river L'Yvel in the Morbihan, and at Le Yaudet, on the estuary of the river Léguer in Côtes-d'Armor. Both fortifications command important routeways, and many have been the residences of the elites.

The subsistence economy was based on farming, with salt production providing an additional marketable resource for those in easy reach of suitable coastlines. But over and above that it was the flow of metal, especially copper and tin, that brought power and wealth to the community. How much copper was produced in Armorica it is impossible to say, but certainly it would not have been enough to meet the needs of society. Supplies had to be constantly replenished, either by acquiring fresh metal in the form of ingots from sources in southern France, Iberia, and the eastern Alps, or as scrap bronze like the accumulations brought together for recycling by the ship's master whose vessel foundered in Langdon Bay near Dover. Such trade would have been organized on many levels. Shiploads of scrap bronze articulated the international trade, but there were many more modest operators. The farmers who lived on the tiny island of Sark in the Channel Islands acquired a new supply of metal, probably from an itinerant trader. It contained about 1.2 kilograms of metal, most of it made up from fragments of ingots of nearly pure copper, probably from an Alpine source, the rest comprising broken axe blades, a piece of sheet, and a fragment of a carp's-tongue sword, all of tin bronze. Small-scale transactions of this kind would have supplied the needs of the many hundreds of farming communities across Armorica.

The distribution of tin raises different questions. Armorica was one of the major sources of tin for western Europe, alongside Cornwall and Iberia, and since bronze was 10–12 per cent tin, the demands on the suppliers must have been considerable. There can be no doubt that the extraction and marketing of tin featured large in the Armorican economy. Control of the tin supply would most likely have been in the hands of the elite and it was by manipulating such resources that the leaders of society maintained their prominent places in the hierarchy. The concentrations of Late Bronze Age metalwork around the mouth of the Loire highlight the estuary as a place of interregional exchange where Armorican tin may have been channelled to the wider world. Later, in the fourth century BC, a Greek writer, Pytheas, refers to there being an emporium known as Corbilo situated somewhere on the Loire estuary, a place to which merchants travelled to acquire tin for the Mediterranean world (below, p. 142). It may well be that Corbilo had its origins centuries earlier, when the Atlantic Bronze Age trade was at its height.

The End of the Old Order

The Atlantic network had connected the entire Atlantic façade for three centuries (1200–900 BC), but in the tenth century things began to change. The prime cause of the disruption seems to have been the appearance on the Atlantic seaboard of Phoenician merchants—Mediterranean-based traders who had established a trading enclave in a major Bronze Age settlement at the confluence of the rivers Odiel and Tinto now beneath the Spanish port town of Huelva. The settlement may have been ancient Tartessos. From there, during the ninth century, they set up trading colonies all along the Atlantic coast from Mogador, near Essaouira, in Morocco to the river Mondego in central Portugal. From their enclaves in Iberia they were able to exploit the rich sources of tin and gold in Galicia and Asturias in the north-west of the peninsula. The increasing Phoenician presence meant that Iberia was now drawn firmly into the Mediterranean sphere, severing the ocean-facing zone of the peninsula from the Atlantic network. The Bay of Biscay now became a divide, but Armorica, Britain, and Ireland still remained interconnected.

The old system continued for another three hundred years (900–600 BC), but during this time new dislocating pressures were beginning to be felt, the most far-reaching being the spread of ironworking after about 800 BC. Iron ore occurs widely and, once the technology for extracting it had been learned, local deposits could be worked, obviating the need to maintain the complex social networks needed to extract and distribute copper and tin. Concurrent with the social and economic reformation gripping western Europe at this time (referred to as the Hallstatt C period), new horse-riding elites emerged, establishing widespread alliances which embraced much of Britain and Ireland and are archaeologically recognizable from the distribution of horse-gear and a type of long slashing sword, the Gundlingen sword, which may have been developed by the swordsmiths of the Thames valley, soon gaining international currency. In the west, however, in southern Ireland, south Wales, the south-western peninsula of Britain, and Armorica, all of which lay outside the Hallstatt C cultural zone, old behavioural practices continued, among them the deposition of bronze hoards. It was in Armorica that this tradition reached its most extreme expression.

The phenomenon of the Armorican axe hoards is remarkable. In the eighth and seventh centuries vast numbers of axes were consigned to the earth. In Armorica, including Manche and Mayenne, some 350 hoards have been recorded containing thirty-eight thousand axes, and there must be many more still to be found. Since 1970 they have been appearing at a rate of more than one a year. Even the hoards so far known incorporate a huge quantity of metal. Roughly estimated, it amounts to 4 tonnes of copper, 1 tonne of tin, and 3 tonnes of lead. The actual quantity of metal consigned to the ground during those two centuries must have been at least three or four times as much. The hoards were usually made up of straight-sided socketed axes that show no signs of having been used. Indeed, in many cases the axes had not been finished or even trimmed after casting. It is as if they had been made specifically for burial. Another characteristic is their very high lead content. Indeed, a few were entirely of lead, making them soft and of little practical use.

But how to explain all this? Some observers have argued that the axes were no longer functional but served as a unit of currency. This may be so, but then the high and differing lead content would have made equivalence difficult to judge. Others have suggested that the panic created by the appearance of iron encouraged the bronze-smiths to increase the perceived value of bronze by taking large quantities

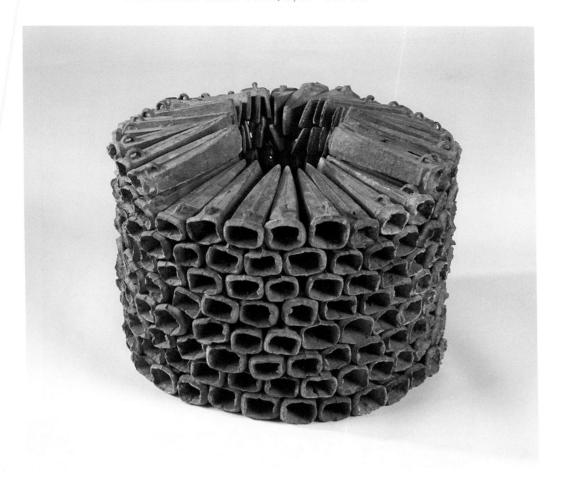

3.19 Cast Armorican axes were made in huge numbers in Brittany in the seventh century and are usually found in large hoards. In this example, from Langonnet, Morbihan, the axes are arranged as they were originally found. Collection musées de Vannes, ancien fonds SPM.

out of circulation, but this does seem a little counter-intuitive. Perhaps the answer lies in the demands of the gods. If the deposition of hoards was bound up in a belief system demanding that the chthonic deities be propitiated with gifts of bronze, then it might be that economic or social traumas, such as recurring famine or plagues, drove the people to dedicate increasing quantities of their wealth to the gods. If it was quantity or weight that mattered most, it would explain the extravagant use of lead substituted for the more valuable tin and copper. Though unresolved, these are fascinating issues helping us to edge closer to an understanding of the people, but we

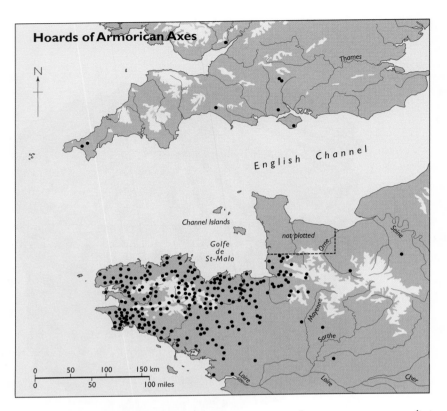

3.20 Armorican axe hoards, so numerous in the Armorican peninsula, must represent a very distinct pattern of behaviour: a compulsion to place large quantities of valuable metal in the ground in the realm of the chthonic deities.

are unlikely ever to appreciate what it was really like to live through this period of rapid change.

By no means all of the Armorican axes made in the eighth and seventh centuries were consigned to the earth. Indeed, they were one of the most successful of the Armorican exports, being found widely across France and southern Britain with a few reaching as far as Scotland. The distribution in Britain suggests several points of entry: Hengistbury Head and Portland–Weymouth in Dorset, Mount Batten in Devon, and somewhere in the extreme west of Cornwall, perhaps Mount's Bay. The ports of Hengistbury and Mount Batten, known to have been in operation at this time, have both produced imported Armorican axes. Clearly the traditional networks were still in operation in the south-west well after the hoarding of bronze in the ground had ceased in the rest of Ireland, Britain, and France. That the west resisted the changes affecting other areas is further reflected in the fact that Gundlingen swords did not penetrate the region. The values and practices of the Atlantic Bronze Age held out here at least until the end of the seventh century.

Interlude, 700–500 BC

In Armorica the practice of depositing hoards of axes continued through the seventh and into the sixth century, by which time a few exotic items were beginning to trickle westwards from northern and eastern France. At Kerléonet, Spézet, in Finistère, two Hallstatt bronze situlae (buckets) of seventh-century type were found accompanied by a hoard of eighty-nine axes. Another similar situla was found at Crossac in the Loire estuary area, while elsewhere knobbed bracelets of Hallstatt type reached Armorica. But the contact with the east seems to have been limited, and life continued as before except that the frenzy of feeding the earth with bronze was now passing.

The two centuries or so that span the end of the Bronze Age and the beginning of the Iron Age are known largely from cremation cemeteries of two different forms: circular graves (*sépultures circulaires*) and small barrows (*tombelles*). The circular graves are found in the southern part of the peninsula with a particular concentration in the southern Morbihan. They consist of clusters of up to twenty cinerary urns placed in pits or small stone cists, each cluster surrounded by a circular or penannular wall 5–10 metres in diameter and about a metre high, the whole buried in a large mound 10–20 metres across. It seems likely that they represent the burials of families or extended families made over a period of time, eventually to be sealed beneath a tumulus when the lineage was deemed to have come to an end. The small barrows also have a predominantly southern distribution and are often found in groups. Cremated remains were placed on the ground surface, occasionally with simple grave goods and covered by small mounds of earth or rubble no more than a metre high. The two groups were broadly contemporary, their differences presumably due to the differing status of their occupants.

The burials in the circular graves were usually placed in cinerary urns with upstanding necks and angular shoulders, suggesting that they are copying metal situlae. An actual bronze situla of Hallstatt type dating to the late sixth or early fifth century was found at Le Rocher, Le Bono, in the Morbihan, covered with a bronze basin, probably of Etruscan origin, dating to the early sixth century. The situla contained the cremated body. Nearby was an inhumation burial accompanied by a cauldron of west-central European type, dating to the late sixth century, and two iron bracelets. Other grave goods from the circular grave are unremarkable, consisting of knobbed bracelets of bronze or iron and occasional glass or amber beads. There is little to suggest the

existence of a wealthy elite, though it is possible that elite status was no longer defined by burial rite.

The overall impression given by the burials and the sparse material culture of this interlude is of a stable society developing in relative isolation. Occasional bronze vessels were arriving in Armorica, very probably along the Loire route, and the cross-Channel route linking with ports like Hengistbury and Mount Batten were being kept open. But exchanges, if they occurred at all, seldom included bronze items. It seems that the Armoricans were allowed to develop largely without the benefit of disruptive external stimuli. The regional nature of the different burial types may hint that tribal confederations, which were to become so evident at the end of the millennium, were now beginning to crystallize out.

3.21 Two bronze vessels used in a burial at Le Rocher, Le Bono, Morbihan. The situla is of Late Hallstatt type and probably comes from west-central Europe, while the basin, dating to about 600–550 BC, was probably made in Etruria. Collection musées de Vannes, ancien fonds SPM.

3.22 Iron dagger in a bronze sheath from Kernavest, Quiberon, Morbihan. It was probably imported from west-central Europe. Collection musées de Vannes, ancien fonds SPM.

Networks in the *Longue Durée*, 2800–500 BC

The span of time traditionally called the Chalcolithic period and the Bronze Age saw the people of Armorica drawn into the many networks that bound western Europe, but the intensity of the different relationships varied considerably over time. The Atlantic network is a case in point. The burst of activity linking Iberia and Armorica in the middle of the third millennium seems to have been associated with prospectors from the Lisbon region searching for new sources of metal. How many people were involved is far from clear, but it was sufficient to introduce a whole new value system to the Armorican elites. But after about 2300 BC there is little evidence that contact was maintained until about 1200 BC, when the long distant networks were reinvigorated, creating the cultural continuum of the Atlantic Bronze Age. It was short-lived, its unity shattered when, in the ninth century, Phoenician entrepreneurs drew Iberia into the Mediterranean sphere, leaving the truncated northern part of the system to continue to function for another two centuries.

The networks linking Armorica to continental Europe were more persistent, though on a much less intensive scale. The Loire–Paris basin–lower Rhine axis remained a significant corridor of communication throughout. It was along this route that the single-grave and battle-axe elements of the Beaker package reached Armorica and, later, items like the Tréboul daggers and the decorated Bignan bracelets of Armorican origin were dispersed to the Paris basin and beyond. Later still, along a similar route, the socketed Armorican axes were exchanged and Hallstatt situlae arrived in Armorica. That the Loire estuary played a crucial part in these exchanges is shown by the very large quantity of bronzework found concentrated along the lower reaches of the river, and it may have been here that the Nantes variety of the carp's-tongue sword was made. Another attraction of the Loire estuary was that it was linked by a short sea-route to the Gironde estuary, leading to the Garonne corridor, giving access to the Mediterranean. As the Greek, and later the Roman, presence in southern France took hold, and the economic reach of the Mediterranean states grew, so the Garonne corridor and the Rhine–Loire route began to take on a new significance, increasing the importance of the Loire estuary both as a route node and as a gateway to Armorica.

Finally, the English Channel. Throughout the whole of the period considered here, cross-Channel maritime ventures of various scales bound Armorica to southern Britain. In the early second millennium the contacts were essentially between elites, but with the development of the Atlantic Bronze Age systems, exchanges intensified, with commodities like bronze being traded on a commercial scale. As the world began to change with the spread of iron technology, the old networks continued to function, though on a reduced scale. The British port of Mount Batten was still dealing in scrap bronze well into the fifth century, when maritime trade with Armorica began to revive. By this time the geopolitics of the world had begun to change. Tin from Armorica and south-western Britain was now in high demand, and the Mediterranean states were beginning to become major players.

4

FACING THE
EXPANDING WORLD
600–50 BC

A T the beginning of the sixth century BC two major developments took place in western Europe: the growth of Etruscan and Greek power in Mediterranean France and the emergence of a zone of powerful chiefdoms centred on eastern France and southern Germany. The two phenomena were closely interlinked through the exchange of commodities. The Mediterranean world could provide wine produced in the region of Marseille together with bronze wine-drinking gear and Attic drinking cups, while the inland barbarians of the Hallstatt D culture could offer in exchange raw materials like metals, amber, and furs, as well as much-needed slaves.

In the last decades of the seventh century, Etruscans began to trade through the communities living in the Rhône mouth region but they were quickly overtaken and displaced by Greeks from Phocaea, who, about 600 BC, founded the colony of Massalia (Marseille). Other colonies followed until, within a century, the entire coast of the gulf of Lion, from the Maritime Alps to the Ebro valley, was ringed with Greek trading towns through which luxury goods from Greek and Etruscan workshops flooded northwards into barbarian western Europe.

The communities who occupied the central part of western Europe were particularly favoured by geography since their homeland encompassed the upper reaches of all the major river systems, the Loire, Seine, Rhône, Rhine, Moselle, and Danube. Thus the major European routes, north–south and east–west, passed through this broad zone, allowing those who commanded them to control the flow of raw materials and other goods. The socio-political system which emerged here is referred to as a prestige goods economy. By controlling ownership of the most prestigious goods, like the wine and wine-drinking equipment coming from the Mediterranean world, and passing items of lesser value to those subservient to them to create bonds of allegiance, the elite were able to maintain their supreme power, but the system would work only so long as the supply of prestige goods continued. Although Massalia was founded about 600 BC, it took a while for the trading networks to develop and it was not until about 540 BC that the Hallstatt D prestige goods economy was fully under way. It was to last until about 450 BC when, as the result of complex and far-reaching changes, power shifted northwards to a broad area stretching from the Loire to the Danube, with new centres of power emerging in the Marne valley, the Moselle valley, and in Bohemia. The change heralds the beginning of the La Tène period.

One region redolent of elite power in both the Late Hallstatt and the Early La Tène period was the territory around Bourges, in the valley of the Loire, sited at the confluence of the Auron and the Yèvre, a tributary of the Cher. The site, now occupied by the modern town, became a centre of power in the fifth century. Attic pottery, both Black and Red Figure Ware, has been found together with the amphorae in which Massaliot wine was imported, and around the settlement four cemeteries have been identified, the dead accompanied by a range of Mediterranean bronze vessels—cordoned buckets, beaked flagons, and stamnoi (handled jars)—all associated with wine drinking. The material spans the fifth century, but thereafter, for the next two centuries, little is known of the settlement. The reason why the elite of Bourges were able to acquire such an array of Mediterranean luxuries lay in their ability to command the short overland portage between the middle Loire and the Rhône–Saône river system, linking Armorica to the Mediterranean, as well as routes leading northwards to the Paris basin and the important centres of power which developed in the Marne region. In other words, their territory was optimally sited to serve as the centre through which commodities coming from the Atlantic—tin, salt, and possibly some gold—were transmitted both to the Mediterranean world and to Late Hallstatt and Early La Tène polities in west-central Europe.

Comparatively little exotic metalwork reached Armorica during this period. We have already mentioned the bronze basin, probably an heirloom, found in a grave in the cemetery at Le Rocher, Le Bono, in the Morbihan, which is likely to be of Etruscan manufacture. Other finds, from west-central Europe, include the cauldron and the situla found at the Le Rocher cemetery, and two antenna-hilted iron daggers from the Donges marshes and the Goulaine marshes at the Loire mouth, as well as a ribbed bucket with an iron handle from Ty-Neuziganned, Caudan, and an iron dagger in a scabbard bound with a highly decorated bronze mount found in a cist with an

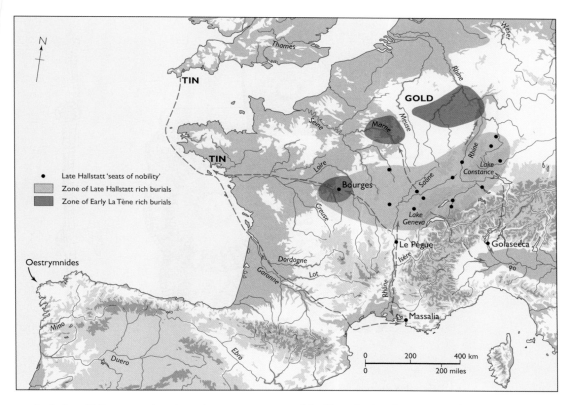

4.1 In the Late Hallstatt period, in the sixth century BC, a zone of chiefdoms developed in west-central Europe, growing rich through exchanging raw materials and slaves with the Mediterranean communities. By the middle of the fifth century, in the La Tène period, the centre of power had moved to the north and west. It was in this context that Bourges developed, benefiting from its position on the overland Loire–Rhône route by which tin was transported to Massalia (Marseille).

inhumation burial at Kernavest, both in the Morbihan. The dagger is of fifth-century date and is comparable to those frequently found in west-central Europe, though this example could have been made in Armorica. All of these items date to the sixth or early fifth century. The only luxury object of La Tène date, which is likely to be an import, is a decorated helmet from Tronoan, Saint-Jean-Trolimon, in the Penmarc'h peninsula. It was made of iron decorated with embossed bronze sheeting enhanced with coral inlay. The helmet, together with the iron swords and spears with which it was found, was part of a ritual deposit buried on the site of what is probably a temple. There has been much debate about its origins. While it could possibly have been made locally, it is more likely to have come from a school of helmet makers active in northern Italy in the fourth century.

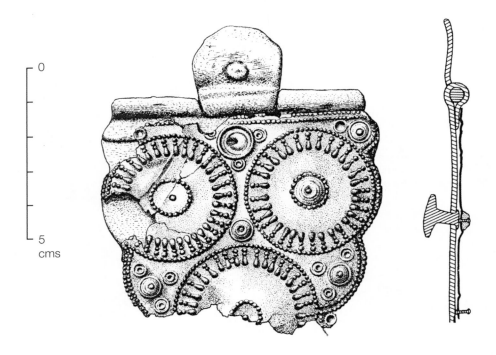

4.2 (*Above and opposite*) Parts of a La Tène-style helmet found at Saint-Jean-Trolimon, Finistère. Late fifth to early fourth century BC. The helmet may have been a gift made to facilitate trade.

Sufficient has been found to show that prestige items were reaching Armorica between the seventh and the fourth centuries, but it is important to remember that what has been found is only the tip of the iceberg: no doubt more lies in the ground to be recovered. Nor should we forget organic materials—fabrics, wooden items, and decorated leatherwork—that may have travelled along the exchange networks. What we can be sure about is that over these four centuries Armoricans would have been exposed to visual and other influences which they chose, selectively, to absorb into their own culture.

Tin remained a much-desired commodity in the ancient world even after the use of iron had become widespread. The establishment of trading colonies on the shores of the western Mediterranean enabled the Greeks to take a more assured control of the tin routes from Galicia, Armorica, and south-western Britain. Herodotus, writing in the fifth century, had heard rumours of tin-bearing islands lying somewhere in the Atlantic off the European coast, though he is careful in his reporting. 'Of the extreme

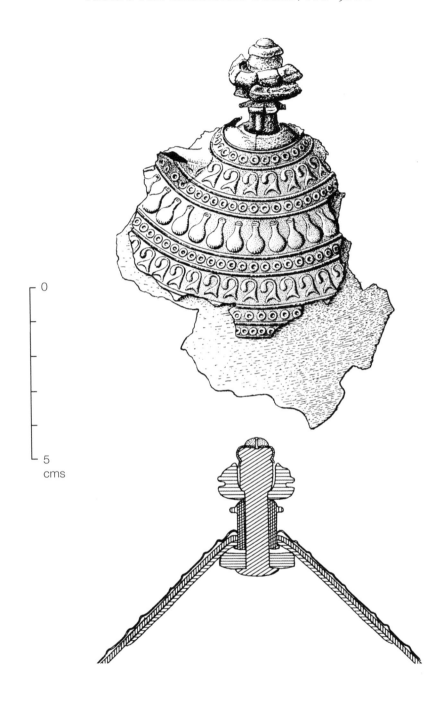

0

5
cms

tracts of Europe towards the west I cannot speak with any certainty . . . nor do I know of any islands called Cassiterides whence comes the tin which we use' (Herodotus 3.115). Another source, probably a little earlier than Herodotus, is the *Massiliote Periplus*, a set of sailing instructions which survived because they were copied *in extenso* in a poem, *Ora Maritima*, composed in the fourth century AD by a Roman official, Avienus. The *Periplus* was evidently the work of a Massaliot ship's captain and gives details of the journey from his home port, westwards along the coast of Iberia to the Atlantic, to acquire tin from the Oestrymnides, which can almost certainly be identified as Galicia. It is possible that the author of the *Periplus* was the Greek trader Midacritus, mentioned by Pliny to have been involved in the transhipment of tin sometime around 500 BC. At this time the Greeks and Phoenicians were trading along the same routes in reasonable harmony, but with the rise of the Carthaginians (who were themselves Phoenicians) and the growing hostility between them and the Greeks, the strait of Gibraltar became a Carthaginian preserve and the Greeks found it increasingly difficult to get access to the Atlantic. Thus it was that tin from Armorica and south-western Britain became increasingly important to the Greek world. The two routes by which the metal was transported from there to the Mediterranean were the Loire–Rhône route direct to Massalia and the Garonne–Carcassonne gap route to Narbo (Narbonne). A first-century BC writer, Diodorus Siculus, no doubt using early sources, says that the journey across France to the mouth of the Rhône took thirty days on horseback. The starting point is not mentioned but it was probably the Gironde estuary. By the late fourth century, with the strait of Gibraltar now barred by the Carthaginians and Celtic tribes causing disruption in parts of western Europe, it became imperative for the Greeks to acquire a better understanding of their supply networks. This may have been the motivation for the journey of exploration made by the Massaliot traveller Pytheas about 320 BC (below, pp. 141–4).

Meanwhile in Armorica

The life of the communities occupying the Armorican peninsula seems to have continued with little disturbance. Contacts with the outside were harmonious and there is no evidence to suggest social disruption of the kind that might have been occasioned by migration or invasions. What stands out from the archaeological record is that during the fifth to third centuries the people occupying the western part of the peninsula, west of a line from the Rance estuary to the estuary of the Vilaine, developed a very distinctive culture that set them apart from those of the rest of Armorica. The culture can be characterized by use of souterrains (underground storage chambers), by their

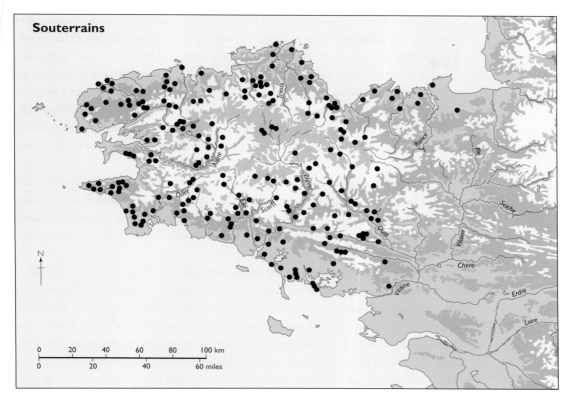

Souterrains

4.3 One of the characteristics distinguishing Iron Age communities in Armorica is the use of souterrains (underground chambers) tunnelled out of the soft bedrock and used for storage purposes. Where the contexts are known, these souterrains form part of settlement complexes.

evident relish for erecting carefully shaped, and sometimes decorated, stelae (standing stones), and by the style and decoration of their pottery.

The souterrains comprise a series of interlinked chambers, varying in number and plan, dug out of the friable bedrock and accessed from the surface by a shaft or steep ramp. The size of the chambers varied from 1.5 to 6 metres in length and between 1 and 3 metres in width with height seldom exceeding 2 metres, but the floors were largely level throughout. Although many souterrains appear to be isolated and without context, where excavation has been on a large enough scale it is clear that they were an integral part of settlements. It is not surprising, therefore, to find that some of them contained domestic refuse. Many ideas have been put forward to explain their function: habitations, places of refuge in times of stress, storage chambers, and even burial vaults, a suggestion based on the occasional discovery of cremated and inhumed human remains. Whatever secondary use they may have been put to, the prime function is most likely to have been for the storage of food and in particular for grain. In southern Britain at this time seed grain was stored in pits sealed to prevent germination. The consigning of seed grain to the soil may have taken with it the belief that the chthonic deities would protect it and ensure its fertility in the coming season. Some such belief may have lain behind the souterrains. Here grain contained in sacks, dried and salted meat, cheese, and other preserves could safely be stored to provide for the community through the long winter months. A similar function may be ascribed to the fogous found in western Cornwall and the souterrains of Ireland and Scotland.

In Armorica souterrains are widely and fairly evenly distributed throughout the western part of the peninsula, but east of the Rance–Vilaine line they are virtually unknown. The divide must surely represent a significant cultural boundary, with those living to the west sharing beliefs and practices which distinguished them from their eastern neighbours.

Another striking characteristic of the western zone is the popularity of stelae, of which two broad types can be distinguished: squat, often roughly hemispherical, and tall, columnar. All were carefully shaped into symmetrical forms about a vertical axis. The tall stelae, which usually taper towards the top, may be circular in cross-section or polygonal with carefully cut facets. In some cases narrow, closely spaced, vertical channels create a fluted appearance. The tallest of the columnar stelae reach 3 metres in height above the ground. The widespread distribution of the stelae and the discovery of some in funerary contexts suggest that we are witnessing an essentially local phenomenon that can be shown to begin as early as the sixth century BC. But what inspired the development we can only guess. One suggestion is that it was a desire to establish links with the distant past, its memory ever present in the Neolithic menhirs that still dominated the landscape. Another suggestion is that the stelae replicate wooden totems carved from tree trunks for which no archaeological evidence now survives. If so, then it could be argued that it was the appearance of iron tools which facilitated the change from wood to worked stone. All this is, of course, speculative and must remain so.

A small subgroup of decorated stelae raises even more fascinating questions. In all, eleven are known, all but two clustering together in Cornouaille in the extreme south-west of Armorica, with a particular concentration on the Penmarc'h peninsula. The two outliers differ from the rest. One, from Sainte-Anne, Trégastel, in the Trégor, is decorated on one side with a double spiral motif framed by two grooves. The other, from Menmeur, Plounéour-Trez, in Léon, is decorated with panels but this time infilled with chevrons. The Cornouaille group, on the other hand, is characterized by horizontal bands of decoration usually at the top and sometimes at the bottom of the

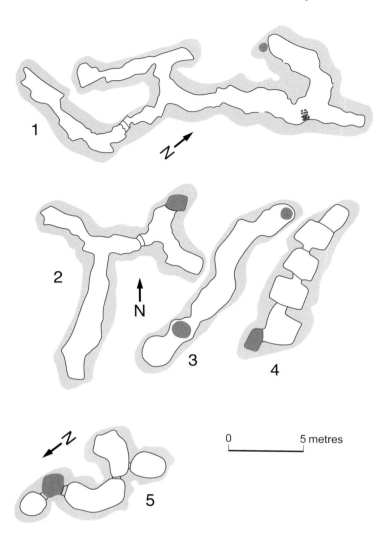

4.4 Souterrains vary in form and plan. All were entered through one or more access shafts. The examples illustrated are all from Finistère. (1) La Motte, Sizun; (2) Kervéo, Plomelin; (3) Pendreff, Commana; (4) Stang-Vihan, Concarneau; (5) Lamphily, Concarneau.

stone. Favoured designs are bands of Greek-key motifs and running spirals. Clearly this group of nine stelae reflects the stylistic preferences of a specific community. But they are remarkable in another way: the combination of Greek-key motifs and running spirals is an exact replica of motifs used to decorate the columns of Greek temples like those of the Ionic temple at Metapontum in southern Italy. More to the point, two of the stelae decorated in this way, Kerviguérou, Melgven, and Roz-an-Trémen, Plomeur,

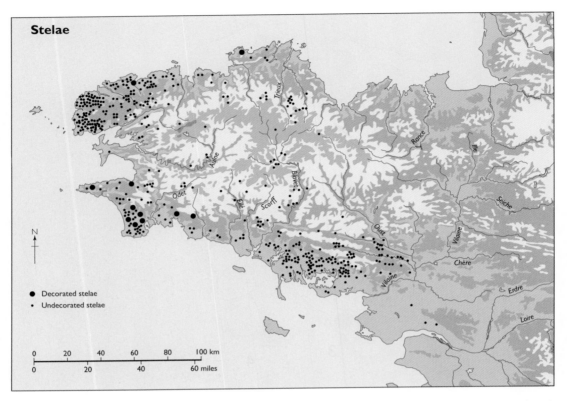

Stelae

● Decorated stelae
· Undecorated stelae

4.5 Stelae, standing stones of both tall and short types, are found throughout Armorica, though with distinct concentrations in the south and west. The few decorated examples known are concentrated in the extreme south-west, with two outliers on the north coast.

are also fluted, as are Greek columns. The similarity, while too close to be a coincidence, is hard to explain. One possibility is that a Greek ship landed in Penmarc'h and the crew erected a temple in timber in honour of their guardian deity and it was this that inspired the local community to make copies of their own in stone. Far-fetched, perhaps, but it is by no means impossible.

The stone stelae occur across the peninsula, but their distribution is uneven. There are three major concentrations, in the southern Morbihan, Cornouaille, and Léon. This applies to both the squat and the columnar types, but the squat types are far more common in the Morbihan than in the other two regions. In these clusters we are unlikely to be seeing simply concentrations of population since the distribution of souterrains implies that the population was more evenly distributed across the peninsula. More likely, they are a reflection of the cultural behaviour of the different communities.

4.6 The Iron Age stela from Croas-Men, Lampaul-Ploudalmézeau, Finistère, was very carefully worked to give it a precise hexagonal form. Much later a Christian cross was added to the top to appropriate it for the new religion.

4.7 The stela from Kermaria Pont-l'Abbé, Finistère, was decorated with four panels of geometric motifs with a band of Greek-key motifs at the top and a continuous scroll at the bottom.

The third category of evidence reflecting on the culture of western Armorica is pottery. As a plastic medium pottery, particularly in its decoration, is expressive of societies' cultural preferences and of changes in fashion over time. Several meticulous studies have been made of Armorican pottery spanning the late sixth to second centuries. The assemblages can be divided into three broad chronological groups. The earliest is characterized by vessels, often with pedestal bases and high necks, decorated with horizontal rows of repetitive stamped geometric motifs arranged in zones. While the form is evidently a development of the large cinerary urns in use in the preceding period, the decoration is new and may be a response to metalwork imported from west-central Europe. This style is probably best dated to the late sixth and fifth centuries. Then follows a period in which horizontal bands incorporating a variety of arc motifs become popular. Stamped impressions, if they are used at all, are much less common. The forms have also changed, the jars becoming less angular with shorter necks and flat bottoms, and dishes are now more common. A mid-fifth-century date is suggested for the beginning of this style, coinciding with the early stages of the La Tène period. The third stage is characterized by the adoption of elaborate curvilinear motifs of the kind used on La Tène metalwork from the fourth century. There are many fine examples known of this style, like the jar from Saint-Pol-de-Léon, characteristic of a style found in the north, and the Kélouer vessel from Plouhinec, typical of those found along the south coast.

4.8 The decorative pattern on the tall stela from Kerviguérou, Melgven, Finistère, shown here with the full design drawn out.

The overall picture to emerge, then, is of a continuous ceramic tradition rooted in the Late Bronze Age, the potters being influenced by decorative ideas emanating from west-central Europe, especially, in the fourth century, from the Marne region. How the inspiring images reached western Armorica is not immediately evident, but the most likely medium was on imported metalwork, of which little now survives. This issue will be returned to again later (below, pp. 139–40).

4.9 (*Opposite*) Selection of decorated pottery dating from the fifth to the third century BC: stamped ware (*top left*), arc-decorated ware (*top right*), and curvilinear-decorated ware (*bottom*). The vessel on the bottom left is from Saint-Pol-de-Léon, that on the bottom right from Kelouer, Plouhinec, both in Finistère.

The three very different sources of evidence, souterrains, stelae, and pottery, combine together in a dramatic way to show just how culturally distinct western Armorica was throughout the fifth to third centuries or perhaps a little longer. While in touch with developments in west-central Europe and the Marne region, quite possibly as the result of the tin trade using the Loire corridor, it retained its highly distinctive identity throughout. There was no obvious physical barrier to cut it off from the rest of Armorica, but perhaps the wide lower reaches of the Rance in the north and the Vilaine in the south, combined with the dense forests of the inner regions between them—the forests of Paimpont and Hardouinais, as they became known in the Middle Ages—were sufficient to make the western part of Armorica a world unto itself, remote from the rest of Europe, accepting only selective influences to be modified and made their own.

Friends across the Sea

After the intense maritime activity of the eighth and seventh centuries, archaeological evidence for exchanges along the seaways decreases significantly, but what little there is shows that journeys were still being made. Most intriguing are fibulae (brooches) of Iberian type dating to the fifth century BC. Two are known in the south-west of Armorica, from Kerancoat, Ergué-Armel, and Roz-an-Tremen, Plomeur, both in Finistère, and three have been found in south-western Britain, one from Harlyn Bay in Cornwall and two from the port site of Mount Batten near Plymouth. While this group has certain similarities with Iberian finds, they are in fact more closely similar to brooches from Aquitania, around the Gironde estuary, and may therefore reflect journeys from south-western France along the south coast of Armorica and across the Channel to ports like Mount Batten which were still active at this time.

A more tenuous cross-Channel link is suggested by two bronze bowls, one from Keshcarrigan, County Leitrim, in Ireland, the other from Rose Ash in Devon. Both have characteristics present on two pottery bowls from Armorica. The bowl from Blavet, Hénon, in Côtes-d'Armor, has a recess on its rim decorated with a zigzag line. This is a direct copy of a metalworker's technique of the type used on the Rose Ash bowl. The bowl from Blavet has a handle made in the form of a recurved horse's head, closely paralleled by a similar handle on the bronze bowl from Keshcarrigan.

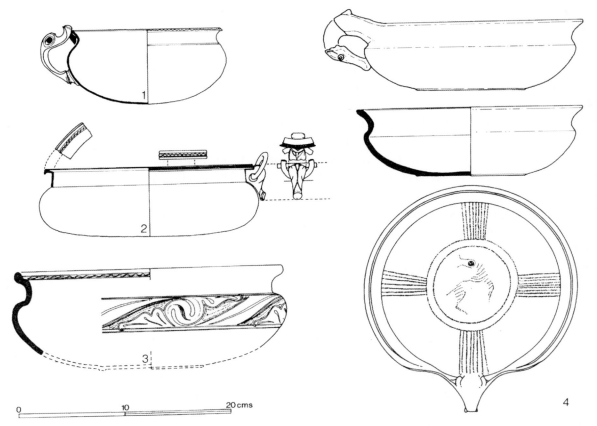

0   10   20 cms

4.10 Metal vessels and pottery copies of the third–second centuries BC. (1) Bronze bowl from Keshcarrigan, County Leitrim, Ireland; (2) bronze bowl from Rose Ash, Devon; (3) pottery bowl from Blavet, Hénon, Côtes-d'Armor; (4) pottery bowl from Hennebont, Côtes-d'Armor.

The comparisons are sufficient to show that Armorican potters in the fourth or third century were copying bronze bowls of the type that were circulating in Britain and Ireland. Where the bronze vessels were originally made and over what area they circulated is unclear, but at the very least the evidence is a reminder that cross-Channel contacts were maintained. Another hint of contact between western Armorica and south-western Britain is the development in Britain of curvilinear ornamented pottery called South-Western Decorated Ware. Although there are significant differences between the styles preferred on the two sides of the Channel, such similarities as there are suggest that the two regions were sharing ideas and values.

There is plenty of evidence in Britain at the time to show that there was a lively trade along the south coast, a cabotage linking one port with another. It remains a possibility that a similar system existed along the north coast of France. Indeed, it is possible that the influences that introduced concepts of La Tène art to Armorica came from the Marne region via the Seine and the sea rather than along the Loire corridor. There is little tangible evidence that this was so, but the distribution of iron ingots with pointed ends—the so-called double pyramidal ingots—offer a little support. These ingots were made in the upper Rhine and upper Danube region in the third to first centuries BC, and it was probably from there that the few found in northern France, and those found at eight sites in Armorica, came. The distribution in the west would be consistent with a route via the Marne and down the Seine to the Channel, then westward by sea to Armorica. Two ingots that found their way to Portland on the coast of Dorset may have arrived by this route. All this is very tenuous, but it at least hints at a sea-route to the La Tène innovating centre on the Marne, along which, perhaps, tin was exchanged for high-quality iron.

Visitors from Afar

The changing geopolitics of western Europe in the fifth and fourth centuries meant that the Greek world had to rely increasingly for its tin supply on the overland routes along which tin ingots were brought from Armorica and south-western Britain following the Garonne and possibly the Loire–Rhône route to the Mediterranean coast (above, p. 130). The processes involved in the traffic are unknown but most likely involved down-the-line trade, with successive middlemen passing the consignments from one to another, the exchanges taking place at recognized ports of trade like the legendary Corbilo at the mouth of the Loire. The Greek merchant waiting patiently in Massalia for the next shipment to arrive was at the mercy of a supply chain over which he had no control and about which he probably knew very little. While this might all have worked well in the sixth and early fifth centuries, when the Late Hallstatt chiefdoms were in power, the late fifth and early fourth centuries were less stable times as La Tène peoples began a series of folk movements—the Celtic migrations—leaving their homelands in west-central Europe, some bands travelling as far as Italy or Greece and Asia Minor. This was a time of disruption and uncertainty.

It may have been these troubled times that persuaded one of the citizens of Massalia, Pytheas, that more had to be learned of the remote region of western Europe. Little is known of him except that about 320 BC he set out on a journey which took him to the Armorican peninsula, around Britain, and possibly as far as Iceland and Denmark, before returning to the Mediterranean to write an account of his journey. His book, *On the Ocean*, was widely read and quoted in the ancient world but no longer survives.

Whether he was an entrepreneur intent on establishing the origin of the tin and amber sources upon which the Mediterranean world depended, or simply an explorer with an insatiable curiosity, we will never know, but the information he brought back, especially about tin working, is vivid, detailed, and first-hand.

While it was for long believed that Pytheas took ship at Massalia and sailed through the strait of Gibraltar, a case can be made that he in fact began his journey overland by following the traditional trade route in reverse direction going from Narbo along the river Aude, through the Carcassonne gap to the Garonne, and then down the river to the Atlantic. It was somewhere in the Gironde estuary that he probably joined a local ship sailing north to Armorica, and by continuing to use local ships and by making overland trips, he completed his remarkable journey.

Since the original book, *On the Ocean*, no longer exists, what is known of the venture and of the places visited comes from the works of later authors who quoted Pytheas as a source. There are therefore many gaps in the narrative, but sufficient survives for sections of the journey to be reconstructed with some certainty. Coming from the Gironde, Pytheas was aware of the Armorican peninsula jutting west into the ocean. He refers to it as *kyrtōma* ('a great hump') 'not less than 3,000 stades' (about 870 kilometres). At its westernmost extremity there were various promontories, 'especially that of the Ostimioi which is called Kabaion, as well as the islands off it . . . the farthest of these, Ou[e]xisame, lies three days' voyage away'. Here we have the first recorded observation of Armorica: the Ostimioi are probably the Osismii named in the first century BC. Kabaion is best equated with the Pointe du Raz, while the island of Ouexisame must be Ouessant, 20 kilometres off the west coast of Finistère. These western promontories and islands would have been seared on the memory of anyone making the dangerous voyage around the peninsula. While it is possible that the journey from the Gironde took a direct route to Kabaion, and perhaps made landfall somewhere there, it is more likely that the vessel he travelled on hugged the coast and that a stop was made in the Loire estuary before journeying onwards. In a rather obscure passage the Greek writer Strabo implies that Pytheas may have known the port of Corbilo, but if he did, there can be no certainty that he landed there.

How much time, if any, Pytheas spent in Armorica is unrecorded, but there is one indication that he visited the north coast. During his journey he made observations of the sun's height so that he could estimate his distance north of Massalia, where he had measured the sun's height at the midsummer solstice before he set out. These measurements were later used by the Greek astronomer Hipparchus to calculate latitudes. The latitude which Pytheas recorded in Armorica is calculated to be about 48° 42′ north allowing a margin of error. It runs across the north coast of Armorica roughly through Lannion and Roscoff. Since the measurement would almost certainly have been made on land, it implies that Pytheas disembarked somewhere along this coastline. Where, we cannot know, but it is tempting to suggest that it may have been at Pointe de Primel at the entrance to the Baie de Morlaix, or at Le Yaudet on the estuary of the Léguer, that he made his landing: both sites were, at the time, large fortified settlements controlling major ports.

From the north coast of Armorica, Pytheas took ship to Britain, landing somewhere on the coast of Cornwall or Devon, and it was here that he probably observed the tin trade in operation. The fullest account of the process is given by the first-century BC writer Diodorus Siculus, who is not known ever to have been outside the Mediterranean but who used the Greek historian Timaeus as a major source. Since Timaeus drew extensively on Pytheas for information about the Atlantic, it is not unreasonable to argue that Diodorus' description was taken from Pytheas' original account. He writes:

> The inhabitants of Britain who live on the promontory called Belerion are especially friendly to strangers and have adopted a civilized way of life because of their interaction with traders and other people. It is they who work the tin, treating the layer which contains it in an ingenious way. This layer, being like rock, contains earthy seams and in them the workers quarry the ore which they then melt down to clean from its impurities. Then they work the tin into pieces the size of knuckle-bones and convey it to an island which lies off Britain, called Ictis; for at the ebb-tide the space between this island and the mainland becomes dry and they can take the tin in large quantities over to the island on their wagons. (And a peculiar thing happens in the case of the neighbouring islands which lie between Europe and Britain for at flood-tide the passage between them and the mainland runs full and they have the appearance of islands, but at ebb-tide the sea recedes and leaves dry a large space and at that time they look like peninsulas.) On the island of Ictis the merchants buy the tin from the natives and carry it from there across the strait of Galatia [the Channel] and finally, making their way on foot through Gaul for some thirty days, they bring the goods on horseback to the mouth of the Rhône.
>
> (Diodorus Siculus 5.1–4)

So vivid are the details that the text must be based on the careful observations of a person who visited Ictis and talked to the local people.

Apart from the fascinating details of extraction, the texts tell us that the traders who came to Ictis took their cargo back across the Channel to a port from where it could be transhipped by land to the Mediterranean. Given that the overland journey took over thirty days, the probability is that the port lay somewhere on the Gironde estuary, perhaps Burdigala (Bordeaux). At this time Corbilo may have been reserved for tin taken to the tribes of west-central Europe. The location of Ictis is usually assumed to be St Michael's Mount in Cornwall and this may well be so, but another site to be considered is Mount Batten, which at the time may also have been cut off at high tide. Extensive deposits of alluvial tin are to be found inland from Mount Batten around the fringes of Dartmoor and there is ample evidence that the port was in active use around the time of Pytheas' visit.

If sea journeys were being made directly between the south-west of Britain and the Gironde, then who were the traders? They were certainly not British. The most likely explanation is that they were southern Armoricans, acting as middlemen, carrying the tin produced by their British neighbours and trading their own tin as well. This gains some support from Caesar, writing in the middle of the first century BC, who notes that the Veneti living in the Morbihan were by far the strongest of the Armorican tribes: 'they have a great many ships and regularly sail to and from Britain' (*Bellum Gallicum* 3.8). He goes on to say that they control all the harbours along the south coast and extract tolls from those using them. Here were a people exploiting their geographical position on one of the major sea-routes much as their ancestors had done for millennia before.

The fleeting visit of Pytheas to Armorica would have caused much excitement to those who met him and his companions but need have left little archaeological trace unless it was he who built a timber temple to his protecting deity in Penmarc'h (above, p. 134) or brought with him the gold coin minted in Cyrène in 322–313 BC which was found at Lampaul-Ploudalmézeau on the coast of Finistère embedded in a root of seaweed. These are tantalizing, but untestable, hints.

The Romans in Gaul

Towards the end of the third century BC, Rome was drawn into conflict with the Carthaginians in Iberia, and even after the cessation of the Second Punic War in 206 BC, when the Carthaginians in the peninsula were finally subdued, Roman armies remained, engaged in bringing the hostile native tribes under control. In 133 BC, following the siege of the native *oppidum* Numantia, a semblance of peace was established and the Roman provinces in Spain could begin to be developed. All this time southern Gaul remained in the control of the Greek coastal cities which provided safe passage and supplies for the Roman soldiers, administrators, and traders travelling between Italy and Spain. But the situation here was far from stable and the

Greek cities were often under attack from hill tribes sweeping down from the interior. On a number of occasions Rome sent military forces to beat back the raiders, but with little lasting effect. It was clear that Rome had to take a firmer control. Matters came to a head late in 125 BC when, in response to a plea from Massalia, two legions were dispatched to deal with neighbouring tribes, the Saluvii, Vocontii, and Ligures. Campaigning continued until 121 BC, by which time the Rhône valley as far north as the Rhône–Saône confluence and eastwards to Lake Geneva was under Roman control. In the next few years the region west of the Rhône was consolidated, culminating, in 118 BC, with the foundation of the citizen colony of Narbo Martius at the old port of Narbo at the mouth of the Aude. A little later, the route to the Atlantic was brought under control when a Roman garrison was planted at the native town of Tolosa (Toulouse) on the Garonne. With a large territory now firmly under control, including the entire Mediterranean coast from the Maritime Alps to the Pyrenees, the Roman province of Transalpina could begin to take shape.

While the events of 125–118 BC had been largely a response to the need to keep the coastal route free for movement between Spain and Italy, the mineral wealth and fertility of the new province and the fact that it controlled the two major trade routes leading into barbarian Gaul—the Rhône corridor and the Aude–Garonne route—meant that it was soon to become a highly profitable addition to the nascent empire. The thrust along the Rhône had been driven by military necessity, but the advance to Tolosa was motivated more by commercial considerations. With both river valleys in her hands Rome was now ready to take control of the trading networks that linked the Mediterranean world to barbarian Gaul and beyond. Transalpina was highly attractive to Roman traders. The land was productive, providing supplies of grain much needed by the burgeoning urban populations of Italy. There were also metals to be had. The hills around, the Montagnes Noires and the Corbières, were rich in copper, silver, and lead, while alluvial gold was available in many of the valleys, especially to the south of Tolosa. Even though the first sixty years following the creation of Transalpina were punctuated by raids and uprisings, some provoked by Roman maladministration, the province flourished. It became a haven for the many who wanted to make a quick profit.

One entrepreneur whose methods became well known is Fonteius, who served as governor of Transalpina in the 70s. His speciality was extorting cash during the transhipment of Italian wine from the port of Narbo to the distribution centre at Tolosa. At each town through which the amphorae passed, a tax was levied, in total increasing the cost by 300 per cent. When challenged about this and taken to court, he was defended by Cicero, whose argument was that it was not an offence because it was the barbarians who had to pay the inflated price. The wine trade was particularly lucrative because wine was produced in considerable surplus on the slave-run estates of northern Italy and it was only a short journey by ship to Massalia and Narbo, from where it could be distributed to the Gauls living beyond the frontiers through ports of trade like Tolosa on the Garonne and Chalon-sur-Saône on the Rhône–Saône corridor. The Gaulish love of wine was legendary, as Diodorus Siculus explains:

> They are exceedingly fond of wine and sate themselves with the unmixed wine imported by merchants; their desire makes them drink it greedily and when they become drunk they fall into a stupor or into a maniacal disposition. And therefore many Italian merchants with their usual love of cash look on the Gallic craving for wine as their treasure. They transport the wine by boat on the navigable rivers and by wagon through the plains and receive in return for it an incredibly high price, for one amphora of wine they get in return a slave—a servant in exchange for a drink.
>
> (Diodorus Siculus 5.26.3)

It might have seemed a bargain to the Romans, but to a Gaul it was an unbelievably good deal. Slaves were cheap—a by-product of the socially embedded system of raiding—while a liberal supply of wine would enable a man aspiring to power to put on a memorable feast, greatly enhancing his status. The very large numbers of amphorae distributed across barbarian Gaul are witness to the accuracy of Diodorus' observation. One plausible estimate, based on the number of amphorae recovered, is that in the first half of the first century BC wine was reaching Gaul at the rate of forty thousand amphorae a year.

There is a distinction to be made between two different types of amphora used in the first century: those classified as Dressel 1A, which date broadly to the late second and early first centuries BC, and the Dressel 1B type, which date to the second half of the first century BC. Although it is not possible to be precise, the change takes place around the time of Caesar's conquest of Gaul. This makes the 1A type particularly useful for characterizing pre-conquest trade.

Wine for the Distant Barbarians

One of the transhipment centres for Italian wine was Tolosa. Here vast quantities of discarded Roman Dressel 1A amphorae have been found, evidence that wine was being transferred to barrels, preferred by the Gauls, for onward transport into the countryside around. But some of the wine remained in amphorae and was taken downriver to Burdigala, where it was loaded onto ships to be sent north to Armorica and beyond. Five shipwrecks, represented by collections of amphorae found on the seabed, chart the passage between Bordeaux and Quimper, one off Les Sables-d'Olonne, one between Île d'Yeu and Saint-Gilles-Croix-de-Vie, two south and west of Belle-Île, and one west of Pointe de Gâvres. The Dressel 1A amphorae that were successfully delivered cluster densely along the south coast of Armorica, but their occurrence on small islands around the western end of the peninsula, Îles Glénan, Île de Sein, and Île Geignog, suggest that trading ships were rounding Armorica to reach the north coast. Considerable numbers were found at the port of Alet (Saint-Servan, near Saint-Malo), but while these might have been brought in by sea, it is possible that at least some of the wine was transported in amphorae across the peninsula by way of the Vilaine and Rance valleys.

As an exotic luxury commodity the wine would, at first, have been manipulated by the local elites to enhance their status, but as the volume of imports increased and wine became more widely available, its perceived value will have fallen until it became a common item of commercial trade available to many.

Sometime in the first half of the first century BC, entrepreneurs from the north-coast ports of Armorica began to ship Italian wine in Dressel 1A amphorae to the southern British port of Hengistbury, a very well-protected anchorage at the confluence of the rivers Stour and Avon (above, pp. 25–9). Not only was Hengistbury a safe port, but its location gave direct and easy access to the heartland of Wessex, which at this time was highly productive of grain and animal products. It was also on the cabotage route along the southern British coast, with easy access to the metal-rich south-west.

The Armorican ship's masters who made the cross-Channel journey, leaving from the north coast, from Alet, the Baie de Saint-Brieuc, or Le Yaudet, probably made first for the island of Guernsey, where the harbour of St Peter Port offered a safe anchorage, to take on supplies of food and water before embarking on the second stage of the voyage. Not surprisingly, amphorae have been found on the island. Approaching Hengistbury the pilot had to manoeuvre eastwards around the dominant headland to reach the protected shelving gravel shores in its lee. Extensive excavations in this area have produced not only quantities of Dressel 1A amphorae but also a surprising amount of Armorican pottery, including Black Corded Ware, graphite-coated wares, and vessels made in a micaceous fabric decorated with horizontal rilling. Nearly 40 per cent of the pottery used at this time at Hengistbury came from Armorica. There are two possible explanations for this: either the vessels were arriving as containers for some desirable commodity such as honey or a special relish, or they represent the resident community of Armorican traders who had brought their own equipment with

4.11 Two types of Italian amphora in which wine was transported to western Europe. The Dressel 1A type (*left*) was in common use from the mid-second to just after the mid-first century BC, while the Dressel 1B type (*right*) was used mainly during the second half of the first century BC.

them for use during their stay. The two explanations are not necessarily exclusive. The suggestion of a community of traders has much to commend it. One can imagine the ships setting out in the spring, the Armoricans establishing a base on the headland for the trading season and there waiting for Britons from neighbouring parts of Wessex and from the south-west to arrive with goods for exchange. A seasonal market of this kind would last for many months. When the deals had been done, the Armoricans would return home before the autumn storms made the crossing difficult.

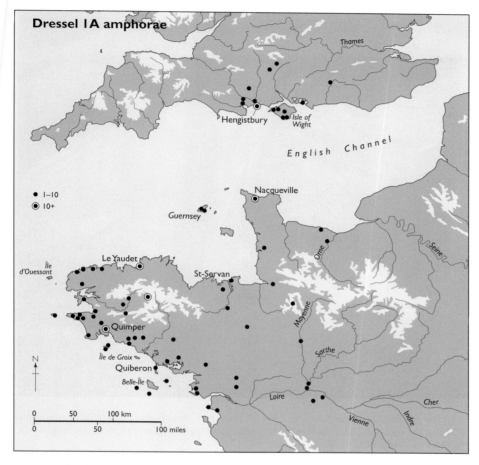

Dressel 1A amphorae

- 1–10
- 10+

Thames

Hengistbury   Isle of Wight

English Channel

Nacqueville

Guernsey

Île d'Ouessant   Le Yaudet   St-Servan   Orne   Seine

Quimper   Moyenne   Sarthe

Île de Groix   Quiberon   Belle-Île   Loire   Vienne   Indre   Cher

N

0   50   100 km
0   50   100 miles

4.12 The distribution of Dressel 1A amphorae in Armorica and southern Britain reflects the extent of the trading of Italian wine in the first half of the first century BC.

The archaeological evidence from Hengistbury provides some idea of the trade goods exchanged. The Armoricans' bulk cargo was wine, but packed around the amphorae would have been their pots, perhaps with marketable content, and smaller high-value goods such as blocks of raw purple and yellow glass, glass bracelets, bronze tableware, and dried figs (identified from a few preserved seeds). In return they were able to acquire grain, livestock (or hides), roughouts for bracelets cut from Kimmeridge shale, wheel-turned vessels of Kimmeridge shale, and a range of metals. Scrap gold was found in the excavations, silver was being refined on the site, and the headland produced iron ore of reasonable quality. It is interesting to compare these archaeologically attested commodities with the list of exports from Britain compiled

4.13 The archaeological excavation in progress at Hengistbury Head (1980–3). The trading community occupied the shelving ground leading down to the sea on the well-protected northern shore of the headland overlooking Christchurch Harbour.

by Strabo at the end of the first century BC (after Hengistbury had ceased to function). He mentions metals, grain, and hides, slaves, and dogs fit for hunting. There is no direct evidence for slaves and dogs at Hengistbury, but while hunting dogs might have been a niche market, we should not underestimate the huge demand that there was in the Roman world for slaves. The strong possibility is that British-procured slaves featured large among the commodities passing through the port.

Roman amphorae and Armorican pots are found in the immediate vicinity of Hengistbury and on at least three sites in the neighbouring Poole Harbour. While some of the Armorican ships may have made direct for Poole, it is more likely that the imports resulted from local cabotage. Poole Harbour would have been the most convenient place to collect the roughout bracelets of Kimmeridge shale quarried on the Purbeck shore. Roughouts occur in some numbers at Hengistbury, from where

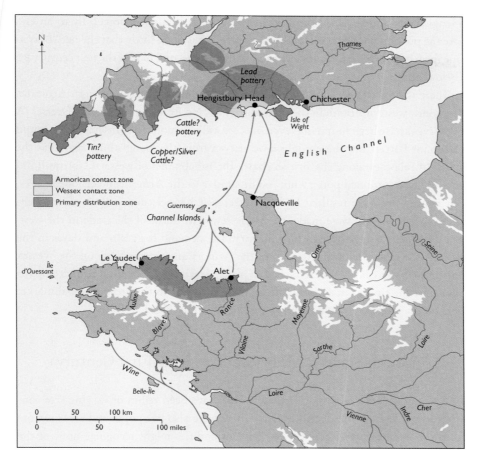

4.14 The trading network in operation in the first half of the first century BC linked northern Armorica with Wessex, probably using Guernsey as a stopover on the route.

they would have been transhipped to Armorica. Some have been found at the port of Alet. Others were carried on the much shorter crossing to Nacqueville, on the north coast of the Cherbourg peninsula, there to be offloaded at a beach market operating in the mid-first century BC.

How long-lived was the trading system focused on Hengistbury it is difficult to say. In all probability it was in operation over a number of years, during which time the Armorican traders will have established lasting relationships with their counterparts and with the agents of the British elite. It might be as diplomatic gifts that the Armorican gold coins found at Hengistbury and along the Dorset coast reached Britain in the years before Caesar's conquest. It is not known when the trade with

Hengistbury ceased. One possibility is that Caesar brought it forcefully to an end after he put down the rebellion in Armorica, but it is more likely that the networks in one form or another continued to function into the second half of the first century BC (below, pp. 176–7).

There is surprisingly little evidence for direct contact between western Armorica and south-western Britain in the first century BC. No Roman amphorae of Dressel 1A or 1B types have been found in Devon or Cornwall. Armorican coins have been found at Mount Batten, but these might have arrived from the Hengistbury region as the result of cabotage along the British coast. The inhabitants of western Cornwall did produce fine cordoned pottery not too dissimilar to the Armorican cordoned wares, but it need not have resulted from direct cross-Channel contact. It is more likely, then, that if voyages were made, they were few, with most of the trade in the western Channel passing through Hengistbury. The demand for grain and slaves in the Roman world focused the attention of the Armorican entrepreneurs on the Wessex chiefdoms, where both were to be had in plenty, leaving it to the local British ships to transport the tin, silver, and hides from the south-west to the great seasonal market held on the sheltered beaches in the lee of Hengistbury Head.

Armorican Society, Mid-Second to Mid-First Century BC

In a region as large as Armorica there would have been tribes of varying size controlled by hereditary or elected leaders. There were also less populated areas remote from the main centres where the settled communities might recognize none of the larger polities or, if they did, might change their allegiance from one to another. The situation was fluid and there were few fixed boundaries. The larger and more powerful polities will have had names to distinguish themselves from others. The earliest recorded name is the Ostimioi, mentioned in the account of Pytheas written at the end of the fourth century BC. These were the people of the western end of the Armorican peninsula. The name means 'the peoples of the west' and is cognate with the Osismii, mentioned by Caesar in the middle of the first century BC. It sounds like an ethnonym—the name that the people called themselves—but it could have referred to a confederation of smaller groups with different names who recognized a kinship because of their proximity in the remote region.

It is Caesar who gives us other tribal names: the Veneti, Coriosolites, Redones, in the peninsula; the Namnetes, allies of the Veneti, in the Loire valley; the Venelli, occupying the Cotentin peninsula of Basse-Normandie; and a number of other tribes further to the east. It was thirty years or so after the conquest, when the emperor

Augustus began to incorporate the disparate tribes of Gaul into the Roman empire, that the tribal boundaries were rationalized and fixed (below, pp. 167–70), but the new map is the rigid creation of administrators. While no doubt broadly correct in its recognition of the more powerful entities, it does scant justice to the fluid and fragmented state of political loyalties in the pre-conquest period. To gain some understanding of this it is necessary to turn to coinage.

The inspiration for the early coinage of Gaul were staters of Philip II of Macedonia (minted 359–336 BC), which are found throughout much of the territory in the following half-century, in all probability brought in by mercenaries returning from conflicts in eastern Europe. These imported types served as models for local coinages issued by Gaulish leaders who wished to be in a position to give away gold, stamped with their authority, in the cycles of gift exchange enacted to maintain a level of equilibrium within society and between polities. The first phase of coins—close copies of the Philip of Macedonia stater—to be found in Armorica was scattered along the Loire valley, suggesting that they may have been associated with Corbilo and used to facilitate exchange at an elite level (not market trading, for which a gold stater would have been far too valuable). The dating of these early copies is uncertain, but they would have been in use sometime between the mid-third to the early second centuries.

The first phase was followed sometime in the middle of the second century with a far more extensive phase characterized by a human-headed horse on the reverse. They were distributed widely on both sides of the lower Loire valley from between Tours and Angers to the Morbihan. Although these coins have traditionally been called Venetic, the distribution better conforms to the territory of the Namnetes as designated by the Roman administrators at the end of the first century BC, and only just overlaps with the Venetic territory defined at that time. The polity that issued the coinage was evidently in control of the network of exchanges that took place along the Loire valley. It may be that the entity split into two, the Veneti and the Namnetes, sometime before the mid-first century. Perhaps it was a reorientation of trade routes, occasioned by the developing wine trade with the Roman world, that led to the emergence of the Veneti of the Morbihan as a separate entity, serving as agents of the new system, thereby bringing about the decline of the polity controlling the Loire corridor, thereafter known as the Namnetes. Strabo says that merchants from Corbilo were among those questioned by Scipio Aemilianus at Massalia around 135 BC about routes to Britain (Strabo 4.2.1). This implies that the port was still functioning there at about the time that the human-headed horse coins were in use. But that no mention of Corbilo was made by Caesar suggests that it may have lost its significance altogether by the mid-first century. These scraps add weight to the suggestion of a major reorganization of power around the beginning of the first century BC.

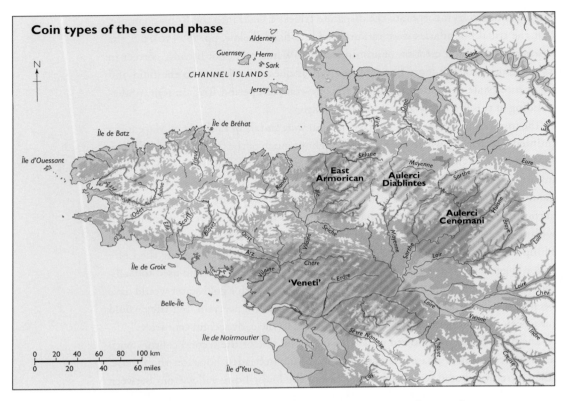

4.15 The major regions issuing coins in Armorica in the second phase of coin production.

Other polities to the north of the lower Loire were issuing distinctive coinages roughly at the same time as the Veneti–Namnetes phase. One group, which extends to peninsular Armorica, characterized as the East Armorican Rider coinage, has a reverse depicting an armed horse rider. This type is found east of the Rance covering the northern part of Ille-et-Vilaine and the southern part of Manche, equivalent to the territory of the Redones and Abricantes as defined in the early Roman period.

The third phase of Armorican gold coinage, spanning the period from the late second century to the mid-first century, is characterized by a fall in weight of the coins and a decline in purity as increasing amounts of silver and copper were introduced into the alloy. This corresponds to a greatly increased volume of production. The coinage is complex and not well understood, but it is now possible to identify series that can be related to tribes recognized in the early Roman period: the Namnetes in the Loire valley, the Veneti, Redones, Coriosolites, and Osismii on the Armorican peninsula, and the Biocasses in Basse-Normandie, as well as other tribes further to the east. Some of the series are complex. For example, the coinage of the Osismii is composed of at least six separate types issued by different authorities at different times. This is a reminder that the minting of coins could have been episodic and related to local circumstances and was not necessarily the sole prerogative of a tribal chief. Nor were the coins issued to facilitate market-level trade since the gold staters were much too valuable, but the huge volumes of lower-value coins issued in the middle of the first century may be a panic response to the threat and reality of Caesar's Gallic Wars. This has been argued for some of the issues of the Coriosolites. Six distinct classes have been identified: I–VI. On the basis that the weight declined over time, the chronological order of issue is likely to have been VI, V, IV, I, III, II. Since there is a distinct break in style between types IV and I and the last three types occur in exceptionally large numbers, it has been suggested that the first three types were in use before Caesar's attack, the last three groups representing a confederate coinage issued in 57 and 56 BC to fund the Armorican resistance. This is plausible but difficult to prove.

How the Armorican tribes were organized and ruled before the threat of invasion became real is not easy to deduce from the surviving evidence. In some parts of Gaul, close to the Roman province, kingship had been abolished and authority over the council of elders was in the hands of two annually elected magistrates. Elsewhere, in the more distant parts, kings or chieftains still held sway. But whichever system was used, in times of stress the tribe, or several tribes together, could elect one outstanding person as a war leader for the duration of the conflict. There is a direct reference to this in Armorica. Caesar tells us that the chief of the Venelli (in Manche), Viridovix, was appointed commander-in-chief of all the tribes who had rebelled against the Romans in 56 BC. No other king, chieftain, or war leader is named, but it is evident that at least some of the tribes had councils of elders. Caesar mentions the Eburovices, Aulerci, Lexovii, and Veneti, but it is not known whether they were under the authority of chieftains or elected magistrates.

4.16 Gold stater issued by the Veneti with the characteristic horse–human motif on the reverse. Found at Arradon, Morbihan. Collection musées de Vannes, ancien fonds SPM.

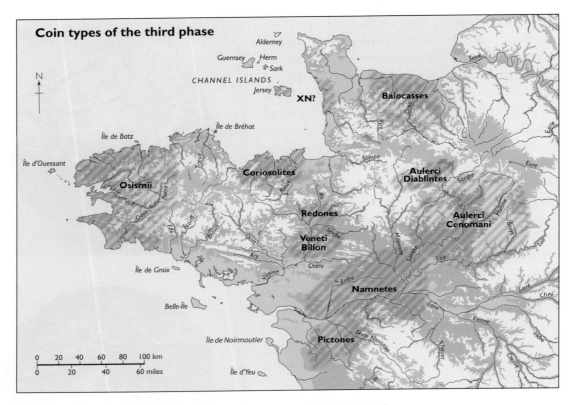

Coin types of the third phase

4.17 The major regions producing coins in the first half of the first century BC.

One highly visible sign of authority in Armorica is the hill-fort, of which there are a variety of types ranging from very large enclaves of many hectares to smaller hill-top fortifications and the cliff castles, promontories jutting into the sea with lines of defence protecting the approach from landward. Fortifications are known throughout Armorica but few have been examined archaeologically. Of the very large enclosures, Le Camp d'Artus at Huelgoat in Finistère has been explored by excavation on a small scale. It was 30 hectares in area, extending for some 2,000 metres along a ridge, with one end more strongly fortified. Both elements were built in the *murus gallicus* style, with a vertical dry-stone wall fronting a rampart composed of soil and rubble laced with horizontal frameworks of timber laid both parallel to the wall face and at right angles to it, nailed together with massive iron spikes where they crossed. Caesar, who gave the type its name, was impressed when he first came across them in central Gaul, noting their resilience against battering rams. The function of Le Camp d'Artus has not been defined, but given its great size it was most probably a place of

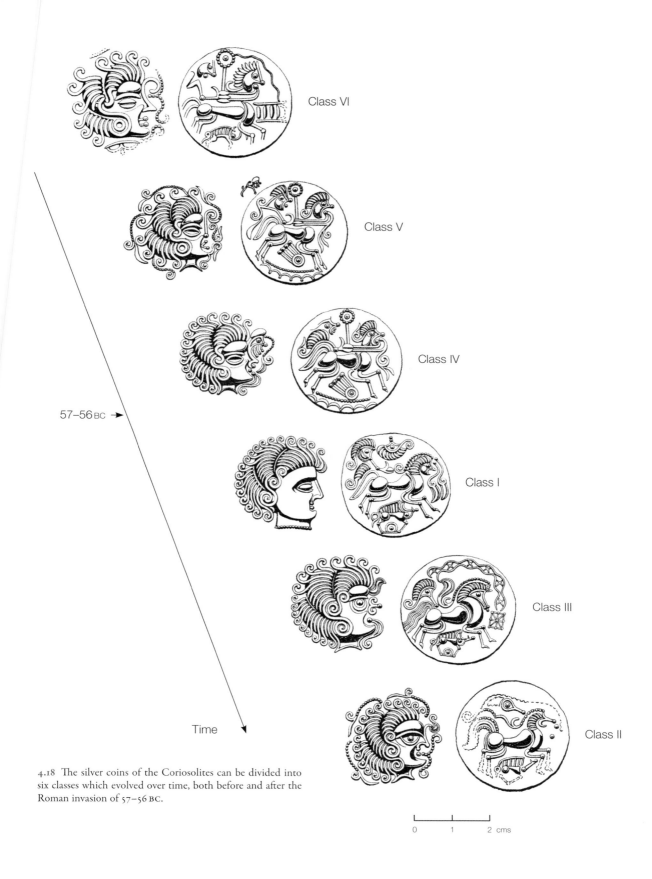

Class VI

Class V

Class IV

57–56 BC →

Class I

Class III

Time

Class II

4.18 The silver coins of the Coriosolites can be divided into
six classes which evolved over time, both before and after the
Roman invasion of 57–56 BC.

0   1   2 cms

4.19 Cliff castles, mentioned by Julius Caesar, are found around the coasts of Brittany. This dramatic example is Castel Meur, Cléden-Cap-Sizun, Finistère. At the neck of the promontory are several lines of banks and ditches protecting the defenders from attack from the land. The pockmarks on the promontory probably represent hut sites of Iron Age date.

4.20 (*Opposite top*) Le Camp d'Artus at Huelgoat was large enough to have served as the principal *oppidum* of the Osismii. Trial excavation in 1938 showed that the defences were built in the *murus gallicus* style described by Caesar, with grids of horizontally laid timbers nailed together to give resilience.

4.21 (*Opposite bottom*) The promontory fort of Le Yaudet, Côtes-d'Armor, was protected by a massive rampart extended on two occasions. The stone wall faces a rampart built in *murus gallicus* style. The rampart was later greatly enlarged, with tips of sand and gravel dumped in front. The addition could have been occasioned by the threat of Caesar's advance.

tribal assembly in use in the first half of the first century BC. The stronger fortification at its eastern end could have been in response to the threat of Caesar's attack. Other large enclosures include Guégon, near Josselin, in the Morbihan (32-plus hectares), in the territory of the Veneti; Poulailler in the forest of Fougères (20 hectares), in the

Le Camp d'Artus, Finistére

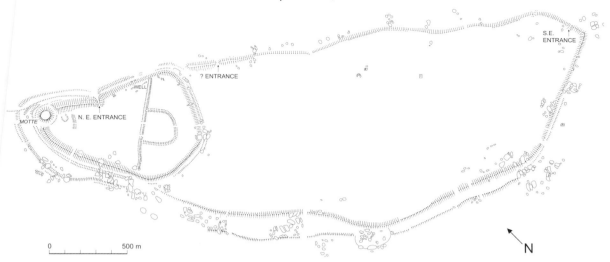

territory of the Redones; and Le Grand Mont-Castre in Manche (18 hectares), in the territory of the Venelli. It is tempting to see these large *oppida* as tribal centres. No inland equivalent has yet been identified in the territory of the Coriosolites, but the cliff castle of Erquy (35 hectares) on the coast of Côtes-d'Armor may have served as a place for tribal assembly.

Among the smaller fortifications, the enclosure of Le Yaudet, on the estuary of the Léguer in Côtes-d'Armor, has the character of a small hill-fort rather than a cliff castle since the fortifications run round the whole of the peninsula. The rampart shows three stages of fortifications, the first two of *murus gallicus* construction, the third consisting of a massive rampart built simply of dumps of soil and rubble, greatly increasing the height and width of the main defence. This last phase may have been an attempt to protect the community at the time of the Roman advance. A broadly similar hill-fort is Le Petit-Celland near Avranches in Manche. It was defended by a single-phase *murus gallicus* rampart but with no sign of later strengthening. These smaller hill-forts, probably spanning the late second and early first centuries BC, were intensively occupied and are probably best regarded as regional focuses within the larger tribal territory, serving as markets, production centres, places for religious worship, and, possibly, the residences of the elite.

Finally, there are the cliff castles, promontories almost surrounded by the sea—wild places exposed to all weathers—where people might take refuge. These are liminal locations between land and sea where the gods might be approached but where few people would choose to live permanently. It was to these places, Caesar tells us, that the Veneti fled as his army approached, but if cornered they would slip away by ship, much to his frustration.

Treaties, Rebellion, and Subjugation

Julius Caesar's conquest of Gaul began in 58 BC and lasted until 51 BC. For the Gauls it was devastating. According to Plutarch, a million had been killed and another million sold as slaves. Given a total population of about six million, the eight-year campaign must have dislocated every aspect of life, ramifying into the remotest of corners.

Caesar's grasp of the geography of Gaul was detailed and his military assessment of it brilliant. He saw Gaul as a central core with a maritime periphery and he understood, from the very beginning, that the most effective way to conquer the country in its entirety was to secure its maritime border first, after which the interior could be quickly wrapped up. Thus it was in 57 BC that he set out to take control of the entire north-western maritime zone from the Rhine to the Garonne. He divided it into two regions: that of the Belgae between the Seine and the Rhine, who he knew would be fierce in their opposition, and 'Aremorica', extending from the Seine to the Loire, whose inhabitants he considered to be more amenable. Further to the south were the Aquitani, who seemed to pose little problem. Saving for himself the glory of beating the Belgae into submission, he left Armorica to a subordinate. 'I had sent Publius Crassus with one legion to deal with the tribes of the Atlantic seaboard—the Veneti, Venelli, Osismii, Coriosolites, Esubii, Aulerci, and Redones' (*Bellum Gallicum* 2.34). He gives no details of Crassus' activities but simply records that after the Belgic campaign was over, 'I received information from Crassus that all these tribes had been brought into submission to Rome.' The troops were set up in winter quarters on the Loire and Caesar returned to Rome to bask in fifteen days of thanksgiving.

Legions had to be fed throughout the winter, a task made difficult by a grain shortage in the region. To manage this Crassus sent military envoys to the Esubii, the Veneti, and the Coriosolites demanding supplies, a heavy-handed act which shattered the fragile diplomacy of the previous year. The Veneti seized the envoys and encouraged other tribes to join them in revolt. This was in late winter or early spring 57–56 BC and Caesar was in Illyricum when the news reached him. Realizing the seriousness of the situation, he acted immediately. First he ordered that a fleet of galleys should be built on the Loire and trained crews brought in. To hold the situation until he arrived Titus Labienus was sent to monitor the Belgae and Crassus was ordered to go to Aquitania to make sure that the Armoricans received no support from the south. Decimus Brutus was given command of the Loire fleet, afforced by vessels requisitioned from the Pictones and Santones, who occupied the territory between the Loire and the Gironde.

Meanwhile the rebels, the Veneti, Coriosolites, and the Venelli, were making their own preparations.

> They fortified their *oppida*, stocked them with grain from the surrounding fields, and assembled as many ships as possible in Venetia, where it was generally assumed I should begin my operations. As allies for the campaign they secured the Osismii, the Lexovii, the Namnetes, the Ambiliati, the Morini, the Diablintes, and the Menapii. And they summoned extra forces from Britain, which lies opposite that part of Gaul.
>
> (*Bellum Gallicum* 3.9)

It is interesting that the rebels were drawing Belgic tribes, the Morini and the Menapii, into the conflict in an attempt to deflect some of the Roman effort. The forces summoned from Britain probably came from the Wessex coastal region between Lyme Bay and the river Arun, where a scatter of Armorican coins may reflect rewards brought home by those troops who eventually returned.

Caesar now faced a full-scale rebellion embracing all the tribes of north-western Gaul between the Seine and the Loire, as well as serious discontent among the maritime Belgae. In spring 56 BC he divided the available land force into two armies, sending Quintus Sabinus with the legions against the Coriosolites, the Venelli, and the Lexovii while he focused his efforts on smashing the Veneti, the leaders of the rebellion. Sabinus faced a large Gaulish force brought together under the war leader, Viridovix. The two armies camped 3 kilometres apart, confronting each other in a tense stand-off. After a while the rebels moved to attack the Roman camp, only to be repelled and soundly beaten. 'All the tribes there immediately surrendered to him for while the Gauls are quick and eager to start wars, they lack the determination and strength of character needed to carry on when things go against them' (*Bellum Gallicum* 3.19).

Meanwhile, in the south Caesar was playing a cat-and-mouse game with the Veneti, who used their experience of the sea to make hasty retreats when necessary. Caesar admits to his inexperience of 'the vast and open sea, where the tides were high and the harbours, if any, were few and far between', but realized that he could only bring matters to a close by defeating the Veneti at sea.

The Venetic ships were formidable.

[They] were built and rigged in a different way from ours. Their keels were some-what flatter, so they could cope more easily with the shoals and shallow water when the tide was ebbing: their prows were unusually high, and so were their sterns, designed to stand up to great waves and violent storms. The hulls were made entirely of oak to endure any violent shock or impact: the cross-beams, of timbers a foot thick, were fastened with iron bolts as thick as a man's thumb; and the anchors were held firm with iron chains instead of ropes. They used sails made of hides or soft leather, either because flax was scarce and they did not know how to use it, or, more probably, because they thought that with cloth sails they would not be able to withstand the force of the violent Atlantic gales, or steer such heavy ships.

(*Bellum Gallicum* 3.13)

The only advantage which the Roman galleys had was their speed and manoeuvra-bility, but their rams were of little use against the solidly built Venetic hulls, whose height made the use of missiles and grappling irons difficult.

Eventually the two naval forces met off the coast of the Morbihan, probably in the Baie de Quiberon: the 220 ships brought together by the Veneti and the mixed flotilla of specially built galleys and locally requisitioned sailing ships under the command of Decimus Brutus. Hostilities opened about ten in the morning and lasted until sunset, by which time the Romans were triumphant: only a few Venetic vessels managed to escape. Roman success was due to two things: their tactic of hacking at the rigging of the Venetic ships with sharp hooks mounted on long poles to bring down the sails, and the sudden onset of a dead calm, leaving the Veneti unable to move. The Roman galleys meanwhile, powered by oars, were able to surround the becalmed vessels and fight their way on board.

The destruction of the Venetic fleet 'marked the end of the war with the Veneti and the peoples of the whole Atlantic coast'. 'They therefore surrendered themselves and all their property to me. I decided that they must be punished with particular severity so that in future Gauls would have greater respect for the rights of envoys. I put all their elders to death and sold the rest into slavery' (*Bellum Gallicum* 3.16). Since Crassus had succeeded in beating down rebellious elements among the Aquitani, it remained only for Caesar to make a show of strength among the Belgic tribes, the Morini and Menapii, who had joined the Armorican rebellion, before returning his troops to winter quarters based 'in the country of the Aulerci and the Lexovii and the other tribes who had recently fought against us' (*Bellum Gallicum* 3.29). There is nothing like the presence of a victorious army, needing to be fed through a long winter, to remind newly conquered peoples of their subservience.

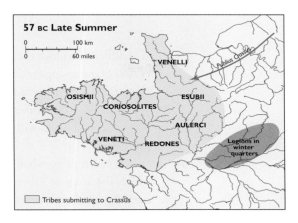

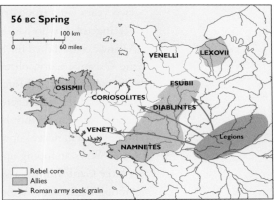

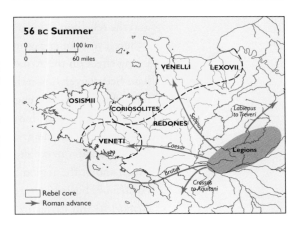

4.22 The campaign of Caesar and his generals against the rebellious tribes of Armorica.

Aftermath: Licking the Wounds

It is difficult to judge the effects on peninsular Armorica of the Roman military successes. Many young men will have died in the confederate army led by Viridovix, in the various skirmishes fought by Caesar against the Veneti, and in the great sea battle. If Caesar is to be believed, the rest of the Veneti were sold into slavery, but a large resentful population will have remained in Armorica waiting for an opportunity to get revenge.

It came in 54 BC when a rebellion broke out in the territory of the Belgae during which the army of Sabinus was destroyed. Encouraged by the news, an Armorican force marched on the winter quarters of the Thirteenth Legion in Basse-Normandie but quickly dispersed when news of Caesar's victory over the Nervii reached them. Two years later troops from all over Gaul flocked to relieve the great war leader Vercingetorix, who had been besieged by Caesar at Alesia. 'All the tribes from the Atlantic coast joined in.' Some fifty-three thousand troops were assembled in all from the Osismii, Coriosolites, Veneti, Redones, Venelli, Caleti, and other Armorican tribes. But the relief forces of nearly a quarter of a million men failed amid 'great slaughter' and Vercingetorix was captured and taken off to languish in a Roman prison for years before being strangled. How many managed to get back to their homes we will never know. But this was not quite the end. In 51 BC, the last year of the Gallic Wars, mopping-up activities in the west sparked further organized resistance. A large Gaulish force assembled in the territory of the Pictones south of the Loire. Among them were 'Armorican tribes who live in the extreme west of Gaul on the Atlantic coast' (*Bellum Gallicum* 8.31), but the force was routed, with heavy losses, and the rebellion faded out.

Seven years of engagement with the Roman army cannot fail to have had a devastating effect on the Armorican communities. Although much of their land seems to have been largely unscathed, so many of their men of fighting age had died or were injured in the various engagements that hardly a village would have been unaffected. The fury of war may have passed, but the trauma of these dreadful years was deep, leaving the sullen and grieving population to nurse its painful memories.

A generation or so after the Gallic Wars there seems to have been another event which shook the region. The evidence is archaeological. Five hoards of Roman silver *denarii* buried sometime between 30 and 20 BC have been found in peninsular Armorica, and it was in the same period that several very large hoards comprised mostly of coins of the Coriosolites were buried on Jersey. One of them, the Le Câtillon II hoard, contained 69,550 coins as well as four complete gold torcs and pieces of at least seven others. Another, much smaller hoard of the same date, including embossed silverwork as well as coins, was discovered on Sark. Although all the hoards could be explained as votive deposits made to the gods in times of stress, the Jersey hoards look very much like wealth stashed away offshore in response to a particular threat.

Perhaps there was an economic downturn driving the prudent to remove their surplus cash from sight, but it is more likely that there was some serious political upset. Gaul was far from calm at this time. The governor, Marcus Vipsanius Agrippa, had spent the year 30–29 BC campaigning against rebellious tribes, among them the Morini in western Belgica, and the next year he had to deal with a revolt among the Treveri. In 28 BC he was fighting in Aquitania, winning a major victory. There is no specific mention of trouble among the Armoricans, but these were unsettled times in the maritime regions and rebellion was in the air. Agrippa may even have thought it wise to move troops to Armorica to keep an eye on dissidents.

To add to all the uncertainty, the emperor Augustus made an extended visit to Gaul in 27 BC to observe the progress of his policy of integrating the tribes into the Roman administrative system. Among the measures he set in train was a national census requiring a detailed assessment not only of population but of the value of all landed property including acreages of arable and pasture land, size of flocks and herds, and number of fruit-bearing trees. This was to form the basis of a new system of taxation. It is little wonder that the natives were restless.

And what of the relations with the Britons? Caesar had made two brief visits to the island and had negotiated treaties with some of the tribes in the south-east, but otherwise the population was left to itself. But one obvious effect of the conquest of Gaul was that trade with Britain was reorganized. The volume of traffic using the long-established cross-Channel route between Armorica and central southern Britain greatly diminished, while new routes were developed between northern Gaul and eastern Britain. This is most clearly demonstrated by the distribution of the Dressel 1B amphorae, common in the second half of the first century BC, which cluster in Britain north of the Thames. That few are found in Armorica or central southern Britain implies that the old route via the Garonne to Armorica and Britain was no longer functioning. Armorica was fast becoming a backwater. These changes may have come about simply as the result of economic factors—the draw of the valuable market offered by the wealthy chiefdoms of eastern Britain—but perhaps there was a political imperative. Armorica was a remote and potentially rebellious territory with close ties to the southern Britons, who had provided troops to fight against the Roman advance. It would have made good sense for the new administrators to reorder international trade so that the links between Armorica and Britain withered, leaving the once rebellious tribes, now isolated, to readjust to the reality of living under Roman control.

5

THE ROMAN INTERLUDE
50 BC–AD 400

I N the famous opening passage of the *Gallic Wars*, Caesar tells us that Gallia
Comata, that is, barbarian Gaul beyond the boundary of the Roman province
of Transalpina, is divided into three parts, one inhabited by Belgae, another by
Aquitani, and the third by 'people we call Gauls, though in their own language they
are called Celts'. The Garonne formed the boundary between the Aquitani and the
Gauls, while the Seine and the Marne divided the Gauls from the Belgae. In the con-
solidation imposed by Augustus, which was completed during his visit in 27 BC, these
ethnic divides formed the basis of the new administrative map except that the Pictones
and the Santones, between the Loire and the Garonne, were assigned to Aquitania.
Peninsular Armorica, along with central Gaul, became the province of Lugdunensis.
Each of the three provinces of Gallia Comata was governed by a legate responsible to
the emperor. Financial matters were in the hands of procurators who also reported
direct to the emperor, but one procurator, based at Lugdunum (Lyon), looked after
both Lugdunensis and Aquitania. While the system offered a useful check on corruption, it inevitably caused tensions.

The provinces were divided into *civitates*—territories based closely on the old tribal
system—and in each *civitas* an urban centre was set up from which the territory was
administered. In Armorica there were five *civitates*, the Redones, the Namnetes, the
Veneti, the Coriosolites, and the Osismii, each a formalization of the prominent
tribes existing at the time of Caesar's conquest. In many parts of Gaul where a suitable

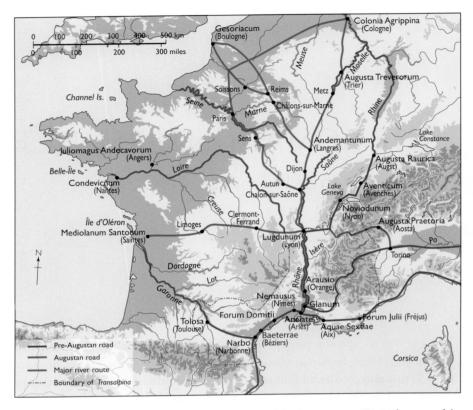

5.1 In the Augustan period (27 BC–AD 14) Gaul, conquered by Caesar, was reorganized as part of the Roman empire. The original trade routes running largely along the rivers were augmented by a new system of roads, and towns were founded at important route nodes.

native *oppidum* existed, the new *civitas* capital was built on the same site or nearby, but in Armorica it seems that the new sites were chosen for the cities, Carhaix (Vorgium) for the Osismii, Fanum Martius (Corseul) for the Coriosolites, Condate (Rennes) for the Redones, Darioritum (Vannes) for the Veneti, and Condevicnum (Nantes) for the Namnetes. It is, however, possible that more thorough excavation may bring to light evidence of pre-Roman occupation beneath these early Roman towns. The possibility is that Nantes may be on or close to the site of Corbilo, but there is no positive evidence of this.

The five *civitates* of Armorica were *civitates stipendaria* (tributary states), each administered by an *ordo* or a *senatus* made up of a hundred *decuriones* elected from prominent members of the native elite. Such men could expect to serve during their career in the many offices responsible for the administration of law and the collection

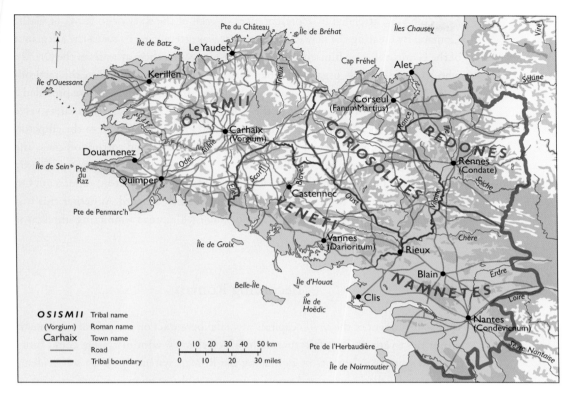

5.2 It was probably under Augustus that the boundaries of the *civitates* of Armorica were formalized, the cantonal capitals were founded, and road systems began to be laid out. The map shows the network of roads that eventually developed.

of taxes, and in the various religious duties required to run an efficient and orderly community. The Roman system was carefully designed to integrate the native elites, rather than simply to impose alien structures. By giving them scope to work within established hierarchies and to express their tribal loyalties, Rome harnessed the energies of the conquered populations to the service of the state. Men who served them well, like Titus Flavius Postumus, a hard-working member of the senate of the Redones, could expect to be rewarded with citizenship. Postumus received his promotion in the late first century AD, assuming the forenames of his patron, the emperor Vespasian.

Augustus spent the years 16–13 BC in Gaul putting the finishing touches to his administrative structure. The completion of the project was symbolized in 12 BC by the dedication of an altar to Rome and Augustus just outside Lugdunum at the confluence of the Rhône and the Saône. It was here that the *consilium Galliarum* was held each year, attended by representatives of each of the sixty or so tribes of Gallia Comata. By creating the new event Augustus was attempting to focus the allegiance of the Gaulish elite on himself and the empire, deflecting them away from the Druids, who had traditionally organized a pan-Gaulish gathering each year in the territory of the Carnutes, between the Seine and the Loire. The occasion may have provided a sense of bonding—of being part of the Roman world—but it was also a safety valve where the provincials could make their views and grievances known to the emperor. And grievances there were not least against exorbitant taxes and corrupt officials. The strength of anti-government feeling that could run high in the provinces is vividly demonstrated by a hoard of coins buried at Port-Haliguen, Quiberon, about 8 BC. On every coin the image of the emperor had been violently defaced. Whether this was the anger of a single individual or a sign of more widespread simmering unrest it is impossible to say.

Becoming Roman

The establishment of the *civitas* capitals was a deliberate act on the part of the Roman authorities to create the infrastructure in which the new administration could function and where the benefits of embracing the Roman system would be self-evident. The fine new urban centres of Armorica were probably set up in the late first century BC or early first century AD by army engineers. A rigorous grid of streets was laid out, with plots reserved for public buildings and others made available for private domestic and commercial development. The other essential facility was an assured water supply. This too would have required the surveying skills of military engineers. The best-known example in Armorica is the aqueduct that supplied Vorgium, bringing water from the Montagnes Noires 13 kilometres away. The aqueduct was significantly longer since it had to follow the contour for much of its length. Within the grid of streets the essential public buildings were erected; the forum and basilica complex would have been the first, providing the economic and administrative heart of the town, followed by such amenities as public baths, theatres, and temples.

Not much is known of the early development of the Armorican *civitas* capitals during the early empire, but Romanization was not without its setbacks. Repressive policies instituted by Augustus' successor, Tiberius, sparked widespread alarm throughout Gaul. What caused most upset was the suppression of Druidism and the ending of tax exemptions for the more important *civitates*. As the discontent became more intense, so the clamour about unfair rates of taxation, high interest rates, and the arrogant behaviour of governors got louder, until, in AD 21, a country-wide revolt

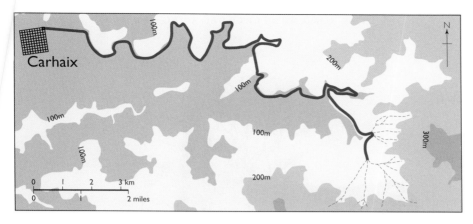

Carhaix

5.3 The creation of new urban centres like Vorgium (Carhaix) required not only a good system of communication but also an assured water supply. The water for Vorgium was brought from hills 13 kilometres away through a carefully engineered aqueduct.

5.4 The aqueduct of Vorgium was probably laid out by military engineers at the beginning of the settlement's life. The underground section, built of masonry, seen here under excavation, had inspection chambers at intervals so that silt and other obstructions could be removed and repairs undertaken.

5.5 The Temple of Mars lies about 2 kilometres from the town of Fanum Martis (Corseul) at Haut-Bécherel. The temple, built in the first century AD, overlooked a spacious colonnaded sacred precinct. The octagonal cella (inner chamber) of the temple now dominates the site. Originally it was surrounded by an ambulatory on three sides. This kind of plan is found widely in north-western Europe and reflects pre-Roman traditions.

broke out, led by two members of the Gaulish elite, Julius Sacrovir and Julius Florus. It may be that the destruction of buildings in Vorgium and in the two smaller towns of Quimper and Alet at about this time was the result of the general unrest spreading through northern and western Armorica.

For the Roman administrative system to work, a network of roads had to be constructed linking the powerful urban centres. Road building was under way as early as the governorship of Marcus Agrippa (39–37 BC). The three main east–west routes along the Armorican peninsula, together with the cross routes joining the main towns along them, were probably laid out at this time. This essential system allowed quick and safe journeys to be made between the main cities and formed the framework on which an intricate network of minor roads could be based incorporating smaller inland settlements and coastal ports.

An improved system of land communication meant that even remote rural areas were now within easy reach of markets, either in the major towns or at settlements that developed at crossroads. The rural population grew significantly, and with it the agricultural productivity of the land. Tin remained a major output. The alluvial deposits at Saint-Renan in Léon and along the south coast, particularly at the mouth of the Vilaine, continued to be worked, while at Abbaretz, Nozay, tin ore was extracted from trenches dug along the lode. Lead, now in demand for plumbing and for pewter manufacture, was mined at Plélauff in Côtes-d'Armor and Donges, Crossac, in Loire-Atlantique, while evidence for iron extraction is widespread throughout the peninsula. Apart from tin, which may have been produced in surplus for export, the lead and iron probably supplied local needs, while copper would have to have been imported.

The sea proved to be a major resource. Salt production, so evident in the preconquest period, continued, though probably now under state control. The main use of salt, apart from flavouring food, was as a preservative for meat and fish, but in Armorica it was increasingly used to make garum, a salty fish sauce used in cooking. Garum was widely produced on the Atlantic coasts of Morocco and Iberia and was first introduced into Armorica in the second century AD, quite probably by entrepreneurs from Iberia who, hearing of the shoals of sardines off the Armorican coast, saw an opportunity to develop a profitable industry. Armorican sardines remain a delicacy today.

Garum works are known, scattered along the north and south coasts, but are found particularly densely clustered around the Baie de Douarnenez in the extreme west, where the small sardines, the preferred fish for making the sauce, shoal in late spring. The installations consist of batteries of up to twenty tanks built of stone and lined with waterproof mortar. The sardines were placed in the tanks together with layers of salt and were crushed and mixed, the resulting mash being left for five or six weeks, roofed over to protect the brew from rain. When the product was deemed to have matured, the liquor was separated from the paste and each was packed into barrels for transport to market. The same processing works also produced barrels of salted fish. Fish products of this kind were much in demand in the Roman empire, and it is quite likely that some, at least, of the output was transferred by ship from Douarnenez direct to British ports and to markets in the Loire and Garonne estuaries.

While there can be no doubt that the Armorican communities enjoyed much the same level of Romanization as the rest of Gaul, the fact remains that they occupied

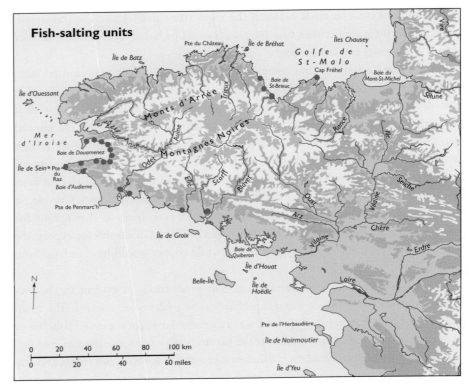

5.6 Fish-salting establishments, producing garum (a fish sauce) and salted fish, are found around the coasts of Armorica. There is a particular concentration around the Baie de Douarnenez within easy reach of the rich sardine shoals encountered in the seas to the west of the peninsula.

the remote outer edge of the empire. Those who lived in the towns or in villas in the countryside around, and may have served on the senate of their *civitas*, understood what it meant to be Roman and what benefits accrued to those who embraced the lifestyle. But they were in the minority. By far the greatest part of the population lived in the countryside and may never have visited a town. At best they might have come into contact with the wider world by using the local markets at the smaller settlements or at major crossroads, or might have visited a fair held at the local temple. These *pagani* (country dwellers) lived among reminders of their ancestors, the megalithic tombs and standing stones: they endured much the same lives as their grandparents and those before them. Life in the *civitas* was far removed from the reality experienced daily by the mass of the population whose loyalty lay with their countryside and with their ancestors.

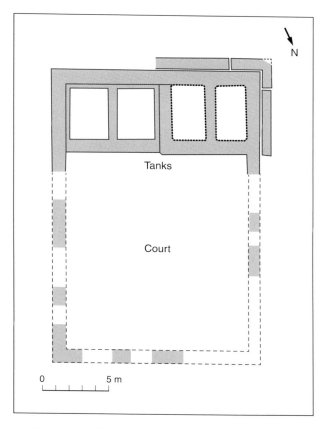

5.7 Fish-salting establishment at Le Resto, Lanester, Morbihan. Small fish steeped in salt were left to rot in the tanks to generate an oily liquid, garum, which was extensively used in cooking.

The Sea Again

In the years following the conquest of Gaul the volume of trade with the Roman world increased dramatically, while its intensity shifted as new economic imperatives began to be felt. The presence of a huge troop deployment on the Rhine frontier that was both consuming and productive encouraged the development of direct routes between the Mediterranean and the frontier zone using the Rhône–Saône–Moselle corridors and the route from the Rhône to Augusta Raurica (Augst) on the upper Rhine. The chiefdoms of south-eastern Britain offered another valuable market that could be reached from the mouth of the Seine or from the newly established port of

Gesoriacum (Boulogne) on the Channel coast in sight of the still-unconquered island. The reorientation of trade to exploit these new opportunities began to overshadow the long-established western routes via the Garonne and the Loire to the Atlantic, a point nicely made by the distribution of the Dressel 1A and 1B amphorae, which show that after the conquest, the movement of Italian wine followed the northern route along the Rhône to northern Gaul and Britain virtually bypassing Armorica (above, p. 165).

But the downturn in Atlantic trade was not to last. Towards the end of the first century BC Mediterranean wine began to reach Armorica again in quantity. Some was carried in Dressel 2–4 amphorae, a type made in both northern Italy and Catalonia, in north-eastern Spain. An analysis of the fabrics of those found in Armorica shows that most, but not all, of the wine transhipped to Armorica in Dressel 2–4 amphorae was Italian. But Catalan wine was being imported in another distinctive form of amphora, Pascual 1, a type found widely distributed in Armorica, particularly along the south coast, arriving throughout the first century AD. The obvious route for this import was overland to the port of Narbo, then along the Aude–Garonne route, and finally by sea to Armorica. The Loire mouth seems to have been largely avoided, with the ships making direct for the port of Darioritum and for Quimper on the estuary of the Odet. At Quimper a hundred Dressel 2–4 amphorae and forty-five Pascual 1 have been found in excavations. But it was not only wine that was being carried. Another commodity was pottery, fine red tableware (*terra sigillata*) made in southern Gaul around the centre of Montans in the upper Garonne region. The products of these southern Gaulish potteries became very popular in western Gaul and Britain, and it seems likely that much of the supply to Britain came via the Atlantic seaways.

The extent of the trade between Armorica and southern Britain in the first century AD is difficult to quantify. Dressel 2–4 and Pascual 1 amphorae, found at Hengistbury Head and in Poole Harbour, were probably brought from the Garonne via Armorica in the early part of the first century AD, and a similar route may have been used by vessels transporting the south Gaulish *terra sigillata* after the conquest of Britain in AD 43, using new ports like Clausentum in Southampton Water or extending the journey to London, which soon became the major port of entry. How much of the trade was in the hands of Armorican middlemen is unclear. While short-haul journeys no doubt continued, many ship's captains probably loaded cargo in the Gironde estuary and sailed all the way to Britain, stopping off along the route to sell some commodities and buy others, returning with the holds full of British products. These men would have included Aquitani or Britons, but a large number of them would surely have been Armoricans benefiting, as always, from their central position dominating the shipping lanes.

A shipwreck found in St Peter Port Harbour, Guernsey, neatly illustrates the complexities of maritime commerce. The ship was on a trading venture sometime in the

AD 280s when it caught fire in the harbour and sank. Included in its cargo were blocks of pitch extracted from pine trees, the most probable source of which (based on the analyses of sand embedded in them) was the Landes, south of the Gironde estuary. The vessel also carried sacks of grain and barrels, the contents of which are unknown (could it have been Armorican garum?). Some hint of the route taken by the ship comes from the pottery found on board, reflecting the ports where the crew brought their crockery. There was an amphora from southern Gaul, bowls from western France, black-burnished jars from Poole Harbour, and pottery from East Anglia that could have been acquired in a port like London. From the bare archaeological facts it would be possible to reconstruct many narratives, but the simplest is that the little vessel tramped the route between the Gironde and the Thames carrying whatever the ship's master thought he could turn to profit. He had taken on a cargo of pitch in the Gironde and was probably making his way to London when the vessel caught fire in the harbour and his livelihood was lost.

One of the pots found on the St Peter Port wreck is a distinctive type of vessel known as *céramique à l'éponge*, manufactured somewhere in western Gaul between the Loire and the Garonne. It is recognizable from its orange-yellow glossy slip, which is sometimes decorated with a darker marbled overslip. The pottery is strikingly original and was traded as a commodity in its own right, to Armorica and southern Britain. In Britain the distribution of *à l'éponge* ware concentrates in the region centred on the port of Clausentum, but finds in Exeter and around the upper estuary of the Severn suggest that cargoes were being offloaded at a number of British ports in the south-west in the late third and early fourth centuries AD. Perhaps the master of the vessel which met its end at St Peter Port had once carried such a cargo and had kept a dish for the use of the crew.

By the third century AD the sea-route between Britain and the Gironde was flourishing, the terminal port of Burdigala growing rich on the proceeds. But a sea journey was always risky and it was as well to try to ensure a safe passage by placating the gods. One cautious traveller was Marcus Aurelius Lunaris, an official who worked in York and Lincoln. In AD 237 he set out to sail to Burdigala carrying with him a stone altar dedicated to the goddess Tutela Boudig(a), the inscription recording his intention to set up the altar to the deity after his safe arrival. Since the altar had been installed in Burdigala, it is evident that the goddess was prepared to bring the ship safely to port, overlooking the bribery involved in the dedication. It is, however, the less successful journeys that provide the best evidence for trade. Sometime in the late third or fourth century a vessel carrying a cargo of lead ingots foundered on Les Sept-Îles, a string of islands off the north coast of Armorica opposite Ploumanac'h. The cause of the disaster is unknown, but either an inexperienced ship's master was trying to sail through a narrow gap between two skerries or the vessel was out of control, driven against the island by a fierce northerly. The cargo comprised ingots of lead weighing from 20 to 150 kilograms, of which 271 were recorded, totalling 22 tonnes of metal. Many of the ingots were inscribed, some with the names of two British tribes, the Iceni and the Brigantes, the implication being that the lead came from these two tribal sources. But there are difficulties. While lead workings are known in Brigantian territory, there are no lead deposits in the territory of the Iceni. One possibility is that the marks indicate not the source of the lead but the *civitates* through which it passed before being taken on board. If so, then the vessel is likely to have sailed from eastern Britain, its journey cut short when it foundered on Les Sept-Îles. Another wreck of about the same date, found off Île de Batz near Roscoff, was carrying ingots of tin, of which five hundred have been recovered. Some are marked with an M, but this gives no clue to their origin. The probability is that the tin was Armorican, coming perhaps from the extensive alluvial deposits at Saint-Renan nearby. The vessel cannot have been long at sea before disaster struck; its planned destination is unknown. That two wrecks have been discovered off the north coast reflects the dangers of these waters and is a reminder that there are likely to be many more waiting to be found.

During the long period of the Pax Romana, from the time of Augustus until the late fourth century, maritime traffic between Armorica and Britain thrived, even during the troubled times at the end of the third century. Alet on the Rance estuary and Le Yaudet on the Léguer have both yielded British pottery, as have Quimper and Kervennénec, both in Finistère. On the British side of the Channel, Clausentum was the main port of entry, but Hamworthy in Poole Harbour was active, and it is also likely that ships were using Weymouth Bay, in easy reach of the town of Dorchester, and Exeter, further west. We can glimpse these links through the archaeological evidence, but we have no sure way of quantifying the traffic that flowed backwards and forwards, creating lasting bonds between the two peoples joined by the sea.

The Ever-Present Ancestors

For the people of Armorica, as for the rest of the Gauls and the Britons, the gods were everywhere, in the rivers and the springs, in the prominent hills, in dominant rock formations, in groves of ancient trees, and in the sky. They had always been there and there they would remain, each divine power known by its ancient name. The only change that Romanization brought was that some of the native gods were conflated with their nearest Roman equivalent. Thus the source of the Vilaine was presided over by the native deity Vicinnonia, who would have been well known and was worshipped in Condate and Condevicnum in temples dedicated to Mars Vicinnus—a powerful marriage of the two deities. Foreign deities were introduced into the major towns, brought in by traders, officials, or time-expired veterans returning from duties in distant lands. But these aliens seldom penetrated the countryside, which remained the preserve of the ancient gods of the ancestors.

Sacred places continued to be revered into medieval and later times. The chapel of St Michel, on a high point in the Monts d'Arrée, commanding sweeping views in all directions, must surely reflect the continued sanctity of a place that even now is imbued with a feeling of awe. The hill near the town of Locronan, the Montagne de Locronan, is still perambulated on the day of the annual pardon, the participants acknowledging points around its perimeter which appear to have celestial significance going back to prehistoric times. Many of the menhirs and stelae are associated with stories and beliefs possibly of ancient origin. In the forested area north of Lannion in Côtes-d'Armor, close to the chapel of St Sampson, is a reclining menhir famous for its ability to cure the back pain of anyone who leans against it. The complex raises many questions. Was the chapel built because of the sanctity of the site? Was the stone always regarded as having curative powers? Or was the story created by someone who found it a comfort to rest against the stone and mentioned it in the local bar? We might like to believe in the continuity of beliefs reflecting the power of a place, but proof is notoriously difficult to come by. That said, the rural population of Armorica in the time of the Roman empire were close to their prehistoric heritage. It would have been difficult to travel far without encountering a standing stone or a megalithic tomb. They dominated the landscape, redolent of meaning, demanding reverence and explanation.

One remarkable moment deserves special mention, the 'menhir-auteil de Kernuz' found at Kervadol, Plobannalec, in Finistère. It began life as an Iron Age stela with four carefully dressed faces, standing nearly 3 metres high. Later, in the Roman period, each face was carved with deities in low relief—a total of six figures in all, Mercury with a child, Hercules, Apollo, Mars, and Minerva or possibly Venus. It is impossible to know what was in the minds of those who transformed the stela with their carving. Were they making explicit the power they believed resided in the stone, or was it simply a convenient block to turn into an altar to the gods? There are different kinds of continuity.

Megalithic tombs were also much in evidence and were responded to in different ways during the Roman period, as is shown by the large number that have produced Roman period finds. Many of these cluster in the Venetic *civitas* and in particular in the coastal region of the Morbihan. While this could be a function of the large number of megalithic tombs in the region, the percentage of those interfered with in the Roman period is much higher than elsewhere and suggests the localized existence of a belief system which regarded the ancestral tombs as places of special veneration.

5.8 The standing stone known as the menhir-auteil de Kernuz, found at Kervadol, Plobannalec, Finistère, was originally an Iron Age stele, which later, in the Roman period, was carved with images of gods: Mercury, Hercules, Apollo, Mars, and Minerva (or Venus). This side shows Mercury holding a caduceus (herald's staff) with a child at his side.

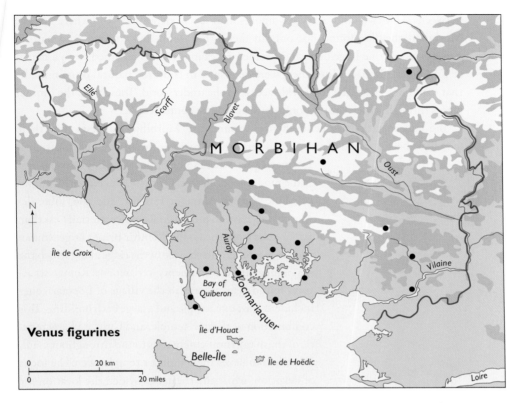

5.9 Roman period Venus figurines, made in pipe clay at workshops in Armorica, provided cheap offerings for a worshipper to dedicate to the gods. They are often found in megalithic tombs placed there to placate the deities of the underworld. Such deposits are numerous in the southern Morbihan.

For the most part the Roman material from megalithic tombs comes from older excavations and is not always well recorded. An exception is Le Petit Mont, Arzon, which commands the narrow approach from the Baie de Quiberon to the Morbihan (above, pp. 55, 57). Here recent work has brought to light quantities of Late Iron Age and Roman material deposited in the Neolithic passage graves within the mound. Pre-conquest finds include Gaulish coins, glass beads, and a glass bracelet, while finds of Roman date include pottery and coins, a large number of pipe-clay Venus figurines, and a small inscribed altar. The inscription on the altar is partly eroded, removing the name of the god, but the suppliant, whose name is also eroded, is recorded to have been the son of Quintus Sabinus, who 'willingly and deservedly fulfilled his vow'.

The Venus figures are of particular interest. They were mass-produced in several workshops in Armorica, including one in Condate, and sold as ex-votos to anyone wanting to make an inexpensive offering at a shrine or a grave. In Le Petit Mont between sixty-two and sixty-six figures had been deposited. Elsewhere in the Morbihan they are found not only in megalithic tombs but in caves and natural crevices, while one large deposit, of some 144 examples, was recorded from a marsh at Kerloquet, Carnac. Most, then, were deposited in contexts, natural or man-made, that could be considered to provide access to the underworld. These were the liminal places through which the chthonic deities could be contacted.

The concentration of Venus figures around the Morbihan suggests that there may have been a ritual centre somewhere in the region. The most likely location is Locmariaquer, where some of the most impressive mega-lithic monuments cluster. Of these, the Neolithic tombs of Mané Rutual, Mané er Hroëck, and the Table des Marchands have all produced Roman material. Less than 200 metres from the Grand Menhir Brisé a large Roman theatre was built into the side of the ridge along which the major megalithic monuments were set out. Roman structures found nearby beneath the village of Locmariaquer include at least one temple and a large bath building. This combination of theatre, temple, and baths is characteris-tic of the many rural sanctuaries found throughout Gaul. In such complexes the temple or temples were the focus of devotion, while the theatre provided the location for pilgrims to assemble to watch religious performances. The baths, in addition to being places for recreation, were also used for curative treatments. Large sanctuaries of this kind would have been locations for annual festivals attracting a constant flow of pilgrims.

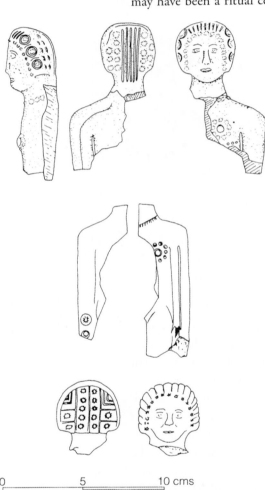

5.10 Fragments of Venus figurines found in the passage grave of Le Petit Mont, Arzon.

The proximity of the sanctuary to a concentration of megalithic tombs clustering round the recumbent Grand Menhir Brisé is hardly likely to have been a coincidence. The sanctity of the place must have been self-evident from the beginning, with people returning time and time again to the old megaliths to wonder at the giants who built them and who raised the great menhir, and to solicit the support of the chthonic deities inhabiting the underworld. The monumentalizing of the place, with all the facilities of a Gallo-Roman sanctuary, was just one stage in the long continuum of religious observance.

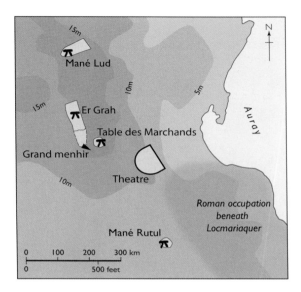

5.11 The cluster of megalithic monuments at Locmariaquer on the gulf of Morbihan became the focus of Roman occupation. The presence of a large theatre, often an adjunct to a temple, suggests that the site may have been a centre of worship in the Roman period, reflecting the long-established sanctity of the location.

Stating Identity

The response of inhabitants of Armorica to the opportunities offered by the Roman empire will have varied according to social status, ambition, and a host of other factors. For those whose life was based in or around the cities embracing the outward and visible signs of *romanitas* was an attractive option, opening the way to enhanced status and wealth as well as offering access to new luxuries and new value systems. With perseverance a city dweller could become Roman. But for the great bulk of the people living in the remote countryside opportunities were far more limited. Here traditional values and loyalties prevailed. With time this divide between town and countryside became wider.

The elites living in the cities or on their estates in the countryside around would also have been aware of their ancestral loyalties, though whether they harboured any nostalgia for the past or wished to construct a new Armorican identity are matters difficult to explore. There are, however, hints of regional cultural preferences expressed in the way in which some chose to decorate their homes. The most obvious manifestation of this is in the fashion for decorating walls of bath buildings with encrustations of seashells set decoratively into the partially dried plaster to enhance the painted geometric designs. Usually the plaster was painted first, before the shells

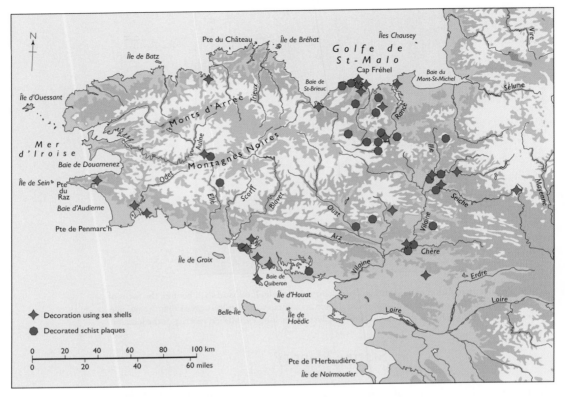

5.12 Roman buildings in Armorica developed distinctive decorative characteristics, notably the use of marine molluscs stuck in the plaster of walls and painted to create a somewhat garish effect. Schist plaques with maritime scenes, used for room decoration, were another Armorican speciality.

were set. After this the projecting part of the shell was either left its natural colour, or was brightly painted to contrast with the background colour. Decorative schemes of this kind are found throughout Armorica in the third century AD in both town-houses and countryside villas. Shells had been used in interior decoration in Italy in the first century, and examples are occasionally found later in Gaul, but it was in Armorica that the style caught on and evidently became the desirable feature of a well-appointed bath suite. A fondness for such garish treatment may simply have been a regional idiosyncrasy, but is there, perhaps, more behind it? Could it be an attempt, in times of increasing empire-wide stress, to create a sense of Armorican identity using the sea as a symbol of their peninsular world?

Another regional curiosity is the use of decorative plaques of schist to enhance wall decorations. Some fifty or so are known in Armorica, with a concentration in the north-east of the peninsula in the *civitas* of the Coriosolites and around Condate.

5.13 Fragments of wall plaster with inset molluscs from the Roman villa at Saint-Cast-le-Guildo, Côtes-d'Armor.

5.14 Schist plaque carved with a triton and seahorse from Broons, Côtes-d'Armor. Third century AD.

Various decorative styles are recognized, some architectural, some geometric, while a number depict marine creatures and mythological aquatic scenes. Here again, the emphasis on the sea may be playing to a nostalgia for a past maritime heritage.

The Looming Crisis

For the Armoricans, the second century AD was a time of growing prosperity and relative peace. Productivity increased, trade flourished, and those able to work the system got rich, reinvesting part of their wealth in their private residences and in public works to adorn their cities, proudly proclaiming their patronage in monumental inscriptions for all to see. Yet behind all this affluence and display were warnings of what was to come. In AD 166 two Germanic tribes, the Quadi and the Marcomanni, broke through the frontier and rampaged as far south as northern Italy, creating panic throughout the empire. They were soon driven back and a long war of attrition followed, but the event was a stark reminder of the ever-present threat of northern barbarians held back only by a flimsy frontier.

Less dramatic, but more insidious, was the growing discontent within the Gaulish countryside as the wealth gap widened and the poor became poorer and more desperate. Afforced by disillusioned army veterans and deserters, and by drop-outs from the middle classes, the undercurrent of discontent gained momentum, in AD 185–7 bursting into an outright rebellion led by an army deserter in Lugdunensis. Rebels 'overran the whole land of the Gauls and the Spanish, attacking the largest cities, burning parts of them and plundering the rest before retiring' (Herodian 1.10.2). Armorica was caught up in the unrest. While the details and extent are unknown, it was serious enough to require the intervention of Legio VI Victrix, supported by military contingents from Britain who, so one inscription from Croatia records, were sent to quell the rebellious Armoricans. The divide between the urban elites and the people of the countryside had now become dangerous and was to get worse.

As the third century progressed, so the crisis in the west grew, exacerbated by increasing barbarian pressures on the Rhine frontier, piracy in the North Sea and the Channel, and political instability among the Roman leadership. Between AD 239 and 251 social discontent throughout Gaul became serious enough to be described as a civil war and had to be suppressed by the emperor. If this was not enough, two years later Franks and Alamanni broke through the frontier and rampaged across Gaul reaching as far south as Arles. The situation was restored by Gallienus, son of the emperor Valerian, but the event had once again brought into stark relief the vulnerability of the Rhine frontier.

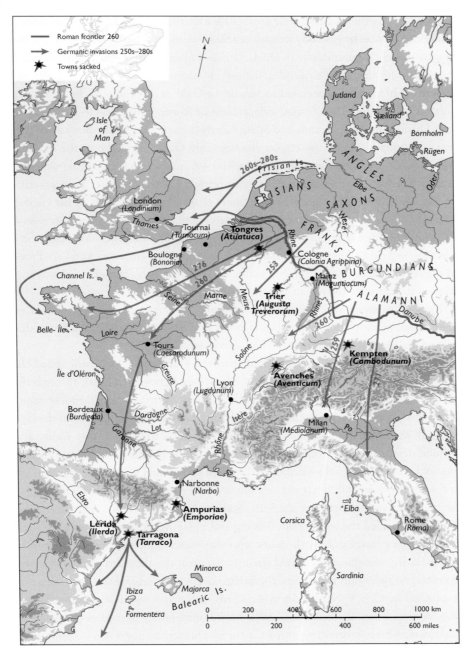

5.15 In the late third century population pressure building up beyond the Rhine frontier forced thousands of Germanic people to migrate, some breaking through the frontier to raid widely across Gaul, others taking to the sea to raid the shores of Britain and of northern Gaul.

It was among the soldiers on the upper Rhine that seething unrest with the Roman leadership eventually gave way to open rebellion when, in AD 260, the frontier troops proclaimed their commander-in-chief, M. Cassianius Latinius Postumus, emperor. Postumus' first act was to send a message to the legitimate emperor, Gallienus, informing him that he intended to remain in Gaul as its protector. By this act he created the empire of the Gauls, independent of Rome, which was to last until AD 274. During this time Britain and Spain briefly became part of the breakaway state but were soon to rejoin the empire, leaving only Gaul. Throughout, the situation was unstable. Postumus was murdered by his own troops in AD 268: other would-be leaders followed, the last being P. Esuvius Tetricus, who had earlier been governor of Aquitania. His Celtic middle name shows that he took real pride in his Gaulish ancestry. Tetricus was sufficient of a realist to see that his fractious breakaway state was undermining the empire it was designed to protect and simply could not last. So it was that, in AD 274, he surrendered power to the legitimate emperor, Aurelian. Proud to the last, Tetricus marched in full Gallic dress in Aurelian's triumph and was later allowed to return to his civilian career.

The Gallic empire was a remarkable interlude. Ill-conceived and opportunist no doubt, born of frustration and ambition, but it is difficult to resist the conclusion that behind it all lay a real resurgence of Gaulish nationalism.

Barely had the empire been reunited than the Franks and Alamanni seized the opportunity of the chaos surrounding the handover of power to break through the frontier and pillage large parts of Gaul. The raids of AD 275–6 were far more severe than those a generation before, and although the situation was contained and the land restored, the event inspired many of the towns of Gaul to face the new reality and to build defensive walls protecting the principal public buildings in their centres. In spite of this display of urban defiance, the situation in Gaul was febrile, particularly in the countryside, and in AD 282–4 a revolt of the *rusticani* (peasants) broke out in the maritime regions between the Seine and the Loire. The rebels, called Bagaudae (Fighters), roamed the countryside looting and pillaging. A panegyric written soon after the event leaves us in little doubt who they were. 'Simple farmers sought military garb, the ploughman imitated the infantryman, the shepherd the cavalryman, the rustic ravager of his own crops, the barbarian enemy' (*Panegyrici Latini* 10.4.3–5; translation by C. E. V. Nixon). In other words, this was a revolt of peasant farmers who took up arms. The 'scourge which afflicted our country' was soon put down by Maximian, who had been appointed Caesar by Diocletian, but it was a reminder of the simmering discontent in the countryside which had burst into open revolt a century before and was to become and ever-present reality during the next hundred and fifty years.

The population pressure building up on the barbarian side of the frontier was exacerbated in the Rhine mouth regions and along the German coast by a rise in sea-level, which forced people from the land. This interplay of pressures drove the maritime communities to mount ever more ambitious raids in the southern North Sea and the English Channel. In AD 285 matters had become serious enough for the Roman authorities to appoint a Menapian sailor, Carausius, to a special post with the brief of ridding the 'seas of Belgica and Armorica' of Frankish and Saxon pirates. That the brief extended to 'the seas of Armorica' suggests that the pirate threat had spread to the western Channel and was now adding to the instability of Armorica. Carausius set up his command centre at Gesoriacum but within a year had fallen foul of Rome. Sentenced to death by the emperor, 'he assumed the imperial power and seized Britain'. Britain offered a secure base for his separatist empire, but he also managed to retain an enclave in northern Gaul until it was retaken by imperial forces in 293. Not long after, Carausius was assassinated by one of his officers, Allectus, who assumed leadership of the breakaway state until 296, when the legitimate army retook Britain, reuniting it once more with the empire.

The second half of the third century had been a traumatic period for the people of Gaul and Britain, as indeed for much of the empire, but the appointment of Diocletian as emperor in 284 initiated a new period of calm. Diocletian not only instituted an entirely new system of government, dividing the empire into an eastern and a western part, each with its own emperor, but he completely overhauled the fiscal structures, bringing a degree of stability to the economy. When his co-emperor Maximian, emperor of the west, brought the breakaway island of Britain back into the fold, it seemed that the stage was set for a period of relative peace and, for some, prosperity.

Armorica during the Decades of Crisis

The broad historical narrative outlined above leaves little doubt that the last four decades of the third century were a difficult time for the inhabitants of Gaul. Political instability, raids by land and sea, economic uncertainty, and an underswell of social discontent among the rural population combined to make these dangerous times, and the archaeological record bears witness to the fact. In the period 270–80, large numbers of coin hoards were buried: sixty have been found scattered throughout the peninsula. That a high percentage were found fairly close to the coast has been suggested to be a response to raids from the sea, but many are found inland and the high numbers along the coasts are more likely to be a factor of the dense population of the maritime zone. If the hoards did relate to insecurity, then it was peninsula-wide.

There is also another factor to be considered. Devaluation was rampant and copper coins were fast losing their value. By the end of the decade it would barely have been worthwhile recovering them.

But one hoard stands out. It was buried in the centre of Condate during the reign of Aurelian (270–5) and included a gold patera (dish) weighing 1.35 kilograms, a gold cruciform brooch, several medallions minted for Postumus' *quinquennalia* in 265, and ninety-four gold coins. The value of the gold in this hoard was considerable, but its overall value was greatly increased by the brooch and medallions, likely to have been gifts from the emperor himself. The owner must have been a man of very high rank. The hiding of the treasure may well have been occasioned by the threat posed by the Franks and Alamanni in 275–6, when so many of the Gaulish towns came under attack. At this stage the towns of Armorica were undefended. It was only in the aftermath of the raids that the authorities of Condate, Condevicnum, and Darioritum

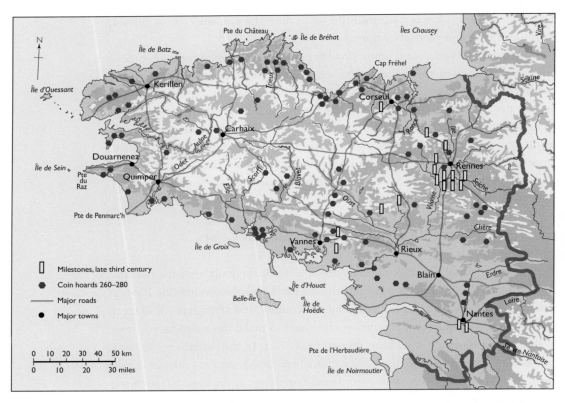

5.16 The barbarian raids caused widespread economic uncertainty and outright panic, reflected in the large number of coin hoards concealed in the ground. Among the responses to the crisis was the enclosing of towns with defensive walls and the repair of roads to allow the rapid movement of troops.

began to enclose their city centres with substantial walls with forward-projecting bastions on which defensive artillery could be mounted. At Condevicnum wall building was still under way during the reign of Constantius (305–6).

That two *civitas* capitals, Fanum Martius and Vorgium, were not defended raises interesting questions. It could be that the authorities considered them to be safe from raids by virtue of their remoteness, but both showed signs of decline in the late third century to such an extent that at Vorgium, when the aqueduct serving the town broke down, no attempt was made to repair it. The clear implication is that among the Osismii and Coriosolites the urban infrastructure was fast coming to an end. But it was in just these territories that new fortified locations defended by masonry walls were now being

0 ⊏▭▭▭▭▭⊐ 4cm

5.17 One of the most spectacular of the treasures buried for safety at the time of the late third-century barbarian raids was a hoard of gold secreted in the centre of Condate (Rennes), including this gold patera weighing 1.35 kilograms. Other items included a gold cruciform brooch and several gold medallions minted in AD 263 and 264. The brooch and medallions are typical of gifts made by emperors to high officials.

5.18 Many cities in Gaul were defended for the first time with city walls in the late third century as a response to the barbarian invasions. This very well-preserved section of Roman wall was built to protect the central buildings of the city of Darioritum (Vannes). The large stone blocks (left) had probably been robbed from a public building. The rest of the structure, of courses of small squared stones interspersed with bonding courses of tile, is typical of late Roman construction.

built. The sites chosen were coastal promontories guarding estuaries. Three have been identified with certainty: Alet on the Rance, Le Yaudet on the Léguer, and Brest on the Élorn. Others may yet be discovered at places like Morlaix and at Cesson near Saint-Brieuc, where late Roman finds have been recovered. At Alet and Le Yaudet excavations have provided details of the settlement. In both cases the new masonry fortifications were built following the lines of much earlier, pre-Roman, fortifications, and both date to the period of the Gallic empire. Alet continued to be occupied thereafter, but Le Yaudet was abandoned around 300 and not reoccupied again until the 340s or later.

The three new forts (and two possible fort sites at Morlaix and Cesson), all commanding major estuaries, were built to ensure that maritime supply lines remained open to serve the northern and western parts of the peninsula during the period of the Gallic empire. In part they augmented the urban infrastructure, but over time they may have begun to replace it. By the middle of the fourth century Alet had begun to take over the factions of Fanum Martius, while the fortification at Brest, later the base for the Maurorum Osismiacorum, had become the main centre of the Osismii, replacing Vorgium. This contrasts with the south-east of Armorica, where the urban system based on the Roman cities of Condate, Condevicnum, and Darioritum was retained and strengthened. This divide is also reflected in the upkeep of roads. Inscribed milestones set at one-mile intervals along the roads were often replaced when the roads underwent major repair. Judging by the number of late third-century milestones recovered, the roads of the south-east were undergoing extensive repair, but no comparable activity was recorded across the rest of the peninsula. For the Gallic empire and immediate successors, it was imperative to keep the communications between the cities of the south-east functioning, not only for economic reasons but to facilitate the rapid deployment of troops when necessary.

Clearly a major transformation was taking place in the late third century, with the communities of north and west replacing the once centralized urban system with something more diverse and decentralized. There are signs, too, that the economic system was in decline in the west. A number of villas were abandoned, and pollen sequences derived from peat bogs in Finistère show this to coincide with a sharp decrease in arable cultivation and a corresponding rise in the regeneration of woodland. The clear implication is that agricultural production was in recession. A further indication of economic disruption is the collapse of the garum-producing industry around the Baie de Douarnenez in the 280s. While this could have been caused by environmental factors, such as changes in the behaviour of the sardine shoals, a more likely explanation is social insecurity leading to the loss of market.

These many scraps of disparate data help build a compelling picture of rapid changes in the last four decades of the third century which created a divide between

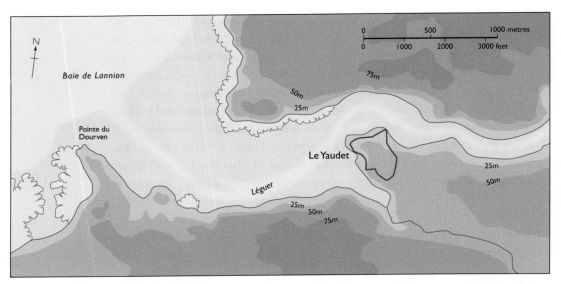

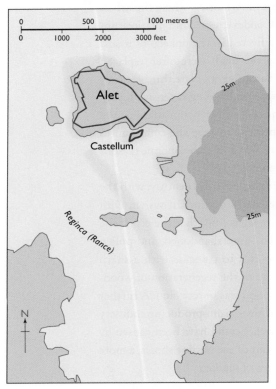

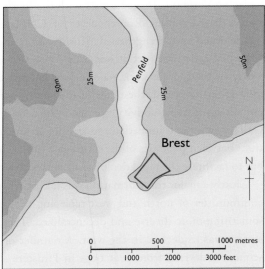

5.19 Several coastal sites commanding important estuaries were fortified with strong walls in the late third century, their purpose probably being to house marines charged with keeping the seas clear of pirates. Examples of these fortifications can be seen at Le Yaudet, Alet, and Brest.

a Romanized south-east, focused on the fortified towns of Condate, Condevicnum, and Darioritum, and the northern and western regions of the peninsula, where de-urbanization was under way accompanied by a marked change in the economy with the demise of large grain-producing estates and industrial production. To some extent it could be argued that the divide echoes tribal divisions evident in the pre-conquest period and the fact that Romanization in the remote west was at best superficial. It may well have been in these regions that the peasant uprisings had most effect in loosening the control of the urban-based administrations. Whatever the reasons, the divide between the south-east and the north and west was, by the end of the third century, becoming very apparent. It was to remain a significant cultural division for many centuries to come.

Raiders from the Sea

To what extent the Armorican coast was threatened by sea raiders in the late third century is uncertain. As we have seen, in 285 Carausius was given the task of ridding the seas of Belgica and Armorica of pirates, a brief that implies that some at least of the Frankish and Saxon sea raiders were operating beyond the eastern reaches of the Channel, but the scale of raiding is unlikely to have been significant and certainly not enough to have brought about the changes we have described. Any suggestion that military detachments were brought in from Britain to support the Armorican community is both unnecessary and without a credible factual base. At worst, any barbarian raids there may have been were but a minor irritant compared with the social convulsions that now gripped much of the peninsula.

The measures that Carausius put in hand to control the pirates included creating a string of very strong forts along the east and south coasts of Britain as far as Portchester Castle on Portsmouth Harbour and an equivalent line along the north coast of Gaul to Cherbourg on the Cotentin peninsula. Some of these forts may already have been in existence: his contribution was to fill gaps and unify the command. So it remained until 293, when the legitimate Roman army retook the Gaulish coastal region leaving the British coastal forts now to serve as a front-line defence of the breakaway British-based empire. It was a confused period but, between them, Carausius and Roman generals who took over after the failure of his rebellion were able to establish firm control over the North Sea pirates and it was not until the 340s that there are signs of further troubles.

The Last Century

The reforms introduced by Diocletian at the end of the third century brought a period of calm to the Roman world: an interlude enjoyed by the Armoricans. There is no mention of pirates in the opening decades of the fourth century, but in the 340s evidence of renewed activity in the British shore forts of Portchester, Pevensey, and Lympne can be detected. This, and the fact that the emperor Constans made a visit to Britain in the winter of 342, suggests that pirate activity was again beginning to pose a threat. Indeed, it may have been during the emperor's visit that the British fleet was placed under the command of the *comes littoris Saxonici* (count of the Saxon shore), a name used in later sources. In Armorica occupation continued at Alet, and the coin evidence from Le Yaudet suggests that the fortified settlement was brought back into use at this time after four decades of abandonment. Taken together the evidence implies that the coastal commands on both sides of the Channel were being reorganized in the early 340s in response to a heightened threat level.

By the second half of the fourth century raiding in the North Sea and English Channel had become endemic, and for Britain it reached a critical point in 367 when Franks and Saxons together with Picts and Scots from northern Britain and Ireland made a concerted attack on the province, capturing the military commander and killing the *comes maritime tractus* (count of the maritime zone). The military situation at the end of the century is recorded in the *Notitia Dignitatum*, a list of military commands throughout the empire. In Lugdunensis III (as the western part of the Gaulish province is now called) two commands are listed, the *magister militum praesentium* and the *dux tractus Armoricani et Nervicani*. The *magister* controlled the inland region with troops based on Le Mans and Condate. There was also a contingent of Frankish mercenaries (*laeti*) stationed in the territory of the Redones, possibly at Condate. The *dux* was responsible for the coastal command stretching from Rouen on the Seine to Blavia (Blaye) on the Gironde estuary not far from Bordeaux. Not all the forts listed can be identified with confidence along the north coast of Normandy but Grannona may be Cherbourg; next follow Constantia (Coutances?), Abricantis (Avranches), Aletium (Alet), Osismis (Brest), Benetis (Vannes), and Mannatias (Nantes). A small fortlet or signal station built on the Channel island of Alderney no doubt belongs to the same system. Although the *Notitia Dignitatum* entries for the western provinces were probably brought together sometime between 395 and 415, they probably reflect troop deployments from some decades earlier. But if, as seems possible, the command was established in the 340s, there may well have been many changes up to the time that the list was finally filed by the administration. What it shows, however, is that in the last decade of the fourth century

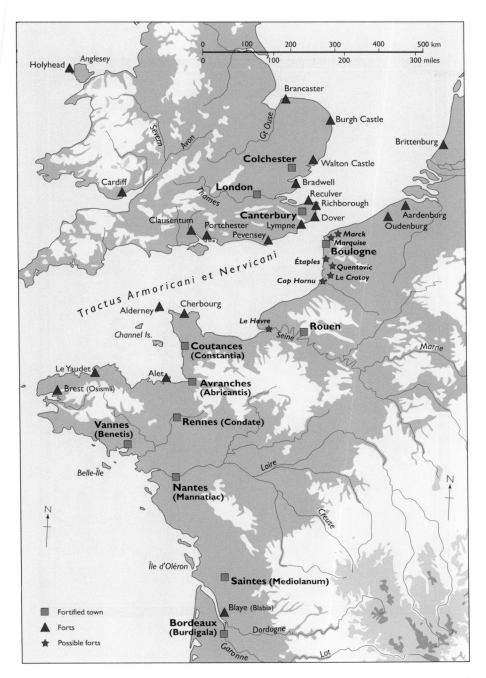

Holyhead

Anglesey

Brancaster

Burgh Castle

Brittenburg

Severn

Avon

Gt Ouse

Colchester

Walton Castle

Cardiff

Thames

London

Bradwell

Reculver

Richborough

Aardenburg

Clausentum

Canterbury

Portchester

Lympne

Dover

Oudenburg

Pevensey

Marck

Marquise

Boulogne

Étaples

Quentovic

Cap Hornu

Le Crotoy

Tractus Armoricani et Nervicani

Alderney

Cherbourg

Le Havre

Rouen

Channel Is.

Seine

Marne

**Coutances
(Constantia)**

Le Yaudet

Alet

**Avranches
(Abricantis)**

Brest (Osismii)

Rennes (Condate)

**Vannes
(Benetis)**

Loire

Belle-Île

**Nantes
(Mannatiac)**

Creuse

N

Île d'Oléron

Saintes (Mediolanum)

Blaye (Blabia)

■ Fortified town

▲ Forts

★ Possible forts

**Bordeaux
(Burdigala)**

Dordogne

Garonne

Lot

0   100   200   300   400   500 km

0   100   200   300 miles

5.20 By the fourth century the coastal defences of north-western Gaul and south-eastern Britain had grown in number and extent and were organized into separate military commands.

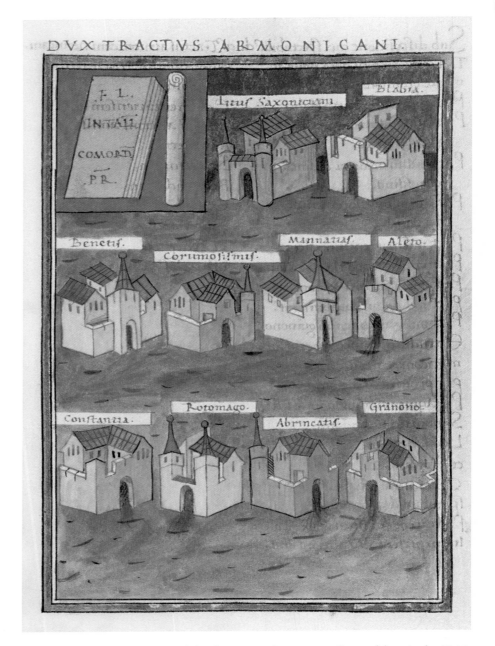

5.21 One of the commands, that of the *dux Tractus Armoricani*, is illustrated here in the *Notitia Dignitatum*, which listed military dispositions at the end of the fourth century. The jurisdiction of the dux stretched from Rouen on the Seine to Blaye on the Gironde estuary. The forts are each named and can be identified.

a systematic attempt was being made to provide some coherent protection for the coastal communities. How effective it proved to be is unrecorded.

By then factors other than sea raiders were beginning to impact on Armorica. In 383 a British commander, Magnus Maximus, set out from Britain for Gaul with a large field army in a bid for imperial power. He was defeated and killed five years later and his army was dispersed, adding to the confusion that now gripped much of northern Gaul. According to several Welsh traditions, composed centuries later, some of his troops settled in Armorica and their leader, Conan Meriadoc, founded a dynasty of Breton kings. There is no confirmation of the legend, archaeological or historical, and indeed it may have been a construct to serve Welsh claims to legitimate links with Brittany, but the possibility remains that some defeated British troops may have made their homes in Armorica and others may have joined them from Britain.

That maritime contacts between Armorica and Britain continued into the fourth century is evident from the general distribution of British-made pottery and from British lead found in the Sept-Îles shipwreck (above, pp. 177–8), but what happened in the second half of the fourth century is far from clear.

So what of the Armorican population in the late fourth century? The ring of coastal fortifications and the garrisons at Condate, supported by the detachment of Frankish *laeti*, afforded some protection from raids from the sea and attacks by land, but within this fragile outer ring there was seething unrest born of economic decline and social inequality. Matters finally came to a head in the winter of 406–7 when a massive force of Alans, Suebi, and Vandals crossed the frozen Rhine and created chaos throughout Gaul. In the wake of the disaster, rival Roman generals competed for power and peasants rebelled. In Britain the historian Zosimus records that the remaining urban administrations were finally overthrown. Then 'all Armorica and other provinces of Gaul copied the British example and freed themselves in the same way, expelling their Roman governors and establishing their own administration as best they could' (Zosimus 6.5). The simmering discontent of the Armorican peasants had erupted once more into outright revolt. This time there was no authority strong enough to restrain them.

6

FROM ARMORICA
TO BRITTANY

400–751

THE two hundred years between AD 400 and 600 saw Europe transformed: the Roman empire had fragmented and people whose ancestors had lived beyond the frontier were now settled in the patchwork of communities making up the new Europe. The causes for such a dramatic change were many, their interaction building to a peak of migration in the first half of the fifth century, their longer-term effects working out over the next hundred and fifty years as new states began to emerge. The unsustainability of the Roman economic model was a significant factor in the revolution. Since the core of the empire was parasitic on the periphery, the boundary had constantly to be pushed outwards, embracing new resources of raw materials and manpower. That could work only until the limiting ecological boundaries had been reached, as they were by the early decades of the second century. Now, bounded by deserts in the east and south, the ocean in the west, and the forest zone to the north, there was no further room for expansion and the demands of the underproductive core of the empire began to sap the energies of the provinces. So the disintegration began.

One result of the growing social and economic stress was a decline in population within the empire. By the end of the third century this had become serious, forcing Diocletian to introduce measures to reduce population mobility and to keep productive people in their traditional jobs. Yet still the decline continued. But beyond the Rhine–Danube frontier quite the opposite was happening. A natural increase in population, together with climate change, reducing habitable coastland, and the arrival of new peoples from the steppe, all created massive pressure against the frontier. The Roman response was to recruit increasing numbers of Germanic people into the army in Gaul, and to bring whole communities into the empire to settle abandoned land to make it productive, and to provide a source of manpower to repel further raids: these communities were known as *laeti*. A panegyric written to Constantius Chlorus at the beginning of the fourth century sums up the situation from a Roman point of view. It talks of *laeti* brought to the towns to be assigned to working the land:

> All of them, shared out among the inhabitants of your provinces in order to serve them, wait to be led to the deserted lands which they must restore to growth . . . This vagabond and this pillager work ceaselessly to bring my land under cultivation . . . What is more, if they are called up into the army, they hurry to join, they are brought to heel by army discipline . . . and they congratulate themselves for having served us as a Roman soldier.
>
> (*Panegyric on Constantius Caesar* 9.3)

Thus the Roman propaganda view: for a dispossessed Germanic community, to be given fertile land to work and the opportunity to serve in the Roman army, the situation might have been seen in a more encouraging light.

The population decline seems to have been empire-wide and there is no reason to suppose that it did not affect Armorica. Indeed, we know that *laeti* were settled in the territory of the Redones. In the western parts of the peninsula the abandonment of Roman villas and arable land, the urban decline, and a general unrest may well have been, in part, driven by the decline in population and the malaise engendered by it. A paucity of skilled people would quickly lead to the breakdown of the infrastructure that sustained ordered life. This in turn provided fertile ground for the peasant revolt that gripped the area in the early years of the fifth century and was to remain endemic for decades to come.

The possibility that military detachments were drafted into Armorica from Britain in an attempt to stabilize the disintegrating situation in the late third and fourth centuries is a theory that has been much discussed but for which there is little supporting evidence. The defeat, in central Gaul in 388, of the army of the British contender for leadership in the west, Magnus Maximus, left a large number of leaderless soldiers roaming the countryside, and it is conceivable that some of them may have decided to settle in Armorica (above, p. 199). Similarly, another British force, brought to fight in Gaul in 407 by the usurper Constantine III, was disbanded on its defeat, adding to the many thousands of disgruntled British troops roaming the Gaulish countryside

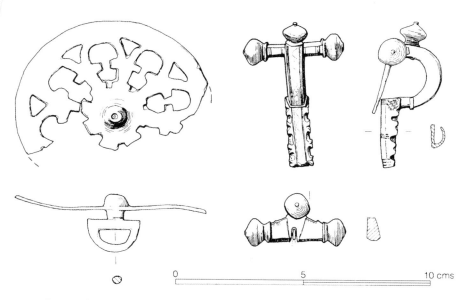

6.1 A selection of late Roman metalwork from Le Yaudet. The disc is a phalera from military horse-gear. The crossbow brooch is a symbol of high status.

looking for gainful employment. There is no particular reason, however, for them to have chosen to make Armorica their home. Scholars who favour the idea of confederate British troops being active in Armorica in the fourth century point to a scatter of artefacts, mainly belt buckles, crossbow brooches, and penannular brooches which were thought to reflect a military presence. In Armorica most have been found in villas, temples, or isolated graves rather than forts, except at Le Yaudet, where a crossbow brooch and a phalera from a horse harness were recovered from a late fourth- or early fifth-century context. It is difficult to know how to interpret these scattered items. While they may have been the equipment of militias employed by the local communities for their protection, there is nothing to imply that troops were supplied from Britain. More likely the local militias, if that is what they are, were recruited from the ranks of the dispossessed and unemployed now wandering the country. At the beginning of the fifth century, then, Armorica consisted of a rebellious west and north bordered on the south-east by the remnants of the Roman *civitates* based at Vannes, Rennes, and Nantes, where some semblance of the old urban administrative order was still in place. While these towns were to hold on as centres of power and *romanitas*, the rest of the peninsula was fast reverting to a far more decentralized way of life.

Armorica in the Early Fifth Century

The rebellion of 407, when 'all Armorica and other provinces of Gaul' ousted Roman officials and took over the running of their own state, was the culmination of the peasant unrest that had been simmering for a least a century and a half in Armorica. There is no positive evidence of how extensive the uprising was. It may well be that the three main cities, Rennes, Nantes, and Vannes, managed to hold out behind their fortifications, but over the rest of the peninsula the last semblance of Roman order had disintegrated. The freedom lasted for a decade, but in 417 we learn that the Roman military leader Exuperantius put an end to the rebellion, re-establishing a degree of order 'to the coasts of Armorica . . . no longer allowing servants to make their masters slaves' (Rutilius Namatianus 1.213–16). That the centre of the Bagaudic resistance was said to have been on the Loire at this time hints that the main concern of the authorities was to make secure the territory of the cities like Nantes and the essential communication routes, leaving the remoter parts of the peninsula to its own devices.

Rebellion broke out again in 435, led by one Tibatto. Two years later his force of Bagaudae was defeated by Litorius, the military commander in Gaul, and Tibatto was taken prisoner. An interesting detail is that Litorius was aided by a detachment of Huns newly arrived on the Gaulish scene. What followed is a little unclear, but the Armorican Bagaudae were active again in 442. This time an army of Alans was sent against them, who were acting as Roman *foederati*, led by Gohar, *rex ferocissimus*. Tibatto seems to have re-emerged as the rebel leader, but in the end the Bagaudae were defeated and he was killed. By now peasant uprisings were spreading to Aquitaine and to Spain, and in 445 the Romans had to use Visigoths to contain them.

The events of the first half of the fifth century are confusing in their detail, not least because the historical sources are few and at best anecdotal, but the broad picture is clear enough. Peasant revolts were now endemic and spreading throughout western Gaul at just the time when bands of barbarians from across the Rhine and from the steppe were moving into Gaul in search of land. The Roman state tried to maintain some control of the situation, though with diminishing resources, but they were forced to employ Huns, Alans, and Visigoths to help them to stamp out the rebellions that kept erupting: Roman generals like Aëtius were nothing if not opportunists. The story that he employed Armoricans in his campaigns against Attila's army of Huns is entirely believable. In the fast-moving situation old enemies could become new allies.

The Arrival of the Britons

By the middle of the fifth century the growing divide in Armorica between the decentralized west and north and the urbanized south-east was growing sharper as the cities became centres for Christianity, each with a bishop presiding over a diocese and administering parishes in the countryside around. Away from the influence of the cities, in the north and west of the peninsula were the *pagani*, the inhabitants of the *pagi* (small rural settlements), a name taking with it the connotation of those without the benefits of organized Christianity.

In the province of Lugdunensis III, of which Armorica formed a part, the principal Christian centre, the seat of the archbishop, was Tours (Caesarodunum), made famous by St Martin in the late fourth century. The first attested bishop was in residence as early as 337–8. Thereafter the south-eastern cities of Armorica all became the centres of diocesan circumscriptions. Nantes had a bishop before 453, Rennes by 461, and Vannes after 463. In November 461 a council was held at Tours attended by bishops from all the towns of the province, except for Angers (whose bishop was recorded as absent) as well as several bishops from outside the region. The bishops from Rennes and Nantes were present, together with Mansuetus, *episcopus Britannorum*. While it is possible that he was a visitor from the island of Britain, a more likely explanation is that he was the bishop responsible for the communities of peninsular Armorica, beyond the jurisdiction of Rennes and Nantes, who, having received an influx of people from Britain, were now known as Bretons.

There were significant differences between this westerly group of Christians and the Gallo-Roman Christians of the urban centres. Sometime between 510 and 520, a letter was sent by the bishops of Rennes, Tours, and Angers to the two Breton priests Lovocat and Catihern complaining of their irregular practices. Not only did they move among their flock from 'hut to hut' celebrating mass on portable altars, but they also used *cohospitae* (deaconesses) to administer the chalice during communion. The letter is fascinating on several counts. It contrasts a simple form of Christian practice, suitable for missionary work and for ministering to dispersed populations before parishes had been organized, with the more organized Gallo-Roman Church. It also displays the superior attitude of the bishops to priests working in the remote west among newly arrived Britons and the indigenous rural population. This divide between the western regions of Armorica and the urban south-east was still evident at the time of the Second Council of Tours, held in 567, when the distinction was made between 'Britannia and Romania in Armorica'.

The arrival in Armorica of immigrants from the British Isles probably began in the early decades of the fifth century and continued over the next two centuries, but of the history and process of the migration we know very little. The romantic view is given by the British monk Gildas. Writing of the chaos and horror experienced by the southern British as the Saxons advanced, he described the distraught survivors fleeing from death and slavery. Some sought safety in the mountain regions of Wales, 'others made for land beyond the sea; beneath the swelling sails they loudly wailed singing a psalm instead of a shanty: "You have given us like sheep for the eating and scattered us among the heathen"' (*De Excidio et Conquestu Britanniae*, 25.1).

It is a vivid image that may even, in part, be true. The Saxon settlement of the southeast of Britain and the migrations of the Irish to Wales and Cornwall created social pressures throughout the fifth and early sixth centuries sufficient to drive communities to flee Britain for the continent. Armorica, because of its familiarity born of centuries of contact and its remoteness from the barbarian inroads affecting the rest of Gaul, would have been a desirable place to make for. How the Armoricans responded to the arrival of the psalm-singing migrants is unrecorded. Those who came in peace with their families may well have been welcomed, especially if the population decline had left large tracts of land unoccupied. But aggressive settlers may well have been opposed. There are hints of this in a ninth-century poem by Ermoldus Nigellus, who writes of the incoming Britons stirring up fierce warfare: 'They returned spears to their hosts instead of rent, a gift of warfare in return for land, for kindness, arrogance.' This could, of course, be little more than Frankish anti-Breton propaganda, but it may reflect some half-remembered troubles. Large-scale immigration is seldom without incident.

Another text throws a rather different light on the migration. In a letter written about 468, the churchman Sidonius Apollinaris refers to a troop of Britanni who, under their chief, Riothamus, were established on the Loire. They were, he said, the most effective troops the empire could call upon. The context of the letter was the trial of the praetorian prefect of Gaul, Arvandus, who stood accused of trying to persuade the Visigoths to attack the Britanni. The same story is referred to some sixty years later by the historian Jordanes, who says that twelve thousand Britons stationed on the Loire under their leader, Riothamus, responded to an appeal from the emperor to move against the Visigoths, who had just invaded Gaul. Taken at their face value the accounts imply that among those who had migrated from Britain in the fifth century were war leaders with bands of followers who were prepared to offer their services to the highest bidder. A few years before, in 451, Aëtius had employed Armoricans in his battle against the Huns. None of this is at all surprising. Large-scale migrations are untidy affairs. Most incomers will have travelled as community groups simply looking for land to settle, peacefully if the conditions allowed, while some, with aspirations to power, would have seized the chance to lead bands of mercenaries in profitable skirmishes, seeing service to the emperor as an opportunity for enrichment. Wherever

FROM ARMORICA TO BRITTANY, 400–751

Riothamus and his followers originated, we meet them not in peninsular Armorica but on the Loire, a convenient place, for mercenaries looking for employment, to assemble to engage with the empire's enemies.

The migration from southern Britain was spread over many generations spanning the fifth and sixth centuries. How it was organized, if at all, is unknown, but we can imagine pioneer groups setting themselves up wherever land was available, establishing workable relations with their Armorican neighbours and creating lasting bonds through intermarriage. Later, more people would arrive seeking out kin to help them find a home, and so the British networks grew. Nothing is known of the total numbers of immigrants involved, nor of the size of the resident Armorican population, but the fact that the Brittonic language became firmly established in much of Armorica suggests that the newcomers soon became the dominant force. It also implies that the migrants came from parts of Britain where Brittonic Celtic was still spoken, places like Devon, Cornwall, and south-west Wales which maintained their own distinctive culture in spite of the four centuries of Roman domination which affected much of the rest of Britain. The similarity between the Breton, Cornish, and Welsh languages is sufficient to show a close cultural link between these three peninsulas born of the migration. This point was carefully considered by Giraldus Cambrensis in the twelfth century. He concludes:

> In both Cornwall and Brittany they speak almost the same language as in Wales. It comes from the same root and is intelligible to the Welsh in many instances and almost in all. It is rougher and less clearly pronounced but probably closer to the original British speech, or so I think myself.
>
> (*Description of Wales*, I. 7)

Naming Places

Place names provide a powerful source of information about the history of settlement, but it is not always easy to tease out the subtleties, and conflicting interpretations can arise. This is true of Breton place names, but fortunately there is a broad consensus on a number of issues. A cursory glance at a map of Brittany is enough to see that a limited number of place name elements predominate: Plou, Lan, Loc, Tre, Ker. All have an insular Brittonic origin and their distribution provides an indication of the areas settled by the British migrants. The names concentrate along the entire northern coastal region and in the south-west of the peninsula, becoming much sparser in the east. The northern zone later became known as Domnonée, while the south-west is

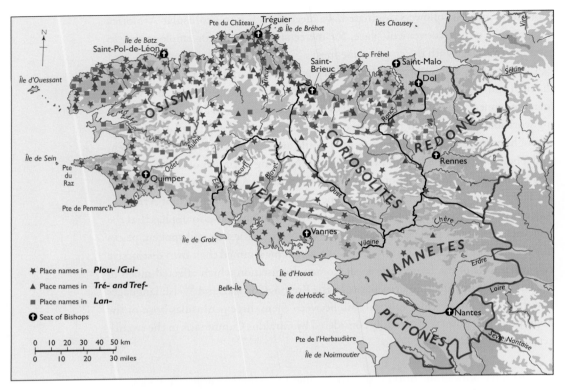

6.2 Two sets of place names reflecting different cultural traditions. The map above shows names introduced by immigrants from Britain in the fifth century; the map opposite shows names derived from Gallo-Roman words..

called Cornouaille, names echoing Dumnonia (Devon) and Cornovia (Cornwall), signposting the homelands from which the migrants may have set out.

The most frequently occurring place name element is Plou, which is derived, via Late Brittonic, from the Latin *plebs* ('the people') and is found in Cornish (*plui*) and Middle Welsh (*plwyf*). About three-quarters of the Plou names in Brittany are compounded with the names of people, invariably men, and of these the majority are religious figures. Wherever these names can be traced they derive from Britain. Although the predominance of religious eponyms might suggest that the *ploue* are religious foundations, it is best to regard them as rural districts in which resided a community and where both civil and religious functions were enacted. Later the *ploue* became parishes, and since the French Revolution, communes. Of the other common names, Lan (Welsh *llan*) and Loc (Latin *locus*, 'place') are often places of religious significance referring to settlements which had grown up around churches and places

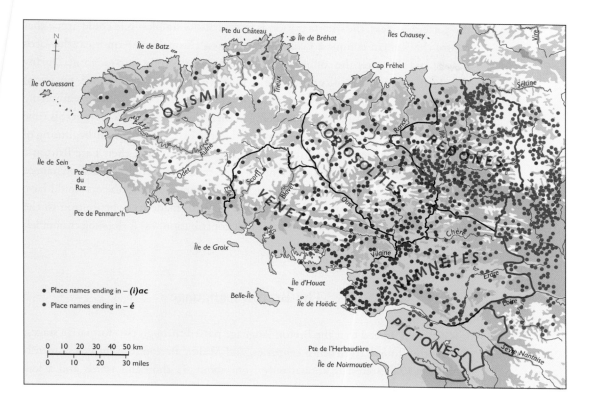

attributed to saints. Tré (Welsh *tref*) is a division of a parish, while Ker (Welsh *caer*) refers to a hamlet. The house of more significant people is called a Lis or Lez (Welsh *llys*). Not all of these words were in common use at the time of the migrations. Loc and Ker become more common from the tenth century, replacing Lan and Tré. Taken together the Late Brittonic place names give a clear idea of the regions in which the impact of the British immigrants was at its strongest.

Another set of place names of Gallic Roman derivation allows us to plot the areas unaffected or less affected by the migration. Names ending in -(i)ac, -é, and -y are ultimately derived from the Gaulish suffix -acos (Latin *acum*), which, as Vulgar Latin evolved, changed first to -ac and later to -é and -y. If these are plotted on a map, the -é and -y names are seen to concentrate in the east, particularly in the *civitates* of Rennes and Nantes. To the west of this zone the -ac names are found but become increasingly rare the further west one travels.

Thus, the place name evidence divides Armorica into two zones: a Late Brittonic zone in the west and a Gallo-Roman zone in the east. The Gallo-Roman zone is itself divided into two subzones reflecting different intensities of Romanization. But while the pattern is clear, the interpretation is less so. At its simplest one could argue that before the Roman conquest Gaulish was spoken throughout Armorica (the -acos names) and that after the conquest the names began to evolve into -ac form. During the third century the cultural divide (which we have discussed above, pp. 151–3) began to appear, with the eastern *civitates* based on Rennes and Nantes embracing *romanitas* while the western regions clung to their Gaulish past. It was from this time onwards that the -é and -y suffixes developed in the east. Finally, at the beginning of the fifth century, immigrants from Britain began to introduce their Late Brittonic dialect of Celtic and with it a different set of place names including the Plou names. Although Brittonic differed from Gaulish, the Britons and Armoricans would have been able to communicate, and in this way Gaulish made its contribution to the development of Breton. How significant that contribution was is the subject of much scholarly debate.

The Breton Language

It is generally agreed that the Breton language passed through two formative stages: Old Breton (fourth to eleventh centuries) and Middle Breton (eleventh to sixteenth centuries). Old Breton is known only from about six thousand words and a few phrases written as glosses on Latin manuscripts, together with place names and proper names. As a living language it was transmitted orally by bards and storytellers and by daily communication until the fifteenth century, when it began to be used in written form. From the eleventh century Breton came to be increasingly influenced by French. Given the paucity of evidence before the fifteenth century, it is difficult to untangle the early history of the language. Today linguists recognize four distinct dialects. Three are closely similar and are known as KLT(G): the dialect of Cornouaille (Kerneu), Léon, and the Trégor (with Goëlo). The fourth, Vannetais, is different in a number of ways. Some scholars believe that the dialects did not begin to appear until after the eleventh century, but others consider them to be much earlier, perhaps even reflecting the pre-Roman situation. They would argue that the migrants from Britain had a significant impact on KLT but would regard Vannetais as being largely untouched and therefore a survival of the Gaulish spoken before the Roman invasion. While it is likely that Gaulish survived in the less urbanized parts of Armorica during the Roman period and contributed to the development of Breton, it is difficult to see why the dialect of the Vannes region should have remained so distinct. However, it was in this zone that the -ac names survived the Romanization experienced by the Nantes–Rennes *civitates*, and it was outside the main concentrations of Late Brittonic place names. Perhaps its position marginal to these two external influences allowed the native Gaulish language to survive. Given the complexity of the subject and the paucity of data, these matters are likely to remain largely speculative.

Neighbours

While Armorica was being transformed by the collapse of centralized Roman authority and the influx of Britons, the rest of northern Gaul was gradually coming under the control of the Franks. The Franks were a confederacy of German tribes who occupied a large territory to the north-east of the lower Rhine in what is now the Netherlands and north-western Germany. Their Latin name, Franci, means 'bold forces'. Their neighbours to the north, along the North Sea coasts, were the Frisians

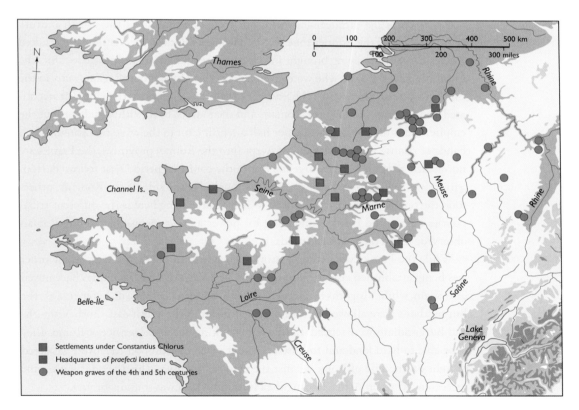

6.3 In the fourth and fifth centuries Franks from beyond the Rhine frontier began to penetrate north-western Gaul. Many will have been incorporated into the Roman empire as mercenaries and settlers by the late Roman authorities to help maintain the stability of northern Gaul.

and Saxons, while to the south, occupying the narrow territory between the upper Rhine and lower Danube, were the Alamanni, another Germanic confederacy made up of many tribes. These were the people who were to put pressure on the Rhine frontier in the early 260s, the Alamanni and Franks breaking through to terrorize Gaul while, over a longer period, the Saxons took to the sea to raid the coasts of southern Britain and northern Gaul.

In the fourth century, as we have seen (p. 196), Franks and Alamanni served in the Roman army as *foederati*, while Frankish *laeti* were settled in family groups throughout northern Gaul to work abandoned land and to serve in militias when called upon. These people, captives and willing migrants alike, were placed under the control of *praefecti laetorum*, whose headquarters were spread throughout northern Gaul, the westernmost being in the *civitas* of the Redones. Something of the extent of these rural militias can be gauged from the distribution of fourth- and early fifth-century graves with weapons, a type found across the whole of northern Gaul.

For a while the arrangement held, but from the middle of the fourth century renewed raids on the frontier zone required Roman military intervention and resulted in Germanic tribes being brought into the empire and given land to settle. One, the Frankish tribe the Salii, who were given land in the Rhine mouth region, were, in the mid-fifth century, to become the leaders of the Franks in northern Gaul. The negotiated arrangement between the Romans and the Franks, both within and without the empire, seems to have held strong for half a century, for in the winter of 406–7, when bands of Alans, Suebi, and Vandals swept into the Roman provinces, the Franks are not mentioned along the insurgents. But in the confused period that followed, from 410 to 430, while some groups of Franks fought on the side of the Romans, others took the opportunity to attack them. What we are seeing here is the different tribal polities among the Franks competing for power among themselves, as one Roman observed, 'urged on by tribal hatreds'.

While the Franks were consolidating their power in northern Gaul, a new order was being established elsewhere in the west. The Vandals and their allies had moved into Spain, while Visigoths had settled in south-western Gaul in 418. Later, in 443, the Burgundians were allowed to take over territories in the south-east. Both Visigoths and Burgundians were settled under their own king but in the service of Rome. They were able to hold land and to raise taxes, but when called upon they were expected to fight on the side of Rome against the empire's enemies. This they did with some success in 451 when Attila, leading the Huns into Gaul, was soundly beaten.

Throughout this time the Franks were extending and consolidating their power in northern Gaul. Sometime about 440 a band of Rhineland Franks sacked the Roman

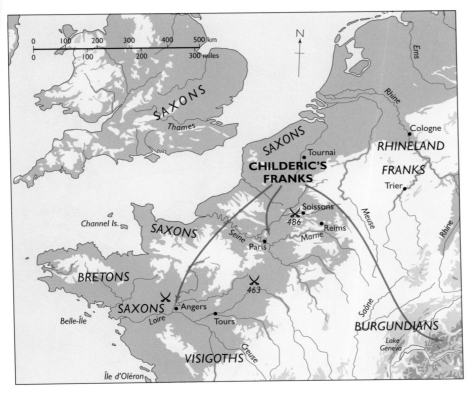

6.4 About 480, Franks who had settled in northern Gaul and had formed a state of their own began a military expansion to the south and west.

city of Trier, causing widespread death and destruction, and ten years later Salian Franks attacked Arras and went on, according to Gregory of Tours, to occupy all the country down to the Somme. The assassination of Valentinian III, emperor of the west, in 455 brought to an end the half-century of unstable equilibrium during which Roman emperors and generals had managed to maintain a semblance of control over Gaul. The way was now open for the Franks to take over virtually the whole of the country.

From about 465 until 481 the Salian Franks led by Childeric were the most power-ful force in northern Gaul, controlling some of the Roman towns and much of the countryside. Other towns seem to have held onto vestiges of their power and remained centres of bishoprics but had no significant military resource. Campaigns were fought in various parts of Gaul. Orléans was attacked in 473. There was an engagement in Angers on the Loire on the border of Visigoth territory, and the Frankish army was also active in the land held by the Burgundians. But it was Childeric's son and successor,

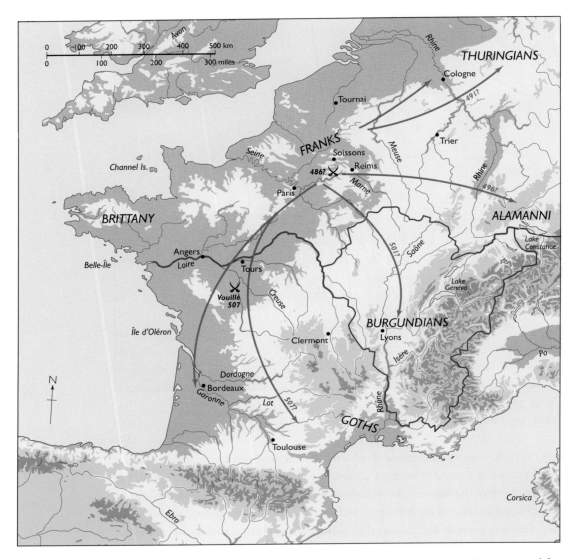

6.5 At the end of the fifth and beginning of the sixth century the Frankish king Clovis instigated far-reaching military campaigns against his neighbours.

Clovis (reigned 481–511), who was to consolidate Frankish control of northern Gaul, campaigning deep into the territory of the Visigoths and Burgundians as well as crossing the Rhine to engage with the Alamanni and Thuringians. Towards the end of his reign Paris had become the residence of the king and the Seine basin developed as the centre of Frankish power under the Merovingian dynasty. After Clovis's death the kingdom was divided among his four sons, who continued to expand the Frankish dominance until, by 563, virtually the whole of Gaul had fallen to the Franks. The only lands to retain their independence were Septimania, a Visigothic enclave in the extreme south, and Brittany.

The Fight for Breton Independence

By the 480s the Bretons living on the Armorican peninsula were confronted on their entire eastern border by settlers of Germanic origin, Saxons occupying the Bayeux region and the lower Loire valley and the Franks in between. The two Saxon enclaves were not large and presented no serious threat, but the Franks, particularly under Childeric and Clovis, were bent on territorial expansion and state formation. For them, the Bretons were a people eventually to be absorbed into the growing empire, but they were of little immediate significance, hardly worthy of the investment of much military resource: first there were more profitable conquests to be made in the south.

The capture of Soissons by Clovis in 486 opened up the west to the Franks, and four years or so later he was on the Loire fighting and defeating a Breton force. How significant was the engagement it is difficult to say, but there was no follow-up, the Franks deciding to push on into Aquitaine, a campaign that culminated in victory at Vouillé in 507 and brought the whole of the middle Loire under Frankish control, further isolating Armorica. It seems that a treaty may have been negotiated with the Bretons at this time by which they agreed to recognize the Merovingian king. A hint of this is given later by Gregory of Tours, who writes that after the death of Clovis, 'the Bretons remained under the domination of the Franks and their rulers were called counts not kings' (*Historia Francorum*, IV. 4). This sounds rather like a non-aggression pact with some token subservience on the part of the Bretons rather than submission. At any event Gregory still refers to the Breton 'kingdom', and from what he says later it is clear that the Bretons remained largely free. For fifty years Franks and Bretons lived in reasonable harmony, the Franks respecting the autonomy of the old Gallo-Roman *civitates* of Rennes, Nantes, and Vannes, and of the Bretons beyond.

In Brittany political power was in the hands of chieftains, among whom there were constant rivalries exacerbated by struggles for power within the ruling families. In the 560s one contender for power, Chanao, slaughtered his three brothers and outlawed the fourth, Macliaw. Macliaw went on to seize the bishopric of Vannes and ally himself to another chieftain, Bodic, but the agreement soured, leading to the murder of Macliaw and one of his sons. His second son, Waroc, taking up his father's quest, advanced with his Breton followers into the country of the Vannetais, assuming command of the territory. It was thereafter known as Broërec (from Bro Waroc) after its conqueror, becoming one of the three major regions of Brittany along with Domnonée and Cornouaille.

Waroc's attitude to the Franks was ambivalent, at one time agreeing to terms, at another reneging on all treaties. His control of the Vannetais put him in a very strong position. From here he could raid the old Gallo-Roman *civitates* of Nantes and Rennes, which offered rich pickings. Gregory of Tours gives the details. In 579 the Bretons attacked the region around Rennes, pillaging as they went, and in 587 they raided the *civitas* of Nantes, acquiring a great deal of plunder from the surrounding country estates. In the wake of these attacks the Frankish king Guntram sent envoys to the Bretons, in doing so recognizing them as equals. At the meeting the Bretons conceded that Nantes and Rennes were part of the Merovingian sphere and said that they would cease their attacks. The agreement also took with it the unspoken acceptance that the rest of Armorica was a Breton preserve. The event was an exercise in diplomacy designed to draw fixed boundaries, but Waroc had little regard for such niceties and in 588–90 he 'widely ravaged the territory of Nantes and Rennes, taking the vintage, devastating cultivated land and carrying off captive the workers on the country estates' (*Historia Francorum*, II. 24). Guntram responded by sending an army against Waroc, but after a disastrous campaign, accepting some worthless undertakings, the Frankish army prepared to depart. As they attempted to cross the Vilaine, many of the retreating troops were massacred or taken prisoner. The bishop of Vannes, on hearing the news, said that once more his flock was forced to accept the 'Breton yoke'.

Thus it was that the frontier between the Bretons and the Franks was staked out, the old *civitates* of Rennes and Nantes acting as a buffer zone between the two powers. But there was a degree of flexibility, with enclaves of Bretons settling in the Guérande peninsula and in the marshland of the Brière north of the Loire estuary, while in the north, in Domnonée, there is some evidence of Frankish penetration, reflected in Germanic place names around Saint-Brieuc. That the Franks claimed some authority over this region is further implied by an incident recorded in 635 in a Frankish chronicle. It tells how the Frankish king, Dagobert, sent a mission to the Bretons requiring them to make amends for a misdeed, threatening that otherwise he would send in a Burgundian army. In response the Breton king, Judicael, travelled to the court of Dagobert, taking gifts and promising that his kingdom would always be under the lordship of the Franks. The submission was accepted and he was given gifts in return, but he refused to dine with the Frankish king, whom he regarded to be too ungodly. In another version of the same event, recorded in the Life of St Eloi, there is no mention of submission: it is simply a negotiation leading to a peace treaty. Two accounts but with different slants on the niceties of protocol: which to believe? Clearly it was a meeting of two men of near-comparable status agreeing on a face-saving formula in the interests of maintaining peace, parading their social differences but not letting them get in the way of a diplomatic solution. The balance between the Bretons and the Merovingian state was, clearly, delicate and when, in 691, there was dissent in the ranks of the Frankish elite, the Bretons took advantage of their enemy's weakness by proclaiming their freedom.

Stories like the Dagobert–Judicael confrontation are few, and the long period from 600 to 750 was largely without recorded incident. An uneasy truce was being maintained, leaving the Bretons to develop their distinctive culture safe in their remote peninsula.

A Land of Saints

It is impossible to travel through the Breton countryside without becoming aware of the saints whose presence is declaimed in place names everywhere to be seen. Some names state the sacred nature of the place like Lan ('church enclave') or Loc ('saint's place'); others embody the names of eponymous saints as in Plougoulm (St Columba), Pleucadeuc (St Cadoc), and Ploerdut (St Illtud). Of the Plou places that embody personal names, two-thirds are of sanctified personalities. Many are known through their Lives, but about half are otherwise unrecorded except perhaps as patrons of a feast day. Who these people were, whose ubiquitous presence is evident throughout Brittany, has given rise to much debate.

The title *sancti* ('saints') in the early Christian Church was used loosely to embrace pious educated people, whether scholars, pilgrims, or rank-and-file clergy. They were the clerics who helped to provide a focus for the community and to whose spiritual needs they ministered. Some set up monasteries, while others became powerful church leaders and travelled widely to spread the ministry. Of the eponymous saints whose names are preserved in the Plou place names, many have an insular British connection. These men travelled to Brittany over several centuries, first from many regions of post-Roman Britain and later from the more restricted western fringes. Of the many hundreds of saints' names known, little more than fifty are commemorated in Lives, texts mostly compiled in the ninth century or later, following the form and conventions of the earliest examples. While the Lives provide a wealth of information about the standards and values of the times in which they are written, they cannot be taken as an accurate reflection of the activity of their subjects or the world in which

6.6 The saints played a significant role in the cultural beliefs of the Bretons and were everywhere to be seen in religious iconography. This retable from the church at Lampaul-Guimiliau, dating to the seventeenth century, shows the death of the Breton prince Miliau, whose head has been severed by his brother Rivas. Miliau, his neck spurting blood, has picked up his head and is carrying it. He became the patron saint of Guimiliau and of Lampaul-Guimiliau. Legends such as this give a vivid picture of the vicissitudes of the life of the elite in the sixth century.

they worked. As history most of them are largely without value other than providing colourful copy for tourist brochures.

The earliest of the Lives is that of St Samson. In its present form it cannot be earlier than the mid-eighth century, but it seems likely that the surviving text is a rewritten version of a seventh-century original which was based on testimony provided by two of the saint's relatives. Given the early date of composition and the near-contemporary sources used, the narrative it provides may well reflect real events in the saint's life. Samson was a member of an aristocratic family based in south-western Wales, where he grew up. In his early years he studied in a monastery, probably at Llanilltud Fawr in Glamorganshire under the tutelage of Illtud. Here he was ordained and went on to become abbot of a small monastery on Caldey Island off the coast of Pembrokeshire. He visited Ireland for a brief period, and after living for a while as a hermit some-where in the Severn estuary he returned to the monastery of Llanilltud Fawr, where he became a bishop. Sometime later, in a revelation, he learned that God wanted him to become a *peregrinus* (travelling monk), so he loaded his books and a cart, which he had acquired in Ireland, onto a boat and sailed across the Severn estuary to Padstow on the north coast of Cornwall with the intention of taking the transpeninsular route to the south coast. On his journey across Cornwall he came upon a pagan gathering worshipping a standing stone, presumably a prehistoric menhir. Having dispersed the group, he carved a Christian cross on the stone, thereby claiming it for God. When he reached the south coast at Fowey, he found a ship to take him, still accompanied by his books and cart, across the Channel to Brittany. A dedication to St Sampson on Guernsey, where a parish is named after him, suggests that he may have stopped at the island on the way.

Once in Brittany he set about founding churches and monasteries, choosing Dol as his episcopal base. It was a wise choice, showing his astute awareness of political geog-raphy. Dol occupies a dominant position in the comparatively narrow corridor of land lying between the sea and the episcopal *civitas* of Rennes, now coming increasingly under Frankish influence. Although Dol was in Domnonée, it was sufficiently close to the Frankish world to serve as a crucial link between two domains. So important was the location that in the ninth century Dol became the metropolis of the independent Breton Church, a status hotly disputed by the archbishop of Tours.

It was at Dol that Samson developed his skills as a diplomat. The most famous incident is his adjudication in a dispute between Judwal, who claimed to be heir to Domnonée, and Commore, whose title, *iudex externus*, suggests that he might have been a contender put forward by the Franks. In the event Samson supported Judwal and took the claim to the court of the Frankish king, Childebert, in Paris. Here he was well received by the king and awarded various estates and privileges. That Samson might not have been entirely unbiased in his judgement is suggested by a note in a ninth-century document recording that Judwal was Samson's cousin. His presence in Paris is recorded again in 553 and 557 in attendance at two church councils where he signed himself 'Samson *peccator Episcopus*' ('Bishop Samson, sinner').

Samson played a significant role in Breton life in the sixth century, not only as a leader of the Church but also as a diplomat accepted at the highest level. The range of skills that he displayed and the authority he exerted were characteristics shared by many of the educated elite who had made the journey from Britain to Brittany in the sixth and seventh centuries.

The Life of St Sampson provides a valuable insight into the origin and mobility of the clerics arriving in Brittany in the early Middle Ages. As the earliest of the Lives it served as a model for the Lives of the saints who followed him, composed several centuries after their subjects' deaths. Such similarities as there are, then, may reflect a desire on the part of the authors to echo the life of an ideal saint. That said, it is clear that many of the saints were born into elite families in Wales, Cornwall, and Ireland and were trained in the British and Irish monasteries in the tradition of the Celtic Church. Like Samson, many brought books with them: the list of insular texts known to have been available to the Bretons is impressive.

Thus it was that the Breton Church developed along different lines from the Frankish Church, which was firmly based on the tradition of Roman Christianity, with each *civitas* representing a diocese led by a bishop presiding in the *civitas* capital. The differences between the two churches is highlighted in a letter sent by Bishop Melanius of Rennes sometime soon after the Council of Orléans (*c.*510–20) to the two Breton priests Lovocat and Catihern complaining of the irregular practices of the Bretons (above, p. 205). Later, in 567, the archbishop of Tours, presiding over a council, issued a decree stating that on pain of excommunication nobody should dare to 'consecrate Breton or Roman bishops in Armorica without consent or written permission of the metropolitan or co-provincials'. The reason for the stern warning was that the bishop of Nantes had recently allowed the Breton chief Macliaw to become temporary bishop of Vannes to escape persecution. The two examples show that the relaxed practices of the Breton Church were not acceptable to the more austere Roman Church. They also provide an insight into the way in which the Roman Church was trying to impose its authority over Brittany.

The Daily Life of the Early Bretons

Archaeology is at last beginning to fill in details about the daily life of the Bretons in the early Middle Ages. In the region around Carhaix a large number of fortified enclaves have been identified representing farms and hamlets occupied for many centuries. One well-excavated example at Bressilien, 5 hectares in extent and surrounded by a substantial bank and ditch, was occupied from the seventh century. Other sites were more modest, like the stone-walled enclosure containing a small rectangular house and a barn found on Île Guennoc, off Landéda, surrounded by fields defined by banks. The complex was in use between 450 and 950.

Excavations within the Iron Age and Roman fortifications at Le Yaudet, a promontory overlooking the estuary of the Léguer, showed that a farming community had been established in the safety of the old defences and was flourishing in the seventh and eighth centuries. The actual habitation area was not identified but it may well have lain in the centre of the site in the vicinity of the present church. What the excavation showed was an area of regularly laid-out rectangular fields separated by stone walls, five of which had been cultivated by the lazy-bed method. This entailed digging parallel trenches 2–3 metres apart and piling the soil from them to form a ridge between. The trenches provided access and drainage, while the low mounds, enhanced no doubt by midden material and seaweed, offered fertile soil for cultivation. In two of the fields elongated stone-lined trenches serving as grain-drying ovens had been constructed, dated by radiocarbon to the seventh century. Charred grain found in the ovens showed that rye and oats predominated, with lesser quantities of free-threshing wheat and hulled barley. Rye and oats are both salt-tolerant crops that could have grown well in local conditions.

The status of the settlement at Le Yaudet is difficult to judge from the excavated evidence. While it could have

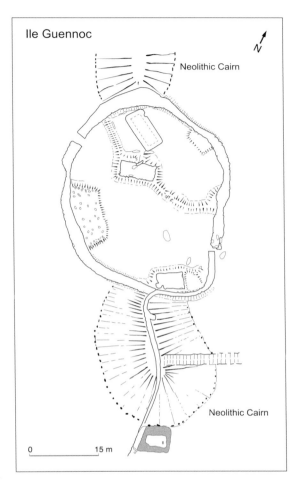

6.7 The early medieval settlement, situated between two Neolithic burial mounds, occupied the centre of the small island of Guennoc. It was enclosed by a boundary wall and surrounded by embanked fields.

been little more than a single peasant family making use of the old defences, it is quite possible that we are dealing with a larger community, perhaps founded by immigrants from Britain, claiming authority from their occupation of an ancestral high-status site. The power of the community is shown by the fact that, at some time before the ninth century, they built a massive stone barrage across the mouth of the inlet, below the flank of the promontory, to create a tidal mill. The sheer scale of the work implies command of a large labour force. Another indication of status was a small decorated

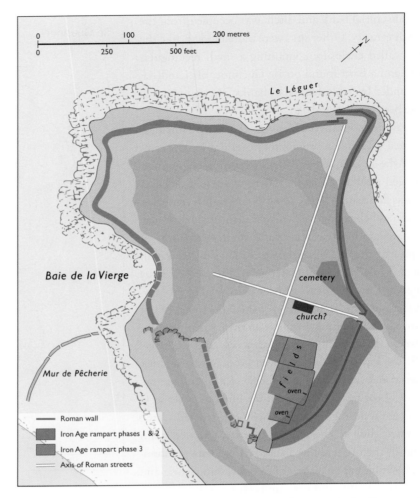

6.8 The promontory of Le Yaudet, defended in the Late Iron Age and again in the late Roman period, continued as a settlement throughout the early medieval period. In one part of the site a series of fields, cultivated by the lazy-bed method, were laid out within the Roman street grid. Corn-drying ovens were found in two of the fields. The church probably lay on or near the site of the present church with its cemetery nearby. The location of the main settlement has not yet been identified.

bronze strap fitting of seventh- to eighth-century date. It was an item of some value made in an insular or Frankish workshop.

Physical evidence of the early religious establishments in Brittany is sparse, but excavations on Île Lavret and at Landévennec give some insights into the beginnings of monasticism. Île Lavret is one of an archipelago of small islands surrounding the larger island of Bréhat, off the north coast, near Paimpol. From the Life of St

6.9 A corn-drying oven constructed at the edge of one of the fields in Le Yaudet, found during excavation. Radiocarbon dates suggest that it was in use in the late seventh or early eighth century.

Guénolé we learn that St Budoc, a disciple of St Maudez, whose monastery lay on a nearby island, decided to set up his own cell on Île Lavret. Excavations on the island show that he made use of the ruins of a small Roman building, to which limited additions were later made. Much later a chapel was built. Close to the religious buildings a cemetery developed, the earliest burials so far discovered dating to the seventh century. St Budoc clearly chose a remote place for his cell, wishing, as many of the early saints did, to devote himself to a life of seclusion. His modest establishment never grew but was of sufficient renown to develop as a small cemetery serving the local community.

The story of Landévennec is rather different. According to tradition it was founded by St Guénolé (St Wingualoei), born of Welsh parents soon after their arrival in Brittany. The archaeological evidence suggests that this foundation took place sometime between 470 and 535, on or close to the site of a Roman villa which was

6.10 The *mur de pêcherie* crossing the bay immediately west of the fortified settlement of Le Yaudet was built as a barrage to retain seawater at high tide, which was then allowed to flow out through sluices powering the wheel of a mill built on the wall. It was probably constructed sometime between the sixth and eighth centuries. Such a considerable undertaking reflects the strength and technical skills of the early medieval community.

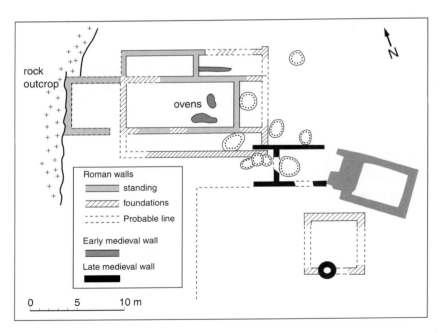

6.11 The Roman building on Île Lavret, close to Île de Bréhat, was developed as a small monastic settlement by St Budoc, pupil of St Maudez. It remained a functioning religious establishment until the later Middle Ages.

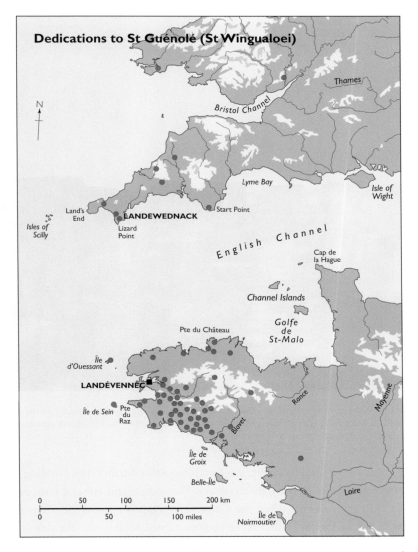

6.12 Dedications to the many saints who travelled the Atlantic seaways indicate the region influenced by their ministry. St Guénolé (St Wingualoei) was born in Brittany of Welsh parents and established the monastery at Landévennec.

later used as a quarry for building stone and brick. At the end of the sixth century the monks moved to the bottom of a nearby valley to make use of a small stream for their drinking water and ablutions. The accommodation for the monks and their oratory was on the north side of the stream, with farm buildings and workshops on the south side. Rebuilding in the late seventh or early eighth century shows something

6.13 The monastery of Landévennec was founded in the late fifth or early sixth century on the site of a Roman villa. It was rebuilt after a Viking attack in AD 913. The location was well chosen, surrounded by rich farmland and with easy access to major sea-routes.

of the vitality of the establishment, its growth requiring further new building works to be undertaken later in the eighth century. The success and fame of Landévennec is reflected in the fact that when the Carolingian emperor Louis the Pious was in Brittany in 818, he visited Landévennec and questioned Matmonoc, the abbot, about the way of life in Breton monasteries, learning that in both discipline and tonsure they adopted Irish ('Scottic') practices. The emperor disapproved and required that thereafter they should follow the Rule of St Benedict. The monastery continued to flourish and was rebuilt on a grand scale in the ninth century.

That the two establishments should have taken such different trajectories is the result of many chances and choices. By moving to a remote island, Budoc was looking for solitude. Guénolé, on the other hand, chose to found his monastery in a fertile land with good maritime connections, providing opportunities for his small community to grow. The intention of the founder was a significant factor in the fortunes of a monastery.

6.14 Many of the standing stones—the menhirs and the stelae—erected in the prehistoric period, reflecting pagan religious beliefs, were taken over by Christians and rededicated. This menhir at Saint-Uzec, Côtes-d'Armor, had a cross added to the top and later was elaborately carved with a figure of a praying woman surrounded by the instruments of the Passion—a clear example of cultural appropriation.

The use of old Roman buildings as sites for religious communities to settle is a reminder that the landscape was full of monuments from the past. Most prominent were the stelae erected in the pre-Roman Iron Age. As monuments to paganism they became targets for the Christians. Some were pulled down and broken up, others Christianized, usually by having crosses attached to their tops, a reminder of St Samson's treatment of the standing stone he encountered on his journey across Cornwall (above, pp. 218–19). Another use of stelae was as grave markers for the Christian community. Of the twenty-six funerary inscriptions surviving from early medieval Brittany, twelve were carved on Iron Age stelae. They vary in date. One of the earliest, until recently in the churchyard at Louannec not far from Lannion, dates to the sixth or seventh century. Its bold inscription reads DISIDERIFILI BODOGNOVS ('of Disiderius son of Bodognous'). Of much the same date, the stone in the churchyard

at Plouagat, near Guingamp, simply records the name Uormuin. By using pagan stelae the early Christians were appropriating the powers once worshipped by their distant ancestors for their own God.

The scraps of archaeological evidence available to us present a varied picture of farming settlements quite closely scattered in the landscape, representing communities of different sizes, from simple single-family farmsteads to larger agglomerations that might have centred around an elite family. It was a typical dispersed pattern of settlement of the kind characteristic of Devon, Cornwall, and Wales. But over and above the patchwork of family holdings was the larger-grained network of the *ploue*—the territorial divisions laid out in the early decades of the fifth century but no doubt based, at least in part, on pre-existing boundaries. In each was a centre, sometimes a monastery but more often a *bourg*, a space where people could meet on market days to buy and sell goods and where a church might eventually be built to serve their spiritual needs. It was a small world in which no one had cause to travel far.

6.15 Some of the Iron Age stelae were used as grave markers in early medieval times. This example from Louannec, Côtes-d'Armor, was set up for Disiderius, son of Bodognous.

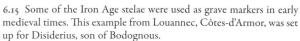

The World Beyond

There can be no doubt that there was frequent movement across the Channel between south-western Britain and Brittany during the fifth to the seventh centuries, but the question of how integrated Brittany was with the rest of the Atlantic maritime network is more difficult to decide. Such evidence as there is consists of a few references to sea journeys in historical sources and archaeological finds of imported pottery. One of the earliest of the stories, preserved in the *Confession* of St Patrick, refers to the escape of the saint from servitude in Ireland in the early 420s. Following God's instruction he made for the sea, where he found a merchant ship carrying a cargo of hunting dogs to Gaul. After three days at sea they landed in Gaul but found the whole countryside in turmoil. Where exactly the ship landed, whether in Brittany or elsewhere on the French coast, is unknown, but the message from the story is that trading ventures along the Atlantic seaways were not uncommon. The Life of Columba makes passing reference to the arrival of Gaulish trading vessels at the island of Iona during the saint's lifetime (*c.*521–597), implying that this was a regular and much-anticipated occurrence. These vessels presumably came from western Gaul via the Irish Sea and may have been carrying wine from the Bordeaux region. A little later, in 610, the Irish cleric St Columbanus was returning home from Burgundy by way of the Loire valley and at Nantes found a ship that had just offloaded a cargo from Ireland and was preparing to return. Another seventh-century source, the Life of St Philibert, mentions Irish traders visiting the monastery on the island of Noirmoutier, just south of the Loire estuary, with cargoes of clothes and shoes.

Taken together these historical sources, while anecdotal, imply that there was lively maritime trade between western Gaul and people living around the Irish Sea. Their principal purpose was trade, but they were prepared to give passage to wandering clerics. The vessels put into major ports like Nantes, but monasteries also offered valuable opportunities for trading. They were rich and could afford the luxuries on offer. More to the point, they also needed a constant supply of wine and oil for communion services. For ship's masters exploiting these needs, a port like Bordeaux would have been a convenient place to take on such a cargo.

The archaeological evidence supports this picture and adds further detail. From about 475 to 550 a lively maritime trade developed between the Mediterranean and the Irish Sea region. It can be traced from the distribution of Mediterranean pottery of two principal categories, fine red-slip bowls and dishes made in western Turkey and North Africa, characterized as A Wares, and amphorae used to transport oil, made in Turkey, Egypt, and North Africa, known as B Wares. The cargoes were probably assembled in west Mediterranean ports like Carthage and then shipped out into the

MATHEVM INCI
PIT PRE FATIO SECVN
DVM MARCVM

MAR
CVS
EVAN
GELIS
TA DEI
ELECTUS

& petri in bab
tis matae filius
atque in diuino
ser mone disci
pulus sacerdo
ciũ misit agens

secundũ car nem leuita conuer sus ad finẽ xp̄i

7

CONFLICTING IDENTITIES
751–1148

For a hundred and fifty years from about 600 to 750 there was a stand-off between the Bretons and the Franks, with the river Vilaine serving as a convenient boundary to keep them apart. To the east lay the old *civitates* (now more conveniently referred to as *comtés*, counties) of Nantes and Rennes, both under Frankish control with their bishops owing allegiance to the metropolis of Tours. To the west was the county of Vannes—the region of Broërec—protected to the north by the dense forest of Brocéliande. Once disputed territory, it had been in the hands of Breton warlords since the late sixth century. It was a period of unstable equilibrium: Bretons mounted raids on the counties of Nantes and Rennes while Frankish rulers required occasional displays of subservience from Breton chieftains. Neither side was strong enough, or sufficiently motivated, to engage on a larger scale; that is, until 751, when everything changed and the Franks began an attempt to bring the Bretons firmly under control.

The long-drawn-out dispute that followed was further confused by the appearance of Scandinavian raiders from Denmark and Norway, commonly known as Vikings. The first recorded raid came in 799 and soon Viking enclaves were established in the Seine valley and the mouth of the Loire. Usually the intruders pursued their own interests but on some occasions fought on the side of the Franks against the Bretons, while on others they allied themselves with Bretons against the Franks: it was a time of confused loyalties. The conflicts, however, strengthened the sense

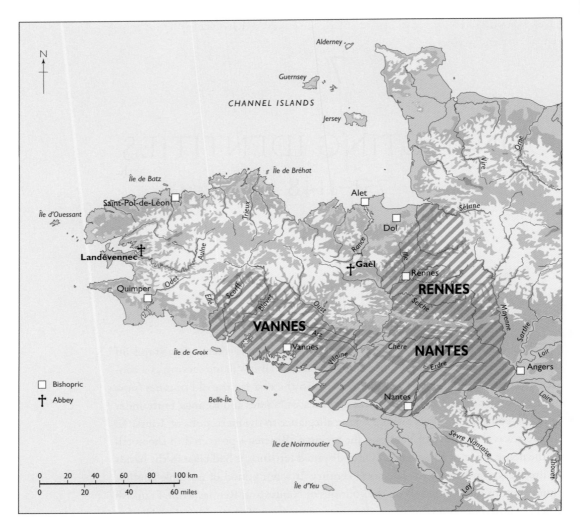

7.1 In the late eighth century the March of Brittany was created, consisting of three *comtés* based on the cities of Vannes, Nantes, and Rennes, now ruled as part of the Frankish empire.

of Breton identity and by about 940 the Viking gangs who had been living off the Breton countryside, following a period of intense raiding beginning in 907, were defeated and dispersed.

In the years to follow, Brittany developed as a feudal state, as did much of the rest of Europe, ruled by fractious dukes. A number of the more entrepreneurial of the Breton lords took their chances with William, duke of Normandy, when in 1066 he invaded England, and were rewarded with large estates in the conquered country.

Later, in the twelfth century, during the English Civil War, they were to play a significant part in the conflict.

The Carolingian Expansion, 751–831

In the middle of the eighth century the fraught political situation in the world of the Franks had resolved itself, allowing the Carolingian dynasty, which had established ascendancy, to focus attention once more on the Bretons, who had begun to raid the counties of Nantes and Rennes. Breton sympathy with the Aquitanians south of the Loire threatened the creation of a new western power block that could be manipulated by Carolingian dissidents who were still contending for power. So it was that in 751 Pippin the Short, who had just deposed Dagobert III, decided to drive a firm wedge between the Bretons and the Aquitanians. As the Annals of Metz record: 'The king Pippin led his army into Brittany, took hold of the fortified town of Vannes and submitted all Brittany to the territory of the Franks.' By adding the county of Vannes to the Frankish-held counties of Nantes and Rennes he had effectively isolated northern and western Brittany from the rest of France, breaking any possibility of alliance between Brittany and Aquitaine. From this position of power he was able to claim some degree of control over the rest of the peninsula.

It was probably at this time or soon after that the March (*Limitis*) of Brittany was created. A march was a military region bordering a territory that was independent and potentially hostile. The March of Brittany was composed of the counties of Rennes, Nantes, and Vannes and was placed under the control of a prefect, appointed by the Carolingian Crown. In peacetime he was based in Nantes but in times of war he assumed command of the whole region. The prefects (or counts), first mentioned in 778, were chosen from a single family, the Widonids, giving the office something of a hereditary flavour.

It was from the March that the Carolingians mounted campaigns against the rest of Brittany with the aim of extracting tribute and booty: this inevitably sparked armed opposition, which drew further intervention. Attacks on the Bretons are recorded on five occasions between 786 and 825. They were usually under the command of a marquis or the counts of the Breton March, but in 818 the king himself, Louis the Pious, assembled his army in Vannes and led it deep into Brittany, defeating the Breton chief, Morvan. It was on this occasion that he met the abbot of Landévennec and, learning something of Breton monastic practices, required them henceforth to follow the Rule of St Benedict (above, p. 226). But trouble flared up again, probably in northern Brittany, this time inspired by the war leader

7.2 The monastery of Landévennec remained a major cultural centre throughout the Carolingian period. It was a repository for many manuscripts, among them the Evangeliary dating to the ninth century. The first page of St Mark's Gospel begins with this spirited figure with a horse's head. It is a visual play on words because 'horse' is *marc'h* in Breton. The manuscript was taken to Boulogne for safety during the Viking raid in 913, where it is still preserved.

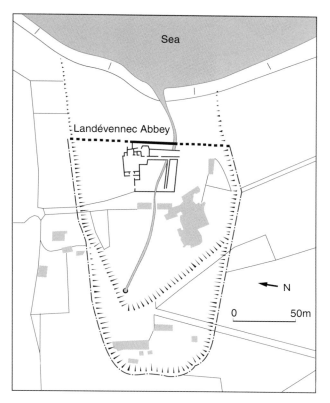

7.3 The abbey of Landévennec was sited on a prolific freshwater source close to the sea. By the Carolingian period it had grown considerably in size.

Guihomarc'h, requiring a series of campaigns in 822, 824, and 825 to contain the rebellion. Although Guihomarc'h was caught and put to death, the unrest continued, and in 830 Louis was driven to assemble an army at Rennes in preparation for another intervention, only to be distracted by the revolt of his sons. By now it was clear that the Bretons could not easily be subdued and a new approach was required.

The failure of seven major Carolingian campaigns, mounted over four decades, to bring the Bretons to heel reflects the strength of Breton resistance. No doubt the difficult landscape of the peninsula worked in the Bretons' favour. Rivers were prone to flood and the forested interior was particularly confusing to invading armies. The camp established by the Bretons in 818 is described as 'in the middle of the forest, surrounded by a river and embedded behind hedges, ditches and marshes, resounding to the sound of arms'. Landscapes like this lent themselves to the guerrilla tactics

7.4 The model represents the main abbey buildings of Landévennec as they would have been in the late ninth century.

favoured by the Bretons and to their very effective use of light cavalry. The fractured nature of the Breton leadership was also in their favour. When one war leader was beaten, another was eager to take up the challenge. But perhaps the greatest of the strengths of the Bretons was their peninsular location: they had nowhere to run to. There was no option but to stay to defend their land. The Carolingians had less incentive to fight. For them the Breton campaigns were something of a sideshow: there were more pressing and more lucrative engagements to be had elsewhere.

The Bretons had had a hundred and fifty years (600–750) to establish their community networks in times of comparative peace. The next eighty years of conflict drove them to become an effective military force. It was in opposition to a common enemy that Breton identity was first beginning to be forged.

Nominoë and Erispoë: Imperial Vassals, 831–857

Until 830 it had been the intention of the Carolingians to subdue Brittany, but the resilience of the Bretons and deep divisions among the Carolingian aristocratic families forced a dramatic change of policy. On 1 May 831 Louis appointed a member of the Breton elite, Nominoë, as imperial delegate (*missus imperatoris*) to represent Brittany. He was to be, in effect, a vassal (*fidelis*) of the emperor. As such he held supreme judicial, military, and ecclesiastical power within his jurisdiction. The county of Vannes was now detached from the March and handed to him as the centre of his power. The arrangement was effective and he remained faithful to Louis until the king's death in 840. But thereafter, until his own death in 851, he grew increasingly willing to confront Carolingian power in the interest of his own county. Nothing is known of Nominoë's origins except that he belonged to the Breton aristocracy and had probably come to Louis's attention in the 820s. But he proved to be a skilled leader. By manipulating the family feuds gripping the Carolingian aristocracy and the disruption caused by the Viking presence in the Loire valley, he was able to extend the territory and the power of Brittany.

The wars between the sons of Louis the Pious, which broke out after the king's death in 840, provided Nominoë with an opportunity to intervene in the affairs of the counties of Nantes and Rennes. His relationship with Louis's successor, Charles the Bald (reigned 840–77), was ambivalent. At first he offered support, but relations soured and Charles, who was now siding with Nominoë's enemies, was defeated in 845 at the battle of Ballon near Redon. A brief truce was agreed, but later, in 846, Nominoë was again campaigning, this time in the Bessin in north-west Normandy. In 850 he raided Rennes, Nantes, and Le Mans, and by March 851 he had reached Vendôme, at which point he died suddenly.

Nominoë was an opportunist who benefited from a degree of Carolingian patronage. By making astute use of the fast-changing political situation on the eastern frontier of Brittany he kept much of the peninsula safe both from the attention of rival Frankish counts and from pillaging Vikings. Away from the battlefield he took an active interest in the affairs of the Church, in 834 supporting the proposal to found the monastery of Saint-Sauveur at Redon. Sited at the confluence of the Oust and the Vilaine, Redon occupied a strategic position on the interface between the Breton- and Romance-speaking worlds. A prestigious religious institution here would serve as a symbol of Breton scholarship and devotion. It would also, as one observant contemporary pointed out, make a useful fortified location. Later, at a synod held at Coitlouh, Nominoë made an even more dramatic impact on the Breton Church. Aware that he now wielded considerable powers, he dismissed the bishops of Alet, Dol, Quimper, Saint-Pol-de-Léon, and Vannes, who owed their appointments to Frankish patronage, and replaced them with Breton bishops: 'men of his own race and language'. There was immediate uproar among the Frankish clergy. The council held at Anjou in 850 issued a decree accusing him of 'having expelled from their see legitimate bishops in order to substitute them for some mercenary intruders not to say more crudely thieves and ruffians, to have violated the right of St Martin to whom the Bretons cannot deny belonging'. His bold act of defiance was to have repercussions for generations to come.

It was inevitable that a man like Nominoë would be eulogized by later historians eager to discern the beginnings of the Breton state. As a leader chosen from the Breton aristocracy he has some claim, but he always acknowledged his vassal status to the Carolingian kings, referring to himself variously as *dux*, *magister*, and *missus in Britannia*, never as *rex*. That said, in his last years he was beginning to show signs of independence, not least in his dismissal of the Frankish bishops. Over the nearly two decades that he held power, he managed to restrict the conflict zone to the eastern frontier region. This left much of peninsular Brittany to develop in comparative peace, demonstrating to Nominoë's fellow Bretons the benefits of a strong single ruler rather than competing rival chieftains.

Nominoë was succeeded in 851 by his son Erispoë. Charles the Bald saw this as a chance to seize back control of Brittany. Amassing a large army aided by Saxon troops, he marched towards the county of Vannes, only to be met by Erispoë's forces at Jengland-Beslé on the left bank of the Vilaine. After three days of intensive fighting Charles fled, leaving his camp to be pillaged and his leaderless troops to be dispersed and slaughtered. It was a significant loss and greatly strengthened Erispoë's bargaining position when later the two leaders met at Angers to negotiate a peace treaty. Erispoë was content to represent himself as a vassal of Charles the Bald but in return he was presented with royal insignia legitimizing the hereditary character of his power base. While his father had been an appointee of the king, he was head of a royal household. In addition, the counties of the March, Rennes and Nantes, were added to his realm together with the Pays de Retz to the south of the Loire, thus giving the Bretons complete control of the Loire estuary. The boundary of Brittany, as defined in the Treaty of Angers, remained unchanged for more than a thousand years until its redefinition in 1941.

Brittany, then, was now a subordinate kingdom of the Carolingian realm ruled by a native aristocracy. But certain checks and balances were needed to maintain equilibrium. In 856 it was agreed that Erispoë's daughter would marry the king's son Louis the Stammerer, who was then only 10 years old. Another of the arrangements, more difficult to explain, was the appointment by Charles of Erispoë's cousin Salomon to 'one third of Brittany'. Under the Celtic system of fosterage it is likely that Salomon had been brought up in the household of his uncle Nominoë and was therefore foster-brother to Erispoë. By insisting on them sharing the responsibilities of the kingdom Charles was strengthening his own control with the option of playing the foster-brothers off, one against each other. The two were able to work in harmony for six years, but eventually, in 857, Salomon murdered his foster-brother and claimed the crown.

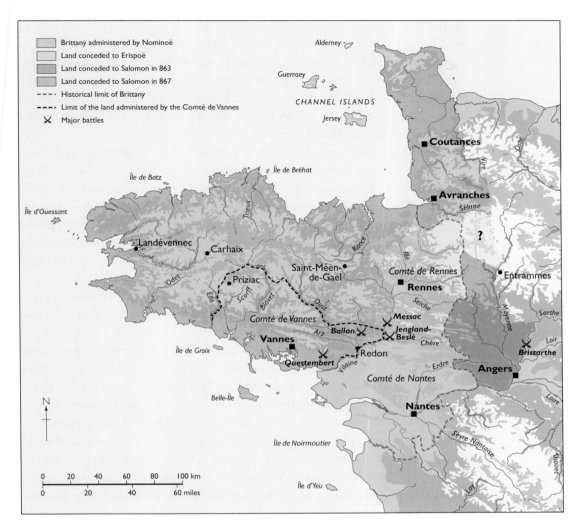

7.5 The growing strength of Brittany under kings Nominoë, Erispoë, and Salomon saw the boundaries of Brittany pushed further east until, in 867, the kingdom reached its maximum extent and included almost the whole of the Armorican Massif.

Meanwhile the Vikings, 799–856

The first recorded Viking raid on western France took place somewhere in the Vendée region in 799, and for the next half-century Viking sea raids were an ever-present third force in the conflicts between the Bretons and the Franks. Sometimes they raided alone but at other times fought on the side of one or other of the two contestants.

At this early stage the Viking bands were made up of fleets of ships carrying fighting men from Denmark and Norway intent on raiding to acquire booty and status. At first they would return home after the raiding season was over, but as time went on many chose to overwinter in their favoured territories ready to start the next season of raiding as soon as the weather improved. Some chose the Friesian coast, some the Seine valley, and others the estuary of the Loire. It was the last who had the greatest impact on Brittany in the early ninth century.

After the first attack in 799 Charlemagne responded by reorganizing the defences of Aquitaine. It may be that the Vikings had used the island of Noirmoutier off the Loire estuary as a temporary base. They certainly did so in 819–20, and the Viking presence on the island became so oppressive in the years between 834–6 that the monastic community, who had chosen the island as a place for a quiet, contemplative life, decided to move off, first to Saint-Philibert on the mainland and then, as the Viking presence became more repressive, to Anjou in the 850s and eventually to the safety of Burgundy in 875.

Taking advantage of the death of Louis the Pious in 840, in the following year a vast Viking fleet sailed up the Seine, pillaging monasteries as they went. Later they tried their luck on the Loire, meeting heavy resistance from the Franks: but this was only a prelude. The next year, 843, the fleet, with the connivance of a rebellious Frankish court, sailed to Nantes and rampaged through the city, killing the bishop and his clergy as well as many of the citizens. They then continued further up the river to Poitou before turning their attention to the coast of Aquitaine. Having overwintered, probably on Noirmoutier, they continued raiding the following year, 844, but were deflected by Nominoë and chose instead to turn their attention to the Garonne. For the next three years they remained in the area, spending the winters on islands off the coast of Poitou and Aquitaine, and then, in 847, they mounted massive raids in the Loire mouth region forcing Nominoë to buy them off. The tactic seems to have brought respite for Brittany and the next year the Vikings made again for the Garonne, besieging Bordeaux.

The raids began again in 853 when Vikings from the Seine, under the command of Godfred, sailed around Brittany and into the Loire estuary, attacking Nantes and Saint-Florent before burning Tours. Godfred's force then set up base on Île de Bièce in the Loire close to Nantes in preparation for a major onslaught on Brittany, but in 854 another Viking fleet, led by Sidroc, arrived and a desperate Erispoë made a deal with them to join in an attack on Godfred's camp. When the attack failed and the Bretons were driven back, Sidroc changed sides, allowing Godfred to sail up the Vilaine with 130 ships. A sudden storm, which wrecked some of Godfred's ships, saved Redon from attack, but the looters rampaged wide, taking large numbers of captives, including the

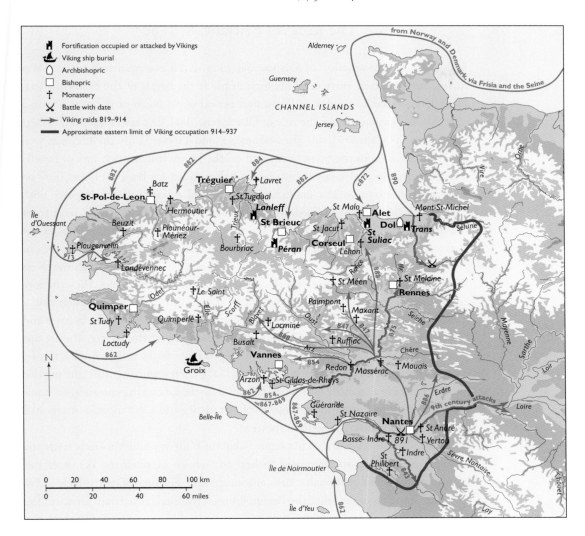

7.6 The Vikings were involved in Brittany for over a century (*c*.840–*c*.960). For much of the time different bands of Scandinavians held the territory between the lower Vilaine and the lower Loire and raided out from there. Other raids were mounted from Viking-held territory in the Seine valley.

bishop of Vannes. The next year Godfred left the Loire for Frisia, but Sidroc returned from the Seine to mount attacks in the Garonne and the Loire. The scene was now set for a more intensive phase of Viking activity. Until this time it had been largely a series of opportunist raids carried out with little forethought. From now on the attacks were to be carefully targeted on centres of wealth and trade.

The Kings of Brittany, 857–907

Following the assassination of Erispoë, Salomon seized power in Brittany and was to rule for seventeen years until his own death at the hands of the Franks in 874. His reign covered a complex and confused period when much of the west was in a state of insurrection against the rule of Charles the Bald. The revolt involved Robert the Strong in Neustria, Louis the Stammerer, and Pippin II of Aquitaine, as well as Viking enclaves in the Seine valley and on the Loire. It was a rich mix of rapidly changing rivalries and loyalties into which Salomon led his Bretons, intent only on protecting his country. But gradually the principal rebels made their peace with Charles, leaving Brittany isolated. By March 863 the royal army was ready to confront the Bretons, but neither side wanted yet another costly battle. Instead they met at Entrammes on the border and agreed terms. Salomon and the other noblemen present pledged allegiance to Charles and in return received a gift of land between the rivers Mayenne and Sarthe together with the abbey of Saint-Aubin d'Angers. The situation, however, remained tense. The following year, at a meeting at Pîtres, Salomon paid a tribute of 50 pounds of silver to the king and two years later, in 866, the Bretons and Vikings joined forces to defeat Charles's arch-enemy Robert the Strong. The actions were sufficient to satisfy Charles of Salomon's good intentions and in August 867 he sent the Breton a crown and other royal regalia, thus recognizing his right to style himself king. He also made over to the Breton state the Cotentin peninsula, a considerable territory including the bishoprics of Avranches and Coutances. Brittany had now reached its greatest geographical extent.

For the last seven years of his reign Salomon built friendly relations with the Frankish court. He also attempted to heal the schism between the Frankish and Breton churches but at the same time encouraged the bishop of Dol to claim archiepiscopal status to ensure that the Breton Church retained its separate identity. The monasteries, too, showed a new vigour and intellectual life flourished. But the Loire Vikings, now led by Hastein (Hásteinn), remained a serious problem. In 869 they mounted a concerted attack in the Vilaine region and were met by Salomon 'and all the Bretons'. Details of the engagement are lacking but a peace treaty was negotiated allowing the Bretons the welcome prize of acquiring part of the Anjou wine harvest. The 870s saw further Viking attacks, one against Alet, but the Franks were now active again and in 873 Hastein and his army were besieged in Angers.

For all his successes Salomon had acquired many enemies at home, not least among his relatives. Those named in the Annals of Saint-Bertin include Pascweten, his son-in-law, Gurvant, son-in-law of Erispoë, and his nephew Guignon, all young men eager for power and willing to work with Franks to see Salomon removed. In June 874 the

7.7 An illustration in the Life of St Aubin, dating to the eleventh century, shows a Norman vessel besieging Guérande. It offers a vivid image of what the Viking ships of the ninth and tenth centuries must have looked like.

plotters struck. Salomon's son (also called Guignon) was taken prisoner and the king fled to seek safety in the monastery at Poher but was handed over to Frankish conspirators, blinded, and later killed. The old regime was now at an end, leaving Pascweten and Gurvant to contest the leadership of the kingdom.

The family rivalries which had led to Salomon's overthrow destroyed the unity of Brittany, emphasizing once more the divide between the north and west, which became the preserve of Gurvant, and the south-east, where Pascweten established his power base. Both men were dead by the middle of 876 but the kingdom remained divided, with Pascweten's brother Alain succeeding to the south-eastern counties while Gurwant's son Judicael took over leadership of the west Bretons. The rivalry between the two leaders continued at first, but renewed raiding by the Loire Vikings eventually brought them together with common purpose. A major joint expedition was mounted in 888 but Judicael was killed in the fighting, leaving Alain in charge of the united army, which he led to a decisive victory at Questembert. The Viking force was dissipated, leaving the surviving flotillas to sail away.

The Loire Vikings were now dispersed, but the Seine Vikings, still a formidable force, began to turn their attention to Brittany in 889 or 890. Alain's rapid response led to the destruction of Viking fleets at Saint-Lô and on the river Couesnon, followed by two decisive victories near Nantes in 891. His success marked a turning point: by the end of 892 the Viking armies had turned away from north-western France to concentrate their efforts on the easier pickings offered by England. From this time until Alain's death in 907, Brittany enjoyed comparative peace.

The events of the second half of the ninth century showed that while Brittany could be united under strong leaders like Salomon and Alain, it was still a divided country, divided between the south-east and the north and west much as it had been in prehistoric and Roman times. While the south-east was more cosmopolitan, ready to absorb the culture of its Frankish neighbours, the north and west remained remote, shielded from continental influences and from the persistent threat of Viking raids. This territoriality, manifest in the regional loyalties of the aristocratic families, created tensions which could burst into outright aggression. But when strong leaders were called upon to face external threats, the factions could unite in common cause.

Life in the Countryside

The foundation of the monastery at Redon at the confluence of the Vilaine and the Oust in 832 created a strong intellectual centre on the interface between the two Brittanys. It looked both ways, to the Frankish-influenced counties of Rennes and Nantes to the east and to the more rural, independent west, serving as a bridge between them. One of its many functions was as a repository for nearly three hundred charters relating to monastic activities. These were copied out in the late eleventh and twelfth centuries and preserved in a cartulary. The charters provide an invaluable insight into the countryside and its organization during the crucial ninth century, when many far-reaching changes were transforming Breton society and its economy.

At the beginning of this period the countryside was divided into communities organized into territorial units known as *plebes*, about 40–50 square kilometres in extent with their centres averaging 6–7 kilometres apart. The focal point of each *plebs* was the *bourg*, where a church was usually sited, but settlement was dispersed through-out the territory, with individual family units living on a landholding known as a *ran* (plural *rannou*). A *ran* was, on average, about 10–25 hectares in extent, though some could be larger, up to 60 hectares. The homestead was usually sited within the arable land but never far from the meadow, pasture, and the *landes*—open heathland and commons where bracken could be cut for animal litter and gorse and broom could be gathered for the fire. Woodland, too, was important, carefully coppiced to provide material for house building and for the manufacture and repair of farm equipment and fencing. The *rannou*, then, were largely self-sufficient.

The social system at this stage was not steeply hierarchical. There were two basic lev-els: the free peasant proprietors (*plebenses*) and the unfree serfs who provided labour. There was also an aristocracy (*principes*), many fewer in number and largely detached from the land but drawing rents and tithes supervised for them by a *machtiern*, an official of authority.

Most peasant proprietors owned a single holding but about a fifth owned more than one though rarely outside the *plebs* in which they lived. Free peasants could also hold land in tenancies paying rent in work and in kind. Before the mid-ninth century the number of tenanted properties was comparatively small, fewer than 10 per cent, but later, as the power of monasteries grew and they acquired more land, the number of tenancies increased. While some were held by men who owned no land of their own, others were taken over by peasant proprietors with holdings.

Some of the smaller *rannou* could be worked by the peasant and his family, but many had at least one serf family to augment their labour. The serf was unfree: he was unable to change his own position and had no freedom of movement. He and his family, with any property which they might own, were alienable and could be given or sold on by his owner. Thus, one land gift to the abbey of Redon in 875 included 'all the serfs living on them, and their progeny until the end of the world'. A serf was a valu-able commodity and if one was killed or injured compensation was due to his master. The serf or serfs would have lived on the *ran* in their own houses and some may have had small plots to work to provide for their own needs, but most of their effort went into cultivating the land of the master. In those rare cases where serfs worked for aristocrats, they were required to pay rents. Altogether it is estimated that about a quarter of the population were unfree.

Each *plebs* was served by a *machtiern*, who may have been resident within the *plebs* or in a neighbouring one. The title includes the elements *mach*, 'surety', and *tien*, 'ruler'. They were men possessing land in more than one *plebs* and their status was hereditary. A *machtiern* provided a range of services for his *plebensis* and exercised considerable powers. He could hold courts, sometimes in the presence of *missi* (representatives of the rulers of Brittany), but could not impose punishments or fines. Their principal function seems to have been to oversee land deals and the general business of the *plebs* and to keep a formal record of sales and ownership. If questions later arose, they could be referred to as the guarantors, and could also be called upon to investigate disputes and to adjudicate when necessary. In other words the *machtiern* was a man of wisdom and experience invested with sufficient authority to enable the *plebes* to run smoothly. They were, however, a feature of the past and by the end of the fast-changing ninth century had all but disappeared to be replaced by a more centralized authority, both clerical and lay answering now to the aristocracy and the king.

Punitive justice and the imposition of fines lay in the hands of judges, men of substance within the *plebes* who were considered to be important. Normally a judge would serve in one *plebs* but might also appear as an important witness in several of the surrounding *plebes*. They therefore formed a loose-knit network, used to working together and in command of an array of case law. In such a system it was important for a person to display good judgement and integrity, and anyone who fell below acceptable standards could easily be excluded. The settlement of disputes was therefore a very local matter and seldom involved representatives of government. The priests, too, played a vital role in the life of the *plebes*. They belonged to the propertied class and might hold several *rannou* as well as own serfs. Each community might be served by several priests, who may have lived communally in the *domus presbyteri*. Besides ministering to the spiritual needs of their people they had business skills and access to money which could be loaned. They could witness transactions, act as scribes, and occasionally serve as impartial witnesses. As literate, educated men, they were vital to the well-being of society. That the priesthood could be inherited, a son taking over from his father, gave a stability to the system and conformed to the norms of the *plebs*.

Above and generally separate from the peasant society was the aristocratic class: the high aristocracy of counts and members of the ruling family, and a lesser aristocracy whose wealth and interests were more restricted. The high aristocracy enjoyed a considerable degree of mobility across north-western France as far east as Maine and Anjou. They also owned property in various places but had nothing to do with the affairs of the *plebes*. The lesser aristocrats travelled less widely and tended to confine their interests to a more restricted territory comprising three or four *plebes*, though they again did not involve themselves in local affairs. On those occasions when contact was necessary, *missi* were used as their representatives, and to ensure the regular payment of rent local agents, *maiores*, provided the necessary services. The aristocracy also exercised seigneurial powers over territories, irrespective of ownership. These were usually fiscal and judicial, and enabled the seigneur to impose taxes and tolls to augment his income. The counts and the lesser aristocrats seem to have spent time in royal courts. The royal leaders were attended by a group of aristocratic companions who were together at all times, but on special occasions more would arrive and join in for a time. Similarly, when a military campaign was being organized, the opportunity for glory and plunder would attract a considerable following.

Standing back from the detail it is possible to discern many similarities between Breton society and that of the Celtic west, in particular Ireland and Wales. Indeed, Julius Caesar's generalization about Celtic social structure is pertinent, distinguishing as it does between the knights, the Druids, and the peasant farmers. The *machtiern*, the judges, and the priests nicely embrace the multiple functions of the Druidic class, while the peripatetic aristocracy are equivalent to Caesar's knights, always ready to engage in a fight when the opportunity arose. From Caesar's lofty perspective the peasants were little better than slaves, but we know enough of the Breton peasantry to see that they were the essential producers whose labours sustained society, allowing the elite their lavish lifestyle and making possible the great cultural achievements of the Breton monasteries.

The Viking Conquest and its Aftermath, 907–939

The strong hand of Alain, 'count of Vannes and king of the Bretons', had kept the Viking threat at bay, partly by military force and shrewd political alliances, and partly by buying off the marauders, but following his death in 907 the raids began again in earnest. The problems were exacerbated when, in 911, following a confrontation at Chartres, the Frankish king, Charles the Simple, granted extensive lands in the lower Seine valley to the Viking leader Rollo (Hrólfr) 'for the defence of the kingdom', the intention being to settle a group of raiders once and for all so that they would create a bulwark to protect the Frankish kingdom from further attack by way of the English Channel. Rollo was probably Norwegian but his army included many Danes who had fought with the Great Army in England. Following the initial agreement, settlers flooded in, not only from Scandinavia and England but also, as the place name evidence suggests, from Ireland, the Hebrides, and Orkney: all territories which the Vikings had already settled. Cultural assimilation through intermarriage led to the creation of Nordmania as a maritime principality of Frankia, the region we now call Normandy. One group of Seine Vikings, not satisfied with the agreement, broke away from the main body and sailed around Brittany to settle in the Loire estuary. Brittany was now confronted by two Scandinavian enclaves, the land-hungry Normans in the north and the Loire valley Vikings still wedded to the excitement and rewards of the raid.

In 912 a new phase of ferocious raiding began against the Bretons, with monasteries being the favoured targets. The monastery of Saint-Guénolé at Landévennec was destroyed in 913 and the monks fled, carrying with them the saint's relics. Attacks on other monasteries followed, their monks fleeing with their treasures to the relative safety of France and England. Many of the Breton aristocracy also took flight, seeking refuge in the courts of the Wessex kings Edward the Elder (reigned 899–924) and Æthelstan (reigned 924–39). Brittany was now seen as easy game. In 914 a large Danish fleet from the Severn estuary began a series of devastating raids, which were to last four years. In 919 another vast fleet, this time of Loire Vikings under the command of a Norwegian, Rögnvaldr, landed at Nantes and went on to take control of much of Brittany, inspiring yet more aristocrats and monks to flee. The Annals from the monastery of Saint-Sauveur in Redon for the year 920 calmly record the tragedy: 'The Northmen devastated all of Brittany, defeating, killing or exiling the Bretons. Then the bodies of the saints who were buried there were carried into diverse lands.' The next year the county of Nantes was formally ceded to Rögnvaldr by the Frankish king, Robert I, in return for the Vikings agreeing to 'receive the faith of Christ'. Having taken control of Brittany, Rögnvaldr joined the Seine Vikings in raids north of the Seine and later campaigned along the Loire, reaching as far as Bourgogne.

The Bretons were not entirely passive throughout this period. In 931, when the Vikings were distracted by a threatened attack by the Franks, the Bretons rebelled, taking the Vikings by surprise, but after some initial successes the Vikings rallied and Brittany was once more secured. It is possible that the Loire Vikings had received some help from the Normans, now led by William Longsword, who had interests in the west. In 933 the Cotentin and Avranchin were ceded to him by the Franks, and he may have acquired additional territory around the Baie du Mont-Saint-Michel. But two years later he had made a firm alliance with the Franks, which meant that from now on the Loire Vikings holding Brittany were on their own.

Among the Breton aristocrats and clerics who had fled to England in 919 were Mathedoi of Poher and his son Alain Barbetorte (Twisted Beard), whose maternal

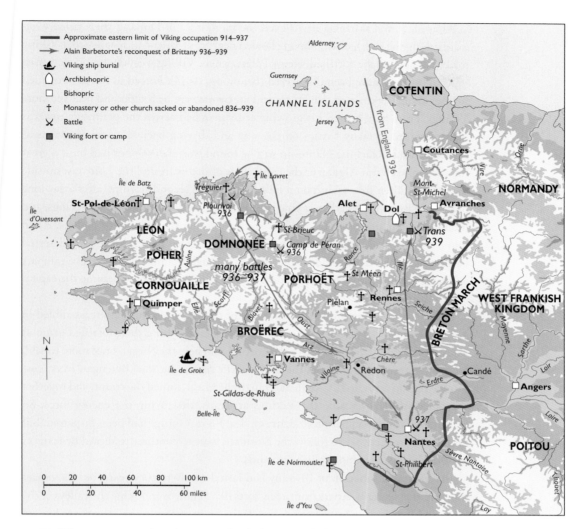

7.8 The Viking presence was brought to an end with the return of Alain Barbetorte and his successful campaigns of 936–9, but sporadic raids continued for another generation.

grandfather was Alain the Great. Alain Barbetorte grew up in the court of the English king Æthelstan and was raised as the king's foster-son. The exiles, meanwhile, were kept informed of events at home by people like Abbot John of Landévennec, who had remained in Brittany. Aware of the increasing vulnerability of the Vikings, Abbot John let Alain know that the time was ripe for his return. Æthelstan approved of the venture and provided a fleet and some troops to augment the expatriate Breton force, and in 936 Alain and his army landed at Dol to begin the reconquest.

After an initial skirmish he relieved the monastery of Dol and then sailed westwards along the north coast. Having landed near Saint-Brieuc he met another Viking force, possibly at the fortified site of Péran, where Viking weapons associated with signs of burning have been discovered (below, pp. 255–6). Forced to retreat, he sailed further along the coast of the Trégor to Plourivo, where he fought and beat yet more Vikings. From here he and his growing army marched across the peninsula towards Nantes, winning many battles on the way and driving back the Scandinavians as they advanced. Reaching Nantes in 937 he found that the Vikings had built a great fortification at Saint-Aignan at the confluence of the Erdre and the Loire just outside the old city. Their first assault on it failed, but on the second attempt, after a day-long battle, the Bretons prevailed, taking the camp, killing large numbers of Vikings, and forcing the remainder to flee to their ships. Entering the old city of Nantes, Alain found only ruined buildings and weed-covered streets. To reach the long-deserted basilica of Saint-Felix he had to cut his way through brambles. A defensive rampart was built around the cathedral to form a citadel and Nantes now became the capital of free Brittany.

But it was not quite over. The remnants of the Loire Vikings had reassembled in 938 and had moved into the county of Rennes, establishing their fortified camp at Trans-la-Forêt in Ille-et-Vilaine to the north. From here they began once more to raid, meeting some opposition from the count of the region, Judicael Berengar. In August 939 the Breton army, led by Alain and Hugh the Great, joined the count, and together they successfully overcame the Vikings at Trans, destroying the enemy force. So ended the Viking occupation of Brittany. The Loire Vikings had been dispersed, but for more than a century to follow the Normans were to continue to regard Brittany as a convenient place to mount lucrative raids.

The Viking occupation of Brittany had lasted nearly twenty years, but its impact was remarkably slight. Apart from a few forts like Péran, overlooking the valleys of the Urne and Gonet near Saint-Brieuc, and Trans no permanent settlements are known and there was no attempt to establish trading ports comparable to Dublin and York, which sustained large resident populations. Nor is there any place name evidence for Scandinavian settlement except for a few in the extreme north-east, which probably relate to a later period. Yet within a few days of reaching Brittany, Alain would encounter three groups of Vikings ready to fight. The implication seems to be that the Scandinavians in Brittany still retained much of the archaic Viking lifestyle, with predatory bands living off the land by raid and extortion. Apart from causing disruption their impact on the Breton community was slight. Their numbers were probably quite small; the only reason that they could continue to dominate the county was lack of effective leadership among the indigenous population. The insurgence of 931 was

7.9 The roughly circular fortification near Plédran known as Camp de Péran was built by the Vikings in the early tenth century and was probably the site of a major battle between Alain and the Vikings in 936. The fortification was a massive structure, with a wall 5 metres thick and 4 metres high. It was laced with timbers, which caught fire, probably when the camp was attacked. Its walls are still clearly to be seen.

easily quelled and led to nothing. But with the return of a charismatic leader, Alain, and the other members of the exiled elite, the scattered Breton resistance could be brought together as an irresistible force to clear the land of Scandinavians in a remarkably short time.

Archaeological evidence of the Viking occupation is comparatively sparse, but two fortifications can, with confidence, be assigned to the period. The first, at Péran, is a roughly circular enclosure defended by a rampart now 3 metres high and originally about 5 metres, fronted by a 4-metre-wide ditch. The rampart was interlaced by vertical and horizontal timbers, which had caught fire and burned fiercely

7.10 The only elite Viking burial known in Brittany was found on Île de Groix. Here a ship had been drawn up on land and was buried together with a range of tools and weapons. One of the items recorded from the burial was an ornament of the kind used to decorate the stern-post of Viking ships.

enough to vitrify the stones of which it was built. Radiocarbon dates centre on the tenth century, which is supported by the discovery of a coin of St Peter of York minted before 925 and a few scraps of metalwork, possibly of Viking armour. It is tempting to relate the destruction of Péran to the engagement between Alain and the Viking force near Saint-Brieuc shortly after his landing at Dol in 936. The other fortifications of possible Viking origin were two earthworks built at Trans about half a kilometre apart, one rectangular, the other circular. The circular fort produced tenth-century pottery. The evidence is slight, but it has been suggested that the circular fort was built by the Loire Vikings and that the rectangular enclosure was constructed by Alain Barbetorte when, in 939, he moved against them in the final thrust. Other rectangular fortifications, like those identified at Saint-Suliac near the Rance and Lanleff near Paimpol, may belong to the early tenth century, but positive evidence is lacking.

The other Viking site of some significance is a ship burial found on the south coast of Île de Groix. The burial was sited close to a sandy bay and was covered by a mound. The ship, some 11–13 metres long, had been dragged to a specially prepared position and set alight. It contained two bodies, a mature individual and an adolescent, possibly a weapon bearer or slave, accompanied by dogs and birds, and a range of gear including weapons, tools, agricultural implements, bronze vessels, an iron cauldron,

7.11 The settlement of Alet continued as a major ecclesiastical and commercial centre until the decision was made to move to the rocky island of Canalch, now Saint-Malo, in the twelfth century. At the end of the tenth century the cathedral of Alet was rebuilt on a grand scale, with apses at each end, replacing the earlier cathedral built in the early ninth century. The apse at the east end still stands.

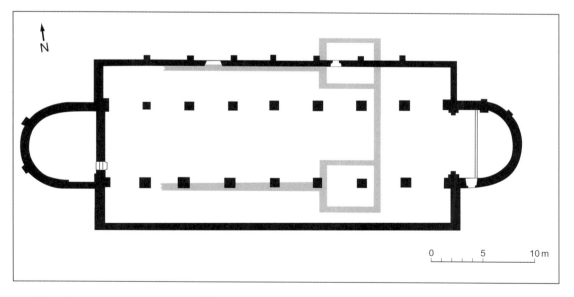

7.12 Plan of the tenth-century cathedral of Alet, with its ninth-century predecessor lying underneath it (shown in grey).

gaming pieces, and jewellery. After the cremation had been completed the remains were covered by a mound of shingle and sand 5 metres high. The exact date of the burial has been a matter of debate but all agree that it belongs to the tenth century, and a convincing case can be made for it belonging to the early decades of that century, contemporary with the Scandinavian occupation.

The Early Dukes, 936–1148

The Scandinavian occupation of Brittany between 913 and 936 brought to an end the *regnum Britanniae*. It was replaced, on the return of Alain Barbetorte in 936, with a system of rule by dukes drawn from rival aristocratic households. Alain, as count of Cornouaille and Nantes, was able to maintain a hold over the whole of Brittany and his reign was relatively peaceful, but after his death in 952 rival factions began to contest the leadership. Alain's son Drogon, widely regarded as the legitimate heir, died after a few years, and in the chaos that followed, Conan I of the house of Rennes became duke of Brittany, his descendants holding the dukedom until 1066, when leadership passed back to the count of Cornouaille and Nantes until the death of Conan III (the Fat) in 1148. The Brittany over which successive dukes struggled to maintain their power was now much reduced. Cotentin, Avranchin, and the parts of Anjou and Maine which king Salomon had ruled were lost. An area south of the Loire had been ceded to Brittany in 942, but it scarcely compensated. Meanwhile, the new power blocks immediately bordering the duchy—Normandy, Blois–Chartres, and Anjou—were interfering with intensifying rapidity in Breton affairs, requiring the attention of the dukes. It was, in many ways, history repeating itself. Facing powerful and aggressive continental neighbours, the Bretons of the peninsula were made increasingly aware of their identity. Once more Bretonness was being forged against 'the other'.

Throughout the two centuries following the routing of the Scandinavians, successive dukes fought to maintain their pre-eminence, not only against outside aggression but against the rising power of the seigneurial class within Brittany itself. Breton society was changing fast from a system that was essentially Celtic to one that was feudal. The changes began in eastern Brittany (Bretagne Gallo), an area in contact with regions where feudalism was already entrenched, and spread rapidly to the rest of the peninsula. One of the factors influencing the change was the return of exiles from France and Britain following Alain's reconquest, bringing with them new ideas of social organization. An immediate result was the emancipation of serfs, a process championed by Alain himself. With the weakening power of the dukes and the counts, the minor nobility of local lords began to build power bases by appropriating land and rights to tithes, which were passed on to their descendants. So it was that the seigneurial class, increasingly divorced from the productivity of the land yet dependent upon it, grew. By the end of the twelfth century they numbered several thousand. These were men who had adopted the chivalric codes of the time and felt themselves free to roam, mostly in France, in pursuit of their ideals, but at heart they were a landed aristocracy tenaciously rooted in their home locality. To French observers, usually hostile to the Bretons, these knights were larger than life. Said to father fifty children from multiple wives, they were renowned for their horsemanship and their boorish manners. While the Bretons guarded their independence from the French with vigour, French observers began to characterize their Breton neighbours as distinctly 'other'.

One of the physical manifestations of the feudal landscape was the motte, a large conical mound built of rubble and soil, flat-topped, with a palisaded fence around the top protecting a fortified tower. At least seven hundred mottes have been identified, and there are, no doubt, more to be discovered. Most were the residences of seigneurial families and date from the tenth to twelfth centuries. In some cases fortified outer baileys were added to provide extra accommodation space for family and retainers, and over time the wealthier lords were able to replace the timber towers on the mottes with masonry donjons, and the earth and timber baileys with stone-built curtain walls. Other motte sites were eventually transformed into manoirs and châteaux. The Bayeux Tapestry offers a spirited rendering of the motte at Dinan under attack by the Normans in the middle of the eleventh century. The mound is clearly depicted surmounted by a timber palisade protecting a central tower with an access ladder to one side. The Breton defenders within are busy throwing spears at an oncoming Norman cavalry charge while, unnoticed, Norman foot soldiers are trying to set fire to the palisade. The rash of mottes that spread across the face of Brittany from the tenth century is a reflection of the desire by feudal lords to display their power in monument building, but the Bayeux Tapestry is a reminder that mottes were effective defences in times when latent aggression was barely contained by social conventions.

In parallel with the development of feudal society, the Church was also undergoing significant changes. The period of Scandinavian occupation had seen the exodus of large numbers of churchmen escaping into exile with their relics and other treasures, but after Alain's successful campaign in 936–7 those clerics who had survived began to trickle back. Under Alain's patronage the monastery of Landévennec, destroyed by the Vikings in 913, was rebuilt on a much grander scale and re-endowed. Further restorations and the foundation of new monasteries followed, encouraged in the early

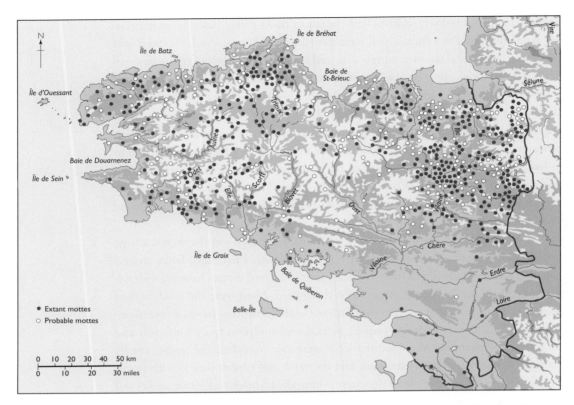

7.13 Troubled times in the eleventh century led to the building of a large number of fortified sites throughout Brittany. The characteristic feature of these fortifications was a large mound, or motte, with a timber or masonry tower on top. Some of the mottes had defended outer baileys.

eleventh century by Alain III (1008–40) and by the more powerful of the seigneurial families. The great majority of the new foundations were in the dioceses that bordered on France—Nantes, Rennes, Dol, and Saint-Malo—but the growing popularity of the eremitical way of life, harking back to the practices of the fifth and sixth centuries, led to an increasing number of hermits seeking solitude in the great forests.

The system of dioceses remained much as before, with Rennes, Nantes, Vannes, Quimper, Saint-Pol-de-Léon, Alet, and Dol continuing to function, but two new dioceses were created in the middle of the tenth century based on the long-established monasteries of Tréguer and Saint-Brieuc. Later, in the twelfth century, the cathedral of Alet was moved to the nearby site of Saint-Malo. Reform of the system led gradually to the disappearance of dynasties of bishops, with appointments now mostly in the hands of the seigneurial families. But at the parish level the traditional practice of

7.14 The motte at Lesquelen, Plabennec, Finistère, is unusual in that the entire outer face was covered with a skin of stonework to prevent erosion and collapse of the earth mound.

the priesthood remaining within the family continued. Entrenched in old ways and deeply superstitious, the priests now offered little pastoral care. Aberrant behaviour was not uncommon. It was almost as though the priests continued to behave much as their Druidic predecessors. The more educated churchmen found much to criticize in the backward ways of the Breton Church. Abelard, a renowned scholar writing at the beginning of the twelfth century, noted that the monks he had encountered spoke only Breton and behaved in an uncivilized manner. About the same time the archbishop of Dol, Baudry of Bourgueil, was being more outspoken in his criticism. Finding Brittany an alien place he wrote, 'I dwell among scorpions, surrounded by a double wall of bestiality and perfidy.' These reactions may be a little extreme, but they are a reminder that, for all their contacts with the wider world, the Bretons did things in their own way.

7.15 (*Opposite*) The Bayeux Tapestry has two depictions of Breton mottes in action. The upper illustration shows a Norman force attacking the motte at Dinan; the lower illustration shows Conan II escaping from the motte at Dol as the enemy approaches.

Bretons in Britain

The exodus of the Breton elite fleeing from the Viking onslaught to the court of the Wessex kings in the early decades of the tenth century suggests that close relations were maintained between the royal households on either side of the Channel. It may well be that some of the émigrés acquired land in England at this time. Certainly Raoul I, lord of Gaël, and Judhael of Totnes held estates in England before the Norman Conquest in 1066. But it was the Conquest itself that unleashed a flood of Bretons on England. The invasion force amassed by William the Conqueror, though predominantly composed of Normans, included lords from Brittany, Boulogne, Picardy, and Flanders: among these the Bretons were the most numerous. By the time of the Domesday Survey in 1086, as much as a fifth of the land of England was in Breton hands.

There were three main groups of Breton holdings, in East Anglia, Yorkshire, and the south-west. In East Anglia, Raoul II, lord of Gaël, was by far the largest landowner. He had inherited estates from his father, who had acquired land in England before the Conquest and had married an Englishwoman. Following the Conquest, new lands were made over to the family. Altogether they owned much of Norfolk and had estates in Suffolk, Essex, and Hertford. After his father's death in 1069 Raoul inherited the title of earl of the East Angles. The second concentration of Breton power was in north Yorkshire, where the honour of Richmond was given by William to Alain Le Roux, who had served with the Breton contingent at the battle of Hastings. Alain, the second son of Eudo of Penthièvre, was William's second cousin. By the time of Domesday in 1086, Alain had become one of the richest and most powerful men in England. The third grouping of Bretons concentrated in the south-west, in Cornwall, Devon, Somerset, and Dorset, extending up into Gloucestershire and Herefordshire. These estates were held by Breton lords from the Dol–Combourg–Fougères region. This was the area of the Breton March, which had recognized the overlordship of William in the 1050s, many of whose elite were prepared to follow him to England.

The Bretons were to play a significant part in English history. In 1075 Raoul II married the daughter of William FitzOsbern, earl of Hereford, but William refused to accept the marriage. Raoul's response was to lead an uprising against the king. The revolt failed, forcing him and his wife, Emma, to flee to Brittany. William immediately confiscated Raoul's East Anglia holdings, passing many of them to Alain Le Roux in recognition of his loyalty. The rest of Raoul's life was not without its excitements. The year after his return to Brittany he campaigned against the duke of Brittany and was besieged for a while in Dol until a rapprochement was agreed. In later life, in 1096, he and Emma went on the First Crusade and took part in the siege of Nicaea, but later in the year both were to die on the road to Palestine.

The two clusters of Breton lords who remained after the rebellion, those from the marches with lands in the south-west of England and those from Penthièvre with estates in the north-east, were descended from, and owed allegiance to, two separate dynasties that, in Brittany, were frequently in conflict. In England these family rivalries remained alive, and in the civil war which broke out between Stephen and Matilda (1139–53) the two groups took different sides: the Richmond–Penthièvre Bretons sided with Stephen while those from the south-west supported the claims of Matilda. Thus the geo-politics of England were directly affected by the rivalries of the Breton lords, nurtured in their distant past. In the English Civil War they sought to settle old scores.

Wandering Bretons

The extension of Norman power provided opportunities for Bretons to move into the wider world. While many of the Breton elite joined William on his English conquest, others followed Robert Guiscard and Count Robert to southern Italy and Sicily. Each would have brought supporters with them and, when given estates, retainers of lower rank would have been encouraged to come and settle, swelling the numbers and attracting kinsmen to join them to explore the opportunities of the new land. In England the survey taken a century after the Conquest shows that there were significant concentrations of Bretons in many parts of the country. William of Malmesbury, writing in the early twelfth century, took a rather jaundiced view of the newcomers. The Bretons, he said, were 'a race of people poor at home who sought abroad a toilsome life by foreign service', adding that 'they decline not civil war if they are paid for it'.

While England attracted many whose seigneurs followed William, others made their own way into France, following traditional routes along the Loire and down the coast to La Rochelle and the Garonne, preferring to settle in cities where there were opportunities for employment as clerks, craftsmen, traders, and labourers. But it was Paris that provided the principal attraction. By the end of the thirteenth century Bretons were the second largest group of émigrés in the city after the British. Why there should have been such an exodus from Brittany is a complex issue. Population growth was certainly a factor, particularly in the counties of Rennes and Nantes. Continual rivalry of the elites created uncertainty and dislocations, while the emancipation of the serfs in the mid-tenth century freed the labouring class, allowing them a new mobility. Social bonds were slackening and the idea of movement, encouraged in part by the Crusades, was in the air: the small world of the Breton *plebes* was now suddenly becoming much larger.

Émigrés finding themselves in alien and often hostile environments bond together to provide mutual support. Bretons who settled in France and England, speaking poor French, or no French at all, were often the butt of derision, creating tensions which encouraged the Breton communities to maintain their cohesion. That they did this with some pride is shown by their names: Haimo *patria Brito*, Johannes Britto *vir literatus*, and Riuallonius *Britannicus gente*. Their language and their nostalgia for the homeland meant that Bretons abroad were able to hold onto and to cherish their peninsular origins.

The extent to which the Breton diaspora was responsible for disseminating the tales embedded in the oral literature of the Brittonic-speaking countries (Brittany, Cornwall, Wales, and Cumbria) is a fascinating issue. That the Old French romances written in the twelfth century by Chrétien de Troyes, Marie de France, and others contain stories and names derived from the Brittonic tradition is not in doubt (below, pp. 384–5). The question is, by what means were they transmitted? One popular view is that it was the wandering minstrels (*jongleurs*) and storytellers (*conteurs*), sometimes travelling under the patronage of Breton lords, sometimes following their own fortunes, that led to the spread of the tales across France and England. This does not, of course, preclude the possibility that some written texts may also have been involved in the transmission. Indeed, Geoffrey of Monmouth, who wrote his famous *History of the Kings of Britain* in the early twelfth century, speaks of having access to an old Breton book which he used to craft the earlier section of his own book (below, p. 382). Whether from old texts or from wandering storytellers, the tales of the Arthurian romance were taken up with enthusiasm by the literate elite of England and France. In these various ways Brittany gained a reputation as a strange, romantic place, its rugged culture very different from that of other parts of Europe.

soleil leuant

Icy assemblent la ripuire de
Villaigne et isle.

La ripuiere d'Albron

de isle

8

OUR NATION OF BRITTANY

1148–1532

G EOGRAPHY matters, and at no time was this more apparent to the Bretons than in the later Middle Ages, when their nearest neighbours, the French and the English, involved in interminable conflict, used Brittany as a pawn—a convenient place to play out their power struggles. From the Breton point of view this was not entirely unwelcome since powerful neighbours could be manipulated by rival dynasties in their contested leadership claims, but it was a delicate game: allies could easily become oppressors. In this way, over four hundred years or so, diplomatic marriages and hastily negotiated alliances gave the English and the French an excuse to send their armies into Brittany when it became expedient for them to do so. For the febrile Breton polities, allying themselves to one side or another may have given them a brief advantage, but it also made them increasingly conscious of their need to preserve their freedom and identity.

In England, following the death of William the Conqueror in 1087, it took some while for the power struggle to settle down. William was succeeded by his third son, William Rufus, and when he died in 1100 his younger brother Henry became king of England. Six years later Henry managed to wrest the dukedom of Normandy from his eldest brother, Robert. The succession following Henry I's death in 1135 proved to be complicated. Henry had no legitimate sons but there was a daughter, Matilda, who had married Geoffrey, count of Anjou. The marriage was very unpopular with the English barons and on Henry's death they saw to it that his nephew Stephen succeeded to the throne. In the nineteen years to follow, with Matilda vigorously contesting Stephen's right to rule, England descended into a period of anarchy and civil war during which, as we have seen (above, p. 264), the different Breton factions holding land in England fought on different sides. Meanwhile, on the continent, Matilda's husband, Geoffrey, conquered Normandy and assumed the title of duke of Normandy. On his death in 1149 their son Henry succeeded to his father's dukedom, two years later becoming count of Anjou. Henry of Anjou was now 19 years old. The following year, in 1152, he married Eleanor of Aquitaine and assumed the title of duke of Aquitaine in 1153. In England, as the trauma of the anarchy continued, the exhausted barons and the nervous Church got together to discuss what would happen on Stephen's death. The solution, most agreed, was to offer the English crown to Henry, the grandson of Henry I. So it was that on 19 December 1154 Henry, duke of Normandy, duke of Aquitaine, and count of Anjou, Touraine, and Maine, was crowned Henry II, king of England.

Through succession and marriage Henry had acquired a huge Atlantic-facing empire stretching from Scotland to the Pyrenees. He had inherited England, Normandy, and Anjou, Touraine, and Maine from his father, and through marriage had gained Aquitaine and Gascony. He could claim authority over the king of Scotland and the princes of Wales, and later he was to go on to attack and largely subdue Ireland and Brittany. His Angevin empire, as it is grandly called, was more a patchwork of disparate territories loosely tacked together. It lacked political coherence, but under Henry's brilliant leadership and that of his son and successor Richard I it was to hold together for half a century. But Richard's early death in 1199 left the succession in dispute once more, the contenders this time being his son John and his nephew Arthur. In the event, John became king of England and retained the dukedom of Normandy until 1204, while Arthur held Anjou, Touraine, and Maine.

The Angevin empire lay between Brittany and the royal domain of France, now under the rule of the Capetian house, whose territories centred on the region of Île de France. The political picture was, however, complicated by the fact that the French king held feudal rights over all the Angevin dukedoms in France. Thus, the English kings Henry II, Richard I, and John owed fealty to the king of France for their continental holdings. This delicate matter was managed quite successfully until 1204, when hostilities erupted and the French king, Philip II, declared war on John. The loss of Normandy in that year marked the beginning of the dismantlement of the English-led Angevin empire.

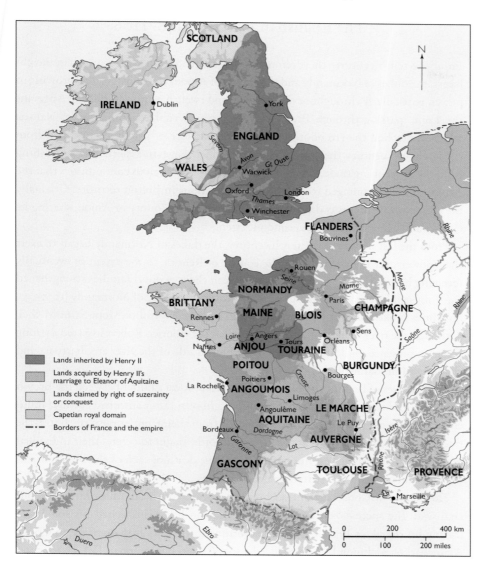

8.1 By inheritance, marriage, and conquest the Angevin empire grew until, by the late twelfth century, Henry II of England ruled over a vast territory stretching from the north of Scotland to the Pyrenees.

The English in Brittany, 1148–1206

From the tenth century, the Bretons had to contend with their immediate neighbours, the dukes of Normandy and the counts of Anjou, who were steadily growing in power, particularly throughout the eleventh and twelfth centuries. For the Angevins the Loire, passing through Breton territory, was a vital economic route. Nantes, which controlled the river-borne traffic, was therefore of prime interest, and from the late tenth century the city was brought under Angevin supervision, flourishing from the burgeoning trade, much of it managed by the religious communities that the Angevins had encouraged to set up their institutions in Breton territory. Gradually the county of Nantes was drawn into the sphere of the county of Anjou, sharing its culture and benefiting from its economic strength.

From the last decade of the tenth century, the dukes of Normandy began to exert their power over their neighbour, the county of Rennes, to the extent of eventually receiving homage. Arranged marriages between the two ducal families strengthened the links still further, but during the reign of Robert I, duke of Normandy (1027–35), hostilities broke out over boundary disputes and the control of Mont-Saint-Michel. Although the river Couesnon was recognized as the frontier, Robert asserted a strong Norman presence, building a castle on the Breton side of the river at Cherrueix and claiming Mont-Saint-Michel.

The counties of Rennes and Nantes continued to form a buffer between the Breton peninsula and their Norman and Angevin neighbours. They absorbed cultural influences from France and benefited economically from their frontier position, but in the fractious politics of the time, as the minor warlords fought to extend their individual power bases, life was at best uncertain, and at the death of each of the Breton dukes the question of succession stirred up deep enmities.

The demise of Conan III in 1148 brought matters to a head, unleashing a vicious civil war. The succession was complicated. Conan had disinherited his son Hoël, leaving his daughter Bertha as principal claimant. Bertha's first marriage to Count Alain, earl of Richmond, had produced a son, Conan (later Conan IV). Her second marriage was to Eudon, vicomte de Porhoët. On Conan III's death, Eudon immediately claimed the dukedom on his wife's behalf. Brittany was now divided between Hoël and Eudon, with other lords taking advantage of the conflict to forward their own interests. During this time Conan, Bertha's son by Alain, had been living in England under the protection of Henry II. In 1156, with Henry's approval, he sailed to Brittany and made for Rennes, driving out his stepfather, Eudon, who fled to France. Meanwhile, the citizens of Nantes had expelled Hoël and power had been seized by Geoffrey, the younger brother of Henry II. When, two years later, in 1158, Geoffrey died, Conan IV made a rapid move to seize Nantes before Henry could reach the city. By this action he reunited the duchy of Brittany but was politically astute enough to acknowledge his subservience to Henry.

Brittany was now part of the Angevin empire and was increasingly to be administered as such, its two chief officers, the seneschal and the justiciar, reporting directly to Henry II while Conan IV retreated to his estates, the lordship of Guingamp in Brittany and the north Yorkshire estate of Richmond, which he visited on a number of occasions. In 1160 Conan IV married Marguerite, sister of the king of Scotland. When their daughter Constance was born, it was agreed that she should marry Henry's fourth son, Geoffrey. This contract firmly linked the two families and gave Henry even greater control of Brittany, until, that is, the two were married in 1181 and Geoffrey became duke of Brittany.

The Breton lords did not respond well to Angevin government, which was far more restrictive than they had been used to. In 1166 unrest grew to outright rebellion, but the insurgents were defeated at Fougères. Over the next fifteen years there were eight further uprisings, all put down with force, resulting in massacres and ransoms generating increasing levels of hatred. Resistance to Angevin rule fostered a greater sense of Breton identity, manifest now in nostalgia for a heroic past embedded deep in the myths of the Arthurian legend, a time when it was believed the independent Bretons had enjoyed their greatest military successes.

Conan IV had died in 1171 and for the next ten years, until his daughter Constance married Geoffrey, Henry II acted as protector of the duchy, intensifying his control of the turbulent Breton lords. After the two were married, things began to change in favour of a more tolerant attitude towards the Bretons, not least because Geoffrey had no love of his father, but his death in a tournament in Paris in 1186 brought the interlude to an end and Constance had to see out the rest of her time as duchess of Brittany under the repressive rule of Henry II, Richard I, and John until she died in 1201. Her concern, and that of her loyal supporters, was that her son Arthur, born after Geoffrey's sudden death, would succeed her, but lacking trust in the English she sent Arthur to the court of the French king, Philip Augustus, where he was brought up with the king's son Louis. It was a bold and provocative move and added a new thread to an already complex network of intrigue.

The French Capetian royalty had kept a distant eye on events in Brittany without taking any direct part for some while, but they had given permission for Henry II to involve himself in Breton affairs. But when Geoffrey, now duke of Brittany, began to quarrel with his father, Henry II, they began to show a more active concern, not least because of the close friendship that had developed between Geoffrey and Philip Augustus. On Geoffrey's death it was understandable, then, that Philip Augustus should look to protect Geoffrey's children. Geoffrey's daughter Aliénor had already been taken virtual hostage by Henry II, but his son Arthur was now safely in the Capetian court and could be used as a pawn in Philip's dealings with the English king, John, who had succeeded Richard I. Philip's grand scheme was to wrest the Angevin state from English control, and events now moved fast. In 1202 the French began their onslaught by campaigning deep into Normandy and Anjou. The following year John retaliated by capturing and murdering Arthur, an act that inflamed the Bretons, who now rose in revolt against the English. Having consolidated his mastery of Normandy and Anjou, Philip moved, in 1206, to take control of Brittany. The duchess Constance had died five years earlier. Of her children, Aliénor was held by the English, Matilda had died, and Arthur had been murdered. This left Alix, the only child of her third marriage, to Guy de Thouars. At Nantes, Philip recognized Alix as the rightful heir to the duchy, a decision which had the support of the leading Breton lords and churchmen, but until the child was old enough to marry, her father was appointed her guardian.

Philip's decisive actions had driven a wedge through the middle of the Angevin empire, bringing Brittany firmly into the French sphere: it was to the Capetian royal house that the dukes of Brittany now owed their allegiance.

The Capetian Dukes, 1206–1341

To consolidate further the link between the dukedom of Brittany and the French royal house, Philip arranged for a member of his family, Pierre, second son of the comte de Dreux, to marry Alix in 1213. Pierre, whose sobriquet was Mauclerc, reflecting his harsh attitude to the Church, was a flamboyant and unpredictable character always looking for a fight with authority, be it with the Breton lords, the clergy, or even the French king. When, in 1237, his son Jean came of age and took over the dukedom, Pierre devoted his energies to privateering adventures against English shipping, and to crusading. He died in 1250 on his way back to France from wounds he had received in Egypt.

The succession passed without upset directly through the male line—Jean I, Jean II, Arthur II, and Jean III—until 1341, creating a degree of stability. The squabbling nobility could now devote their excess energies to minor land disputes, overseas service, and crusading, leaving successive dukes to focus on reforms that strengthened the Breton state, curtailed the right of the clergy, and enabled them to increase substantially their own wealth and power. All this was played out against a robust diplomacy balancing the rights and demands of the French royal house with the possible advantage of alliances with the English. Personal power dominated everything: without it the dukes were at the mercy of their feudal lords. From the outset, Pierre Mauclerc imposed his authority with force, and violent confrontations continued throughout the reign of his son Jean I, but Jean also adopted more subtle means of control by making generous loans and then confiscating estates when repayments were not forthcoming. By weaponizing money in this way, the level of outright violence decreased and wasteful destruction was avoided.

Mauclerc was not afraid to tackle the Church, which had grown excessively rich through ecclesiastical taxes. The tax of *tierçage*, which allowed the parish priest to claim one-third of the furniture of the deceased and the post-nuptial tax of 40 sols on every marriage, was abolished at a meeting of the feudal lords held at Redon in 1227. The Pope immediately responded by excommunicating the duke and banning all religious offices and sacraments, an act which caused dismay throughout Brittany. Three years later, under considerable pressure, the decision made at Redon was revoked in return for the Pope lifting the excommunication and the ban. But the battle to restrict the power of the Church was continued by Jean I and Jean II and was not resolved until the reign of Arthur II (1305–12) when *tierçage* was cut to one-ninth and the post-nuptial tax was reduced for all and abolished altogether for the poor.

Relations with the French court were delicate. The dukes of Brittany were vassals of the French kings and Mauclerc was content to accept this throughout the reign of Philip Augustus and Louis VIII, but after Louis's death he began to develop closer ties with Henry III of England. Henry had helped to persuade the Pope to lift sanctions on Pierre and the Bretons, proving himself to be a useful ally. In 1230 Mauclerc wrote to the new king of France, Louis IX, saying that he did not consider himself to be subservient to the king and would no longer pay homage to him. Encouraged by appeals from Breton lords opposed to Pierre's Anglophile tendencies, Louis marched on Brittany with a powerful army. The two sides met at Saint-Aubin-du-Cormier, where a truce was agreed and the French withdrew, having been assured that the pro-French Breton barons would keep Pierre in order. But Mauclerc continued his negotiations with Henry III, who offered him the inducement of the Richmond estates in Yorkshire. France responded in 1234 by sending three large forces against Brittany, in the face of which Mauclerc submitted. His flirtation with the English had been brief and had come to nothing, but the response of the Breton lords had shown that many of their number were strongly pro-French and totally opposed to those whose interest lay across the Channel: it was a foretaste of things to come.

Later, dukes occasionally displayed an interest in links with England. When, in 1294, war broke out between France and England, Jean II briefly sided with the English, but when the English and Welsh started to raid the Breton coast, he thought better of it. Later, Jean III accepted the Richmond estates, thus becoming a vassal of the English king. But these were minor episodes. For the most part the dukes were content with the relationship of trust and interdependence that was growing with the French.

Over time Brittany acquired a level of independence. In law, for example, appeals against judgments would pass from the first court to more senior courts ending with the seneschals of Nantes and Rennes, and from there to the Parlement of Brittany. The final court of appeal lay with the Parlement at Paris. In 1297 it was agreed that only cases claiming false judgment or denial of justice should come before the king. In the early fourteenth century the laws of Brittany were first codified in *La Très Ancienne Coutume*. About the same time there is the first mention of the Chambre des Comptes, the office that oversaw the ducal accounts. The dukes also issued their own coinage from mints in Rennes and Nantes but with occasional oversight from France to maintain parity. Gradually, then, Brittany acquired some of the attributes of a state, but still the dominating power of France remained. To prevent the dukedom from being drawn further into the orbit of France, Jean III managed to obtain a charter laying out the privileges enjoyed by Brittany. In this document Breton administrative autonomy was confirmed and guaranteed.

The hundred and forty years or so of comparative stability under the Capetian dukes had allowed Brittany to become a more coherent polity. After the disruptive squabbles among the elite that characterized the regency of the over-energetic Pierre Mauclerc, the country had settled down under dukes whose interests lay primarily in building the state. The uncontested succession from father to son and the fact that the reigns were long (Jean I held the dukedom for forty-nine years) created conditions in which society could begin to build a network of systems that bound it together offering a new stability. In such times the economy could flourish and the people could begin to appreciate the benefits of peace.

The War of Succession, 1341–1365

On 30 April 1341 Jean III died. There being no legitimate children from his three wives, the succession was in doubt. Jean had believed that the solution was for the duchy to pass to the French king, but the idea was unanimously rejected by the Breton Parlement. There were two possible lines of succession, either through his brother Guy or through his half-brother Jean de Montfort. Guy had died ten years earlier but had a daughter, Jeanne de Penthièvre, who had married Charles de Blois. Under the customs of Brittany, which allowed female succession, Jeanne was the legitimate heir, but under French feudal law Jean de Montfort, the closest relative, had the strongest claim. Since both contestants believed themselves to be the rightful heir, the scene was set for another bloody conflict.

What followed was directly influenced by the deteriorating relationship between France and England. In 1328 the last of the Capetian kings of France had died and the throne passed through his daughter to Philip VI of the house of Valois. One of the possible claimants to the French throne was Edward III of England, who still held the dukedom of Gascony, a remnant of the now dismembered Angevin empire. Edward decided at the time not to contest the succession, instead paying homage to the new king for his Gascony holding. All this changed in 1337 when Philip seized Gascony. Edward's immediate response was to claim the throne of France, and thus began the long-drawn-out conflict that became known as the Hundred Years War. Brittany, by virtue of its position commanding the sea-route between England and Gascony, was of direct strategic interest to England. It also offered the attractive prospect of opening up another front with France, drawing forces from other regions where the war between England and France was now raging. For this reason Edward III decided to engage in the Breton conflict by taking the side of Jean de Montfort, since Philip VI had offered French support for Charles de Blois. Although the battle lines moved over time, the north and east of Brittany tended to support de Blois while the south and west sided with Montfort. This can, to some extent, be explained by the fact that de Blois had the support of the Francophile counties of Rennes and Nantes in the east and his wife's estate of Penthièvre lay in the north. The ports of the south and west, on the other hand, benefited from the lively maritime trade between Gascony and England. Although the political players were different, it was a reflection of the old geographical divide, which had moulded Brittany since prehistoric times.

For an account of what was to follow one has to rely largely on the *Chronicles* of Jean Froissart (*c*.1337–*c*.1405), a court historian born in the Low Countries who spent time travelling through western Europe, including seven years or so in the court of Edward III. Froissart was in love with the chivalric age and lavishly embroidered his *Chronicles* with the daring deeds and romance of the genre, but beneath it all is a narrative that seems to be reasonably reliable. At the outset, in July 1341, before any decisions were made about the succession, Edward sent an envoy to Montfort, then installed in Nantes, offering his support. It was a clear signal that the English were prepared to use the opportunity to confront French interests in Brittany. A commission appointed by Philip VI to advise on the succession finally reported in early September in favour of Charles de Blois, and Montfort, who was in Paris at the time, fled for Brittany to rally support for his cause, his resolve strengthened when, later

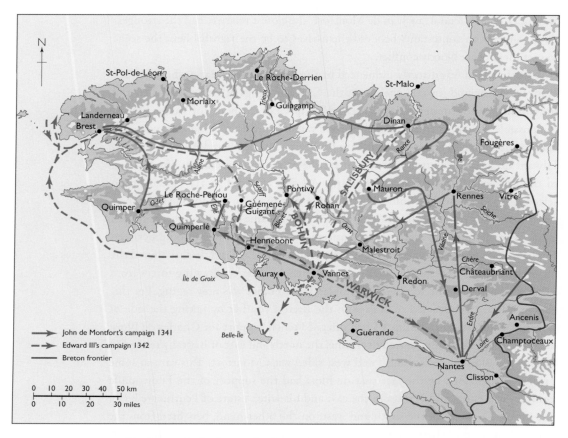

8.2 The Breton Civil War was fought out between 1341 and 1365 by armies supporting different contenders for the duchy of Brittany. Military campaigns embraced the whole of the country. The English were intimately involved.

in the month, Edward awarded him the estates of Richmond, which had been the preserve of the dukes of Brittany. So the battle lines were set.

Shorn of its chivalric embellishments the outline of the story may be briefly told. In a rapid move Philip VI sent his son John, duke of Normandy, with a large army to besiege Nantes. Within three weeks the town had surrendered and Montfort was taken prisoner. Thereupon his wife, Jeanne de Flanders, took over leadership of his cause, entering into a formal alliance with Edward III. Throughout 1342 several English detachments arrived, the last, led by Edward himself, landing at Brest at the end of October. The English then set about establishing a series of fortified positions around the south and west coasts from Guérande to Morlaix while the Franco-Bretons consolidated their hold on Nantes and took Rennes and Vannes. Engagement began when Edward made an unsuccessful attempt to capture Vannes, but Philip VI, who was now leading the Franco-Breton forces, refused to meet the English in the field. A stand-off followed, during which mediation by the Pope's representatives resulted in a truce signed at Malestroit in January 1343. The two kings then departed, leaving senior officers in charge of the field armies, Edward taking with him Montfort's wife, Jeanne, and her two children.

The truce was broken by both sides, resulting in a number of minor actions, which allowed the English to capture Vannes. Then, early in 1345, Montfort escaped from Paris, where he had been held prisoner, briefly rejoining his family at the court of Edward III before returning to Brittany in June with another English force. A few months later he was dead, brought down by an infected wound inflicted some years before. Since his son and heir, Jean, was now only 5 years old, Edward remained the proxy leader of the Montfort faction. Two years later, at La Roche-Derrien, Charles de Blois was captured and sent to England, leaving leadership of Franco-Breton partly to his wife, Jeanne de Penthièvre.

And so the war dragged on, the Anglo-Bretons and Franco-Bretons slogging it out, interrupted by ineffectual truces and weakened by the Black Death that took its toll in the years 1348–9. Few parts of Brittany escaped the effects of the war. Towns were besieged, ransoms were demanded, and, as always in these situations, it was the ordinary people who suffered. Among the main players, Jean de Montfort, now 16, was brought to Brittany in 1355 by the duke of Lancaster and took part in attacks on the Penthièvre estates before returning to England. It was little more than a political gesture, but seven years later, in 1362, he was sent back to Brittany by Edward III, deemed mature enough now to assume his position as claimant to the duchy. The end finally came in 1364 when an army led by Charles de Blois (who had been allowed to return to Brittany after paying a huge ransom) met an Anglo-Breton force besieging Auray. In the ensuing carnage Charles and many of his followers were killed and others were taken prisoner. The war had now been going on for twenty-three years and exhaustion and disillusionment had set in. On hearing news of the battle, Charles's wife, Jeanne de Penthièvre, decided to concede defeat, either because she wished to end the suffering of the Breton people or because she was just too tired to go on. That the battle was decisive and the Montforts had won the right to the dukedom was also conceded by the French king, now Charles V.

The treaty announced at Guérande on Easter Saturday 1365 confirmed Jean de Montfort as the successor to his uncle Jean III, while Jeanne de Penthièvre, who had so valiantly defended the claim of her family, was allowed to retain her land and her title, duchess, on the understanding that the family would make no further claims to the dukedom unless the Montforts failed to produce a male heir. On 13 December

8.3 The doublet worn by Charles de Blois, who contested the dukedom against Jean de Montfort.

1366 Jean IV reluctantly paid homage to Charles V, acknowledging Brittany's subservient position to the French Crown.

The War of Succession had been long and costly, driven by the ambitions of the Breton ruling households and manipulated by the English and French kings in their long struggle for supremacy. In Brittany it had enlivened the old divide between east and west, between those comfortable to sit close to the continent and to France and those for whom the sea offered freedom of action. For the elite the conflict offered the opportunity to enhance status and to expand estates; for the poor, unwillingly involved, there was little to gain and much to lose.

Characters in Action

The narrative of the long-drawn-out civil war was enlivened by acts of chivalry selected and embellished by near-contemporary chroniclers like Jean Froissart and retold with additional flourishes in the ballads that proliferated in the aftermath of the conflict. Over time these brightly lit acts of valour became the story, while the drudgery and sheer horror of it all faded from memory. One of the characters to be given prominence as the heroine of the hour was Jeanne de Flanders, the wife of Jean de Montfort. When Montfort was imprisoned in Paris, she became leader of his cause. Having mustered an army and captured Redon, she went on to Hennebont, where her force was besieged by Charles de Blois. One night, seeing the enemy camp unguarded, she led a raiding party of three hundred men and set fire to the camp (earning the sobriquet Jeanne la Flamme). Her return cut off, she marched to Brest, took the town, and returned with reinforcements to Hennebont to await the arrival of the English relieving force she had requested from Edward III. When it arrived, she took ship to England to seek further help from Edward. Given an assurance of support, she returned to Brittany, but the English convoy in which she was travelling was attacked by a force loyal to Charles, and in the sea battle that ensued Jeanne took part in the fierce hand-to-hand fighting. The English won and went on to take Vannes and besiege Rennes. Her heroics impressed Froissart: she had, he said, 'the courage of a man and the heart of a lion'.

Another of the flamboyant characters of this time was Bertrand du Guesclin (1320–80), who spent his life fighting for the French king in France, Brittany, and Spain. In Brittany he was a supporter of the Penthièvre claim. One of the stories told of him is that, when he learned that his younger brother had been dishonourably captured by the English knight Thomas of Canterbury during the siege of Rennes in 1365, he demanded the satisfaction of a duel. In hand-to-hand combat Thomas was killed. Honour redeemed, Guesclin went on to lead the relief of Rennes. Whether the duel ever happened is in doubt, but it was a good story, one that readers of Froissart were happy to believe.

But perhaps the most famous event of the War of Succession was the Combat of the Thirty. In one of the many stalemates during the war, two neighbouring towns, held by different factions, confronted each other. Ploërmel was controlled by the Montforts under the command of Robert Bemborough, and Josselin was held by the

8.4 The Combat of the Thirty took place at Chêne de Mi-Voie in 1351 between troops loyal to de Blois and Montfortists commanded by an Englishman, Robert Bemborough. It was a pre-arranged set-piece combat between men chosen from the rival forces, conducted according to the best chivalric tradition. The illustration comes from the *Compillation des cronicques et ystoires des Bretons* by Pierre Le Baud, published in 1480.

Blois faction, led by Jean de Beaumanoir. To relieve the monotony, Beaumanoir challenged Bemborough to single combat. Bemborough replied by suggesting a tournament involving thirty knights on each side. Froissart chose to present it as an act of chivalry fought for the honour of the ladies of the two contesting parties Jeanne de Flanders and Jeanne de Penthièvre. So on 26 March 1351 at Chêne de Mi-Voie, midway between the towns, the two teams of combatants met. Beaumanoir commanded thirty pro-French Bretons while Bemborough led a force of twenty English, six Germans, and four Bretons. The engagement lasted all day. After several hours a halt was agreed for refreshment and first aid. The fighting then resumed and by the end of the day Beaumanoir was declared the victor. Nine of the English side were dead, including Bemborough, and at least three of the French. The survivors all suffered horrific injuries. Honour had been done and those taken prisoner were released for a small ransom. All were agreed it was a supreme example of the finest chivalry. But it had achieved nothing.

Froissart was writing his *Chronicles* at a time when the chivalric age was coming to a close. He dwelt with evident nostalgia on the more colourful flourishes of the War of Succession. These events were to become part of Breton folk culture, helping later generations to visualize and to verbalize their Breton identity. For some the Combat of the Thirty was the triumph of the Bretons (Franco-Bretons) over the foreign English invader; others, opposed to French domination, were more wary of applauding the result. Yet, while the ambivalence remained, the war allowed the Bretons to place themselves as a distinct ethnic entity in the centre of the great events that were shaping Europe.

The Last Dukes, 1365–1461

When Jean IV knelt before Charles V of France in December 1366 and the bishop of Saint-Brieuc read out a statement saying that the duke was performing homage 'in the manner and form in which it used to be offered and rendered by his ancestors', the Bretons were making it clear that their subservience to the French monarch, though acknowledged, was of a minor register. Later dukes emphasized this by standing armed during the ceremony. But it was in both sides' interests to maintain harmonious relations as far as possible. For Jean IV this was not easy. He owed his victory to English support, and his mother, Jeanne, remained confined in England by Edward III until her death in 1374 at the age of 79. He still depended on the Richmond estate for part of his income, but perhaps of more pressing interest was the flourishing trade with England, which brought prosperity to many Breton towns. Clearly there was a careful balance to be maintained, made more delicate by the still raw memories of the war that had divided the Breton nobility into pro-English and pro-French camps.

In 1369, when hostilities erupted again between France and England, Jean IV entered an ill-advised alliance with the English, but this proved to be very unpopular. The arrival of French troops in Brittany in 1373 forced him to flee to England and Guesclin was installed as constable to rule Brittany on behalf of the French king. When it became clear that the French were intent on confiscating the duchy altogether, an influential group of Bretons made up of nobility, churchmen, and representatives from the towns appealed to Jean to return, and on 3 August 1379 the duke landed at Dinard to an enthusiastic reception. The unwillingness of Guesclin to engage in another civil war, coinciding with the death of the French king, meant that there was little resistance, and in April 1381 a second treaty was agreed at Guérande by which Jean IV renounced his alliance with the enemies of France and renewed his homage to the king. Thereafter he and his successors were able gently to play off the English and French without provoking retaliation, while gradually enhancing the status of Brittany on the international stage through careful diplomacy and well-chosen marriage alliances. The foundation of a university at Nantes in 1460, with the support of the Pope, was an important symbol of the duchy's growing maturity as a state.

Jean V (1399–1442) was a master of the balancing act between England and France. He had married a daughter of Charles VI and had sent Breton troops to Agincourt, yet was able to remain on reasonably good terms with the English kings Henry IV and Henry V. That said, English ships raided the Breton coast causing much damage at Pointe Saint-Mathieu, Penmarc'h, and Guérande, while the Bretons retaliated, attacking Jersey and Guernsey and venturing as far as Plymouth and Dartmouth. These were largely pirate-led raids, and both countries worked to suppress them. But there were more extended involvements. In the autumn of 1400 a disenchanted Welsh landowner, Owain Glyndŵr, inspired a revolt against English rule and claimed the title of prince of Wales. The grievances of the rebels grew from the exploitation of tenants by the marcher lords and the rebellion spread quickly, its ramifications rumbling on until 1408. In the winter of 1405–6 a force of 2,500 Bretons landed at Milford Haven to support Glyndŵr. They were active in helping the Welsh take Carmarthen and Cardigan and also took part in the siege of Hereford. Although it is tempting to see this episode as Breton support for a Celtic neighbour against English repression, it is more likely to have been a French-inspired action, a tactic used to harass the English on their own island in the context of the ongoing Hundred Years War.

In 1420 an attempted coup by the lords of Clisson, heirs of the Penthièvre estates, threatened the stability of Brittany. Jean V was captured and imprisoned for some months, but the rebels were defeated by forces rallied by the duke's wife, Jeanne, with the help of the English king, Henry V. Accused of treason, the rebels' estates were confiscated and the Montfort dynasty emerged strengthened. The coup had been supported by the French king, and Jean V retaliated, moving more decisively to the English side by joining an alliance with the English and the duke of Burgundy in 1423 against Charles VII. Subsequent dukes, François I, Pierre II, and Arthur III, however, carefully redressed the balance by assisting the French cause in various ways as the Hundred Years War dragged to a close with the French conquest of Normandy and Gascony (1449–53). By skilful diplomacy Brittany had kept itself largely independent of France for nearly a hundred years. All this was about to change.

8.5 Many castles were built in Brittany during the Middle Ages and most had chequered histories. Tonquédec, commanding the valley of the Léguer south of Lannion, is a typical example. The original castle was built in the early thirteenth century but was dismantled by order of Jean IV in 1395. The present castle began construction in 1406 but was eventually dismantled by Richelieu in 1622.

The Beginning of the End of Breton Independence, 1461–1488

The accession of Louis XI to the French throne in July 1461 marked the beginning of the end of Breton independence. Nicknamed the Universal Spider, Louis was devious, manipulating, and determined. His web of intrigue was flung wide, entrapping many of the Breton nobility, whose pro-French leanings were strengthened when the king began to offer generous pensions to his supporters. His intention to absorb Brittany into the French state was made clear when, in 1480, he bought from Nicole de Bretagne, heiress of Penthièvre, her right to the duchy. Since the duke of Brittany, François II, had produced only daughters, Louis XI was preparing his claim to Brittany under the terms of the agreement that had concluded the Wars of Succession. He died three years later, but his death did not diminish the threat to Breton independence. While the French became emboldened, tensions between the pro- and anti-French parties in Brittany intensified. In 1487 French troops invaded, besieging Nantes. The response was a popular uprising throughout Brittany. More than sixty thousand Bretons, mostly from the west of the peninsula, together with sailors from Quimper and Guérande, marched on Nantes and relieved the siege. The next year the French were back and, having taken a few border towns, awaited the approach of the Breton army, a motley and disorganized band including English, Germans, Gascons, and Spaniards. On 28 July 1488 battle took place on the heathlands near Saint-Aubin-du-Cormier. The Breton army was defeated, with some six thousand losing their lives, and the towns of Saint-Malo and Dinan were taken. The duke, François II, now seriously weakened, was forced to agree peace terms arranged at Le Verger near Rennes a few weeks later. He swore allegiance to the French king, made over several towns and fortresses, agreed that his daughters were to be married only with the persuasion of the king, and accepted that the king's claim to the dukedom should be submitted to legal opinion. Three weeks later he was dead—the last duke of independent Brittany.

Meanwhile, an Uninvited Guest

In the late spring of 1471, François II, resident in Nantes, received two unexpected visitors: the Welshman Jasper Tudor and his 14-year-old nephew Henry Tudor. Henry had a distant claim to the English throne through the second marriage of his grandmother Katherine of Valois, widow of Henry V. He was therefore a Lancastrian, and it was from the defeat of the Lancastrian army at Tewkesbury in May 1471 that Jasper and Henry were fleeing. They had escaped to their native Wales, making for Tenby, where they boarded a ship intending to sail to France to join the court of Louis XI, who was Jasper's first cousin. Weather and currents took over, and instead of landing safely on French territory, their ship finally made land at Le Conquet in the west of Brittany. Their only option was to seek the hospitality of Duke François.

Their arrival in Brittany created an interesting political situation and they became pawns in the delicate three-sided relationship between the Bretons, French, and Yorkist rulers of England. While granted asylum by Duke François, their movements were restricted. They were first given lodging in the ducal château de Suscinio in the Morbihan, overlooking the sea, but were later moved to greater safety inland, Jasper to the château de Josselin and Henry to the château de Largoët in Elven, where there was no danger of them being captured by an English raiding party. At Largoët the young Henry Tudor was under the protection of Jean, lord of Rieux. That Henry's distant

8.6 Henry Tudor, who after the battle of Bosworth in 1485 became Henry VII of England, spent his youth from 1471 to 1483 in exile in Brittany under the protection of Duke François II. Though treated as an honoured guest, he was a pawn in the intrigues between the Bretons, the French, and the English. The portrait, by an unknown French painter, was made while Henry was in Brittany.

relation Owain Glyndŵr had been a supporter of Jean's grandfather will have given them something to talk about during the long winter evenings.

To the Yorkist house, now ruling England, Henry Tudor, free on the continent, posed a potential threat and they were keen to have him back under their control in England. Political overtures were made and eventually, in 1476, eager to establish good relations with the English king, Edward IV, François agreed that Henry should

8.7 For the early years of his exile Henry Tudor was housed in the ducal castle of Suscinio (pictured here) close to the Morbihan coast but was later moved inland to Largoët to be safe from potential kidnappers coming by sea.

be returned, assuaging his conscience with an assurance from Edward that he would restore Henry to his inheritance and arrange a good marriage for him. Henry was taken to Vannes and handed to English envoys, who took him to Saint-Malo to board a ship to England, but Henry managed to escape and took sanctuary in the cathedral, giving François's advisers time to persuade the duke that it was probably not wise to extradite him after all. The chastened duke apologized to Henry for his misjudgement and faced the fury of the Yorkists for his change of heart. For the next seven years Henry remained an honoured hostage of the Bretons.

In April 1483 Edward IV died, and in the chaos that followed, the king's younger brother Richard claimed the crown to become Richard III. Many, including Yorkists, were unhappy with this turn of events and began to look to Henry Tudor to replace the unpopular Richard. Seeing opportunity in the fast-changing situation, Duke François allowed Henry, whose value had suddenly increased, more freedom, and welcomed the English dissidents who were now arriving in Brittany to support Henry's cause. The situation had been transformed, and late in the year, at Vannes Cathedral, Henry swore to lead his supporters and to claim the English throne. Later, at Rennes, to strengthen his claim he pledged to marry Elizabeth of York, Edward's eldest daughter, and thus to unite the warring factions and bring the Wars of the Roses to an end.

If Henry were to become king of England, the Breton dukedom would gain a powerful ally in their struggle against the French. Some in François's court, however, believed the future to lie with Richard III and began to plot to hand Henry over to the English king. Hearing of this, Henry, Jasper, and their supporters decided to flee to the comparative safety of France and in September 1484 crossed the border to seek the support of Louis XI, which was willingly given. After eleven months of preparation, on 1 August Henry's force sailed from Honfleur for Pembrokeshire. Three weeks later, having defeated Richard III on the battlefield of Bosworth, he was declared king of England.

Henry Tudor, now King Henry VII, had good reason to remember the support he had received from Duke François during his thirteen-year residence in Brittany. When he had heard of the plot against Henry, François had been outraged, sending his apologies and giving safe passage to Henry's followers who had remained in Brittany. He also sent financial support. No doubt the rules of hospitality required such recompense, but François knew that he was backing a winner and could expect some return from his investment.

The Final Decades of the Dukedom, 1488–1532

The death of Duke François II in September 1488 meant that the country's fate now rested with his elder daughter, Anne, who was 11 years old. While the politicians immediately began marriage negotiations and a reluctant and rather stubborn Anne, now Duchess Anne, established herself in Rennes, French forces invaded Brittany. Within a few weeks they had taken Guingamp, Lannion, Morlaix, Brest, and Carhaix in the north and Concarneau and Vannes in the south. The immediate response was another popular uprising in the west supported by six thousand English troops who had landed in Morlaix. Presenting the English intervention to the Pope, the English papal ambassador explained that Henry VII was 'compelled at present to defend the Breton interests, both on account of the immense benefits conferred on him by the late Duke in the time of his misfortunes, and likewise for the defence of his own kingdom'.

8.8 In 1522 a flotilla of sixty English ships carried out an attack on Morlaix in retaliation for a raid on Bristol made by Breton corsairs. Recognizing the vulnerability of Morlaix, a fort, the château du Taureau, was built on a rocky island further downriver to protect the approaches to the town by sea. The fort was in operation by 1544.

Though acknowledging his debts to the Bretons, the king was careful to insist that they must bear the cost of the English intervention.

Two weeks later two thousand Spanish troops arrived, and by July 1489 the French holdings were reduced to a few border towns and the port of Brest. Anne, meanwhile, having promised Charles VIII to expel foreign troops, raised a force to contain the rebellion. Brittany was again polarized into pro- and anti-French factions with the pro-French supporters coalescing around Anne. The failure of Henry to send the reinforcements he had promised weakened the resolve of the Breton rebels, and by the winter of 1491 all serious resistance was spent.

A year earlier Anne had symbolically married Maximilian of Austria. Now, after five years of debilitating conflict, her advisers realized that the only way out of the impasse was for her to marry Charles VIII. And so at Langeac, on 6 December 1491, the duchess of Brittany married the king of France, in effect bringing to an end Breton independence.

8.9 The Duchess Anne (1477–1514). Anne became duchess of Brittany at the age of 11. Her marriage to two kings of France in succession, Charles VIII in 1491 and Louis XII in 1498, was the first step in the integration of Brittany and France, which was formalized by an Edict of Union in 1532. The illustration comes from a painting by Jean Bourdichon and dates to between 1503 and 1508.

Henry VII had not quite given up, and in October 1492 he landed with a huge army at Calais threatening to invade France. It was an impressive show of strength and could in part be presented as a response to the French taking control of Brittany. However, the promise of a massive annual payment from the French encouraged him to withdraw. For the English, the power game had moved on and Brittany was no longer of any real consequence.

The process of integrating Brittany with France was to take forty years to complete. Charles VIII died in 1498 and the following year Anne married his successor, Louis XII. By the time Anne died in 1514 the political union of Brittany and France was well under way. In the absence of male children the dukedom passed to Claude, the daughter of Anne and Louis XII, but the legal situation was still delicate. To bring matters to a conclusion, Claude's husband, François I (king of France 1515–49), encouraged the French États-Généraux (General Assembly) to debate the issue of union with France. This they did in August 1532, the meeting ending with a vote in favour of the union. The edict signed on 8 September 1532 at Le Plessis-Macé near Angers declared 'the perpetual union of Brittany and France' and guaranteed the 'privileges, rights and exemptions' of the Breton people. Brittany was to keep its own États-Généraux and Parlement with their own administration. No new taxes could be imposed without the agreement of the Breton États. Bretons would be tried by Breton courts and no Breton would be eligible for military service outside Brittany. Ecclesiastical positions in Brittany would be held by Bretons. Representatives from the États would serve on the French États, and in Brittany the French king would be represented by a governor appointed from either the Breton elite or the French royal family. For many in Brittany, exhausted by the perpetual struggle with France, this must have seemed a reasonable deal, with the real prospect of bringing to an end the destructive bouts of conflict which had devastated the country over the past centuries. For others it was an act of treason, selling the independence for which many had so long fought and died.

Brittany and the Sea

Geography determined that Brittany should play a significant part in the maritime commerce that developed during the Middle Ages. The creation of the Angevin empire in the twelfth century set in motion a steady trade between Gascony and England, principally driven by the demand for wine, huge quantities of which passed through the two principal Gascon ports, Bordeaux and Bayonne. But the two ports were rather different. While Bayonne was frequented by its own native sailors, who were prepared to carry goods for anyone, the ships using the harbour of Bordeaux came from many different countries. In one year in the fourteenth century for which reliable figures are available, of the two hundred ships leaving the port only five belonged to locally based entrepreneurs. The rest came from England, the Low Countries, Brittany, and Bayonne, with the English outnumbering all the others. At least thirty-five British ports, stretching from Milford Haven to Newcastle, traded with Bordeaux, and in 1409–10 two hundred English ships left for Bordeaux. But the quantity of wine imported into England was much greater than that. Port records from Bristol show that only half the wine arriving at the city came in Bristol-based ships, the rest being brought mainly by vessels from Bayonne and La Rochelle. By the mid-fifteenth century, the annual export of Gascon wine to England reached three million gallons, amounting to about a third of the total value of England's imports.

The Gascon trade had grown exponentially, with Bordeaux doubling in size by the end of the thirteenth century. As English vineyards were allowed to go out of production, so more and more land in the Bordelaise was given over to wine production. Both countries were now dependent on each other. Gascon wine flowed into England, while English cloth, grain, fish, and dairy products were unloaded at Bordeaux. The changing fortunes of the Hundred Years War caused the volume of trade to vary and there was real decline in the closing years, but it was of such importance to both countries that even after Bordeaux had been captured by the French, trade continued, and after the conflict was brought to a close with the Treaty of Picquigny in 1475, it quickly regained its former energy.

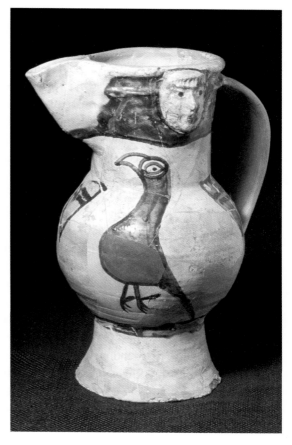

8.10 The wine trade between Bordeaux and Britain was at its height in the late thirteenth and early fourteenth centuries. In addition to casks of wine, the ships also carried polychrome pitchers for pouring the wine, which were made in the Saintonge region and became very popular in Britain and Brittany. This example, from Cardiff in south Wales, dates to 1275–1320.

The Gascon trade, important though it was, accounted for only part of the maritime commerce that fed the Atlantic ports. Castile and Portugal were important players. Early in the thirteenth century, ships from Castile were visiting English ports as well as Bruges and Arras, and ships from Oporto and Lisbon were sailing to England in increasing numbers after hostilities had broken out between England and Castile in 1340. The actual number of Portuguese ships making the journey in any one year was not large, in the peak years of 1378–80 never exceeding ten, but English shipowners were keen to develop the trading possibilities of Portugal. In the last quarter of the four-teenth century, about two-thirds of the vessels leaving Bristol were bound for Portugal carrying English cloth in return for wine. Trade increased throughout the fifteenth century, boosted by the new opportunities opened up by Portugal's colonization of the Atlantic islands, from which came sugar, oranges, pomegranates, and almonds.

Another factor boosting Atlantic trade was the Reconquista in Iberia as the Castilians gradually began to drive out the Muslim rulers. A crucial moment came in 1248 when Seville was taken by Ferdinand of Castile, thus opening up maritime routes between the Mediterranean and the Atlantic, allowing the Genoese and the Venetians access to the Atlantic trading system. In a pioneering voyage in 1277 Nicolozzo Spinola sailed his galley from Genoa to Sluys, the port for Ghent and Bruges, initiating a system that was to flourish for two hundred years. Thereafter fleets of galleys made the annual voyage from the Italian ports to England and Flanders laden with silks, damasks, luxury metalwork, fruit, spices, and alum (for processing fabrics), returning with raw wool, cloth, and tin.

This flood of maritime activity cannot fail to have had an impact on the lives of the Bretons. The Breton ports, particularly those along the south coast, provided welcome havens for ships to shelter and to take on provisions, and even if vessels leaving Galicia chose to sail across the Bay of Biscay, they would have had to contend with the terror of rounding Ushant. For some Bretons piracy offered a profitable lifestyle; others made a living from scavenging from wrecks. One lord of Léon claimed, in the thirteenth century, that a single well-located offshore rock brought him in a very comfortable annual income. The right to material recovered from shipwrecks (*lagan*) was valuable for coastal communities, but for the shipowners and those who employed them to carry cargoes it could spell financial ruin. To encourage trade and to safeguard the entrepreneurs, the Angevins who ruled Brittany between 1166 and 1186 introduced a system of offering *brefs de mer* in ports like Bordeaux and La Rochelle. These were safe conducts promising protection against piracy and the right to salvage in the event of a shipwreck. The *brefs* were issued under the authority of the dukes of Brittany and remained a substantial source of income throughout the Middle Ages.

Breton ports benefited considerably from maritime commerce. Nantes was the larg-est by virtue of its position on the river Loire. At the end of the fifteenth century it was providing for between fifteen hundred and two thousand vessels a year carrying an estimated cargo of about 20,000 tons, mostly of wine and salt. Nantes and other ports on the south Breton coast were also frequented by ships on the Atlantic route, particularly vessels like the Italian galleys which, because of the large complement of rowers they carried, were obliged to put into port several times to restock with food and water on the long journey from the Mediterranean. Having set sail from El Ferrol on the north coast of Galicia, the Venetian galleys made for La Rochelle or Nantes before rounding Brittany. The route taken by the galleys of their Genoese competitors tended to avoid the ports used by the Venetians. After leaving La Coruña they favoured smaller Breton ports like Quimperlé and Quimper. Captains plying the wine route between Gascony and England had their own favoured routes. Ships leaving Bordeaux would hug the south coast of Brittany before sailing round the Pointe du Raz and sighting Saint-Mathieu. From there, they would follow the coast of Léon, striking off north to Cornwall, Plymouth, or the Isle of Wight before completing their journey along the English coast to their port of disembarkation. In the early fifteenth century the journey from London to Bordeaux could take 100–150 days allowing for stopovers. But journeys and journey times could vary and some captains chose to leave out Brittany altogether. In 1488 a merchant ship, the *Margaret Cely*, left London for Plymouth, from there sailing direct to Blaye on the Gironde estuary not far from Bordeaux in twenty-two days. The ship's master was evidently intent to avoid Brittany at the time when the war between the invading French army and the Breton resistance was coming to a head.

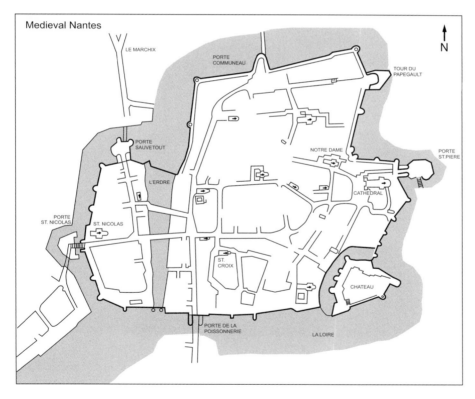

8.11 The fortification of Nantes by the late medieval period.

8.12 The strongly fortified city of Rennes commanding the crossing of the Vilaine in an illustration of 1543.

8.13 The salt-pans of Guérande contributed considerably to the local economy and salt was widely exported. In later medieval and early modern times salt was used in quantity for salting fish and became increasingly important as the Breton fishing fleet began to develop the Icelandic and Newfoundland fishing grounds.

In times of comparative peace the Breton ports, in addition to providing facilities for foreign ships in transit, were also the home bases of Breton sailors, who were becoming increasingly involved in trade. Bretons, like the men of Bayonne and the Basques, were known to be reliable carriers, prepared to shift cargoes for anyone wishing to employ them. By the late thirteenth century between a fifth and a quarter of the ships found in Bordeaux or Bayonne were Breton. They might arrive with cargoes of salt from the salt-pans in the estuary of the Loire and around the Baie de Bourgneuf, dried fish from the *sécheries* of Finistère, and linen and sailcloth from Léon, and return home with wine, wood, and iron ore. The more adventurous made for the Mediterranean. They were few at first. A vessel from Groix arrived in València in 1413, and in 1439 two Breton ships were recorded as having visited Genoa, but after 1480 the numbers making the journey rapidly increased. Breton shipwrights were also spreading knowledge of different styles of shipbuilding, especially the skeleton-first method of building carvels. About 1459 a Breton shipwright at Zealand in the Low Countries is said to have taught the locals the art of carvel building. By the early sixteenth century Bretons were known throughout western Europe as skilled and reliable sailors. Their involvement in the Atlantic system gave those who lived on the coast a keen sense of their independence and an awareness that in mastery of the sea lay their freedom.

'Our Nation of Brittany'

These words used by Duke Jean IV in 1364, in a pardon given to the bishop and citizens of Quimper for supporting Blois, are the earliest occasion when aspirations of nationhood are explicitly mentioned. The state grew gradually by accretion throughout the thirteenth and fourteenth centuries. The raw power of individuals had to be curtailed by the creation of systems of government giving consents and offering judgments while the increasing complexity of the duchy required specialists to ensure its efficient administration. In 1297 the king had formally recognized Jean II as duke of Brittany and as peer of France, an honour that required the duke to perform liege homage to the sovereign. While these obligations were largely symbolic, the king and his officials had the right to intervene in the running of the duchy. Subsequent dukes were intent on restricting these intrusions and the most effective way to do this was to introduce a parallel state structure to provide the appearance of autonomy.

The Parlement of Brittany was in existence by 1288: it met irregularly and was largely a judicial forum. The duchy was divided into eight bailliages, each presided over by a ducal seneschal who could receive appeals from the lower court. Appeals from the bailliages were referred upwards, the more contentious eventually appearing before the Parlement. Only in the cases claiming false judgment or denial of justice could a final appeal be made to the Parlement of Paris. The États-Généraux de Bretagne, in existence by 1352, was a formalization of the group of ducal advisers. It was made up of members of the nobility (First Estate), clergy (Second Estate), and representatives sent by the urban bourgeoisie (Third Estate). They met at least once a year in one of the major towns and their main function was to ensure that rights and privileges were maintained. Proposals to introduce new taxes and other restrictive measures required their approval. Another sign of state development was the creation of the Chambre des Comptes, which from the 1360s was responsible for levying certain taxes and for dealing with all public accounts, now separated from the private finances of the ducal household. Finally, the Chancery, an office where letters were issued in the name of the duke, which had originated in the early thirteenth century, rose to become a powerful organ of the state by the end of the fifteenth century, covering all matters from international relations down to the most trivial of administrative detail.

Alongside the increasingly complex administrative infrastructure, successive dukes were adopting the pretensions of kingly power: elaborate ceremonies, the creation of chivalric orders, and the right to ennoble and enfranchise. By the end of the fourteenth century the dukes had formed Brittany into a sovereign principality with its own separate identity, now powerful enough and wealthy enough to stand up for itself against the French king. It was in the interests of successive dukes to maintain the Breton state to counter the French threat, but they tended to do it by replicating the trappings of statehood practised by the French and Burgundian courts: there was surprisingly little direct reference to Breton's past. Admittedly, Charles de Blois, for all his pro-French leanings, was content to have himself portrayed in the window of a convent alongside Salomon and the other kings of Brittany, while Jean IV made payments to care for the relics of St Grallon. Nor should we forget the popularity of the name Arthur among the ducal family, used in homage to a mythical ancestor. But there was little sense of the more distant Celtic past or any stated reverence for the Breton language. Indeed, Breton was in retreat as French came to be widely accepted in the east of the country. In the ninth century Breton was spoken west of a line from Mont-Saint-Michel, via Rennes, to Saint-Nazaire. Three centuries later French had advanced westwards to a line between the mouth of the Vilaine and Saint-Brieuc.

The People and their Beliefs

The historical evidence, which deals largely with the actions of the elites, gives little hint of how the ordinary Bretons felt about their identity but a consideration of their religious beliefs and practices leaves no doubt that, in this aspect of their culture at least, the population of the Breton-speaking regions behaved in a very distinctive way. The Christian religion pervaded all aspects of life and was evident in the stone crosses that were everywhere to be seen, put up in liminal places where danger was believed to lurk, like crossroads and bridges and at the many springs and wells—entrances to the underworld—that in pre-Christian times had been presided over by Celtic deities. In many of the churchyards more elaborate crosses, calvaries, were erected, enhanced by scenes from the Crucifixion and other biblical stories to serve as open-air preaching aids. The intricacy of the carving of the intractable granite shows the skill and patience of the craftsmen. Church buildings, too, became highly decorated, many with open-work spires carved to look like lace, each parish vying with its neighbours to display its affluence. In the sixteenth and seventeenth centuries the assembly of religious

8.14 As the economy of Brittany flourished in the fifteenth and sixteenth centuries, money poured into the churches, largely through tithes but also by gift. It was used to aggrandize church buildings, which became blatant expressions of the communities' affluence. Craftsmen benefited, like the carpenter Olivier Le Loergan, who, about 1480, made this flamboyant Gothic rood screen for the chapel of Saint-Fiacre, Le Faouët, Morbihan.

8.15 As commissions multiplied, stonemasons became increasingly skilled in working granite to make intricate forms. The great calvary at Tronoën, Saint-Jean-Trolimon, Finistère, dating to about 1450–70, is a fine example of their skill.

buildings known as *enclos paroissiaux* (parish closes) became increasingly elaborate, reflecting the growing prosperity of the rural communities (below, pp. 309–12). Inside the churches the exuberant originality of the stonemasons who carved the capitals and the carpenters who crafted dragon-headed beams and flamboyant Gothic rood screens spoke of an intense devotion and of a community prepared to commit a significant tithe of their meagre resources to the glory of their god.

People felt a deep need to express their piety in public. One means by which this was done was in the pardon, an annual pilgrimage ending in a penitential ceremony. Pardons were a feature of western Brittany west of Guingamp, and were held on the feast of the patron saint of the church or chapel, usually between March and October. The more popular could be attended by many hundreds of people. At the pardon held on 23 and 24 June at Saint-Jean-du-Doigt near Morlaix, people came from all over Brittany, attracted by the famous relic believed to be the forefinger with which John had pointed to Christ. The much-travelled finger eventually ended up in Plougasnou, where, in 1440, Duke Jean V founded a church to house it. One of the attractions of visiting the church at the time of the pardon was the belief that water in the nearby holy well, when stirred by the finger, was particularly efficacious in curing diseases.

There is something distinctly pagan about many of the beliefs associated with pardons, suggesting links with a pre-Christian past. At Motreff the ceremony focused on a hill-top where a great fire was lit by a pure virgin and the most ancient of the villagers chanted the Prayer of the Fire. When the fire had died down, the ashes were collected by the worshippers because of their curative value. A pardon held in honour of St Gelvest in the Monts d'Arrée on 13 May was dedicated to ensuring that the grain crop was protected from pests, while at Plougastel children were purified by passing them across a fire on Midsummer's Day, a practice that has its roots in Celtic religion. Others offered more specific benefits. St Eloi was the patron saint of horses. The statue of the saint, near Landerneau, had to be approached on horseback and the horse be made to bow its head on passing. The penitent then had to leave a knot of horsehair on the altar. For more conventional Christians these eclectic beliefs and practices associated with the pardons, so reminiscent of paganism, were upsetting, particularly so to Welsh Calvinists, who, in the late nineteenth century, did their best to put a stop to them.

Apart from being an act of devotion, the pardon was a significant social event which brought people together from far and wide, reuniting kin groups, allowing family business to be transacted, and providing an occasion when the wider community could be made to feel a strong bond, one with another and with the locality. Brittany also had its own version of the more demanding pilgrimages that were so popular in the medieval world. Called the Tro Breizh it required the participant to visit seven cathedrals, Dol, Saint-Malo, Saint-Brieuc, Tréguier, Saint-Pol-de-Léon, Quimper, and Vannes, a journey that would take about a month.

A deep reverence for the dead pervaded Basse-Bretagne and is still evident today in the care with which graves are tidied and provided with bowls of fresh chrysanthemums for All Saints' Day (1 November), the time when many believe that the spirits of the departed visit their living relations. It was common in the nineteenth century for a bowl of cream to be put out at night for the spirits to sup with the living. The belief in a liminal period when spirits escape from the confines of the other world had its origin in the Celtic ceremony of Samhain, celebrated on the night of 31 October, marking the end of the old year and the beginning of the new. Like all liminal periods it was a dangerous time when the powers unleashed had to be carefully placated.

Bretons believed that the last man to die at the end of the old year became the Ankou (Death) and was destined to roam the countryside for the next twelve months, hovering to gather the souls of the dying. The Ankou was ever present and much feared, and was made starkly real to people through depictions of him as a skeleton often carrying a scythe. There is a fine wooden sculpture of the Ankou in the church at Ploumilliau and he appears again in a painting on the wall of the church of Kermaria-an-Iskuit, Plouha. The Kermaria painting, dating to the late fifteenth century, is a *danse macabre*, showing death leading the living, everyone from popes and kings to common

8.16 The Breton obsession with death is expressed in the many representations of the Ankou, the grim reaper, who travels the country gathering the souls of the dying. The Ankou (*left*) is preserved in the church of Ploumilliau. The figure (*right*) is now in the Museum of Morlaix.

8.17 The parishioners using the church of Kermaria-an-Iskuit, Plouha, Côtes-d'Armor, were constantly re-minded of their mortality by the fifteenth-century *danse macabre* painted on the inside walls of the church. Its message is that, however rich and important you may be in life, in death you are as everyone else.

peasants, to their graves. For those attending the church it was a constant reminder of the transience of life and the ultimate irrelevance of social status.

The cult of death, which pervaded Breton life, was also manifest in the treatment of human remains. Bodies were seldom left buried for long—only long enough for the flesh to decay—and were then exhumed and stored in ossuaries within the church enclosure before being disposed of in other ways. This procedure was under way in the medieval period. How far back in time it goes is difficult to say, but it is tempting to wonder if, in some way, it harked back to the practice of collective burial evident in megalithic tombs. Direct continuity seems unlikely, but it may have been a revival of practices long past but still dimly remembered. A particularly vivid description of burial rituals, observed at Trégastel in the late nineteenth century, is given by Charles Le Goffic. He tells how bodies were left in the ground for six or seven years and were then exhumed and the bones stacked in the ossuary. After a longer period of time, when there was no more space in the ossuary, the final ceremony took place, which he observed first-hand. A large pit had been dug and linen sheets had been laid on the ground just outside the ossuary. Inside the building were

> a little girl and a boy of twelve years up to their armpits in the mouldy fragments; they were cleaning the bones and passing them to a troop of little fellow-workers of both sexes, who received them reverently in their aprons, and carried them to one or other of the sheets.

He goes on to describe how, through the night, the heaps of bones were protected by a circle of candles, then at first light a mass was said for the dead and the procession left the church led by the celebrant and the clergy. As they passed the bone pile, each person picked up a bone.

> It was a grey autumnal morning, and the candles of the choir burnt like phosphorescent points of light. The procession moved twice around the churchyard, and then halted at the pit. There the official placed the first bone in it and all followed in silence, bowing themselves and gently lowering the fragments, after kissing them, into the hole.
>
> (Charles Le Goffic, *Sur la Côte* (1897), 78–9)

It was in these deeply held beliefs and practices that the people of western Brittany expressed their identity. Bound to the land, tradition and the comfort of ritual gave reassurance, enabling them to live out their lives in some degree of harmony.

A Nation Divided?

The long, gruelling Middle Ages, during which so many fought and died for their own ideals and for the ideals of others, revealed again the old divide between the east and the west evident in prehistoric and Gallo-Roman times. During the War of Succession (1341–65) it was intensified still further with Bretagne-Gallo (Haute-Bretagne), French-speaking and dominated by great lords largely controlled by the Penthièvre faction, contrasting with Bretagne-Bretonnante (Basse-Bretagne), the Breton-speaking land, a region of lesser lords who supported the Montfortist claim. It is this region where religious observance embraced the pardon and showed particular reverence for the spirits of the dead. The divide persisted throughout the later Middle Ages, manifesting itself most clearly in 1487 when tens of thousands of men from the west marched to relieve the siege of Nantes imposed by the pro-French faction. Many of them were sailors from the southern ports, particular Quimper, men who from habitual contact with fellow seamen from England, Gascony, Spain, and Italy were driven by their rather more outward-looking, cosmopolitan attitude to oppose what they saw to be the domination of the Francophone elite. It was a peasant uprising of the kind that was to recur many times in the centuries to come.

9

FOUR REBELLIONS
AND A REVOLUTION
1532–1802

THE union of Brittany and France proclaimed on 18 September 1532 must for many have seemed a chance worth taking. A few weeks before, when the question was debated by the États-Généraux of Brittany, emotions ran high and opinions were divided. On the one hand there was the pro-French faction, who believed that union would bring them increased wealth and opportunity for advancement; on the other were the *opiniâtres* (the 'obstinates'), who saw only loss of freedom and with it a whittling away of the Breton identity. Between the two extremes were those, tired of the interminable conflict with France and mindful of the new prosperity which the dukedom was enjoying, who were prepared to embrace union so long as the terms were right. In the end they won the debate, and the king of France, anxious to bring the conflict to an end, agreed to 'guarantee the privileges, rights and exemptions conceded by the Duke of Brittany'. On the face of it, it was a good deal for the Bretons. The contract bound the king to respect the traditional freedoms of Brittany embodied in the États, the Parlement, the Chambre des Comptes, the Chancery, and the fiscal system. Together they offered a robust defence against royal interference.

Until the beginning of the Revolution in 1789, the rebellions that erupted from time to time were not so much against union with France, though the cry for independence was sometimes heard, but more specifically against the erosion of traditional rights. The first of these came in 1553 when the Pope vested in the king of France the power to make ecclesiastical appointments. The immediate result was that Breton bishops were replaced by Frenchmen. Such opposition as there was proved ineffective, but threats to other rights, when they came, were more robustly challenged, sometimes leading to outright rebellion. There had been uprisings and internal conflicts in the past, but usually they were orchestrated by the elite to forward their own interests. The rebellion against the rule of the Angevins in the twelfth century and the War of Succession in the fourteenth century were about ducal rights and the struggle among the higher nobility for power. The common people were of little relevance except as battle fodder. But society was changing and becoming more complex, and when a French army moved into Brittany in 1489 it was met by a popular uprising in the west that drove the invaders back (above, p. 287). The power of the people was now a factor that could determine events, and that power was now in the ascendancy.

Union changed the geopolitical balance. On the broader world stage the politics of Brittany were now those of France, and the enemies of France—the English, the Dutch, and the Spaniards—were, at least in theory, the enemies of Brittany. This meant that when disputes arose between the French king and the duchy, the old game of playing off the English against the French was no longer an option. This does not, however, mean that the English and the Spanish were unwilling to involve themselves in Breton affairs when the opportunity arose and it suited them to do so.

Population and Prosperity

The two factors to have most impact on the social complexity that Brittany was now experiencing were population growth and increasing prosperity. By the fifteenth century Brittany had a relatively dense population compared with the rest of France, though it was kept in check by a series of epidemics, which ravaged the towns and the countryside. Towards the end of the century there were signs of significant growth. In some parishes more than 50 per cent of the population were children. This, and the rising price of cereals and demands for new tenancies, was all a reflection of an expanding population. Population continued to rise during the sixteenth century and even more rapidly in the seventeenth century, outstripping much of the rest of France. Figures from Léon show that in some parishes the number of baptisms doubled over the first eight decades of the seventeenth century. But the population was by no means evenly distributed. By the end of the century, the main concentrations, outside the major towns, lay in a corridor between Vitré, Rennes, and Saint-Malo and in the Trégor and Léon, where densities in excess of fifty inhabitants per square kilometre were recorded: in some parishes in the interior the figures were less than twenty-five. The towns grew rapidly in size. Nantes increased in population from fourteen thousand in 1530 to forty thousand by 1650.

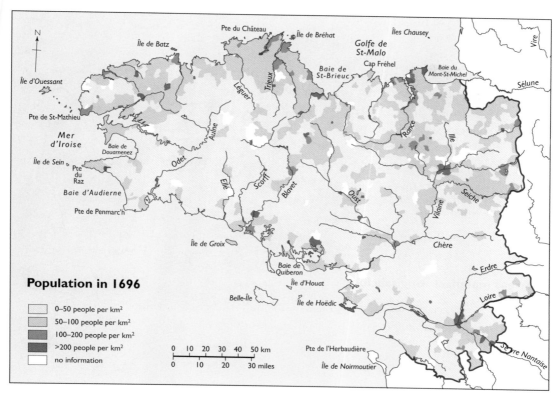

Population in 1696

- 0–50 people per km²
- 50–100 people per km²
- 100–200 people per km²
- >200 people per km²
- no information

0 10 20 30 40 50 km

0 10 20 30 miles

9.1 The population of Brittany in 1696 was concentrated in the main towns and along the north coast, where the communities enjoyed the dual benefits of easy access to the sea and a very fertile hinterland.

In that year Rennes was the largest city in Brittany with forty-five thousand, and the bishopric of Rennes included more than thirty towns with populations exceeding a thousand. By 1696 it is estimated that the urban population of Brittany was 280,000.

The growth of towns created urban populations distinct from the countryside. Many of the large landowners lived in the towns together with the legal and judicial elite and merchants who also owned land. They were served by master craftsmen, journeymen, day labourers, and casual workers. Most of this urban population was not directly involved in basic production but provided the infrastructure, legal and mercantile, and the other services that were needed to maintain the increasingly complex socio-economic system. In the small town of Ancenis, for example, there were thirty-nine taverns serving a population of two thousand, while in the Nantes region one person in every 100–150 ran a tavern.

The economy flourished throughout the sixteenth and well into the seventeenth century. Brittany at this time can be divided into a number of different economic zones,

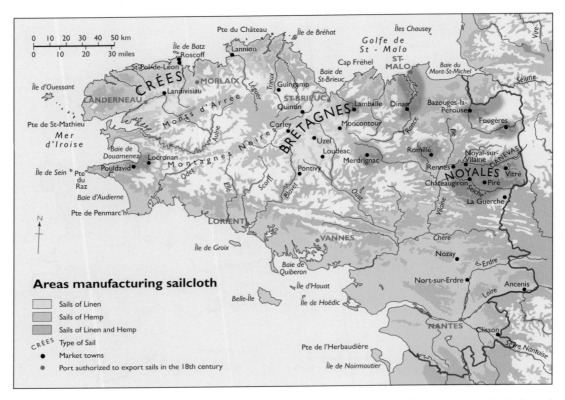

Areas manufacturing sailcloth

- Sails of Linen
- Sails of Hemp
- Sails of Linen and Hemp
- CRÉES Type of Sail
- ● Market towns
- ● Port authorized to export sails in the 18th century

9.2 The growing of flax and hemp enabled some regions to produce cloth for sail making. As the demand for sails increased with the development of maritime commerce, so the Breton economy flourished.

but the primary divide was between the coastal region with its many small ports, and the vast areas of *landes*, or heathland and forest, extending through the interior. The coastal region falls naturally into four discrete zones: a southern zone extending from the Baie de Bourgneuf to Crozon focused on Nantes, and three northern zones, Léon with Morlaix as its main port, a cluster of small ports around the coast of the Trégor to the Baie de Saint-Brieuc, and Saint-Malo with its urban hinterland extending as far inland as Rennes, Vitré, and Fougères. Grain production and livestock rearing were practised widely across the peninsula and grain was exported in quantity. Then there were regional products: wine in the Loire valley, salt around the Baie de Bourgneuf, Guérande, and the southern Morbihan, and dried fish from the *sécheries* along the coast between Quimperlé and Audierne. The northern ports specialized in the export of sails and other fabrics made from linen and hemp. Linen (made from the flax plant) was intensively produced in Léon and exported via Morlaix, with other areas of production in the Trégor between Guingamp and Lannion and in the inland region south of

9.3 The church at Pleyben, Finistère, built about 1580, is typical of the highly ornate churches of the region proclaiming the wealth of the community, much of it coming from linen production. The monumental calvary dates from 1550–1650.

Saint-Brieuc. Further east, particularly around Vitré, hemp was intensively produced to make sailcloth. The Locronan region also produced sails of hemp, but during the seventeenth century linen gradually replaced hemp in popularity. By the end of the century the sails made in the Saint-Brieuc hinterland were widely exported to Latin America while, of those from Léon, between 80 and 90 per cent went to the English market.

The wealth which sail making brought to the community is reflected in the elaboration of the parish churches and the ensemble of buildings associated with them. Already by the late fourteenth century rural communities were aggrandizing their churches (above, pp. 297–9). From the fifteenth to the seventeenth century those in the west became even more elaborate, with the full development of the *enclos paroissiaux*, each with its ornately decorated church accompanied by a calvary and an ossuary, all set within a walled enclosure entered through a monumental gate. The grandeur of these structures, with their towering spires visible from miles away, proclaims not only the vitality of the local economy but the extraordinary power of the Church. The

9.4 The parish close at Saint-Thégonnec, Finistère, entered through a triumphal arch, contains a church (*right*), an ossuary (*left*), and a calvary. The calvary, erected in 1610, depicts scenes from the Passion, providing a valuable visual aid for the preacher.

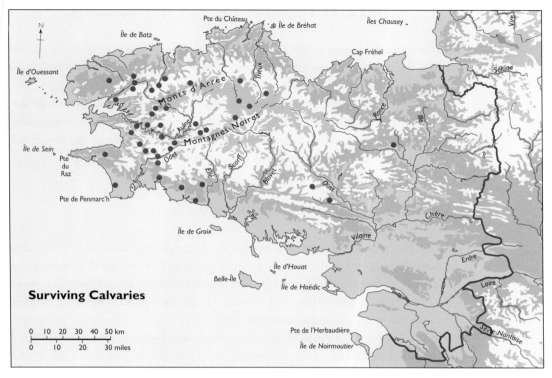

Surviving Calvaries

0 10 20 30 40 50 km
0   10   20   30 miles

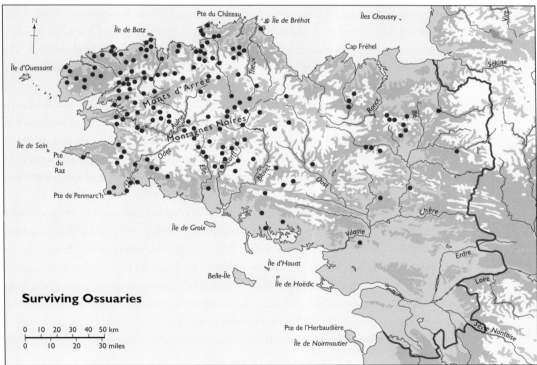

Surviving Ossuaries

0 10 20 30 40 50 km
0   10   20   30 miles

9.5 With the growth in rural prosperity surplus wealth was increasingly invested in aggrandizing the parish churches. The parish close—an enclosing wall with an elaborate gate within which lay the church, the calvary, and the ossuary—now became the outward and visible sign of a community's wealth and the strength of their devotion.

distribution of elaborate parish closes, clustering in the west of the peninsula, in part reflects the productive capacity of the region but it also maps the region in which the hold of the Church on people's lives was at its most intense.

The sixteenth and early seventeenth century, then, was in so many ways a golden age for Brittany: a stable flourishing economy, a growing population, and burgeoning towns, all a reflection of the comparative peace that union with France had brought. It was also an age of exploration in which Bretons were to play a creative part.

The Empowering Sea

The thriving economy brought a new prosperity to the coastal towns, all of which were in some way engaged in the import–export trade as well as fishing. The smaller ports were more concerned with cabotage: moving commodities to and from the larger ports like Nantes, Saint-Malo, and Morlaix, which were main centres for overseas trade. In the sixteenth and seventeenth centuries the Atlantic networks prospered, with Brittany playing an increasing role linking Spain, Portugal, and western France to Ireland, England, the Low Countries, and Germany. Breton cloth, grain, and wine were everywhere in demand, but with rich cargoes on the move, piracy was rife. Freebooters based on La Rochelle became a serious threat between 1570 and 1620, requiring the intervention of the French navy, while in the English Channel ship's captains from Saint-Malo were left free to prey on Spanish, Dutch, and English ships. The town grew rich on the proceeds, and in 1590, during a time of unrest, declared itself to be a republic, adopting the motto 'we are not French, we are not Breton, but Malouin'. The republic lasted three years. Like all ports, Saint-Malo was an unruly place. In 1654 the town council installed a police force, explaining that police 'are very necessary in the town of Saint-Malo because it has great commerce and is filled with many seamen who are ordinarily very rude'. Because the town embraced an 'infinity of persons of different nations and professions', disagreements among them 'can lead to disorder and to blows'.

The world was now changing fast. In the remarkably brief span of three decades from 1492, when Columbus made his Atlantic crossing, to 1520, when Magellan reached the southern extremity of Patagonia, virtually the whole of the Atlantic coast of the Americas had been explored and plotted by Spanish, Portuguese, and English seamen. France came late to the scene, showing little interest until, in 1524, the king invited a Florentine sailor, Giovanni da Verrazzano (1485–1528), to reconnoitre the coast of North America. Little seems to have come of it, but ten years later, determined to join in the race to establish a northern route around America to the Indies, the king commissioned Jacques Cartier (1491–1557), a native of Saint-Malo, to lead an expedition for France. Cartier was already familiar with parts of the American continent, and in 1534 he set out for Newfoundland. In three expeditions, 1534, 1535–6, and 1541–2, he thoroughly explored the gulf of St Lawrence and sailed up the St Lawrence river, visiting the native sites that were later to become Montreal and Quebec. Claiming the new land for France, he named it the Country of Canadas (after an Iroquois word referring to two native settlements).

But it was not until the seventeenth century that the French consolidated and expanded their discoveries in North America. The foundation was laid by Samuel de Champlain (1567?–1635), who was first sent out in 1604 and for the next sixteen years explored widely. In 1608 he established a permanent colony at Quebec, where, from 1620 until his death in 1635, he supervised the growth of New France. Meanwhile, with the enthusiastic support of Cardinal Richelieu, French colonial enterprise intensified, particularly in the West Indies, where French settlement had begun on St Kitts in 1623. Other colonies soon followed, producing tobacco and cotton at first, but after African slave labour was introduced in 1649, sugar began to increase in importance. A new impetus came in 1661 when Louis XIV assumed control of the French government. Yet for all the effort, the American colonies were precarious, largely because of the comparatively small number of colonists sent out. Nonetheless, determined to reinforce his hold on America against the English, in 1707 Louis ordered the colonization of Louisiana (named after him). The age-old conflict between France and England could now be fought out on two continents.

The establishment of overseas colonies dramatically changed the fortunes of Brittany after the middle of the seventeenth century. As cross-Atlantic trade increased, so the west coast ports of France, particularly Saint-Malo, Nantes, La Rochelle, and Bordeaux, flourished. In 1670 Nantes was given a monopoly of ships returning to France from the West Indies and by the eighteenth century it had become the second port in France (after Bordeaux), growing rich on the burgeoning slave trade. Saint-Malo also benefited from North American trade, but its sailors ranged wide wherever opportunities for amassing wealth beckoned. They are credited with discovering the Falkland Islands, which they named Les Îles Malouines (whence the Spanish, Islas Malvinas), but never settled there. The establishment of the new port of Lorient in 1666, on the south coast at the confluence of the Blavet and the Scorff, was a direct result of new French settlements in India. Lorient, with its spacious approaches protected by the fortress of Port-Louis, was given a monopoly of the trade with India managed by the French East India Company. It was here that the company's ships were built. One of the first, the thousand-ton *Le Soleil Orient*, more usually known as *L'Orient*, gave the town its name. By 1720 its growth was affecting the fortunes of

BREST.

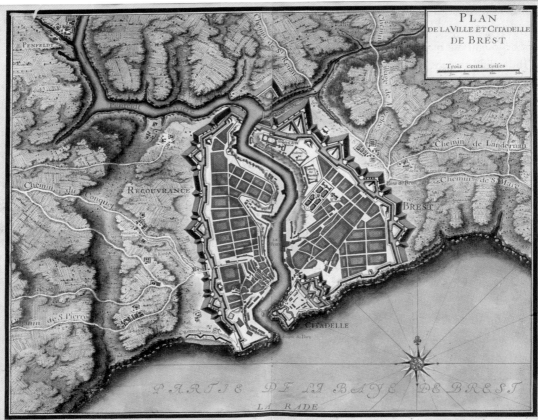

PLAN
DE LA VILLE ET CITADELLE
DE BREST

Trois cents toises

PENFELDT

Chemin de St Kerau

village de L'isle

Chemin de Landernau

RECOUVRANCE

Chemin du Conquet

Rüe de Brest

Chemin de St Mar

BREST

Chemin de St Pierre

CITADELLE

PARTIE DE LA BAYE DE BREST

LA RADE

9.6 (*Opposite*) Brest became a thriving port, both commercial and naval, with the most up-to-date fortifications defending positions on either side of the estuary of the river Penfeld, which opens into the Rade de Brest, a huge enclosed inlet where large fleets could anchor in safety. The engraving, dating to the eighteenth century, gives a clear idea of the topography and shows that the Penfeld estuary was being used for ship repairs. The map shows the fortifications in the seventeenth century.

Saint-Malo, which thereafter began to decline. Lorient's monopoly lasted until 1769, when the Indian trade was disrupted by the English.

Besides trade, Breton ports were havens for the fishing fleets, which had fished the inshore waters at least since the Roman period, bringing in great hauls of sardine and herring. Fishing continued to be a vital part of the economy, the *sécheries* of the south-west coast producing large quantities of dried fish for local consumption and export.

Plan et profil de SAINT MALO ville Episcopale et Port de la Haute Bretagne
fait par Aveline Avec Privilege du Roy

9.7 Saint-Malo, too, prospered. Built on a rocky island joined to the mainland by a strand of sand and shingle, the city was defended by formidable walls with a castle guarding the approach from the land. Though access from the sea was not easy, and was sometimes dangerous, ships could dock in safety in the extensive bay nearby. The illustration shows the city in the seventeenth century.

9.8 Saint-Malo today, its grandeur carefully restored after devastating destruction during the Second World War. It remains a busy commercial and passenger port.

Towards the end of the fifteenth century, Bristol fishermen had learned of, and were exploiting, the exceptionally rich cod shoals off the Newfoundland Banks. At first the secret was well kept, but with the opening up of North America, following the discoveries of John and Sebastian Cabot and, later, Jacques Cartier, Breton fishermen from the northern ports flocked to the new fishing grounds. It was an arduous regimen requiring them to be at sea for months at a time during the year. Boats from Saint-Malo, Erquy, and Saint-Pol-de-Léon were already fishing off Newfoundland by the 1520s. Other ports were soon to follow, and fishing in the North Atlantic became a major occupation for men from the northern ports until the early twentieth century. The demands and dangers of the fishermen's existence provides the background to Pierre Loti's famous novel *Pêcheur d'Islande*, a memorial to all the many hundreds of men from Paimpol lost at sea during Atlantic fishing expeditions (below, pp. 376–7).

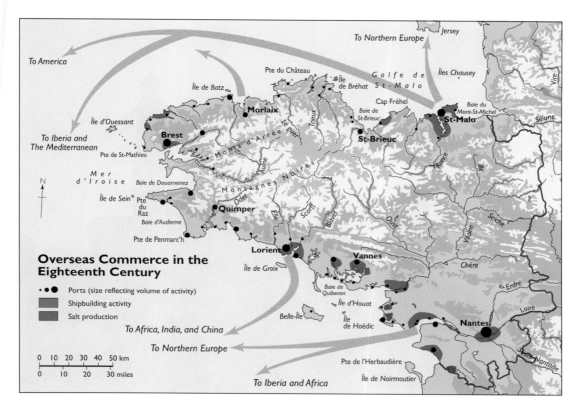

9.9 In the eighteenth century shipbuilding became a major industry focused particularly on the ports along the south coast together with Brest and Saint-Malo. The economy of Brittany flourished as trade with America and the Indies developed.

Union with France meant that the ports of Brittany were now an integral part of the coastal defences of the French state, but it was not until Cardinal Richelieu (1585–1642) became the First Minister of State for France in 1624 that the implications of this were fully realized and acted upon. Richelieu's overarching aim was ambitious: to consolidate royal power, crushing all factions, and to transform France into a strong centralized state. Besides being First Minister, he became grand-master of navigation in 1626 and governor of Brittany in 1632. He was therefore in an ideal position to oversee Brittany's coastal fortifications. He appreciated at once the crucial importance of Brest, a promising site overlooking a large, well-protected expanse of water, the Rade de Brest, where the entire fleet could anchor in safety. Brest also lay close to the western extremity of Brittany, commanding the shipping lanes rounding Ushant. From the safety of the Rade a squadron could easily sail out to protect, or to prey on, vessels making this difficult and dangerous passage. Understanding these advantages,

9.10 While sea travel along the north and south coasts was comparatively safe, rounding the western extremity of the peninsula was often dangerous. Coming from the south, once safely through the passage between the Pointe du Raz and Île de Sein, ships made for the next hazard to be negotiated, the headland of Saint-Mathieu, given enhanced visibility in the Middle Ages by its great medieval abbey and, more recently, by its lighthouses.

and mindful of the fact that the English had occupied Brest for a number of years during the Wars of Succession, Richelieu decided to make Brest a permanent base for the French navy. His preparations began in 1631 and were later continued by the French finance minister Jean-Baptiste Colbert. The massive fortifications were completed in 1680–8, when the great military engineer Sébastien Le Prestre de Vauban was brought in. The decision was sound, and Brest has remained one of the country's prime naval bases to the present day.

People on the Move

Increased trading activity in the sixteenth and seventeenth centuries brought with it a new mobility among the population, with individuals, often whole families, willing to relocate and set up livelihoods for themselves in foreign countries. A detailed survey of the counties of Devon and Cornwall shows that there was a very substantial community of immigrants, called 'aliens' and 'strangers', resident in the early sixteenth century. In Cornwall most of them were from Brittany, while in Devon, although the Bretons were the most numerous, immigrants also came from other parts of France, the Low Countries, Germany, and Italy. For the most part they served as labourers, servants, fishermen, and tin miners, but some were craftsmen, a significant number of them being carpenters or wood carvers. Most of those who settled in the Cornish parishes were young men in their late teens who had probably come to raise money

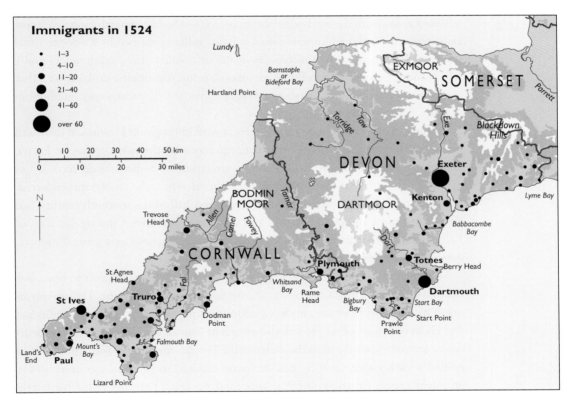

9.11 In the sixteenth century large numbers of immigrants from Europe, mainly craftsmen and workers, settled in Cornwall and south Devon. A high percentage of them were from Brittany. The map, based on information from the Lay Subsidy Rolls, shows where the immigrants were settled in 1524.

before returning home to get married. A few women are also listed, working usually as servants.

The south-west of Britain at this time was prosperous and there was much work to be had, particularly in the refurbishing of churches, which were benefiting from the economic prosperity of the region. It is here, in the carved rood screens and other church fittings, that the work of Breton craftsmen can be recognized. At Bodmin in Cornwall records of 1529–30 mention the 'Bretouns' who constructed seats in the church. Two Bretons were responsible for mending the steeple door and the church clock in 1572–3, and at North Petherwin, also in Cornwall, the parish accounts for 1524 record, 'we paid the Brytons for our rood loft at 24s the foot'. The total bill, which came to £54 13s., shows it to have been a significant contract.

An even more impressive piece of work was a four-storey timber-framed house known as King John Tavern, which stood in South Street, Exeter, until its demolition in the 1830s. Records of the building and surviving timbers show it to have been a *maison à pondalez* of the kind otherwise restricted to Morlaix in north Finistère. These elaborate structures, with superimposed wooden galleries reached by a wooden spiral staircase, were built for rich merchants or minor nobility. The circumstances under which one came to be built in Exeter are unknown, but the simplest explanation is that it was constructed for an English merchant, familiar with contemporary buildings in Morlaix, by craftsmen from the city.

Breton carpenters and wood carvers were at work throughout Devon and Cornwall in the early sixteenth century, with concentrations in the main towns of Exeter, Dartmouth, and Plymouth. In Plymouth a street known as Bretonside, recorded as early as 1493, hints that there may have been ghettos where the immigrants clustered. Immigrant numbers increased throughout the first half of the sixteenth century, but rising resentment among the English and hostility to the French during the Wars of Religion meant that after the middle of the century immigrants were generally unwelcome and their numbers began to decline steeply.

Movements of craftsmen from England to Brittany are more difficult to trace, but the case of Robert Dallam (1602–65) and his family deserves mention. Dallam was an organ maker of some repute, his work adorning King's College Chapel, Cambridge, and Gloucester Cathedral. He was also an ardent Roman Catholic who felt it expedient to leave the country with the onset of the Puritan revolution. Sometime in 1641 he fled with his wife, mother, and six young children to Brittany, a country where he might expect to maintain his religion and his craft. Fortunately for his family his skills were much in demand and he was contracted to build organs in Quimper Cathedral, Saint-Jean-du-Doigt, Plestin-les-Grèves, and Lesneven, and, with his son Thomas, in Saint-Pol-de-Léon Cathedral. Robert returned to England in 1660 after

9.12 Among the Bretons who settled in south-western Britain were skilled wood carvers, whose work is to be seen in many churches. This section of a rood screen, in the church at North Petherwin, Cornwall, was created by Breton craftsmen between 1518 and 1524.

the Restoration and continued his career, but Thomas remained in Brittany, living in Lannion. He built seven organs in the west of Brittany, working until his death in 1705. He was married four times and had twenty children, one at least of whom returned to England and continued the family tradition. Another member of the family, Robert's son-in-law Thomas Harrison, who accompanied them to Brittany, was also an organ builder, working at Roscoff, Brélévenez, and Morlaix between 1648 and 1681. It was a

9.13 Sometime around 1641 Robert Dallam, a skilled organ maker, and his family fled to Brittany to avoid religious persecution in England. One of the organs he made, for the church in Plestin-les-Grèves, was later transferred to the church at Lanvellec, where it is lovingly cared for and still played.

prolific family which served Brittany well at a time when much of the wealth generated from the Breton countryside was being invested in aggrandizing its churches and cathedrals.

The Wars of Religion

The rise of Protestantism throughout Europe in the middle decades of the sixteenth century posed a major threat to the Catholic Church. In England, Henry VIII finally broke with Rome in 1534, instituting the Anglican Church. In the years to follow, Luther was active converting the Germans, Calvin, in Geneva, was setting up the Reformed Church, while in Scotland, Knox was founding the Presbyterian movement. To Catholics throughout Europe it seemed as though the tide was turning against them. This was particularly evident in France, where the power of the Protestant Huguenots was growing stronger. Tensions sparked into a long-drawn-out conflict known as the Wars of Religion. Hostilities began in 1562 when Protestants started to seize towns across the country, and ended in 1598 with the Edict of Nantes, which formalized a truce between the two religions offering guarantees to both sides. In the thirty-six years of conflict three million people died from violence and from the disease and famine that accompanied it.

Brittany was caught up in these events, but the discontent which fed the religious confrontations was nuanced. Resentment over union with France still ran strong, as did the old rivalries between the houses of Montfort and de Blois dating back to the Wars of Succession. To add to this, in 1553 the Pope had given the king the right to appoint French bishops, overturning an agreement in the Edict of Union which had allowed ecclesiastical appointments to be left in the hands of the Bretons. Brittany was fertile ground for those who wanted to use the religious conflicts for their own ends.

In 1582 the French king, Henry III, appointed Philippe-Emmanuel, duke of Mercœur (1558–1602), to be governor of Brittany. Mercœur was a leader of the Catholic League (or Holy League), founded in 1576 to prevent seizure of power by the Huguenots and to eradicate Protestantism. He had a particular interest in Brittany because his wife, Marie of Luxembourg, as a direct descendant of the house of de Blois, held the title duchess of Penthièvre, and thus had a claim to the dukedom of Brittany. It is not clear what Mercœur's aspirations were, but in all probability his intention was to restore an independent Brittany to be ruled by his family. By referring to his son as 'prince and duke of Brittany' he was blatantly staking his claim. In 1589 he began to establish his authority by taking over the towns of Brittany, making Nantes his capital. Only Rennes, Vitré, and Brest held out for the royalists. His actions were no doubt

PHILIPES EMANVEL DE LORRAYNE, DVC DE MERCVEVR ET DE PENTHEEVRE, PAIR DE FRANCE, PRINCE DV SAINCT EMPIRE ET DE MARTIGVES, ET GOVVERNEVR DE BRETAIGne.

MERCVRIVS Princeps, clarus lauroque, togaque,
EMMANVEL isthæc ora PHILIPPVS habet.

9.14 Philippe-Emmanuel, duke of Mercoeur (1558–1602). He was made governor of Brittany in 1582 and led an unsuccessful attempt to win independence for Brittany from France.

encouraged by the death of his one-time patron Henry III and the accession of the Protestant Henry of Navarre as Henry IV. He could now claim that he was leading Catholic Brittany against the scourge of a Protestant France.

Meanwhile, Georges d'Aradon, bishop of Vannes, was also building support for an independent Brittany, but his idea was that the dukedom should be offered to the Infanta Isabella, daughter of Philip II of Spain, and he wrote to this effect to the Spanish king. Philip's response was to seek Mercœur's opinion. Mercœur was ambivalent. The king, he said, should disregard the 'secret practices of some Breton ministers', but he kept open the option of installing Isabella and accepted the assistance of seven thousand Spanish troops, who subsequently landed at Port-Louis, where they established the fortress. The insurrection in Brittany had now taken a serious turn and Henry of Navarre had little option but to confront the separatists directly.

The action took place at Craon, Mayenne, on 22 May 1592. Henry's force, led by the duke of Montpensier, was supported by twelve thousand English troops and eight hundred German mercenaries. In the end Mercœur and the Spaniards won the day and the royal army was forced to retreat. The English soldiers captured in the engagement were all executed in retaliation for the behaviour of the English against survivors from the wreck of the Spanish Armada four years earlier.

Mercœur now hesitated, in part because of a concern for the growing arrogance of his Spanish allies. His indecision led to loss of support and when, in July 1593, Henry of Navarre embraced Catholicism, Mercœur's crusade against the threat of a Protestant takeover was totally undermined. The following year Henry, now Henry IV, king of France, sent an army to Brittany to re-establish control, but it was not until the last town was taken by the royalists, in February 1598, that Mercœur finally submitted. Two months later the Edict of Nantes was signed. Mercœur spent the remaining four years of his life in exile in Hungary using his energies in fighting against the Turks.

The war in Brittany that raged for a decade (1589–98), notionally against the French state and in the name of religion, was really a hangover from the old rivalries of the Middle Ages. It was driven by the ambitions of the elite contesting the right to rule and, as in early conflicts, they were manipulated by foreign powers, in this case the Spanish and the English fighting proxy wars. No doubt, in the minds of some, the good old days of Breton independence were an ideal to cling to, but that Brittany was now flourishing as part of France weakened the desire to break away. Yet for others, especially the peasants in the rural west, the Holy League was a cause that gave hope in the constant struggle against the rich and privileged. In the early years peasants willingly took part, in 1590 taking over the town of Carhaix and burning castles and two years later attacking Brest, then occupied by royalists. But as the war dragged on and the leaders lost their purpose, peasant support fell away and the chance to build an effective independence movement was lost. It was only the sailors of Saint-Malo with their short-lived republic who, briefly, broke the political mould (above, p. 312).

Social Structure, Social Tensions

By the beginning of the seventeenth century the social structure in Brittany had become complex. There had been two principal ways of classifying society, by orders (a legal and social hierarchy) and by classes (an economic hierarchy), but, in reality, the two were now combined. The real divide was between those who owned land and those who did not. Landowners at the top of the hierarchy included the titled nobility, the legal and judicial elite, and merchants. Between these classes there was now a degree of mobility. A merchant might expect to be able to educate a son sufficiently for them to join the legal profession, and from there, with ability, luck, and a degree of ruthlessness, a young man might acquire enough money to buy land, and then, by providing services for the state or the monarch, the more favoured might aspire to titles. To this extent, then, the upper levels of Breton society functioned as a meritocracy, but for an artisan to become a merchant was very much more difficult. An artisan created the products that he sold; a merchant dealt in goods produced by others. One was a worker, and other was a facilitator: herein lay the real class barrier.

Of workers there were many kinds. In the towns the hierarchy included master craftsmen, journeymen, shopkeepers, day labourers, and casual workers, and these classes made up more than 80 per cent of the whole population. In the countryside there were ploughmen, millers, cottagers, and day labourers. Between these classes there was a degree of mobility.

Power was generated through the ownership of land, the prime concern of the landowners being to accumulate, in their own hands, the surpluses generated by the labour of their lower-class tenants. In this way the elite sustained and enhanced their status, but for the system to work it required that order be maintained. The greatest threat to order lay not in outright rebellion but in the passive resistance of the working classes through refusal to pay taxes or to submit to corvée labour (a day's unpaid work due to a feudal lord). It was in the interests of the landowning class, therefore, that the taxes falling on the lower classes and demands for their labour were kept to acceptable levels. While they had it in their power to moderate the latter, taxes were ultimately in the gift of the king. But herein lay another delicate balance. Since the stability of the monarchy rested on the co-operation of the elite, the elite had the power to call for lower levels of taxation if the king was tempted to make excessive demands.

One of the greatest causes of discontent in the countryside was the system of tenancy known as *domaine congéable*. In this system the initial fee to be paid by the peasant on entering into an agreement was much higher than for other types of tenancy. This was hard enough, but the main problem lay in the terms: the tenant had to pay an annual rent of one-third of the gross revenue of the holding rather than half the net revenue. This meant that he would be hit severely by any increase in direct taxation that the state decided to impose. Another disadvantage of the system was that under the lease, which usually ran for nine years, the landlord retained possession of the land and of large trees, while the tenant owned the buildings and the rest of the woodland. At the end of the lease the landlord had to repurchase the buildings and woodland, paying for any improvements that had been made. Since, however, the landlord had to give permission for improvements, the fact that he had to pay for them when the lease was terminated disinclined him to do so. In such a system there was little opportunity for the peasant to do more than scratch a living from the soil, a situation made more desperate as the tax burden increased. It is no coincidence that it was in Basse-Bretagne, where the *domaine congéable* was the common form of tenancy, that peasant unrest was to burst into open rebellion.

The socio-economic system was delicately balanced in a state of unstable equilibrium highly vulnerable to outside forces. Two were to have an impact on Brittany in a disastrous way: the Thirty Years War (1618–48), which drained the resources of the French state, and the excessive demands of the king, Louis XIV (reigned 1643–1715), to pay for his wars and for his ambitious building programmes. The king deeply resented the special privileges enjoyed by the Bretons, guaranteed by the treaty of 1532, and with the enthusiastic support of his ministers Mazarin and Colbert, he determined to undermine Breton independence and to bring the country more directly under royal authority. So began Brittany's economic decline.

Many factors combined to damage the country's prosperity. Richelieu's replacement of the Breton navy with a French navy affected shipping, trade, and the fishing industry; prohibition of trade with England devastated the linen industry; while the loss of markets to Dutch enterprise after 1660 struck another blow, further limiting Brittany's trading capacity. But worst of all was the king's demand for increased revenues through taxation. Some control was exercised because, according to the terms of the union of 1532, no new taxes could be imposed without the agreement of the États-Généraux. Louis XIV, however, got over this minor impediment by demanding instead direct gifts. In 1661, while visiting Nantes, the king asked for the colossal sum of four million livres and was content to compromise on three million. In 1663 and 1665 further gifts were demanded. The only way that the États could raise such sums was by imposing taxes. The overall effect of these combined assaults was that rents and tithes increased dramatically through the seventeenth century. In the Nantes region, for example, they doubled between 1610 and 1650, and in the decades from 1640 to 1660 the Breton economy went from stagnation to decline. By 1700 most of Brittany was severely depressed to such an extent that it was to take two hundred years to recover.

In the face of the multiple pressures, the États had little option but to raise revenue by putting increasing demands on landlords through additional taxes, the burden of which was passed down to the lower classes. The ones who suffered most were the better-off peasants, who were required to pay higher entry fees for leases, higher tithes, and higher direct taxes: the poorer peasants produced little to no tax. By the early 1670s the situation in the countryside was tense, particularly in the west, where *domaine congéable* leases were the most common. To the peasant, remote among his fields and livestock, the fault was seen to lie with the landlords. In the towns, too, there was growing discontent. Declining productivity and rising taxes were a lethal combination, driving both rural and urban workers to the brink.

The Rebellion of 1675

The Franco-Dutch War (1672–8) and Louis XIV's extravagances at home led to a continuing and growing demand for revenue. To meet this Louis's minister Colbert instituted a series of new taxes, on stamped paper, tobacco, and pewter, and there was the suggestion that the tax on salt (*gabelle*), which in Brittany had been much lower than in the west of France, would also be raised. All this was without reference to the États-Géneraux. Stamped paper was essential for all legal transactions, and to tax it at a high rate would affect all levels of society. The tax on pewter would hit the food and drink industry, while the tax on tobacco was universally unpopular, particularly among the tobacco merchants. If the salt tax in Brittany was brought in line with the rest of the country, where it was about forty times higher, not only would the workers of the coastal salt-pans suffer, but so, too, would the entrepreneurs who made a good living by smuggling it across the border. It is little wonder that the tax rises, actual and threatened, were unpopular and led to outright rebellion.

The rebellion began in Rennes on 18 April 1675. The events were reported to the Parlement the next day by the *procureur*. He blamed 'vagabonds and persons unknown and without occupation' from outside the city who gathered together,

> first pillaging the office of the tobacco monopoly and that of the marking of pew-
> ter, and then the offices of land registers, deeds, and suits over land, and of the

stamped paper, and prepared themselves to pillage several houses of individuals
and to commit other great disorders and violences.

(translation by James B. Collins)

From Rennes, the uprising extended to Saint-Malo and Nantes. In Saint-Malo the
decision to keep on selling tobacco until the fishing fleet left for Newfoundland
averted major trouble, but in Nantes on 23 April the tobacco office and pewter office
were pillaged and the rebellion spread. Troops were brought in to re-establish order
and six hundred cavalry were billeted on the town. But troubles continued. A week
after the initial riot Rennes was again in uproar, beginning when Jesuit students led
attacks on Protestant targets. The mob then threatened to burn down the prison and
one observer believed that they were intent on 'a universal pillage of the richest individuals of the city and the bureaux in which they believed they would find money'.
Rebellion flared up again on 17 July when the palace was attacked and the office where
the stamped paper was distributed was ransacked.

It is difficult to distinguish who was responsible for the uprisings in the eastern
towns but some in the Parlement played a part in organizing events and the duke of
Chaulnes, governor of Brittany, was convinced that the legal professionals (*procureurs*)
were 'the first authors of the seditions'. But among the people who were arrested and
put on trial, in addition to members of the legal profession, there were artisans, hoteliers, fishwives, butchers, masons, blacksmiths, and a second-hand clothes dealer: the
lower classes were the foot soldiers of the uprising. The man accused of leading the
rebellion on 17 July was a violinist: he was quartered and his body parts displayed at
the four main city gates. In Rennes many hundreds of people were hanged and whole
neighbourhoods razed. The Parlement was exiled to Vannes until 1690, but, worse still,
ten thousand soldiers were billeted in the city and allowed to murder, rape, and rob as
much as they pleased.

In May and June unrest spread to Basse-Bretagne and there were uprisings in many
of the towns, Guingamp, Lamballe, Quimper, and Châteaulin, mostly targeting the
bureaux of stamped paper, tobacco, and pewter. Other towns were to follow: Daoulas,
Landerneau, Carhaix, Pontivy, and Concarneau. But by now the nature of the rebellion had changed as peasants from the countryside were caught up in the clamour.
Their list of grievances was long: the abuses of the courts and the high cost of justice,
the abuse of seigneurial rights, particularly with respect to demands for corvée labour
and hunting, and abuses by priests charging excessive fees for masses and burials. It is
interesting that they were not complaining about paying fair taxes and rents but were
against all those in authority who were manipulating the seigneurial system for their

own benefit. The rebellion in the west was largely about justice, not the overthrow of the class system.

The rebels were a mix of the lower classes: labourers, farmworkers, artisans of all kinds, hoteliers, and even some merchants; one of the leaders, Sebastian Ar Balp, was a notary working in Carhaix. Women also played a significant part, some in leadership roles. Together they presented a formidable force united by their hatred of injustice and identified by the *bonnets rouges* (red hats) that many of them wore. Violence spread throughout the countryside. Two hundred houses of the nobility were attacked and pillaged, and some of them burned and a number of the owners injured. Many of those in authority understood and even sympathized with the peasant demands. The governor of Brittany, de Chaulnes, writing to the First Minister, Colbert, explained that the rebels were complaining about 'the exactions that their seigneurs have made against them and the ill treatment they have received'. In extracting money and corvée labour from them the seigneurs had 'no more consideration for them than for horses'. The baron de Névet summed up the situation: the peasants, he said, 'demand justice from the evil nobility, judges and tax farmers'.

The revolt seems to have taken a new turn in September when Ar Balp, who had gathered a force of thirty thousand in Carhaix, decided to attack the thriving port of Morlaix. His aspirations came to nothing, but there is the suspicion that he may have been hoping to link up with the Dutch fleet now in the Channel: the Dutch were still at war with France at the time. That there may have been some attempted collaboration is given credence by the fact that the *bonnets rouges* who escaped to the Îles Glénan after the rebellion had collapsed were rescued by the Dutch fleet. At any event, the matter ended in confusion when Ar Balp was killed at Ty Meur, Poullaouen, by the marquis de Montgaillard, whom he had been trying to persuade to lead the rebels. Without a charismatic leader the rebellion began to lose impetus. The governor, de Chaulnes, now began a decisive move against the rebels supported by six thousand troops sent from France.

The autumn and winter of 1675 saw reprisals on a massive scale. Indiscriminate violence and mass killings were commonplace. As a reminder to all, the trees along the roads to Quimper were hung with the bodies of peasants. Even de Chaulnes was forced to agree that the French soldiers were behaving as though Brittany was enemy territory. The south-west took the brunt of the retribution. Around Pont l'Abbé the bells of the churches which had called the rebels to arms were melted down and the ravaged belfries left as a reminder that rebellion would be met by brutal force.

The rebellion of 1675 was a fascinating episode. This was not a nostalgic movement asking to return to former times when Brittany was independent, nor was it an attempt to overthrow the social order. It was simply a demand by the lower classes for the

9.15 Charles d'Albert d'Ailly, duke of Chaulnes (1625–98). The Fat Pig, as he was known, was responsible for bringing in the French army to crush the revolt of 1675.

multiple abuses rained on them by the landowners, the clerics, the legal profession, and the state to be brought to an end: it was a revolt for fairness, not for the overthrow of the elite. Whether it could have been developed into a full-scale social revolution with suitable leadership is a debatable point. Its rapid and violent suppression brought it to an end before the rural peasants and the urban workers could make common cause. The difference between eastern and western Brittany was now more evident than ever.

9.16 The vicious reprisals that followed the suppression of the revolt of 1675 included the removal of church bells from the churches whose communities had supported the revolt. The chapel of St Philibert at Plonéour-Lanvern, Finistère, still proudly displays its mutilated steeple.

As one member of the nobility, the marquis de Lavardin, remarked of Basse-Bretagne, 'it is a rude and ferocious country, which produces inhabitants which resemble it. They poorly understand French and scarcely better, reason.' The ferocity of the repression did nothing to encourage the peasants to become otherwise: the west remained a poor and depressed region for generations to come.

Nobles in Revolt, 1718–1720

The death of Louis XIV in 1715 left France with enormous debts. Since his successor, Louis XV, was a minor, the affairs of France were controlled by a regent, Philippe II, duke of Orléans, whose first task was to pay off the country's debts by levying higher taxes. The États-Généraux, regarding this as a direct challenge to the rights guaranteed to Brittany, refused to pay and was dismissed. Three years later, on 6 July 1718, the regent reconvened the États at Dinan. Again they resisted the demands, and some of the lesser nobility began to discuss ways of seeking greater independence from France. When knowledge of this reached Philippe a number of the dissidents were arrested and exiled, but those who remained were defiant and circulated a document, 'Act of Union for the Defence of the Liberties of Brittany', which demanded the safeguarding of the privileges of the nobility. Whether coincidentally, riots broke out in some of the towns of Haute-Bretagne.

Meanwhile, the duke and duchess of Maine, angered by the unfavourable way, from their point of view, in which Louis XIV's will had been interpreted, began to organize a conspiracy to overthrow the regency with the help of Philip V of Spain. Both the duke and duchess were arrested on 29 December 1718, but news of the conspiracy had reached the marquis de Pontcallec, a member of the Breton nobility who was planning to organize a rebellion in Brittany. An envoy was sent to the Spanish to explain the situation and was met with an offer of Spanish troops and money to aid the overthrow of the regent.

Aware of growing unrest in Brittany, the government in Paris sent an army of fifteen thousand men to Rennes in September 1719 under the command of Pierre de Montesquiou, marshal of France. He soon learned of the magnitude of the conspiracy. Pontcallec's plan was to gather forces and march on Rennes, but support failed to materialize and when it became known that the Spanish had sent only two thousand Irish troops, the rebellion collapsed. The Irish quickly re-embarked, taking with them some of the conspirators. Of those who remained, Pontcallec among them, many were arrested. In the subsequent trial held in Nantes, twenty were condemned to death. Of these, sixteen were on the run but the four in custody, including Pontcallec, were beheaded.

The conspiracy was doomed to fail. Since it involved only the nobility and the safeguarding of their rights, it was of little concern to the population at large. Moreover, its aims were confused and its organization muddled in the extreme. The conspirators were victims of their social class, a class that was becoming fragmented and irrelevant in the fast-changing world.

The Seven Years War

In the middle of the eighteenth century Britain and France were at war again, the two countries contesting the supremacy of the Channel and Atlantic seaways and control of the colonial settlements in America and India. This conflict, the Seven Years War

(1756–63), was to have a major impact on Brittany. The strategy adopted by the British prime minister, William Pitt (the Elder), was to control the sea-lanes and hinder French reinforcements from reaching the colonies, where the British were having spectacular successes, in Canada taking Quebec in 1758 and Montreal in 1760. The French, meanwhile, were planning an invasion of England.

Crucial to Pitt's strategy was to maintain British supremacy at sea by blockading the French fleets in the ports of Brest and Toulon, where they had taken shelter. The task of containing Brest was assigned to Admiral Sir Edward Hawke commanding a squadron of twenty-three ships of the line. In November 1759 the blockading fleet was forced by bad weather to seek shelter at Torbay on the south Devon coast, and there to hold to while the gales abated. This gave the French admiral time to escape from Brest when the weather improved, and to sail south around the coast with Hawke in hot pursuit. The two fleets eventually met in the Baie de Quiberon, where the French were making for shelter. The engagement began at two o'clock in the afternoon and raged

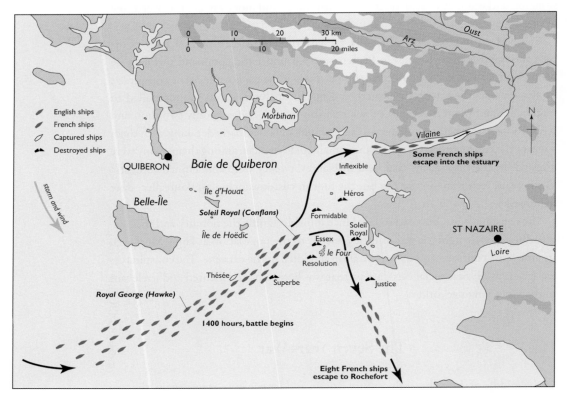

9.17 On 20 November 1759 Sir Edward Hawke successfully led the British fleet in an attack on the French navy in the Baie de Quiberon, destroying and capturing many ships and dispersing others.

until the next morning, by which time eleven out of twenty-one major French ships had been sunk or captured, the rest escaping, some to the Vilaine estuary and some to the port of Rochefort. It was a significant victory for the British and the invasion threat was now averted, but to ensure the safety of British merchant shipping along the south coast of Brittany, a British force was landed on Belle-Île in 1761. The island was occupied until the end of the war in 1763, when it was exchanged for Menorca.

Attacks on the mainland of Brittany were less successful. In 1759 the duke of Marlborough landed with a force at Cancale with the aim of destroying French vessels in the port of Saint-Malo. Apart from burning a few ships at Saint-Servan, the expedition was a failure. Later in the year another attempt was made, this time by landing a force of ten thousand at Saint-Briac. Again it was a failure, and the decision was made to re-embark at Saint-Cast-le-Guildo, but at that moment the French attacked, killing two thousand English and taking 730 prisoners.

Peace was eventually negotiated in 1763 in Paris. By the terms of the treaty, France gave up Canada, Nova Scotia, and Cape Breton Island, but retained the small islands of Saint-Pierre et Miquelon off the south coast of Newfoundland. In the Caribbean

9.18 In the eighteenth century trade in American tobacco brought prosperity to Morlaix. Tobacco factories were established along the quay in the 1740s. In 1788, the year before the Revolution, 750 people were employed in the tobacco trade.

they continued to hold Guadeloupe and Martinique. The impact of all this was to weaken French trade. Some sugar and tobacco continued to arrive from the West Indies, while the islands of Saint-Pierre et Miquelon provided a base for the Breton cod fishing fleets, but Britain now controlled the lucrative fur trade. With the loss of the trading settlements in India to the British and the consequent demise of the French East India Company in 1769, Lorient lost most of its trade but was soon to be redeveloped as a naval port. The war and its outcome had caused substantial disruption in Brittany's overseas trade, but all was not gloom. Morlaix continued to thrive on the importation of tobacco, its grand quayside warehouses proclaiming a new-found prosperity, while the ports of Nantes and Saint-Nazaire became successful shipbuilding centres.

Prelude to the Revolution

The economic impact of the Seven Years War was a significant factor behind the social changes now gripping Brittany. With maritime commerce growing in importance, a bourgeoisie was emerging, separate from the old elite, with an identity of its own. This was to have an increasing impact on political events in later decades of the eighteenth century, in particular in the so-called Brittany Affair, when the Breton Parlement once more confronted the authority of the monarchy over the vexed issue of increased taxation. The principal character in the story is Louis-René de Caradeuc de La Chalotais (1701–85). He was a jurist and for sixty years had served as *procureur général* in the Breton Parlement. La Chalotais was a modernizer and bitterly opposed to the power of the Jesuits, who had a stranglehold on education. In 1763 he published his *Essay on National Education* calling for a scientific programme of study. His views won the enthusiastic approval of Voltaire.

In 1764 the États-Généraux refused to agree to new taxes ordered by the governor of Brittany, the duke of Aiguillon, on behalf of the king. The Parlement, led by La Chalotais, backed the États, issuing decrees forbidding the imposition of new taxes. The king responded by annulling the decrees, at which point most members of the Parlement resigned. In the recriminations that followed, La Chalotais was arrested and jailed, first in the fortress of Taureau in the Morlaix estuary and later at Saint-Malo, from where he was able to issue his memoirs. After it became clear that charges against him were unlikely to stand in a court of law, he was exiled to Saintes, in south-west France. On the death of Louis XV in 1774, the new king, Louis XVI, attempted to calm the situation. The Breton Parlement was recalled and La Chalotais, allowed to return from exile, chose to speak at the new Parlement on the rights of the Breton nation, a concept that was beginning to gain widespread support.

The Brittany Affair was in many ways a minor episode in the long struggle of the Bretons to maintain their rights in the face of the French monarchy's drive for absolutism. Its interest lies in the fact that it happened at a time of social change. La Chalotais was speaking not for the nobility or the clergy but for the new bourgeoisie, who shared his dislike of the power of the Jesuits. The voice of the bourgeoisie was now being increasingly heard. In 1776 the Third Estate, angry at the tax exemptions and other privileges enjoyed by the nobility and the clergy, demanded a revision of the tax system. Social discontent grew, and in January 1789 riots broke out in Rennes between the deputies of the Third Estate and supporters of the nobility.

France, crippled by debts resulting from the Seven Years War and its costly involvement in the American War of Independence, and suffering from a succession of poor harvests, was now caught up in the fury of social unrest. The Ancien Régime was about to be swept away.

Revolution

The Revolution that gripped France and ramified into much of Europe is an event of immense fascination: a sudden surge of human energy destroying the old rules and desperately trying to establish new ones, guided and misguided by leaders driven by their own egos. Once the mischief was unleashed, it took its own surprising course. Few who had witnessed the fall of the Bastille on 14 July 1789 could have anticipated the pomp of Napoleon's coronation on 2 December 1805. The Revolution lasted from 1789 to 1799 and can be divided into two broad phases: the Constitutional Monarchy, which continued until September 1792, and the First Republic that followed, in the early months of which Louis XVI was guillotined. The Constitutional Monarchy began on 4 August 1789 following the establishment of the National Constituent Assembly in Paris. At its first session (4–11 August) the feudal system was formally abolished. This meant that the nobility (the Second Estate) lost their seigneurial rights, and the Catholic clergy (the First Estate) could no longer gather their tithes. The judicial system, administered by the thirteen regional *parlements*, was suspended and abolished the following year. The original intention was that the peasants were to pay the landowners for the release of seigneurial dues. Most refused to do so, and four years later the obligation was lifted. The abolition of tithes paid to the Church, and later the transfer of all church property to the ownership of the nation, meant that since the Church was now without financial means, the state had to shoulder

9.19 Cartoon of the Third Estate (the working people) carrying the First and Second Estates (the Church and the nobility) on its back. The caption reads, 'You should hope that this game will be over soon.' It was published in the year of the Revolution, 1789.

responsibilities for paying the clergy and providing for the sick and the poor. This was formalized in the Civil Constitution of the Clergy, passed on 12 July 1790. The clergy were now state employees, and both parish priests and bishops were to be appointed by election. Moreover, from November that year all clergy were required to swear an oath of loyalty to the Civil Constitution. Those who did so were declared 'constitutional'; the many who refused were deemed 'refractory'.

On 26 August 1789 the Assembly published *The Declaration of the Rights of Man and of the Citizen* as the first step in working towards a constitution. When the various relevant laws had been collected together into a single document and the resulting Constitution had been approved by the king, the work of the National Constituent Assembly was at an end. It was replaced by a Legislative Assembly, a body elected by four million voters made up of all men taxed above a certain level. It met for the first time on 1 October 1791 but was short-lived. Financial problems, difficulties in working with the king, the intervention of the Prussian army, and insurrection in Paris caused widespread chaos and carnage. To resolve the crisis it was agreed that the king should be suspended and a new constitution drawn up. This was entrusted to a National Convention, elected by all Frenchmen over the age of 25 who were living on the product of their own labour. The Convention met on 20 September 1792. The next day the monarchy was abolished. France was now a republic.

One of the first acts of the Convention was to put the king on trial. He was found guilty and beheaded on 21 January 1793, unleashing a fury of bloodletting. In the Reign of Terror which followed, more than sixteen thousand people were executed for counter-revolutionary activities and probably as many as forty thousand died in prison or were executed without trial. Most of the French departments expressed opposition to the central government in Paris and some, including Brittany, were now in open revolt. Meanwhile, intrigue among the political leaders and near-famine in the army and in Paris were adding to the sense of despair. In response to the failures of the National Convention a new Constitution was drawn up and approved on 27 September 1795. It created a Directory with two chambers: a Council of Five Hundred, which initiated laws, and a Council of Elders to approve or reject them. Executive power was in the hands of five directors. The Directory came under constant pressure, caused not least by growing tension between the royalists and those who wanted to revert to Reign of Terror tactics. With France still waging wars throughout Europe, the Directory came increasingly to rely on the army in both foreign and domestic affairs. Matters came to a head in November 1799 when, in a coup d'état, the executive was reduced to three consuls: Emmanuel-Joseph Sieyès, Roger Ducos, and Napoleon Bonaparte. The creation of the Consulate, with Napoleon as First Consul, effectively marked the end of the Revolution. In the following years Napoleon consolidated his power and on 18 May 1804 was granted the title of emperor of the French.

The febrile and dangerous political situation developing in France was played out against a background of almost constant warfare between France and Britain, with other European countries becoming involved for shorter episodes. This long period of warfare divides into two: the Revolutionary Wars, beginning in 1792 (with Britain entering the conflict on 1 February 1793) and ending with the Treaty of Amiens in

1802; and the Napoleonic Wars, beginning in 1803 and ending with Napoleon's defeat at Waterloo in 1815. Throughout the conflict, command of the sea was energetically contested, especially in the waters around Brittany. The royalist leanings of many Bretons offered the British the possibility of opening up a new front against the Revolutionary government of France by landing forces in the peninsula to support those wishing to reinstate the monarchy.

Brittany and the Revolution

In May 1789 a group of Breton representatives, called to attend the États-Généraux held at the château de Versailles, formed an association, the Club Breton, to campaign for the abolition of the feudal system. It was a popular cause and the club rapidly outgrew its original regional affiliation. By October, when the club moved to Paris and set up its headquarters in the refectory of the monastery of the Jacobins in the rue Saint-Honoré, it had become a national movement soon to be known simply as the Jacobins. The Jacobins quickly became a driving force in the Revolution.

The members of the original Club Breton should have been careful what they wished for. They were no doubt overjoyed that the first meeting of the National Constituent Assembly held in August abolished the feudal system, removing seigneurial rights and the right of the Church to demand tithes. But less palatable was the Assembly's suspension of all regional *parlements*, which were abolished altogether a few months later. This swept away the autonomy that Brittany had enjoyed in legal and fiscal matters since union with France in 1532, an autonomy that Bretons had fought to preserve for centuries against the predations of successive French kings. Many in Brittany viewed this loss of freedom as unacceptable. Further disquiet came when the Civil Constitution of the Clergy was enacted on 27 November 1790, requiring all clergy to swear loyalty to the Civil Constitution. Brittany was a deeply religious country used to its old ways and there was much popular support for the many priests and bishops who refused to take the oath. A final blow came in 1793 when the *levée en masse* (mass national conscription) was instituted, requiring all able-bodied men aged 18 to 25 to be conscripted. The Edict of Union of 1532 had specifically stated that Bretons were free from any obligation to serve in the French army. Though many welcomed its social reforms, the Revolution had now swept away all of Brittany's traditional claims to independence.

In all regions of France, opposition to the dictates of the Revolutionary government in Paris grew, and in 1793 many areas were in open revolt. The most serious opposition came from the Vendée (the coastal region south of the Loire) and from Brittany, where

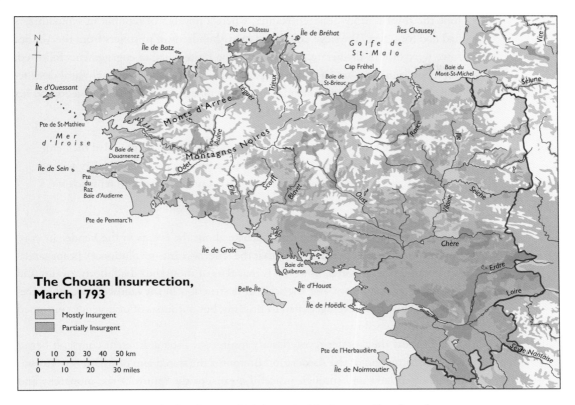

The Chouan Insurrection, March 1793

Mostly Insurgent
Partially Insurgent

0 10 20 30 40 50 km
0 10 20 30 miles

9.20 The insurrection against the Revolution, which began in March 1793, affected south-eastern Brittany, but many areas, particularly in the west, had revolutionary sympathies.

the pro-royalist movement became known as the Chouans, from the name adopted by one of the leaders of the insurgents, who used the call of the tawny owl (*chouette hulotte*) as a signal of recognition. The revolts in the Vendée and in Brittany were separate manifestations adopting different methods, but there was a degree of overlap and co-operation, especially when refugees from the Vendée fled to Brittany in the winter of 1793–4.

In the Vendée the uprising was triggered by the introduction of conscription. In March 1793, instead of joining the republican army, many young men opposed to the aspirations of the republicans formed an army of their own, the Royal and Catholic Army, to become the spearhead of the counter-revolutionary movement. The force was composed of two thousand irregular cavalry and a loosely organized rebel infantry using mainly guerrilla tactics. The Republic's response was to dispatch an army of forty-five thousand troops to the region. There followed a series of engagements. In

June the royalist army besieged Nantes, where a number of republican sympathizers had fled for safety. The siege failed, and many hundreds of prisoners from the Vendée force were shot or deliberately drowned in the Loire. Further engagements followed, the republicans now under orders to pacify the region by complete physical destruction. By December the commander of the republican army was able to report to his masters in Paris:

> the Vendée is no more . . . According to your orders, I have trampled their children beneath our horses' feet; I have massacred their women, so they will no longer give birth to brigands. I do not have a single prisoner to reproach me. I have exterminated them all.

Needless to say, there has been much debate about the events in the Vendée in 1793, some claiming it as genocide, others that the letter was anti-revolutionary propaganda. What cannot be doubted, however, is that tens of thousands died, both royalist and republican sympathizers, and the scale of destruction in the landscape was unprecedented. Many royalist refugees fled to Brittany, but outbursts of insurgency continued in the Vendée until 1799.

In Brittany the counter-revolutionary insurgency took a different course. It began with the formation of the Association Bretonne, the stated aim of which was 'to contribute essentially, and through peaceful means, to the return of the monarchy and to the salvation of the rights of the Province, of the properties, and of the honour of Brittany'. To this end representatives were appointed in each parish to act as co-ordinators, but the movement lacked impetus and after 1792 the Chouans began to take power, their insurgency spreading quickly through the Breton countryside. It was particularly strong in the south-east of the country, with active pockets along the eastern border, and around Saint-Brieuc and in Léon. The Chouans tended to work in small local cohorts using guerrilla tactics to harass the revolutionary troops and to take control of communication. Where possible, open battles were avoided. In the Breton countryside, with its small embanked fields, woodlands, and marshes crossed by numerous rivers, guerrilla warfare was an effective tactic, but lack of a centralized command structure made it difficult to co-ordinate actions. To try to improve matters, and his own prospects, one of the more prominent of the Breton leaders, Joseph de Puisage, led a mission to London in September 1794 to meet the émigré French monarchists, including the future king Charles X, and with the support of the British prime minister, William Pitt (the Younger), had himself appointed general-in-chief of the Royal and Catholic Army of Brittany with power over royalist supporters in the whole of the region north of the Loire.

9.21 The Chouans in action. Drawing by Léonce Petit (1839–84).

To counter the insurrection the Convention first established three army commands: the Army of the West, based in Nantes, which controlled the territory south of the Loire; the Army of the Coasts of Brest, based in Rennes or Vannes, with command of most of Brittany north of the Loire; and the Army of the Coasts of Cherbourg, based at Saint-Malo, with responsibility over Basse-Normandie and the north-eastern corner of Brittany. In December 1795 the commands were combined to become the Army of the Coasts of the Ocean under General-in-Chief Lazare Hoche. In addition to the military, the Convention also sent *représentants en mission* charged with maintaining civil order in the departments. These men were given unlimited power, which often expressed itself in excessive violence against counter-revolutionaries. The insurgency continued largely unabated until the royalists in Paris asked the Chouans to cease the fight. A peace treaty was negotiated and offered for signature in April 1795, but only twenty-one of the 121 Chouan leaders signed. When General Hoche ordered all those who had not signed to be arrested, hostilities began again.

The involvement of Britain in the affairs of Brittany continued when, on 23 June 1795, a British fleet landed an émigré army of 3,500 men at Carnac to join a fifteen-thousand-strong Chouan force. Disagreements, causing delays, allowed Hoche to attack, driving the counter-revolutionaries onto the Quiberon peninsula, but the British ships transported some of them to landings behind the republican lines. Others took ship and returned to England. In spite of further reinforcements sent to join the émigrés, Hoche won the day, taking more than six thousand prisoners. The only lasting effect of the episode was to demoralize the Chouan fighters and to divide their leadership. Hoche followed up his success by promising amnesty to Chouans who surrendered: many accepted the offer, including several of the Chouan leaders.

But still the insurgency continued, erupting into violence from time to time. A new law, passed in July 1799, allowing the imprisonment of the relatives of anyone suspected of causing trouble inspired the Chouans to attack a number of towns including Redon, Saint-Brieuc, and Nantes, and in December 1800, Bretons were involved in an abortive attempt to assassinate Napoleon in Paris. It was the last desperate gesture of defiance. By the following year Chouannerie was all but dead. In 1801 Napoleon, now in power as First Consul, signed a concordat with the Pope marking the end of the persecution of the clergy: those who had refused to sign the oath of allegiance could now return. This removed one of the main grievances of the counter-revolutionaries. To further the cause of reconciliation, an amnesty was now offered to all royalists. After fifteen years of conflict and bloodshed, which had divided the country between royalist and republican, the Bretons could now settle back to try to make the best of the new world in which they found themselves.

Retrospect

For many in Brittany the union agreed in 1532 gave them the guarantee they wanted: their country would have a reasonable degree of autonomy while enjoying the benefits of being part of a larger and stronger France. The nobility and the clergy retained their power and their sources of income through rents and tithes. For them the lower classes were of little concern so long as the general tax level was not allowed to impact too heavily on the peasants' productivity, a resource upon which the elite depended. Yet aside from these practical considerations there remained a fierce pride in being a Breton, in sharing a cultural tradition rooted in the land of the peninsula. At an elite level this manifested itself in hereditary titles and nostalgia for the heroic events of the past. For the peasant classes in the remoteness of the countryside it was their language and the intensity of their religious beliefs and practices that provided the comfort of identity.

Two hundred and fifty years later, with the whole of France on the verge of revolution, much had changed. Throughout this time there had been the constant threats of French absolutism eating away at the freedoms guaranteed in 1532. These had to be fought off by the elite, overtly for patriotic reasons, but also in the awareness that the productive lower classes should not be destabilized by over-taxation. But other forces were now coming into play: increasing resentment among the lower classes burdened by the abuses of the seigneurial system, and the gradual emergence of a bourgeoisie. The uprising of 1675, though sparked by taxes imposed by the French state, was fed by the tavern owners and fishwives of the towns and the millers and better-off peasants in the countryside. No longer was opposition to French autocracy restricted to the elite of Haute-Bretagne. The uprising was, in part, fuelled by a deep resentment of the seigneurial system, with its increasingly extortionate entry fees for leases and its demand for corvée labour, and the 10 per cent tithe on produce due to the Church. It is no surprise that, in the frenzied early months of 1789, Bretons were in the forefront of those calling for the abolition of feudal rights.

Yet when the Revolution came, many in Brittany were ambivalent; others were outright hostile. The state takeover of the Church was bitterly opposed. It was, perhaps, only then that the Bretons became aware of the depth of their religious beliefs. The very distinctive form of Catholicism practised in Brittany was an essential part of their identity. For their priests and bishops to be answerable to a secular government in Paris was unthinkable. And then the second blow, universal conscription, hit, tipping large areas of Brittany into counter-revolutionary insurgency. While the Chouan movement, ineffectually led, faded away, it created a potent image of Brittany, strongly Catholic and royalist in stark opposition to the ideals of Revolutionary France. It was an image that was to persist, reminding the Bretons of what made them a people.

10

OURSELVES AS
OTHERS SEE US
1789–1900

OUTSIDERS looking in on Brittany saw a people very different from themselves. The Bretons dressed differently, spoke their own incomprehensible language, and were highly superstitious, their lives dominated by a sense of ever-present death. In short, they were altogether more primitive, more *sauvage*. It was a caricature, of course, but like all successful caricatures it contained an element of truth.

In 1788, the year before the fall of the Bastille, an Englishman, Arthur Young (1741–1820), spent a month travelling around Brittany on horseback. He was a gentleman farmer and a writer on agricultural matters and his purpose in visiting France was to gather information about the 'cultivation, wealth, resources and national prosperity' of the country. To this end he made three journeys, in 1787, 1788, and 1789, publishing his findings in 1792. For part of the time in Brittany he stayed with the local elite, to whom he carried letters of introduction, but he also lodged in local inns, being more concerned about whether his horse would be comfortable and well fed than with his own well-being.

For him Brittany was a land of 'privileges and poverty'. Having crossed into the country at Pontorson, he wrote:

> There seems here a more minute division of farms than before. There is a long street in the episcopal town of Dol, without a glass window; a horrid appearance. My entry into Brittany gives me an idea of its being a miserable province.

The next day was no better:

> To Combourg. The country has a savage aspect; husbandry not further advanced, at least in skills, than among the Hurons; the people as wild as their country, and their town of Combourg one of the most brutal, filthy places that can be seen.

But the larger towns he found more acceptable, enthusing in particular about the thriving ports of Brest and Lorient and the cultured atmosphere of Nantes. What seems to have depressed him most was the backwardness of the agriculture, particularly in the remoter parts. The extent of uncultivated land is a recurring theme, culminating in a cry of disbelief at 'all the wastes, the deserts, the heath, ling, furz, broom and bog' he had travelled through for three hundred miles before finally reaching the civilized city of Nantes. For Young, a comparatively unbiased outsider, Brittany was different, its land was under-developed, and its people lived primitive lives.

A View from the Centre

There was much the new Revolutionary regime in Paris did not like about the Bretons, not least the adherence of many of them to the ideals of the Ancien Régime: feudal power, the rights of the aristocracy, and the stranglehold of the Church on all aspects of life, especially education. Not all Bretons, of course, held to these values. In the 1760s the politician and philosopher La Chalotais had railed against the power of the Jesuits and the uselessness of the monastic movement, but the resistance to revolutionary change which had flared up in many areas of Brittany under the name of Chouannerie had shown just how reactionary much of the population was. Chouannerie was not a unified movement; it was disorganized and fractious, a series of often isolated insurrections responding to different perceived injustices like compulsory recruitment in the army and the demand that clerics swore allegiance to the state. Support for the causes of individual aristocrats acting in their own interests added to the chaos. While there were enclaves of staunch republicanism, especially in some of the towns, the overall impression was that Brittany was a reactionary province set against the ideals of the Revolution. The view from Paris is nicely summed up by Bertrand Barère (1755–1841) in his report for the Comité de Salut Public written in 1794. In Brittany, he writes, ignorance perpetuates the yoke imposed by the priests and nobles; there citizens are born and die in error: they do not even know yet that new laws exist. The inhabitants of the countryside only understand Breton; it is with this barbaric instrument of their superstitious ideas that the priests and the intransigents hold them under their sway, direct their conscience, and prevent citizens from knowing the laws and from loving the Republic.

This was part of a broader argument he was making that all the local languages and dialects spoken in France should be suppressed and replaced by French in the interests of educating the people in the benefits of the republican ideal. He was no doubt mindful of the surprising statistics published a few years earlier, in 1790, showing that only a fifth of the population of France could speak French well and over a third knew no French at all. If communication of the laws and diktats of the Revolution was the imperative, then clearly the polyglot nature of the inhabitants was a problem that had to be overcome. For Barère, French was 'The most beautiful language of Europe, the first to have consecrated the rights of man and the citizen, and the language which is charged with the role of transmitting to the world the most sublime thoughts of liberty and the greatest political speculations.' And so began the move to replace the Breton language (see below, pp. 352–3).

At the outset the leaders of the Revolution realized that uniting France required the old structure of provinces, each enjoying a degree of self-government, to be abolished. Thus it was that in November 1789 the province of Brittany ceased to exist and its États and Parlement were disbanded. A review was then held, and on 22 December five new departments (*départements*), roughly comparable to the English county, were announced: Finistère, Côtes-du-Nord, the Morbihan, Ille-et-Vilaine, and Loire Inférieure. Their extent was based as far as possible on existing boundaries, and together the five departments covered the territory that had been Brittany since the ninth century. A similar reorganization was carried out across the whole of France, resulting in ninety-five departments. Each was administered by a prefect appointed by the central government in Paris, to which he was required to report. In a single sweep the slate had been wiped clean. The old administrative system, which had gradually crystallized out of the chaos following the collapse of the Roman empire, was now replaced by a number of smaller units, each directly linked to Paris. Old allegiances were torn apart and ancient rights and privileges were no longer recognized. It was a highly effective way of breaking down regional identities and loyalties where reactionary, counter-revolutionary tendencies could fester. It also greatly strengthened the hold of the central government on every aspect of life.

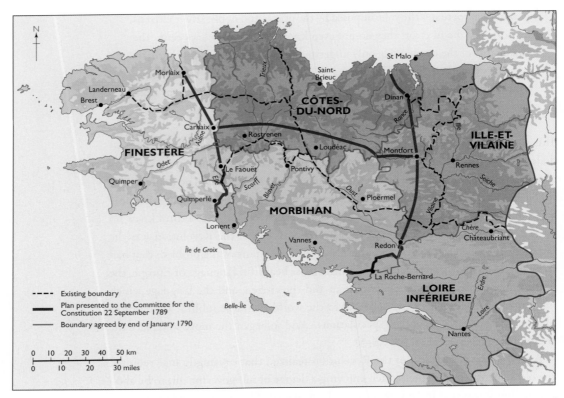

10.1 With the Revolution came massive organizational change throughout France with the setting up of new administrative units called departments (*départements*). In September 1789 the Comité de Constitution put forward a proposal for the division of Brittany. Modifications were made and by January 1790 the boundaries were finally agreed, creating the departments of Finistère, Côtes-du-Nord, the Morbihan, Île-et-Vilaine, and Loire Inférieure.

The revolutionaries had also to take control of the power of the Church. As we have seen, this was done by requiring clergymen to swear allegiance to the state. Across France only about 55 per cent chose to comply, though in Brittany it was only 25 per cent. These were referred to as the Constitutionals. Those who refused to take the oath, known as the nonjuring priests, were frequently persecuted, and in one year alone, 1799, more than nine thousand were arrested and deported. In this mood of anti-Christian fervour churches were closed, Sundays were abolished, and time was no longer calculated from the birth of Christ: in Revolutionary France the year of the beginning of the Revolution became year 1. To a deeply religious people like the Bretons this wholesale dismantling of their religion struck at their very identity.

By the time Napoleon became First Consul in 1799, it was clear that there was widespread disquiet over the suppression of religion. As one commentator advised, 'The mass of the French people want to return to their old habits and it is no longer the time to resist this nationwide tendency.' Napoleon acted quickly and negotiations were opened with the Pope. The Concordat which eventually resulted after much hard bargaining was signed in July 1801. It stated that the Roman Catholic religion was 'the religion of the great majority of the French people and citizens could now worship freely'. The Pope was to liaise with the French government to remap the dioceses to reduce their number. All the existing bishops were to resign and new bishops were to be appointed by the First Consul and invested by the Pope. All churches not previously nationalized would be available for worship, and the state would pay the salaries of bishops and priests. In April 1802 churches reopened throughout France and the ringing of church bells resounded across the country. Although relations between Napoleon and the Pope subsequently became extremely strained, leading to Napoleon's excommunication, the Pope was prepared to agree that 'the Concordat was a healing act, Christian and heroic'.

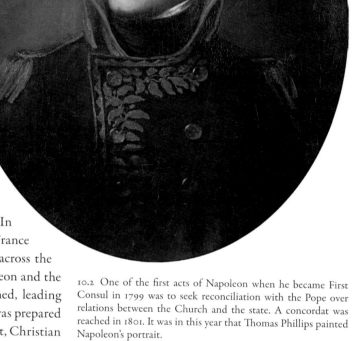

10.2 One of the first acts of Napoleon when he became First Consul in 1799 was to seek reconciliation with the Pope over relations between the Church and the state. A concordat was reached in 1801. It was in this year that Thomas Phillips painted Napoleon's portrait.

For the Bretons, it meant that after twenty years of repression they could begin to reconstruct the ecclesiastical network that was so much a part of their way of life. The cathedrals at Quimper, Vannes, Saint-Brieuc, Rennes, and Nantes continued to serve as the episcopal seats of the newly formed departments, but four of the original nine, Dol, Saint-Malo, Tréguer, and Saint-Pol-de-Léon, lost their status. With the churches open, the priests could continue their work as teachers, but under the Consulate and First Empire much was beginning to change.

The Future of the Breton Language

Before the Revolution schools were run by the clergy, who received payment from those who could afford it but were prepared to take a number of poorer pupils for free. All teaching was based on the catechism, beginning with Latin and moving on to French. Only later were pupils taught to read and write Breton. But in the early eighteenth century a teacher from Léon pioneered the idea that teaching should begin with the known, Breton, and only then move on to the unknown, Latin and French. The method was adopted widely throughout Basse-Bretagne. But with the Revolution came the directive to teach French. At the same time a bill was introduced to send special French teachers to all areas where patois, 'idioms', dialects, and foreign languages were spoken. They were to be paid by the state and were tasked to give extra French lessons and to teach the responsibilities and benefits of citizenship under the Republic. In Brittany the special teachers were required to know Breton so that they could translate orally when required. The experiment did not last for long. State funding dried up and the special teachers were soon absorbed into local systems, but by the end of the republican period French had become the national language.

While it was generally accepted from the beginning that Breton could be a useful aid to teaching, the emphasis to be put on the teaching of Breton as a living language was hotly contested. The debate lasted throughout the nineteenth century, and indeed is still very much alive today. With the Concordat of 1801 the Church began to reassert its control of education and the argument grew that since, in rural areas, the preaching of the catechism in church was in Breton, it should be taught in Breton in schools. The link between language and faith was strong. In 1863 school inspectors in the Brest region noted that some priests were concerned that the emphasis on French teaching would weaken people's Catholic faith and warned that if teaching the catechism in French was enforced, children would stop attending church. In 1879, having received complaints from some republicans that teachers were using Breton texts, the prefect suggested that schools might consider using bilingual catechisms. But, as the bishops pointed out, there were four different Breton catechisms, reflecting the different dialects of the old dioceses. There was little chance of agreeing on reducing them to one language and the printing costs of producing them all would be excessive. This was to some extent a diversionary tactic, but the matter was decisively clarified when, in 1880, it was decreed that only French should be used in school.

In some schools the suppression of the Breton language was taken to extremes. One of the methods adopted was the use of the *symbole*. Any child who was heard to speak a word of Breton was made to wear a token around his or her neck, often a block of wood or sometimes a sabot (wooden clog). Only when they reported another child speaking Breton would the *symbole* be transferred. How extensive the practice was is unclear, but in 1889 the inspector-general of primary education, Irénée Carré (1829–1909), ordered that it should cease. Carré presented a wide-ranging report on Breton schools, offering advice on teaching methods. He stressed the importance of French but agreed that Breton could be used in class, though in a restricted way. Children, however, should be allowed to speak it freely while at play. His critique of the value of the Breton language, however, was devastating. He had learned, he said, that Breton children were neglected, ill-nourished, and ill-clothed, and hardly spoke at all in the home except in 'a few words of prayer morning and evening'. The neglect meant that the children were retarded and taciturn, the average Breton child having a limited vocabulary of only about five hundred words. Thus, his or her language skills, before attending school, were minimal and hardly worth building on. This was the view of an educated Frenchman: the Breton peasants as others saw them.

No doubt there was an element of truth in what Carré's informants had told him. The language of Breton peasants was hardly suited to education. With four basic dialects and many regional variants it lacked orthography and had been bastardized by the incorporation of increasing numbers of French words. It was for this reason that scholars like Jean-François Le Gonidec (1775–1838) and, later, Théodore Hersart de La Villemarqué (1815–95) worked on Breton dictionaries to distil ideal Breton, reconstructing it where necessary even if it meant borrowing from Welsh and Cornish. But this was academic Breton, the language of scholars writing in their studies, not peasants chatting in the fields. For Carré and his fellow educationalists popular Breton was the limited, mumbled language of a depressed underclass. He was writing nearly a century after Barère, but their views were much the same. He would have agreed with Barère that the Breton language was 'the barbaric instrument of [the] superstitious ideas' of 'the inhabitants of the countryside', and also with his famous statement that 'Federalism and superstitions speak Breton.' The negative connotations of speaking Breton were now firmly established in the mind of the outside observer.

So, the British Come

The French Revolution and the Napoleonic Wars which followed made travel in most of Europe a hazardous prospect, but with Napoleon's defeat at Waterloo in 1815

Europe began to settle down and once more the English upper classes began to look at the Continent as a suitable place to while away their leisure time. Brittany had much to offer. In the year before the outbreak of the Revolution, Arthur Young had made a month-long tour of the country (above, pp. 347–8). He had been well received by his contacts, and in his *Travels in France* presents a lively, and generally encouraging, account. A casual reader could not fail to be curious about a people and country so very different from England. It was the otherness of the place and its inhabitants that, in the post-war era, began to draw a growing stream of visitors.

One of the earliest British visitors to write about his travels in Brittany is quite open about his fascination for the place: 'To the student of man, and his history, the Breton peasantry present an object of observation, as interesting and as suggestive as the fossilized remains of extinct races of organized beings can to the physiologist.' These were the words of Thomas Adolphus Trollope (1810–92), the elder brother of the more famous writer Anthony. In 1839 Trollope set off with the artist Auguste Hervieu to spend the summer months travelling throughout Brittany to record their impressions of the country and its people. The following year *A Summer in Brittany* was published in two volumes. It was Thomas's first book, a work presided over by his formidable mother, Frances, who is acknowledged on the title page as editor in a type considerably larger than that naming her author son.

Trollope was by no means a pioneer. The English were already well entrenched, particularly in the little town of Dinan, close to Saint-Malo, the favoured port of arrival. Dinan was, he writes,

one of those towns which have become colonies of English emigrants. It is very pretty and conveniently situated, and was very cheap; and so a tribe of our wandering countrymen 'marked it for their own'.

No Egyptian ever dreaded the approach of a swarm of locusts more than the native residents of the little towns of France do the settling down of a flight of English. For the result in both cases is the same—scarcity and dearness of every article of consumption . . . I met, in the remoter parts of Brittany, three or four old Englishmen, many years resident in the country, who constantly retreat before the advancing flood of their countrymen like the squatters, those pioneers of civilization in the western forests of America; well knowing that to live cheaply they must find some part of the country where English gold has not yet penetrated.

At Dinan the English have a place of worship and a resident clergyman. . . . Notwithstanding the English, you may live very comfortably at a tolerably good hotel for £3 a month . . .

10.3 One of the earliest travel guides to Brittany in English was Thomas Adolphus Trollope's *A Summer in Brittany*, published in two volumes in 1840. The influence of his domineering mother, Frances, is obvious from the title page.

That there was already a colony of English expatriates in Brittany is interesting, as is his implication that they kept arriving. Perhaps here we are seeing refugees fleeing from the steeply rising taxation and increasing industrialization of their native country.

Trollope's account of Brittany and the Bretons is generous and effusive: everything delights and interests him, even the squalor and the smells. He is always descriptive rather than critical: 'Two nearly naked children were sprawling on the earth . . . and close to them, were three or four fowls seeking their food among the quantity of filth and rubbish of all kinds which loaded the floor of the whole apartment.' Perhaps the most moving of his descriptions is that of the pardon of Saint-Jean-du-Doigt. He contrasts the movement of the healthy pilgrims, walking or going on hands and knees around the outside of the church, with the static group of mendicants hoping for alms, displaying their 'hideous deformity and frightful mutilation', their 'loathsome filth, and squalor, vermin-breeding corruption'. Then inside the church the scene changes to jostling crowds struggling to get close to the altar kept in control by a man high above them with a long cane, 'whacking the most violent and impatient of the crowds over their heads and shoulders in the manner that a Smithfield drover regulates the motions of an irritated and over driven herd of bullocks'. It is an uncensorious, good-humoured account drawn with all the skills Dickens would master many decades later.

He observes with the eye of an anthropologist, at one moment writing of how in church the sexes separate out, the men clustering in the nave while the women occupy the aisle and the space in front of the altar; at another, how the peasants prefer to drink their milk, curdled with a large lump of butter added and then boiled. Nor is he prepared to accept the dismissive stereotypes of the Breton character offered by Paris-based observers. The Bretons may be different, he says,

> But with all the faults, which result from backwardness in the race of improvement and civilization, the natural character of the Breton has much in it to admire. Honest, frank, loyal, hospitable, and religious . . . He is idle, it is true, but contented with the small produce of his easy labour.

And again,

> They have many good qualities which are indigenous to the race, and above all, the principles of religion have not yet, as in almost every part of France, been sapped and destroyed in the minds of the people.

To our modern ear this sounds patronizing—the Bretons as noble savages—but it was a far more subtle and gentle way of describing Bretons as 'other' than that which had emanated from Revolutionary Paris. When he feels it necessary to give his reader some sense of the character of the Breton, he does so by stressing qualities that might be considered admirable, balancing the description with a caricature of himself as an arrogant, impatient Englishman.

> The stillness of demeanour, the grave, severe manners, and a pathetic silence of the Bas-Breton peasants, is one of their most striking characteristics. Unless when strongly excited by some powerful feeling, there is a degree of ste[a]dfast immobility about them, which forms the strongest possible contrast to the habits and temperament of the peasants of the rest of France. I have been assured also that their bodily insensibility is correspondingly remarkable. My own experience of the difficulties of making my way through a Breton crowd, would lead me to think them utterly destitute of the sense of feeling. The most vigorous punches in the ribs, and most determined application of the whole force of the back and shoulders against his person, will fail to make a Breton peasant move out of your way, or even look round.

Trollope is alert to the social changes going on around him. The growth of towns had created differences between urban and country dwellers. 'Not only their manners and way of life, but their character and modes of thinking upon all subjects are altogether at variance.' This 'general feeling of opposition and separation' he puts down to differences generated by the Revolution. There were also regional differences. Finistère had changed little over the years, but in Tréguer 'the Celtic character, language and costume are slowly submitting to the same process of change, which has at length rendered the upper province [Haute-Bretagne] to so great a degree French'. All this careful observation of the people is presented against lyrical descriptions of countryside. In this he was following the aesthetic ideals of the Romantic movement, given prominence by writers like William Gilpin in the 1770s, which encouraged English travellers to analyse and communicate the countryside through which they journeyed according to the rules of the picturesque. Some of Trollope's descriptions of the Breton landscape are minor masterpieces.

Trollope was not the first British traveller to write a description of post-Revolutionary Brittany. In 1834 Leitch Ritchie published his *Travelling Sketches on the Sea-Coasts of France*. Focused mostly on Normandy, he made visits to Mont-Saint-Michel and Saint-Malo but is more interested to describe monuments and give details of local history than to write about people. A far more interesting early visitor was Thomas Price (1787–1848), a Welsh clergyman, linguist, and antiquarian. Price was a good friend of La Villemarqué and helped organize his trip to the Eisteddfod at Abergavenny. His passion for the Celtic world led him to travel widely in Ireland, Scotland, Cornwall, and Brittany. He learned Breton and supported the call for the Bible Society to publish a Breton translation of the New Testament. But perhaps his greatest achievement was to demonstrate the close cultural links that there were between the Welsh and the Bretons.

His impressions of his visit to Brittany in 1829 were eventually published as 'Tour through Brittany Made in the Year 1829' in *The Literary Remains of the Rev. Thomas Price* (1854). His interest in the language is evident throughout, and he writes with particular fondness of the Breton people, their dress, and their countryside, his most lasting memories, he says, being simple things like 'the march of cows through the village of Chamouni' and the sound of the sabots in the marketplace of Morlaix. For him, in the isolation of Brittany survives the Romantic spirit, which elsewhere in Europe had been stifled by the heavy hand of Rome and 'the knell of the Gothic curfew'. Nor had he any time for the derogatory remarks made by the French:

> the truth is, that the Bas Bretons . . . so far from being the arrant savages those French cockneys would have us believe, live in as comfortable farmhouses as the same class of people in any other part of France, and to outward appearance, as well constructed as those of the small farmers in many parts of England.

He feels bound, however, to add the qualification,

> But although accusation of barbarism is false . . . Yet it must not be concealed that there are some remote corners in the western department . . . in which the condition of the people would seem wretched.

Between them Trollope and Price provide an unrivalled insight into Brittany in the 1820s. They wrote under different imperatives: Price as a Celtic scholar stressing the unity and uniqueness of the surviving Celtic peoples, and Trollope as a fledgling author stretching his wings as a Romantic, excitedly communicating the exotic nature of the Bretons. As pioneers their writing has a freshness that is lacking in so much of the later British travel writing about Brittany, which becomes lazy and formulaic, repeating the same tired tropes, painting the Bretons as simply quaint.

The Illustrators

It was not unusual for travellers to Brittany intent on publishing their observations to be accompanied by artists to provide the necessary illustrations. Thomas Trollope took with him Auguste Hervieu (*c.*1794–1858), who had served as tutor to his family and was a confidant to his mother, Frances. Hervieu was trained as an artist in France but had been exiled in 1823 for his anti-royalist politics. Although he was allowed to return following the death of Louis XVIII in 1824, he chose to settle in London and made his living as a painter and book illustrator. Accompanying Trollope on his summer travels in 1829, Hervieu must have made many sketches, but only fourteen of them were turned into engravings. They are for the most part rather dreary and claustrophobic, adding little to the text.

The value that appropriate illustrations can add is nicely shown by a book published fifty years later, *Breton Folk: An Artistic Tour in Brittany*, by Henry Blackburn. It was illustrated by Randolph Caldecott (1846–86), an artist and illustrator best known for his children's picture books, his work characterized by clean lines and simple use of colour. *Breton Folk* contains 170 of his drawings, greatly enlivening an otherwise unremarkable text. Beautifully observed, lively, and often amusing, they touch upon every aspect of Breton existence. Here, for the first time, the reader is presented with a view of people happily engaged with their daily lives, shorn of all the gloomy foreboding with which they were traditionally associated.

The earliest British photographic expedition to Brittany appears to be that organized by the Reverend John Mounteney Jephson in 1859 to accompany his five-week walking tour. The result was a book written by Jephson on his travels, *Narrative of a Walking Tour in Brittany*, accompanied by a box containing ninety photographs in stereo pairs. Jephson prepared carefully for his trip, taking advice from a friend, 'himself a noted pedestrian', who guided him on the equipment which he needed to take:

PEASANTS IN PRAYER AT THE GRAVES OF THEIR RELATIVES

10.4 Trollope was accompanied by the French artist Auguste Hervieu, who produced illustrations for *A Summer in Brittany*, mostly dismal scenes that were almost caricatures of the dour life of the Bretons. This graveyard scene stresses the deeply religious beliefs of the people, with the skulls of ancestors in the ossuary looking on in approval at the piety of a newly bereaved couple.

This consisted of a suit of stout grey tweed, a light cap, a pair of moderately strong French elastic boots, a light waterproof paletôt, and a waterproof knapsack,

containing shirts, spare trousers, slippers, and dressing materials; a pocket tel-
escope, a note-book, an ink-bottle, writing materials, mariner's compass, and
hazel-handled umbrella completed my equipment.

He was shadowed, at a distance, by a friend, Lovell Reeve:

He himself, accompanied by a professional photographer, travelled in a hired
carriage, stopping at the principal towns, and making stereographs of any object
of interest to be met with on the road, while I took the same, or nearly the same
route on foot. It so happened that we occasionally met in the course of our trip,
but we were quite independent of each other.

Reeve gives an account of what the photographic expedition involved:

Our apparatus consisted of a small double-lens landscape camera, by Ross,
a black tent, about four feet square and seven feet high, fitted with table and
sink, the whole folding up into a moderate-sized portmanteau, and two boxes
of chemicals, one for use and the other for store, with a third box, containing
in a small compass a gross of glasses, comprised in six inner boxes of two dozen
each. It was decided to confine our operations to the wet collodion process, and
to defer varnishing the plates until our return home. Great care was necessary so
to economize our hours of travelling, as to have the fairest weather and the best
description of light at our disposal while at work with the camera. The first thing
to be observed on entering a town or village, was the position the sun would
be in, with respect to the objects selected, at the time we should be prepared to
photograph them, the points of view to be taken, and the most effective arrangement of foreground; the next consideration was to select a place for our tent in
the nearest proximity to two or more views together. The result was, that we
visited thirty towns and villages within the space of thirty days, pitching our tent
about a hundred times, during which period my active photographer, Mr. Taylor,
could not have taken fewer than two hundred pictures, from which the present
ninety have been selected for publication. Our evenings were fully occupied in
looking over the day's harvest, clearing away the day's disorder, and preparing
plates and chemicals for the next day's work, though I fear I contributed little
myself in this respect.

It must be admitted that the photographs that survive seem hardly to have justified the
effort, but as an attempt to make a photographic record of Brittany, only twenty years

10.5 A far more cheerful illustrator was Randolph Caldecott, whose sketches enliven Henry Blackburn's *Breton Folk*. Here the artist depicts himself calmly enjoying the fascination that his activities are causing among the locals.

GOING TO THE PARDON AT CHÂTEAUNEUF DU FAOU.

10.6 Caldecott's illustrations are full of movement, often with touches of humour but never condescending. His artistic skills were admired by Gauguin.

after the birth of photography, the achievements of this little expedition were notable. The Victorian family could now sit in the comfort of their home viewing the sights of Brittany through their stereoscopes as a prelude to planning their holidays.

The Floodgates Open

Until the early 1860s, travellers to Brittany had to travel by coach, on horseback, or on foot as Jephson chose to do, but the arrival of the railway changed everything. The main French rail network had reached Nantes by 1851 and Rennes by 1857. From Nantes the line was extended along the southern side of the peninsula, arriving at Quimper by 1863, and from Rennes a northern route was laid, reaching Brest in 1865. Thereafter the network spread, criss-crossing the country. The track from Auray to Pontivy was opened in 1865 and extended to Saint-Brieuc in 1872, and the route from Quimper to Landerneau was in operation in 1867. Other intermediate lines followed, opening up the country, providing quick and inexpensive travel. For a visitor coming from Paris the journey took about fourteen hours. From London, taking the train to Southampton and then a steamship to Saint-Malo, it took about the same time, in 1880 the journey costing £2 2s. return.

The extension of the rail system encouraged tourists to arrive in ever-increasing numbers, and Brittany changed from being a mysterious place, attractive to the intrepid traveller, to a comfortable holiday destination known for its sea bathing facilities. The writer of a guide book published in 1875 mentions meeting 'many tourists, from England, Prussia, Austria, Spain and America as well as from all parts of France'. English-speaking tourists were well catered for. Between 1860 and 1910 more than thirty books were written to introduce them to the delights of the country. Most were very general, and not a little derivative, with titles like *Summer Holidays in Brittany*, *Rambles in Brittany*, and *The Bretons at Home*, but others were designed for the more demanding traveller: books such as John Kemp's *Shooting and Fishing in Lower Brittany* (1859) and Edward Davies's more adventurous *Wolf-Hunting and Wild Sport in Lower Brittany* (1875), the last being of sufficient specialist interest to be translated into French. The Bretons were now beginning to experience the dubious benefits of mass tourism introducing a different, and in many ways more insidious, challenge to their sense of identity.

10.7 The coming of the railway in the middle of the nineteenth century opened up Brittany to a flood of tourists, attracted, as the poster suggests, by the landscape, particularly the beaches, the monuments, and the curiosities of the local culture. The poster was printed by the Paris–Orléans Company in 1891.

Enter the Archaeologists

A few of the British travellers to Brittany came for reasons of serious study. One of the first was Alexander Logan, who spent September 1825 examining the monuments of Carnac. His conclusion, published five years later, was that the stone rows represented a serpent and were part of a Druidic temple. A similar claim had been made by William Stukeley, a century before, about Avebury, and Logan drew a parallel between the two monuments. A little later, in 1831, the Reverend John Bathurst Deane spent time at Carnac making a far more accurate plan but broadly supporting Logan's interpretations. Bathurst and Logan were antiquaries of the old school steeped in romantic

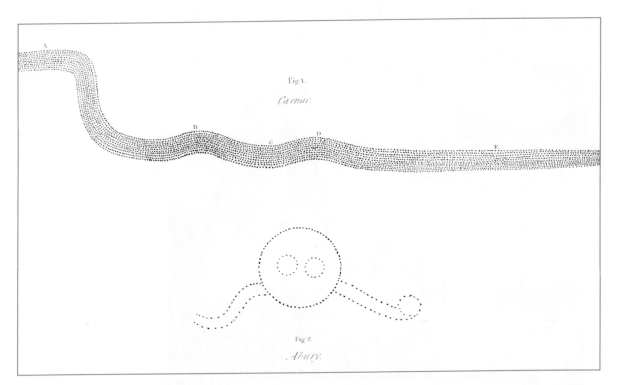

10.8 The Carnac alignments were a great source of fascination for British antiquaries. In 1825 Alexander Logan made a sketch plan of the stones, likening the sinuous form of the monument to Avebury in Wiltshire (below) which William Stukeley had interpreted as a coiled serpent constructed to serve as a Druidic temple—a Dracontium.

views about Druidism, which were fast being overtaken by a more objective approach calling for detailed and accurate recording.

The first British men to respond were Alexander Blair and Francis Ronalds, who visited the Carnac region in 1834 and made a number of accurate drawings of the stone rows and other monuments, but there matters rested until 1864, when the Reverend William Collings Lukis and Sir Henry Dryden began an ambitious programme with the aim of recording all the megalithic monuments in the Carnac region. As Lukis modestly explained, 'I passed a portion of seven summers, four of them being consecutive, ending with the year 1872, exploring the neighbourhood of Auray.' Those seven summers were highly productive, yielding several hundred accurate drawings of all the principal monuments in the region. Their importance is that they record the sites as they were before damage or modification caused by more recent agricultural and other activities. The collection has never been published, but the original drawings, now shared between the Society of Antiquaries in London, the Ashmolean Museum in Oxford, and the Guernsey Museum, offer an incomparable record.

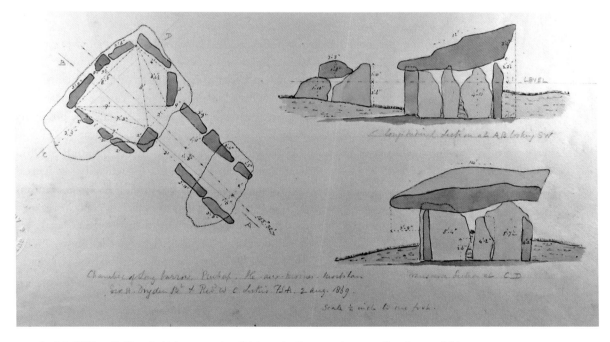

10.9 In 1864 William Collings Lukis began a series of visits to the Carnac region, recording the megalithic monuments with great accuracy. This drawing of the tomb of Penhap, Morbihan, was completed on 2 August 1869.

Three years after his final field season, Lukis, mindful of the growing public interest in prehistoric monuments of Brittany, published a little book, *A Guide to the Principal Chambered Barrows and Other Pre-Historic Monuments* (1875). It is a small volume, fitting neatly in the pocket with a hard cover to ensure that it would survive heavy use in the field. It was written, said Lukis, for tourists attracted by Brittany's 'widely-famed Rude Stone Structures' rather than 'ordinary tourists, who had no definite object in view, or who desired to be present at some of the great religious gatherings, or Pardons, and to take a brief glance at the manners, customs and holiday costumes of the Bretons'. The requirements of such people, he says, were met by the many other guidebooks available. To facilitate the visit he presented six itineraries. Notes are provided about travel arrangements and distances and also about hotels. At Auray, for example, the Hôtel de la Poste is recommended, its patron, 'Mon. Hédan', being 'an active enterprising man' who has 'sufficient knowledge of the English language to be able to come to the relief of an English tourist'. Some of the itineraries were demanding, requiring an early start that allowed a number of monuments to be ticked off before breakfast. Nonetheless, it would be worth it, and Lukis was encouraging, telling his readers that 'the journey to Locmariaker will fill him with wonder, and impress him with awe, on beholding gigantic tumuli and enormous menhirs'.

Another visitor to fall in love with Brittany was James Miln (1819–81), a wealthy Scot who had travelled widely in China, India, and New Zealand. In the summer of 1875 he disembarked at Saint-Malo to begin a tour of the country. Whether he intended to get involved with archaeological fieldwork is unclear, but at Carnac he heard of a proposal to excavate a Roman site on a nearby piece of moorland called the Bossenno, and offered to take over the work himself. He then went on to excavate other sites including the massive Neolithic burial mound, Mont-Saint-Michel, promptly publishing his work in 1877 in two volumes, one in English and one in French. His later excavation on the stone alignments of Kermario was published in 1881. As a man of means he could afford to carry out ambitious excavations and to publish lavishly at his own expense, but he clearly understood the moral responsibility of an excavator to make his results available through speedy publication. As a further legacy he left money in his will to endow a museum at Carnac where his collection could be displayed to the public. The first guardian of the museum was the young Zacharie Le Rouzic (1864–1939), who had been his assistant and went on to become a highly prolific archaeologist in his own right.

A British visitor of a very different kind was Augustus Lane-Fox, who, in 1880, took the name Pitt-Rivers on inheriting an estate on Cranborne Chase in Dorset. Lane-Fox was an archaeologist who, in his later excavations on his Dorset estate, was to set extremely high standards of recording and publication. He was also an

CROSS ON THE MONT ST. MICHEL.

10.10 This final image from James Miln's book, *Archaeological Researches at Carnac in Brittany*, shows that the author could not resist adding the mandatory image of pious Breton life to satisfy his British readers.

ethnologist and a keen collector of items of material culture from around the world. Much of his collection now forms the basis of the Pitt Rivers Museum in Oxford. In October–November 1878 and March–April 1879, Lane-Fox toured Brittany to visit sites and monuments. He was, in fact, waiting for the Ancient Monuments Act to pass through the British parliament, after which he understood he was to become inspector of ancient monuments. His tour through Brittany, visiting monuments and making records of them, was something of a dry run for the work he was expecting to do in England. He had heard of Lukis's fieldwork and wanted to see the sites for himself.

Lane-Fox's notebooks show that in 1878 he spent most of his time in the Morbihan, followed by a short stay in Dinard. The next year he began in Dinan before returning to the Morbihan and then travelling along the south coast and through Finistère and Côtes-d'Armor. While his prime interests were megalithic monuments, churches, and hill-forts, he also indulged his passion for ethnography, buying objects of material culture everywhere he went, treating Brittany as an ethnographic field study. The collection was extensive, including carved wooden panels, coifs (female head coverings), embroidery, hair ornaments, an array of tools including a potter's wheel and a spinning wheel, even down to crêpe-making utensils and a coffee grinder. He also indulged his fascination for folk magic, collecting amulets, wax models of arms, ears, heads, legs, and breasts, and amber beads, of which he says, 'an uneven number are worn around the neck . . . to cure sore throats'. He records that at the Church of St Leonard, Guingamp, 'snails are used as a cure for fever'. Here he acquired two little cotton bags containing 'earth, fibres and snail shells'. In making the collection Lane-Fox was not regarding the Bretons as an exotic backward people but was gathering comparative material to demonstrate that humans behaved in similar ways across the world.

Visitors like Lukis, Miln, and Lane-Fox were not casual tourists who flocked to Brittany for a cheap holiday and a chance to observe quaint peasants: they were serious scholars who went to study Breton culture and its remarkable prehistoric and medieval monuments. Their contributions did much to change the more enlightened tourist's perception of the Bretons and to strengthen links between scholars on both sides of the Channel.

The Search for *la Vie Sauvage*

From the 1850s painters began to discover the delights of Brittany: its picturesque otherness, the brilliance of the light in the coastal regions, and, most importantly, the low cost of living. With the extension of the railway to Quimper in 1863 the number of painters increased, creating schools in coastal towns, notably Pont-Aven, Concarneau, Douarnenez, and Camaret, and on Belle-Île. Of these the most famous was at Pont-Aven. Its attractions, well away from the main tourist scene, were discovered by a group of American painters from Philadelphia led by Robert Wylie who arrived for the summer of 1866. Others joined them from America, Britain, and

France and later from Canada, the Netherlands, and Ireland. In 1880 the English illustrator Randolph Caldecott, who was preparing illustrations for Henry Blackburn's *Breton Folk* (above, p. 359), spent some time there. His crisp, energetic style and use of plain slabs of colour were a revelation to many of the artists and were later to influence Paul Gauguin.

By now Brittany had become the favourite summer location for art students from Paris escaping from the constraints of the École des Beaux Arts. It was in the summer of 1886 that Gauguin made his first visit. He was tired of the Impressionists—'confetti painters', as he called them—and was looking for a change. In a letter to his wife, then in Denmark, he wrote:

> I have succeeded in finding some money for my trip to Brittany, and am living here on credit. . . . At the hotel we pay 75 francs a month for full board and lodging—and the food is enough to make me feel blown out every time I sit down for a meal. . . . If I can arrange to get a small, certain and regular income from my pictures, I shall come and live here throughout the year . . .

But money worries continued to concern him and he returned to Paris later in the year to recuperate after what may have been a mild heart attack and to work up the drawings he had made into finished paintings. The most important of these was *Les Quatre Bretonnes*, in which it is possible to see the simplicity he was searching for combined with a strength in composition. The wildness of Brittany had begun his liberation.

After a period working in Martinique he returned to Brittany in January 1888. 'In Brittany . . . I can work for seven or eight months without a break, saturated with the character of the peasants and the countryside, something essential for good painting.' A month later he writes to his friend Émile Schuffenecker, 'I love Brittany. I find here the savage and the primitive. When my sabots clang on the granite earth, I hear the dull, muffled tone, flat and powerful, that I try to achieve in painting.'

It was a few months later that he met the younger but highly talented painter Émile Bernard, who had with him a series of greatly simplified drawings of Breton subjects, in part inspired by stained-glass windows, the figures often defined by black outlining. It was a style which one reviewer referred to as Cloisonnism. Bernard also favoured the use of areas of plain colour. There was much in the younger man's style that appealed to Gauguin and it is quite possible that Bernard's *Le Pardon de Pont-Aven* (1888) directly influenced Gauguin's *La Vision après le Sermon*, painted the same year. Both men were clearly stimulating each other in this intensely creative period. From the collaboration

10.11 On his first visit to Pont-Aven in 1886 Gauguin made many sketches of Breton dress. This study of a Breton girl was worked up for his painting *Les Quatre Bretonnes* (1886) and was also used to decorate his *Vase with Breton Girls* (1886–7).

10.12 Gauguin's *La Ronde des petites Bretonnes* (1888), illustrating a dance performed at haymaking time, sets the figures in a typically Breton landscape.

emerged the style known as Synthetism: compositions free from all unnecessary detail using flat areas of pure colour without shading, depicting scenes created from the artist's memory combined into a single, new vision. This is what Gauguin had been striving for when he used the words 'flat and powerful'.

At the end of October, Gauguin left Brittany to stay with Van Gogh in Arles, returning to Brittany again in the autumn of 1889. He remained for about a year, going back to Paris a few months after Van Gogh's suicide. Pont-Aven was now too crowded with artists and the growing throngs of tourists attracted by their presence, so Gauguin, in the company of Paul Sérusier and the wealthy Dutch artist Meijer de

10.13 The style of painting known as Cloisonnism was developed by Émile Bernard. It is evident in his *Les Bretonnes dans la prairie* (1888), which had a significant influence on Gauguin's developing style.

Haan decided to set themselves up at Le Pouldu, some 15 kilometres along the coast from Pont-Aven. Gauguin was now much involved in exploring the more primitive aspects of the Breton landscapes: 'I scrutinized the horizons, seeking that harmony of human life with animal and vegetable life through compositions in which I allowed the great voice of the earth to play an important part.' This sudden awareness of the power of the Breton land is apparent in most of the paintings of 1889–90. So, too, is his use of the religious iconography he saw all around him in the churches and the calvaries. His three great works *Le Christ jaune*, *Le Christ vert*, and *Le Christ au jardin des oliviers*, all painted in 1889, are redolent of Breton piety. He also gained inspiration

10.14 Gauguin's *La Vision après le sermon* (1888) shows a clear reference to Bernard's style. It also shows his interest in the religious culture of Brittany, which will become increasingly apparent in his later work.

from wood carvings to be seen in plenty in churches and adorning domestic furniture. His response was the laboriously carved wooden panel *Soyez amoureuses, vous serez heureuses*. It is almost as though only on this third visit did Gauguin open himself fully to all aspects of his Breton environment, in doing so perhaps exhausting his enthusiasm for this small exotic world now too easily reached from Paris. In a year he was on his way to a new *vie sauvage* in Tahiti.

Gauguin returned to Pont-Aven and Le Pouldu again in April 1894 to try to repossess some paintings and sculpture he had left with his innkeeper, but it ended in a lawsuit, and his visit was further marred by a drunken brawl with sailors in Concarneau.

His last visit to Brittany had not been a success and early the next year he left Europe for the last time for Tahiti.

The large number of artists who had flocked to Brittany in the years between 1860 and 1900, the majority of them foreign, cannot fail to have made an impression on the Bretons. The seaside towns where they stayed benefited financially, and the cosmopolitan society, Americans, Canadians, British, and Scandinavians, introduced notions of the wider world. But these curious visitors had come to enjoy the otherness of Breton culture, the dress and behaviour of the people, their deeply held religious beliefs and practices, and their colourful folklore steeped in mystery. The fascination of the outside world for all things Breton caused the locals to pause and reflect upon themselves.

Novel Fodder

French novelists, too, gained inspiration from the Bretons and their harsh way of life. One of the first to develop the theme was Honoré de Balzac (1799–1850) in his justly famous book *The Chouans* (1829), which provides an intricate insight into the problems and intrigues of the Revolutionary years. His intention was, he wrote, 'to relate the events of one of those sadly instructive incidents in which the French Revolution was so prolific'. His research was thorough. His father had lived and worked in Brest in the years before the Revolution as a civilian in charge of army supplies and had stories to tell of the skirmishes between General Hoche and the royalists during the insurgency in the Vendée. These will have inspired the young Honoré, but the real research was done in the autumn of 1828, when he spent several weeks near Fougères with a family friend, the baron de Pommerœul. The baron had been a general in Napoleon's army and was a source of stories about the Chouannerie; so, too, were the local people Balzac talked to. From them he would have gathered first-hand accounts of the execution of the anti-revolutionary insurgents in 1792 and the peasants' attempt to take Fougères in 1793. His exploration of the alleyways and fortifications of the town and of the countryside around provided the physical setting for the story. Balzac returned to Brittany for his short story 'A Tragedy by the Sea' (1834), the tale of a family played out on the coast near Le Croisic, an unrelenting father drowning his depraved son while the young man's mother looked on in desperation, unable to intervene. This powerful image of peasant life on the Breton coast cannot fail to have impressed his readers with a vision of Brittany as a brutal and primitive country.

A later writer, Guy de Maupassant (1850–93), added to this impression with his awful story 'The Christening' (1885), a narrative of drunken, superstitious peasants, uncaring clergy, and the death of a newborn child. Maupassant had made a long journey through Brittany in the autumn of 1879 and another in 1882, gathering tales and impressions of the landscape, which he used in other short stories. For the most part Brittany is presented as a slightly strange world towards the edge of civilization, different but generally benign, yet a place where horrors could occur.

Gustave Flaubert (1821–80) also made a tour through Brittany as a young man. In 1847, accompanied by a fellow writer, Maxime Du Camp, he travelled along the Loire and then explored the Breton coast. The two men kept a journal, taking turns to write alternate chapters. Those written by Flaubert were gathered together and published posthumously as *Over Strand and Field: A Record of Travel through Brittany* (1904). The journey took three months. Flaubert delighted in what he saw, describing châteaux along the Loire, a boat trip to Belle-Île, the first aid they gave to two women engaged in a domestic dispute at Pont-l'Abbé, bear-baiting and dogfighting in Brest, together with a visit to the red-light district, the magnificence of Mont-Saint-Michel, ending with an emotional description of the château de Combourg, birthplace of Chateaubriand. Flaubert's youthful enthusiasm offers clarity. As a comparatively unbiased and uncensorious description of Brittany in the middle of the nineteenth century it is difficult to better.

Quite a different picture of Brittany from that offered by Balzac, Flaubert, and Maupassant is given by Émile Zola (1840–1902) in his amusing short story 'Shellfish

10.15 Gustave Flaubert (1821–80) was one of many French writers who sought inspiration from Brittany. As a young man, accompanied by a friend, Maxime Du Camp, he made a three-month journey round Brittany in the summer of 1847. His observations were not published until 1904. The photograph, by Carjat and Co., was taken in 1875.

for Monsieur Chabre' (1878). Set in Piriac on the Guérande, it tells of a gentle seaside holiday and a romance that leaves all three characters satisfied. Here, what Brittany has to offer is not the human cast but the theatre: the intertidal landscape where the tide itself drives the narrative. It allows Zola to tell a story very different from his doom-laden norm. Zola had spent a holiday at Piriac, which might explain the lightness of the mood. The next year, 1877, he wrote another short story, 'Priests and Sinners', which begins in the same coastal region of Brittany, a place where 'the wretched villagers

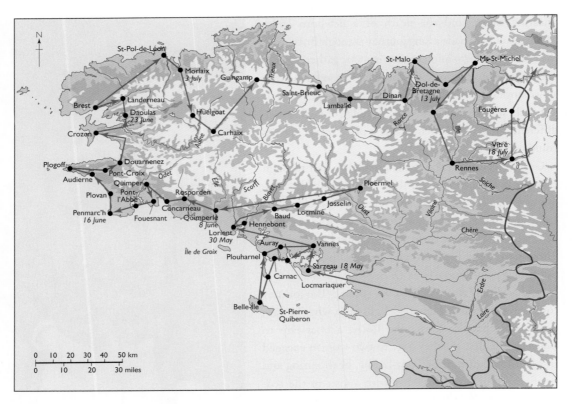

10.16 The extent of Flaubert's travels in 1847.

seemed to belong to quite a different world from that of the average Frenchman'. He could not resist reverting to the conventional picture of a peasantry repressed by the Church, describing an exorcism in which a child dies. It is a world pervaded by 'the icy chill of superstition, the helpless ignorance of people crushed by life's adversity'. The priest 'ruled like God himself, like some old rough-hewn, wooden idol with power to dispense thunderbolts and horrible diseases'. It is what his readers had been led to expect of the Bretons.

For many writers it was the coast and the life of those whose existence was bound up with the sea that so characterized Brittany. This was no more so than in the work of Pierre Loti (1850–1923). Loti was a sailor. He had joined the naval school at Brest at the age of 17, reaching the rank of captain in 1906 and serving until the age of 60, when he went onto the reserve list. One of his earliest works, *A Tale of Brittany* (*Mon Frère Yves*, 1883), is partially autobiographical and deals with the sailor's life. But far more emotive of the sea is his masterpiece *An Iceland Fisherman* (*Pêcheur d'Islande*, 1886)

BRETAGNE *(Collection E. Hamonic)*
531. – Goëlette pour la Pêche d'Islande

Sortez le lard et les galettes,
Tirez du cidre frais !
Au large on voit des goëlettes :
Ce sont les Islandais !

Botel

10.17 Pierre Loti's famous book *Pêcheur d'Islande* (1886) brought instant fame to the fishing port of Paimpol. Visitors came to see the goëlettes, the schooners in which the fishermen braved the North Atlantic. These little vessels were home to twenty or more sailors, who spent many months together at sea each year.

about the lives of the fishermen of Paimpol. Every year in the spring the little fishing boats set off to fish cod in the North Atlantic, returning in the autumn with their salted catch. It was a dangerous existence. The sea took its toll of those who ventured on it. In the churchyard of Ploubazlanec a long wall devoted to memorials lists the boats that never returned and the men who went down with them. Loti would have been familiar with all this and chose the nearby headland of Pointe de la Trinité as the location of the final scene of his book, where his heroine, Gaud, waits forlornly for her lover's ship to return, mocked by the ebb and flow of the sea. Loti's portrayal of the fishing community of Paimpol shows a deep sympathy with the tough life of the people and he writes in admiration of their resilience. This was no lazy caricature of the Bretons but a generous appreciation of their culture. His dramatic depiction of the Icelandic fishing expeditions has given Paimpol an irresistible focus for its thriving tourist industry.

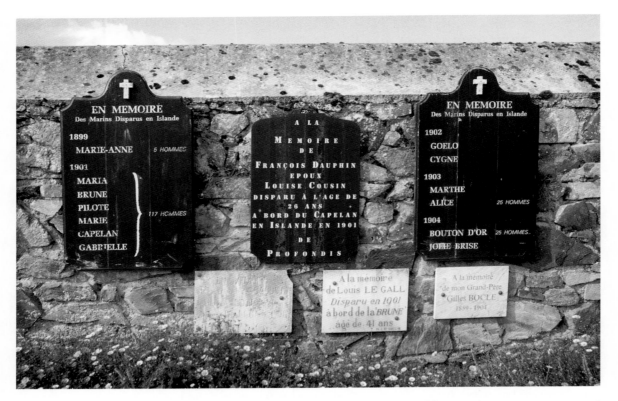

10.18 The fishermen who failed to return from the Icelandic fishing expeditions were commemorated in memorials attached to the churchyard wall at Ploubazlanec, a village to the north of Paimpol. The original memorials were dispersed in 1939 but the names of the ships and the numbers of their crews who lost their lives were recorded on boards lining the 'wall of those who disappeared'. Between 1852, when the first ship, *Occasion*, sailed for Iceland, and 1935, the last year of the Icelandic expeditions, 120 ships were lost and two thousand fishermen drowned.

The travel writers, artists, and authors who came to Brittany in search of inspiration crafted a vision of the land and its people that set in high relief their distinctive characteristics. This inevitably fed back into the consciousness of the people themselves, providing them with a vision to which to aspire. Thus it was that the fascination of foreigners encouraged the Bretons to become even more Breton.

11

CREATING IDENTITIES

HUMANS across the world have a need to relate themselves to a vision of the past shared by their community: it gives a sense of identity, of deep-rootedness and an assurance that we 'the people' are different from 'others'. For this reason, origin myths abound. For Christians it all started in the Garden of Eden; Romans imagined their ancestry beginning with the legendary Romulus, suckled by a wolf, who became the first king; while the Scythians had several versions of their origin story, usually involving the liaison of a hero god with a semi-serpent woman. These various myths lay at the beginning of long narratives leading to the present, created from a mélange of myth and hazy folk memories of actual events: narratives that were transmitted orally and, in literate societies, were eventually codified into texts.

In England it was a monk, Geoffrey of Monmouth (d. 1154/5), living in a religious community of Osney on the outskirts of Oxford, who produced the first written account of the history of Britain. It began with the mythical Brutus, grandson of Aeneas, landing at Totnes, and ended with the last of the British kings, Cadwaladr, who in the seventh century finally submitted to the Saxon advance. The *Historia Regum Britanniae* (History of the Kings of Britain) appeared sometime about 1135. As its title implies, its focus was on the succession of kings, which provided a narrative history and gave legitimacy to the ruling house. Some of the material that Geoffrey used was gleaned from earlier sources. From Nennius, who had written three hundred years before, he took the story of the landing of Brutus (who gave his name to the British), embellishing it with much detail generated by his own fertile imagination. From Gildas came stories of the Saxon attack and settlement of England in the fifth and sixth centuries. But much of the content of the *Historia* had never before been heard and was derived, wrote Geoffrey, from 'a certain very ancient book, written in the British language' acquired 'outside the country', which had been given to him by Walter, archdeacon of Oxford. The implication is that the book came from Wales or, more likely, Brittany. This work, Geoffrey claimed, he translated into Latin, using a précis to form the basis of his text. But did such a book ever exist, or was the *Historia* largely a fiction created by an under-employed monk to fill his hours of solitude? That the mysterious book was not referred to or seen by any other scholar might suggest the latter. A fellow historian, William of Newburgh, writing about 1190, had no doubt: 'It is quite clear', he said, 'that everything this man wrote about Arthur and his successors, or indeed about his predecessors from Vortigern onward, was made up, partly by himself and partly by others either from an inordinate love of lying or for the sake of pleasing the Britons.'

The existence or otherwise of the 'very ancient book' is unlikely ever to be resolved, but that Geoffrey might have had access to Breton sources is a strong possibility. As we have seen (pp. 263–4), there was a significant influx of Bretons into Britain at the time of the Norman Conquest. In many areas of the country Breton lords were established in extensive fiefdoms, creating conditions highly conducive to the movement of people and ideas. This mobility increased still further with the development of the Angevin empire under Henry II. In such times scholars were on the move, serving in courts of the nobility or in monastic communities. Their cherished books as well as their esoteric knowledge will have travelled with them. In the *Historia* Geoffrey took a particular interest in Brittany and showed a decidedly pro-Breton attitude. This raises the interesting possibility that he may himself have been of Breton ancestry, his parents perhaps arriving in the wake of the Norman Conquest, taking up residence in Monmouth, where Geoffrey was born. The fact that in later life he was appointed to the Welsh see of St Asaph suggests that he was not a Welshman since the Anglo-Norman monarchy is most unlikely to have appointed a native to a Welsh bishopric.

One of the themes that Geoffrey developed with evident relish in the *Historia* was the life of King Arthur, a local leader born in Britain at the time when the Roman order was breaking down and the Saxons were invading. Armed with his magic sword, forged on the Isle of Avalon, Arthur routs the Saxons in a battle near Bath and drives them from the country. After twelve years of peace he decides to conquer Europe. Starting with Norway and Denmark, he moves on to Gaul and takes control of extensive tracts of Roman territory, reaching Burgundy, but before he can consolidate his rule he has to return to Britain, now in revolt. Eventually he crushes the rebellion in a battle fought at the river Camel in Cornwall but is mortally wounded and is carried off to Avalon, perhaps to become immortal. It is a rich fable full of vivid characters like Merlin the magician, Gawain the knight, the treacherous Mordred, and many others. Told with pace and energy, Geoffrey's text served as a basis of the Arthurian romances that were to spread wide throughout the medieval world in subsequent centuries.

How much of Geoffrey's Arthurian narrative derived from his own imagination and how much from earlier sources is a complex issue, difficult to untangle, but he clearly had access to Welsh sources and the possibility remains that Breton stories were available to him, either as written texts or as oral tradition transmitted in verse or song. That Arthur and the attendant characters of the story feature so strongly in the Breton folk memory raises other questions. Was there a historic Arthur who in the early fifth century was active in both southern Britain and Brittany, or was he a British-based resistance leader whose stories were brought to Brittany with the British migrants arriving in the late fifth and sixth centuries? It is a field that has generated much lively and ingenious scholarly debate with little real prospect of resolution. From our point of view what is significant is simply that stories of Arthur and his fellows were deeply embedded in the folk traditions of Brittany, echoing a bygone golden age that could be looked on with pride and nostalgia. When Henry II's grandson was born, heir to the Angevin empire, a deputation of Breton nobles petitioned, successfully, that he be named Arthur.

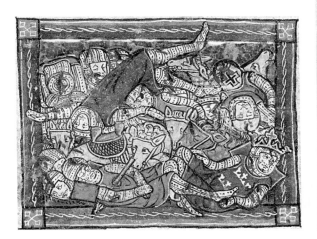 

11.1 Two illustrations from the fourteenth-century manuscript *Le Roman de Lancelot du Lac et de la mort du roi Artus*. *Left*: The battle of Camlann, where Arthur meets and kills Mordred, and *right*: Gifflet casts Excalibur into the water, where it is caught by the Lady of the Lake.

The Transmission of the Arthurian Tradition

The publication of Geoffrey's *Historia Regum Britanniae* about 1135 introduced to a receptive world a compelling story of heroism and chivalry. By leaving open the question of Arthur's death, and his possible immortality, Geoffrey offered the enticing spectre of a redeemer who could appear at any moment to lead his people once more to victory. It is hardly surprising that the Arthurian theme became popular among the Bretons at a time when they were resisting the invasions of the French.

One early exponent was the poet Wace, whose surname (if he ever had one) is unknown. He was born in Jersey about 1110 but was brought up in Normandy, in Caen, and spent his last years as canon of Bayeux, dying sometime not long after 1174. His two surviving works, written in Old French, are the *Roman de Brut* (*c.*1150), a retelling of the history of Britain closely based on Geoffrey's *Historia*, and the *Roman de Rou* (*c.*1160), devoted largely to William the Conqueror and the Norman invasion of Britain. The importance of the *Roman de Brut* is that, while it relies heavily on the *Historia* for the Arthurian story, it contains new material, which, he implies, he gathered from oral traditions transmitted by Breton storytellers. He is the first to mention the Round Table and to name Arthur's sword, Excalibur, and he introduces the idea of the 'Breton hope' of Arthur's return from Avalon to lead his people to victory against the oppressor. In the *Roman de Rou* is to be found the first mention of the legendary enchanted forest of Brocéliande in the centre of Brittany, where many of the events of the Arthurian romances take place, and frightening characters like Merlin, Morgan Le Fay, and the Lady of the Lake disport themselves. He also mentions the fountain of Barenton, deep in the forest, where, by throwing water on a nearby stone, it is possible to summon up rain. Thorough historian that he was, Wace travelled to Brittany to see these things for himself: 'I saw the forest and the land and looked for marvels,' he wrote, 'but none I found.'

By writing in Old French, Wace was able to reach a much wider audience than Geoffrey, who chose Latin, and it was through his *Roman de Brut* that Arthurian stories began to become known throughout the French-speaking world. His near-contemporary Marie de France (*fl.* 1160–1215) also chose to write in a French dialect, Francien, spoken in the region of the Île-de-France. Marie claimed to have come from France, but she spent most of her time in England, closely associated with the court of Henry II. Her exact identity is unknown, but she was evidently well connected with the English elite, one possibility being that she was abbess of Shaftesbury and half-sister of the king. Her most famous work, known as *The Lais of Marie de France*, was a collection of twelve narrative poems based, she tells us, on stories she had heard from Breton minstrels. The poems were a few hundred lines long and were about characters who, unwittingly, find themselves bound up in adventures set in a world which flits from the real to the supernatural where one might at any moment encounter fairies or werewolves. Two of the poems, 'Chevrefueil' and 'Lanval', deal with Arthurian themes. 'Chevrefueil' describes the passionate romance between Tristan and Isolde in an enchanted forest, while 'Lanval' explores the adventures of a young noble who had left Arthur's court and falls in love with a fairy. Though tempted by Guinevere, the pair are happily united on the Isle of Avalon.

While Marie de France was writing in the English court, another great poet, Chrétien de Troyes (*fl.* 1160–90), was at work in the court of the comtesse de Champagne, daughter of Louis VII and Eleanor of Aquitaine, and later at the court of the count of Flanders. In five major poems, among them *Lancelot; or, The Knight of the Cart* and *Perceval; or, The Story of the Grail*, he greatly elaborates the Arthurian legend, using the narrative to expound the ideals of French chivalry. What sources he used is unclear. The works of Geoffrey of Monmouth and Wace no doubt provided some material. But there is so much that was new in his poems, not least major characters like Lancelot, that he must have been using tales and ballads emanating from Brittany, brought to the courts of the French elite by itinerant storytellers.

The Breton *lais* to which Chrétien and Marie had access offered a rich source of stories reflecting a past half-remembered, half-created. The corpus must have been built up over a very long period of time, with new themes and characters introduced from other sources encountered by the performers or written anew to reflect contemporary concerns. These tales, in lyrical or narrative form, were communicated widely by harpists, minstrels, and storytellers. They were the folk history of the people, exposing human nature in all its variety, from heroism and romantic love to perfidy and wanton violence. While they offered examples of proper behaviour, and challenged the listener to reflect on it, they also provided the history, the heroes, and the landscapes that gave the medieval Bretons their sense of identity.

Enter the Celts

In the sixteenth and seventeenth centuries the desire to understand the past was quickening, inspired by the growing availability of Greek and Roman texts, the realization that monuments and artefacts had a significant story to tell, and a greater awareness of 'primitive' people encountered during the exploration and colonization of other continents. In Britain, John Leland (1503–52) planned to write a great book, *De Antiquitate Britannica*, and travelled extensively to visit sites, monuments, and libraries, but he was overtaken by madness before he could complete the work, leaving only an account of his journeys to be subsequently published in the early eighteenth century. It was left to William Camden (1551–1623) to produce the first account of British antiquity, based on empirical study, in his great volume *Britannia*, first published in 1586. It was a turning point, sweeping away the myths and speculations of medieval antiquaries and setting entirely new scholarly standards for research. In France the focus was different. Caesar's detailed account in his *Commentaries on the Gallic War* provided a convenient starting point to the country's story and was used in several early works, including Noël Taillepied's *Histoire de l'état et république des Druides* (1585). But the Caesarean episode raised a problem of interpretation. Should Gaul be presented as the victim of the Roman invader or as the proud heir to Graeco-Roman culture? It was an ambivalence that was to persist well into the nineteenth century.

In the opening passages of the *Commentaries on the Gallic War*, Caesar states that people known to the Romans as Gauls occupied the central part of France, adding that 'In their own language they are called Celts.' The antiquaries of France and Britain made little of this until the end of the seventeenth century when two scholars, Paul-Yves Pezron (1639–1706), a Breton cleric who studied in Paris, and Edward Lhuyd (1660–1709), a Welshman working in Oxford at the Ashmolean Museum, began to take an interest in the Celtic question, but from very different points of view. Pezron was a scholar who liked to tackle big historical themes. His first major book, *L'Antiquité des tems rétablie et défenduë* (1687), dealt with the history of the world following the Creation in 4004 BC. In it he moulded the biblical story of Noah and his sons into a wide-ranging narrative history. It was very much of its time and had little new to say, but in his next book, *L'Antiquité de la nation et de la langue des Celtes* (1703), he offered an entirely original hypothesis. The Celts, he said, arose in Asia Minor, not far from Mount Ararat, and were the direct descendants of Gomer, son of Japheth, son of Noah. From there they spread west, conquering the Greeks and Romans before becoming the overlords of much of Europe. The Bretons and the Welsh were the survivors of these conquering Celts and it was 'a singular fact that so ancient a language should now be spoken by the Armorican Bretons in France and by the ancient Britons in Wales'. Pezron was constructing an entirely new creation myth for the Bretons, giving them the most distinguished of roots. For a scholar born in Hennebont in southern Brittany and educated in a seminary in Rennes, the results of his researches must have given him a degree of satisfaction. The French could take some comfort in knowing that their Gaulish ancestors were also Celts, but their culture had been adulterated by Roman conquerors and waves of Germanic invaders. Only the Bretons preserved the purity of the ancestral Celts.

11.2 Edward Lhuyd (1659/60?–1709), keeper of the Ashmolean Museum at Oxford. Antiquary and Celtic scholar.

Pezron's ideas had surprisingly little effect on French antiquarian thought at the time and have been barely acknowledged since, but they were to have an immediate impact in Britain, where Edward Lhuyd was gathering material for his proposed multi-volume work *Archaeologia Britannica*. Lhuyd was aware of Pezron's research and knew that he was also working on a Breton dictionary, but the two men were never in direct communication. Pezron's *L'Antiquité de la nation* greatly impressed Lhuyd and he helped to organize an English translation. The task was taken on by the historian David Jones, and three years later, in 1706, its title carefully modified to appeal to the British public, *Antiquities of Nations: More Particularly of the Celtae or Gauls, Taken to be Originally the Same People as our Ancient Britons*, was published. It was immediately successful, running into several editions over the next century.

Archæologia Britannica,

GIVING SOME ACCOUNT

Additional to what has been hitherto Publish'd,

OF THE

LANGUAGES, HISTORIES and CUSTOMS

Of the Original Inhabitants

OF

GREAT BRITAIN:

From Collections and Observations in Travels through
Wales, Cornwal, Bas-Bretagne, Ireland and *Scotland.*

By EDWARD LHUYD M.A. of *Jesus College,*
Keeper of the ASHMOLEAN MUSEUM in OXFORD.

VOL. I.

GLOSSOGRAPHY.

OXFORD,
Printed at the THEATER for the Author, MDCCVII.
And Sold by Mr. *Bateman* in *Pater-Noster-Row, London*: and *Jeremiah Pepyat*
Bookseller at *Dublin.*

11.3 The title page of the first (and only) volume of Edward Lhuyd's *Archaeologia Britannica*, published in
1707. It deals exhaustively with Lhuyd's research into the language, which he called Celtic, spoken along
the Atlantic façade.

Lhuyd's interest lay largely in the linguistic implications of Pezron's work. He had already, by 1692, made a comparative study of Welsh and Irish and was in contact with John Toland, who was preparing word lists comparing Welsh with Irish. Lhuyd saw language as the key to understanding the origin of the British, and his extensive fieldwork in Cornwall, Wales, the Scottish islands, Ireland, and Brittany gave him the opportunity to study the languages of the native speakers of these regions. He recognized at once the similarities between these languages and, inspired by Pezron's work, decided to refer to them as Celtic. In 1707 the first volume of *Archaeologia Britannica* appeared, entitled *Glossography*. In it, using word lists and grammars of 'the original languages of Britain and Ireland' together with Brittany, he set out to demonstrate their close affinities. It was a scientific work presented in a scholarly and objective fashion, quite unlike the rambling speculations of Pezron. The intention was for the *Glossography* to be the first volume of a series presenting the antiquity of the British people. The ambition was never fulfilled and Lhuyd died in 1709.

  Both Pezron and Lhuyd had their own political agendas. Pezron wanted to give his people, the Bretons, a worthy ancestry rooted deep in the past to help to differentiate them from the French. Lhuyd's great work was published in the year the Treaty of Union was signed, uniting Scotland to England and Wales. As a Welshman he was concerned that his people would begin to lose their identity. By calling them Celts rather than Britons he was setting out to distinguish them from the inhabitants of the rest of the country, whose ancestry had been compromised by the flood of Germanic immigrants arriving in the fifth and sixth centuries AD. The concept of the Celt, then, became a symbol for the minorities of the western extremities of Europe who were striving to maintain their way of life and language against the inroads of French and English culture.

Celtomania

In the British Isles an enthusiasm for all things Celtic grew rapidly and it was not long before the antiquaries began to develop a particular fascination with Druids, the priests of the Celts, mentioned by a number of classical authors. John Toland, who had studied the similarities between Irish and Breton, wrote his *History of the Druids* in 1719, but it was not published at the time, appearing later in his collected papers in 1726 and 1747. Meanwhile, the Druid theme was taken up by William Stukeley (1687–1765) and became his life's passion. In 1723 he began work on a proposed four-volume study, 'History of the Temples of the Ancient Celts', fascinated by the belief that Avebury and Stonehenge were Druidic 'temples'. Eventually he published his ideas in two volumes, *Stonehenge* in 1740 and *Avebury* in 1743. By now he was obsessed by Druids, seeing them as the successors of the ancient patriarchal religion going back to biblical times. As Druidomania took over, his objective observations, made during fieldwork, became increasingly distorted to fit his growing fantasies.

In France, Celtomania gained momentum towards the end of the eighteenth century and Bretons were to play an important role in it, in large part because megalithic monuments, then considered to be Celtic, were found in such abundance in the country. The first significant publication was *Origines gauloises, celles des plus anciens peuples de l'Europe* (1796), written by the distinguished Breton soldier Théophile Malo Corret de La Tour d'Auvergne (1743–1800). Born in or near Carhaix-Plouguer, he was familiar with megaliths and with the Breton language and suggested using the Breton word *dolmen* (or *dolmin*) for megalithic tombs and *menhir* (from the Breton *ar-men-ir*) for standing stones. His nomenclature was quoted with approval by his near-contemporary Pierre Jean-Baptiste Legrand d'Aussy (1737–1800) in his *Mémoire sur les anciennes sépultures nationales*, first presented before the influential Institut de France in 1799. By the time of its eventual publication in 1824 both words were in common usage.

The other great figure of these formative years was Jacques Cambry (1749–1807), who was born in Lorient and became a great supporter of the French Revolution. He combined his passion for historical research and writing with a career as an energetic civil administrator, at one time being responsible for setting up the new department of Oise established by Napoleon. One of his official tasks was to tour western Brittany assessing the large hauls of property confiscated from the nobility and the monasteries during the Revolution. The journey inspired him to write a highly influential book, *Voyage dans le Finistère*, in 1799. It was an astonishing work for a civil servant to write, an emotional and evocative outpouring romanticizing the Breton countryside, especially its seascapes, and the Celtic heritage of its people, becoming a major influence on subsequent French writers. His deep interest in the Celts led to the publication, in 1805, of *Monumens celtiques; ou, Recherches sur le culte des pierres*, a book which he dedicated to his hero, Napoleon. For Cambry the dolmens were constructed by the Druids and the stone rows of Carnac constituted 'the most ancient and the grandest monument in the world'. This extravagant praise for the monuments of his homeland was matched by his enthusiasm for all things Celtic. To forward the study, in 1804 he and two colleagues, with the blessing of the emperor, set up the Académie Celtique. It held its inaugural meeting the following year, with Cambry as president, its task being to research the culture and language of the Celtic heritage of France, using historical, archaeological, linguistic, and folkloric evidence. This focus on Celtic culture was

O qui me gelidis in vallib Hæmi | Atqꝫ metus Omnes & inexorabile Fatum
Sistatꝗ ingenti ramorum protegat umbra! | Subjecit pedibus, strepitumꝗ Acherontis
Fœlix qui potuit Rerum cognoscere causas! | avari. Virg.

11.4 The antiquary William Stukeley (1687–1765) carried out extensive research on Stonehenge and Avebury, which he believed to be Druidic temples. He intended to publish 'The History of the Temples of the Ancient Celts', for which this is his title page, prepared in 1723. The work never appeared, but separate volumes were published later, *Stonehenge* in 1740 and *Avebury* in 1743.

Pl. 3.

11.5 The stones of the Carnac alignments were eternally fascinating to the early antiquarians and grew, in the imagination, to gigantic proportions as in this illustration from Jacques Cambry's *Monumens celtiques; ou, Recherches sur le culte des pierres* (1805).

thought to be particularly appropriate 'in an era when the French have demonstrated themselves worthy of their ancestors, when, for the last ten years, Napoleon has led us from victory to victory . . . bringing their [the Celts'] vast empire back to life' (*Mémoires de l'Académie Celtique*, 1, 1807). Such sentiments were, of course, entirely acceptable to Napoleon, who had been styled 'Emperor of the Gauls' by the Italian poet Melchiorre Cesarotti, and who had thought it appropriate to transfer the famous statue *The Dying Gaul* from Rome to Paris.

The Académie Celtique's main claim to fame is that it initiated serious studies in the field of French folklore, but many felt that it had become too much the domain of the Celtomanes and in 1813 it was restructured as the Société des Antiquaires de France with a much wider remit to include the classical and medieval world.

Another Breton influential in archaeological research was Armand-Louis-Bon Maudet de Penhouët (1767–1839). Unlike Cambry, he was a staunch royalist and, indeed, had served as an officer in the Vendée fighting in the resistance against the revolutionary forces in 1790. His interests lay firmly in Breton antiquity, upon which

11.6 The first recorded excavation of a megalithic tomb in Brittany was carried out by Armand-Louis-Bon Maudet de Penhouët in 1814 at the Table des Marchands at Locmariaquer. The work is published in his *Recherches historiques sur la Bretagne d'après ses monuments anciens et modernes*. The proportions of the stones are greatly exaggerated.

he wrote a number of papers including *Essai sur les monuments armoricains*, published anonymously in 1805, and *Recherches historiques sur la Bretagne* (1814). In the latter he included accounts of the first scientific excavations of the megaliths, carried out 1811, at the Table des Marchands and Pierres Plates at Locmariaquer. Earlier in his life he had visited south Wales and had written an account of his travels in *Letters Describing a Tour through Part of South Wales* (1797), stressing the close historical links between the Bretons and the Welsh.

The contrasting approaches of Cambry and Maudet de Penhouët nicely reflect the divide appearing in the way in which the concept of the Celt was being used by French antiquarians. Cambry, believing passionately in the values of Revolutionary France, saw the Celts as the ancestors of the French unifying the country irrespective of regional differences, while the royalist Maudet de Penhouët emphasized the

uniqueness of the Celts of Brittany and stressed their close relations with their overseas cousins like the Welsh and thereby, implicitly, their differences from the rest of
France. The concept of the Celt, then, took with it a convenient ambiguity, allowing it
to serve quite different political ideologies.

By the middle of the nineteenth century the worst extremes of Celtomania were
abating. The multi-volume work *Antiquités de la Bretagne*, compiled by the chevalier
de Fréminville and published between 1827 and 1837, was far less emotive, presenting
the megalithic monuments simply as the tombs and monuments of Gaulish warriors.
In 1835 Prosper Mérimée, a man of many talents, travelled through Brittany in his
capacity of inspector of historic monuments, the following year publishing his findings in *Notes d'un voyage dans l'ouest de la France* (1836). His careful scientific approach
and critique of the wild theories of the Celtomanes marks the beginning of a more
rational era in archaeological research and also a concern for the proper conservation

11.7 Prosper Mérimée, who became inspector of historic monuments in France, travelled through
Brittany in 1835 and published his findings in *Notes d'un voyage dans l'ouest de la France* in 1836. His
gouache of the Carnac alignments shows him to have been a competent artist and to have been content
to show the stones as they actually were.

of the monuments. But not all could resist the lure of imagining megaliths as Druidic altars upon which the entrails of sacrificial victims were examined. Looking back on the more imaginative excesses of the Celtomanes, the French archaeologist Salomon Reinach (1858–1932) could not resist offering a succinct caricature:

> The Celts are the oldest people in the world, their language is preserved practically intact in Bas-Breton; they were profound philosophers whose inspirational doctrines have been handed down by Welsh Bardic Schools; dolmens are their altars where their priests the Druids offered human sacrifice; stone alignments were their astronomical observatories.

His tongue-in-cheek brevity nicely sums up the beliefs of the antiquarian world at the turn of the eighteenth century.

Celts and the Romantic Movement

In Britain in the eighteenth century the growing awareness of a deeply rooted Celtic heritage raised the intriguing possibility that, in the more remote parts of the island, ancient oral traditions might survive in songs or folk tales still being sung and recited. The expectation was met in 1760 when a young Scottish poet, James Macpherson (1736–96), published *Fragments of Ancient Poetry, Collected in the Highlands of Scotland and Translated from the Galic or Erse Language*. Amid excited acclamation a subscription was raised to enable him to travel to the western parts of Scotland and the Western Isles in search of more. Much to everyone's delight he was soon able to announce that he had found an entire epic poem written by a bard, Ossian, about the life of his father, Fingal, a third-century AD Scottish king. The publication of *Fingal* in 1762 was an immediate success. News spread throughout Europe and the work was translated into many languages. Then, a year later, Macpherson announced the discovery of another manuscript by Ossian, which he quickly published as *Temora: An Ancient Epic Poem, in Eight Books. Together with Several Other Poems* (1763). His sources, he said, were manuscripts of the fourth or fifth century. The rapturous reception by some readers was matched by criticism and accusations of fraud by others. One of his sternest detractors was Samuel Johnson, who made his famous journey to the Western Isles partly to examine the evidence for himself and wrote a scathing criticism of the two epic poems in his *Journey to the Western Islands of Scotland* (1775) claiming that Macpherson had gathered some fragments of poems and stories and had embedded them in a romance totally of his own creation.

I believe [the poems] never existed in any other form than that which we have seen. The editor, as author, never could show the original, nor can it be shown by any other; to revenge reasonable incredulity by refusing evidence is a degree of insolence with which the world is not yet acquainted; and stubborn audacity is the last refuge of guilt.

11.8 The Romantic Ossian legend, created by James Macpherson, became widely popular throughout Europe. It was much admired by the emperor Napoleon. The theme was celebrated by Romantic painters like Nicolai Abildgaard in his *Ossian Singing* (1787).

While the controversy about the authenticity of the poems raged, Macpherson kept a low profile, but he continued writing, producing two creditable works, a translation of the *Iliad* (1773) and a *History of Great Britain* (1775), finally retiring to obscurity in 1780 when he became a member of parliament. The original manuscripts that he claimed to have found were never produced.

After his death in 1796, an enquiry into the poems was launched by the Highland Society of Scotland. Although serious doubts were recorded, no firm conclusion was reached. But the controversy continued and by the end of the nineteenth century sufficient proof had been amassed to show that the Ossian poems were the product of Macpherson's creative imagination, inspired by scraps of stories he had come across, driven by the desire to give his beloved country an epic in the Homeric tradition. He was writing only a few years after the English forces had crushed the Jacobite Rebellion in 1746, forcing Bonnie Prince Charlie to flee and leaving Scotland in a demoralized state subject to active Anglicization. The Ossian epics not only lifted the Scottish soul but inspired freedom movements across the world. Macpherson's poems gave Scotland a national voice, but they also did much more. They created the persona of the lone sentimental poet recounting wistful stories of a heroic past wrapped in a misty Celtic nostalgia. The poems were a major inspiration to the Romantic movement, now beginning to grip Europe, and were widely admired, not least for their lyrical prose style. Napoleon caught the mood. He carried a copy of Melchiorre Cesarotti's Italian translation of Ossian with him, saying, 'I like Ossian for the same reason that I like to hear the whisper of the wind and the waves of the sea.'

Not to be outdone, the Welsh soon joined in the search for authentic folk poetry. In 1764 Evan Evans (1731–88), a Welsh poet and antiquarian, published *Some Specimens from the Poetry of the Ancient Welsh Bards* (1764), a serious scholarly work focusing attention on the importance of the bardic tradition. But other, less scrupulous individuals were at work, people like Edward Williams (1747–1826), a Welsh stonemason who preferred to be known by his bardic name, Iolo Morganwg. Apart from forging a number of supposedly ancient Welsh texts, which confused serious scholarship for decades to come, Williams created a fake Druidic ceremony, the Gorsedd, initially to provide a bonding event for expatriate Welshmen working in London. The *Gentleman's Magazine* records the meeting that took place on Primrose Hill on 23 September 1792, the autumn equinox. The ceremony involved a circle of stones, 'in the middle of which was the *Maen Gorsedd*, or Altar, on which a naked sword being placed, all the Bards assisted to sheathe it'. It was all, of course, invented nonsense and would have been of no concern were it not for the fact that, with all the consummate skill of a conman, Williams managed to have his Gorsedd ceremony attached to the long-established Eisteddfod at its meeting held in Carmarthen in 1819. Thereafter his

Primrose Hill pastiche has clung parasitically to its genuine host. As the archaeologist Stuart Piggott has written, 'The Gorsedd was now assured of a future as an integral part [of the Eisteddfod], nicely calculated to appeal to nationalists and romantics, the credulous and the pompous.'

11.9 Romantic fantasies about the prehistoric past abounded in the nineteenth century. This engraving by Georges Devy, *La Danse des korriganes, près des menhirs* (1887), is typical.

The Search for a Breton Literary Tradition

The search for an oral tradition rooted in the distant past was well in train in Britain in the last decades of the eighteenth century, and its apparent success did not go unnoticed in France. Indeed, with the foundation of the Académie Celtique in 1804, the hunt for oral tradition got quickly under way, not least because the French antiquarian world, led by the emperor, was now gripped by Ossianic enthusiasm. That there was a lost, or undiscovered, Breton literature to be found was championed by the medievalist Gervais de La Rue (1751–1835), who in his *Recherches sur les ouvrages des bardes de la Bretagne armoricaine* (1815) urged those working in Brittany to begin the necessary fieldwork to discover this treasure.

One man who took up the challenge was Émile Souvestre (1806–54), a prolific novelist who worked as a journalist and teacher. Souvestre was born in Morlaix and spent his early life in Brittany before finally settling in Paris. It was in Brittany that he gathered together folk tales and worked them into stories set within emotionally drawn Breton landscapes. These collages of country life appeared in two major works, *Les Derniers Bretons*, published in four volumes between 1835 and 1837, and *Le Foyer breton* (1844). In both the land features large: it is a place where the past is alive, echoing with the sound of people and their song; nature in her various guises is always present. Thus,

> On a lovely summer evening [the traveller] crosses the hills of Cornouaille listening to the song of the shepherds. At every step the voice of a child or an old woman carries from afar a scrap of one of those ancient ballads, sung to tunes such as are no longer made, recounting a miracle from a past era, a crime committed in the valley, a passion which ended in death. The couplets echo from boulder to boulder, lines dancing in the air like evening insects; the breeze whips them into your face in gusts, with the scent of buckwheat and wild thyme.
>
> (*Les Derniers Bretons*)

Le Foyer breton, with its varied array of stories often set in a world pervaded by magic, was an immediate success. To what extent Souvestre edited the tales he collected to emphasize this Bretonness is unclear, but the two great works stand at the beginning of a long tradition of gleaning the literary remnants of the Breton past.

While Souvestre pioneered the collection of Breton folk tales, it was a Breton aristocrat, Théodore-Claude-Henri Hersart de La Villemarqué (1815–95), who was to make the greatest impact. Born in Quimperlé, La Villemarqué left for Paris at the age of 18 and there became part of a group of Breton expatriates whose fervour for their country was

11.10 Émile Souvestre (1806–54) was the first to gather the folk tales of Brittany together and to present them in published form in his *Les Derniers Bretons* (1835–7) and *Le Foyer breton* (1844).

accentuated by this self-imposed exile. His recompense was to write nostalgic accounts of the Breton countryside, interweaving them with themes taken from Breton folk songs. In this he was clearly influenced by the first volume of *Les Derniers Bretons*.

By 1835 he began actively to collect songs and manuscripts for himself on trips through the Breton countryside, inspired by La Rue's belief that there existed a lost literature there for the gathering. In that year Prosper Mérimée was completing his tour of Brittany and the two must have met. What transpired we will never know, but in October unattributed reports appeared in local newspapers claiming that Mérimée had appropriated an ancient manuscript recording the prophecies of the bard Gwenc'hlan, found in a church in the Montagnes Noires by a young student. It then became known that the student was La Villemarqué, who had presumably informed the press. Mérimée denied the accusations and responded by challenging him to a duel. The duel did not materialize; neither did the manuscript, and the affair was soon forgotten. But four years later La Villemarqué's book *Barzaz-Breiz: chants populaires de la Bretagne* was published. Its opening poem was 'The Prediction of Gwenc'hlan'. How to interpret this curious incident is unclear, but one critic has, unkindly perhaps, suggested that it may have been a publicity stunt engineered by La Villemarqué to increase the sales of his forthcoming book.

Barzaz-Breiz was composed of songs and stories which La Villemarqué had gathered on his various journeys. He visited fellow collectors, hunted for unknown manuscripts, and copied down songs and stories from country people. Many, he believed, were very ancient, stretching back to the Dark Ages, and told stories of famous people like Arthur, Merlin, and Nominoë, the heroes of the Celtic Bretons in their struggle against the Franks and other Germanic intruders. In La Villemarqué's hands Breton Celticism was idealized and used in support of a nationalistic agenda. *Barzaz-Breiz* was an immediate success and appeared in various editions through La Villemarqué's lifetime. It was Brittany's answer to Scotland's Ossian, a comparison with which the author will have been all too conscious. Indeed, the folklorist Anatole Le Braz, writing half a century later, suggested that La Villemarqué's original intention may have been

11.11 Théodore-Claude-Henri Hersart de La Villemarqué (1815–95), the author of *Barzaz-Breiz*, was one of the towering intellectual figures in the search for Breton identity in the nineteenth century. Although his work came in for much criticism from some of his peers, it helped to focus attention on Breton folk culture and on the place of Brittany in the Celtic world. Painted by Alexandre Le Bihan.

to present the bardic prophet Gwenc'hlan as the narrator in the same way Macpherson had used Ossian. If so, the spat with Mérimée may have changed his mind.

La Villemarqué was enamoured by all things Celtic. In 1838, at the age of 23, he travelled to England and Wales, making a pilgrimage to Stonehenge. He spent time in Oxford studying Welsh manuscripts and later met Lady Charlotte Guest, translator of *The Mabinogion*, but the highlight of his visit was taking part in the Eisteddfod held that year at Abergavenny. The event included the Druidic nonsense of the Gorsedd invented by Williams and grafted onto the original revered ceremony eighteen years before. La Villemarqué was overwhelmed and wrote a highly excited letter to his father: 'I am a bard now, truly a bard! A "titled bard!" and I have been received according to the ancient rituals of the 5th and 6th centuries, handed down to our own times.'

On his return from the British Isles, with his reputation as a scholar growing, La Villemarqué took on the task of re-editing the *Dictionnaire celto-breton* first assembled by Jean-François Le Gonidec and last published in 1821. Le Gonidec had tried to purge the Breton language of its 'dialectal chaos' and distortion caused by the intrusion of French. La Villemarqué continued this process of cleansing in an attempt to get back to the purity of the original Celtic language. He was not, however, averse to drawing on Welsh where gaps were to be filled. His new edition was published in 1850. As its subtitle proclaims, the dictionary was 'enriched by the addition of an essay on the history of the Breton language'.

Even at the beginning there were doubts about the authenticity of *Barzaz-Breiz*. The original was offered for publication to the Comité Historique in Paris, but, mindful of the controversy over Macpherson's Ossian, they had refused to accept it, leaving La Villemarqué to publish it himself. Although the volume was widely welcomed and won honours for its author and an ardent following, criticism grew, particularly in the 1860s. Matters came to a head at the first meeting of the Inter-Celtic Congress, instigated by La Villemarqué and held at Saint-Brieuc in 1867. The conference had been called to stress the unity of the Celtic-speaking peoples. La Villemarqué appealed to his 'compatriots' from Wales, 'brothers' from Cornwall, and 'cousins' from Ireland and Scotland to attend. It was a blatant attempt to build a pan-Celtic movement to counter the power and influence of France and England. To coincide with the Congress the archaeologist R. F. Le Men published a new edition of *Le Catholicon*, a Breton–French–Latin dictionary, in which he made a devastating criticism of La Villemarqué's credibility and scholarship: 'Play the bard, play the arch-bard and even the Druid,' he wrote, 'but do not attempt to falsify history with your inventions.' The criticism was taken up by other delegates at the meeting. La Villemarqué's response was rapid. The book was seized and legal action threatened, resulting in the offending passage being covered up. But the damage had been done and the floodgates of censure were open.

By the time of the next Congress, held in Saint-Brieuc in 1872, a new generation of folklorists had begun to engage in the debate. One was François-Marie Luzel (1821–95), who had been a follower of La Villemarqué but was now becoming doubtful about his methods. Luzel wrote a polite note to La Villemarqué informing him that he proposed to speak on the 'authentic history' of Breton popular songs in order to initiate a critical discussion. La Villemarqué, seeing this as a personal attack, chose to withdraw from the Congress, leaving Luzel to give his lecture and to respond to the storm of disapproval from supporters of *Barzaz-Breiz*. Luzel's paper, containing a rigorous critique of La Villemarqué's methods and assertions, was published in

Saint-Brieuc later in the year as *De l'authenticité des chants du Barzaz-Breiz de M. de La Villemarqué*. In it he laid out clearly his serious doubts concerning not only the validity of La Villemarqué's sources, but the way in which he had manipulated them.

The debate continued for some years, but by the time of La Villemarqué's death in 1895 his reputation as a reliable scholar had been largely discredited. There matters rested until the 1960s, when La Villemarqué's original notebooks were discovered, showing the care with which he had recorded the folk traditions in the field and the extent to which he had reworked them. The new study has gone some way to restoring his reputation.

Luzel's approach to presenting the folk tradition of Brittany was quite different from La Villemarqué's. In the second volume of *'Gwerziou Breiz-Izel': chants populaires de la Basse-Bretagne* (1874), which contains a number of plays, songs, and folk tales from the Trégor, he is explicit about his methods and intentions. He gives the Breton texts exactly as he had collected them from the performers, offering different versions of the same song if he knew them. His translation was as literal as possible and he exercised 'great sobriety in the commentaries, historical or otherwise'. In other words, he was stressing that his approach was the antithesis of everything he had criticized in La Villemarqué's work. In his two volumes of *gwerziou* (ballads) and his other publications he claimed he had gathered 'virtually all of this type of poetry that is to be found among the people of Lower Brittany'. But other collectors were also at work: Jean-Marie de Penguern (1807–56), based in Lannion; Guillaume-René Kerambrun (1813–52), who worked with him; and Madame de Saint-Prix (1789–1869), who collected material from around Morlaix and Callac. These and other collectors scoured the Breton countryside and gathered every scrap of folk literature and song they could find. Gervais de La Rue, who had urged just such an endeavour in 1815, would have been proud of them. But what Luzel and his co-workers had discovered was that the oral traditions they were able to record were not the remnants of a deeply rooted historical narrative as La Villemarqué had claimed, but a reflection of the folk culture of the Bretons which had been augmented over time. That said, it had a distinctive quality and value of its own in helping to characterize the Breton identity.

The Celtic Dilemma

The story of the Celts which Pezron was able to construct from his knowledge of the Bible and classical texts, greatly enhanced by his own inventive imagination, presented a very acceptable origin myth for the Bretons and the British, and Lhuyd's scholarly study of the native languages of the west not only reinforced Pezron's basic thesis but added a new depth to it by stressing the close cultural connection between the Bretons, the peoples of the western extremities of Britain, and the Irish. Thus, in the first decades of the eighteenth century the concept of the Celts was transformed. For those who saw themselves as persecuted by their French and English neighbours, it provided a comforting sense of identity. A growing interest in field monuments opened up a new source of speculation by providing a physical context for the Celts and especially for their priests, the Druids, fuelling the growing Celtomania. The search for ancient historical texts, both manuscripts and in oral form, generated a new enthusiasm, in Britain culminating in the Ossian creation in the 1760s and in Brittany in *Barzaz-Breiz*, popular from the 1840s to the 1860s. Both countries, then, developed their Celtomania roughly in parallel.

The concept of the Celts provided for the Scots, Irish, Welsh, Cornish, and Bretons a welcome focus around which to define their identity. For those in Britain and Ireland this was comparatively straightforward in that they could style themselves as the direct descendants of the Celts in opposition to the Anglo-Saxon and Norman intruders. It was a simple them-and-us. But for the Bretons it was much more difficult because the French, too, saw themselves as Celts (Gauls), a concept strongly supported by the republicans and, later, by Napoleon. How, then, could the Bretons distinguish their Celtic ancestry from that of the French? For royalists like La Villemarqué the way was to stress the links between the Bretons and the insular Celts, particularly the Welsh. It was a theme that could be developed further by recalling the historically attested movement of Bretons to Brittany in the fifth and sixth centuries. In one version of this scenario a flood of Celtic Britons from Devon and Cornwall and from Wales, barely touched by the hand of Rome, poured into the Armorican peninsula, reinvigorating the local Celtic population, giving it the strength eventually to overthrow the Roman oppressors and to resist the oncoming Franks. A more extreme version of the story saw the incoming Celts from Britain as conquerors exterminating the existing Gaulish Celts, effete because of centuries of Romanization, and repopulating Armorica, now Brittany, with a vigorous new Celtic strain. These old politically motivated debates still reverberate within discussions about the formation of the Breton language. So it was that the ambiguity surrounding the Breton population played into the continuing conflict between royalists and republicans. The republicans were content to see the Bretons as the descendants of the pre-Roman Gauls, demonstrating that Brittany was part of France, while the royalists stressed the close ties between Brittany and Britain, pointing to the similarities between the Breton and Welsh languages and the shared Arthurian tradition. These underlying political allegiances added vigour to the long-drawn-out debate about the authenticity of *Barzaz-Breiz*, a work that continued to serve as a guiding light for Breton nationalists.

From the 1790s until the middle of the 1870s the vision of the Breton as Celt was changing. To the revolutionaries, Brittany was peripheral and distinct and its people uncivilized, volatile, and reactionary. It contrasted with the centrality of France and the cultured, stable, forward-looking people of the Revolution. To the Bretons, different oppositions were in play. The hard masculinity of the French, driving forward in the certainty of a rational world, was the antithesis of themselves, a lyrical people living a spiritual life in harmony with the landscape that moulded their existence. There are clear echoes of this in the writings of Émile Souvestre in the 1830s, but the most explicit exposition was that of Ernest Renan (1823–92), a Breton-born priest, in his *Poésie des races celtiques* (1854), quoted in full above (p. 3), in which he contrasts the gentle, visionary Breton with his refined religious instincts to the fat, vulgar, egotistical Norman. For Renan it was the landscape of Brittany, 'tough and full of vague sadness', that created the Breton. By using these structural oppositions Renan was defining Bretonness.

Polishing the Image

One person who well understood the popular mood in Brittany was Anatole Le Braz (1859–1926). Born and raised in Côtes-d'Armor and trained at the Sorbonne, he returned to Brittany first as a teacher at a *lycée* in Quimper and later as a professor of French literature at the University of Rennes. While at Quimper he met Luzel, and the two worked closely together until the latter's death in 1895. Le Braz's contribution to Breton culture was considerable. In 1892 he published *La Chanson de la Bretagne* and a decade later his *Essai sur l'histoire du théâtre celtique*, both serious academic works. But he also well understood the need to communicate to a broader audience, and in a series of books he retold, in an engaging if somewhat sentimental style, the stories he had gathered as a folklorist. Their emotive titles, *La Légende de la mort* (1893), *Au pays des pardons* (1894), and *Contes du soleil et de la brume* (1905), were designed to attract a general readership and were a great success, with several translated to satisfy his avid English and American audiences. He understood what his public wanted and was not afraid of a little self-mockery:

> You take several openwork steeples, a few calvaries, a tune for the *biniou*, a couple of notes of *bombarde* (highly recommended, the *bombarde*!); you add a sprig of broom, a bouquet of gorse, some wind, mist and sea; mix it all up, shake vigorously . . . and you have Brittany.

11.12 The marquis de L'Estourbeillon resplendent in Breton dress, here photographed at the Celtic Congress held at Caernarfon in 1904. He was one of the founders of the Union Régionaliste Bretonne in 1898 along with Anatole Le Braz.

The French government recognized Le Braz's skills as a communicator and dispatched him on a number of cultural missions, mostly to America and Canada.

The other big literary figure in the Breton cultural renaissance at the turn of the century was the poet, novelist, and historian Charles Le Goffic (1863–1932), who was born in Lannion and kept close ties with the Trégor during his long teaching and literary career. He wrote extensively on Celtic and Breton culture and identity and is credited with having introduced the Great Highland bagpipes to Brittany.

Inspired by scholars like Le Braz and Le Goffic, the Breton cultural movement began to gain momentum, especially in the last decade of the nineteenth century, culminating in the foundation, on 16 August 1898, of the Union Régionaliste Bretonne following a festival of Breton culture held in Morlaix. The Union's aim was to preserve Breton cultural identity and to obtain regional independence. Its first president was Anatole Le Braz, and Charles Le Goffic became one of its ardent supporters. Two years later, following a Union meeting in Guingamp, the Gorsedd of Brittany was created with the aim of reviving Celtic bardic traditions. It was modelled on the Welsh Gorsedd and adopted the same self-aggrandizing flummery, requiring each participant to assume a bardic pseudonym. Some felt that such backward-looking nostalgia was ill-suited to a serious modern cultural movement. In 1903 the Union went further, adopting a new Breton national anthem based closely on the Welsh song 'Mae Hen Wlad fy Nhadau' ('Old Land of my Fathers'); its Breton title is 'Bro Gozh ma Zadoù'.

Many Bretons were dismayed with the direction that the Union was taking. It was dominated by the nobility and the clergy, and its ideas were rooted in the past, reflecting values upheld by royalist counter-revolutionaries of the late eighteenth century. In seeking to preserve a Catholic, Breton-speaking, peasant society subservient

11.13 Following a meeting at the Union Régionaliste Bretonne in Guingamp in 1900 the Gorsedd of Brittany was instituted in a contrived ceremony designed to revive the Celtic bardic tradition. The postcard of the Gorsedd held at Saint-Brieuc in 1906 gives the flavour of the occasion.

to an aristocracy, its conservatism sat ill with many activists, and in 1899 the Ligue des Bleus de Bretagne was founded with the avowed aim of promoting the ideals of the Enlightenment and of the French Revolution in Brittany. By choosing the colour blue as their symbol they were making direct reference to the revolt in the Vendée when the troops of the Revolutionary government wore blue uniforms, the counter-revolutionaries being identified by their whites. It was a movement of the liberal, urban middle classes with its strength largely focused, at least in the beginning, in the east of Brittany. While there were significant social differences between the Union and the Ligue, they shared similar cultural aspirations to such an extent that Le Braz found no problem in being a member of both.

And so, at the beginning of the twentieth century, we see the old divide between Haute-Bretagne and Basse-Bretagne once more apparent. The one, urban-based, French-speaking, and sharing the ideals of Europe, the other, essentially rural in its attitudes, fighting to maintain traditional values and culture. The geography of the peninsula was once more asserting itself, reminding us that there have always been two Brittanys.

Postscript

Among the more active members of the Union Régionaliste Bretonne were two men interested in photography: Joseph Villard (1818–98) of Quimper and Émile Hamonic (1861–1943) of Saint-Brieuc. Both were to turn their attention to the production of postcards of their native country. The first issues appeared in 1896 and between them they produced about eighteen thousand different images frequently depicting some aspect of Breton folk culture or Breton dress, photographed, where appropriate, in a landscape setting. Other producers soon joined in. Armand Waron of Saint-Brieuc began a series, 'La Bretagne pittouresque'; J. Sorel of Rennes published 'Costumes bretons' as well as wonderfully animated series of village life. National producers were also quick to cash in on the lucrative market: Neurdein Frères with their 'Coutumes, mœurs et costumes bretons', and Lévy Lucien Fils with 'Mœurs et types bretons'. In all it is estimated that in the brief period when postcards were at their most popular, between 1900 and 1920, some six hundred thousand different images of Brittany were generated.

389   TYPES BRETONS. - *Femme allumant sa pipe.* - ND

11.14 (*Above and next page*) Many of the postcards produced in the period around 1900 focus on the Breton way of life, emphasizing the quaint and the curious. They were designed to amuse the tourist market, but as a record of life and landscape at the turn of the century they are of incomparable value.

For editors like Villard and Hamonic the initial intention was to record and to popularize Breton culture, and they proudly used the Breton language for the text on the reverse side of the cards, but as the visiting holiday-makers took up the craze of sending and collecting postcards, so French was used and the images became more varied, often verging on the caricature, with aged, toothless crones smoking clay pipes and suggestive young females disporting themselves in *lits-clos* (box-beds). So, once more, competing oppositions: genuine homage to Breton culture through a desire to proclaim it proudly, counterpointed with a willingness to satisfy the

30. - DOUARNENEZ
Une ronde joyeuse aux Plomarchs

COUTUMES, MOEURS ET COSTUMES BRETONS
467 — Départ pour le Marché (PLOUGASTEL). ND Phot.

preconceptions of outsiders looking for easy stereotypes of 'the other'. The craze for postcards was a remarkable phenomenon. It produced an incomparable record of the Bretons and their landscape at the final moment before so much of traditional Breton folk culture disappeared. It also ensured that images of the people and their country spread across the world.

EPILOGUE

THE long nineteenth century culminated with the First World War, marking, for so many in Europe, both an end and a beginning. For the Bretons it was an awakening to a new reality. They had responded in large numbers to the call to arms. Some three hundred thousand Bretons out of a total population of 2.6 million had joined the army to fight for France. They died in disproportionate numbers. Of the Breton conscripts, 22 per cent were killed. From the rest of France 16–17 per cent died, and from Paris, 10–12 per cent. Why the disparity has been hotly debated: inferior equipment, inability to understand French orders, deliberate deployment in especially dangerous situations? Whatever the cause or, more likely, causes, the fact that Bretons died for France in huge numbers is not in dispute.

Emboldened by this, the right-wing politician the marquis de L'Estourbeillon, founder and president of the Union Régionaliste Bretonne, presented a petition to the French government at the Versailles Peace Conference entitled 'Le Droit des langues et de la liberté des peuples', in which he argued for proper recognition of the Breton language and a return of some of the rights enshrined in the Edict of Union of 1532, notably the right of Bretons to speak for themselves in the international forum. He based his petition on statements made by President Woodrow Wilson in favour of self-determination for all nations, citing the strength of the Bretons' undiluted Celtic spirit and their disproportionately high mortality rate in the recent war. The stunning rebuff which followed, accompanied by the cruelly dismissive 'So, you are twice French!', left those with regionalist or autonomist views in no doubt about the entrenched attitudes of the powers they were now confronting.

But the world was now very different. The young men who had returned from the war, many of whom had never before ventured more than a few kilometres from their homes, had suddenly been introduced to a much wider world, where values were very different from those of the communes in which they had grown up. Moreover, confronting the German enemy had enhanced their new-found French identity. On their return home they attended the ceremonies of dedication at monuments to the war dead, which every village proudly erected, and many would have taken pride in the inscription telling the world that the children of the community had 'died for France'. There were others, of course, for whom these words were bitterly ironic.

And so the struggle to create a degree of regional autonomy and to make Breton a vibrant living language continued, to be played out against the ever-changing currents driving European, national, and regional politics.

Defining Identities

This book has been about identity, presented, not in theoretical constructs, but as a narrative to display the dynamic diversity of the subject. We each have many identities that come into focus and fade again as our circumstances change. Identities are dependent on a range of disparate factors: on geography, our attachment to location, rural or urban, maritime or land-based; on genetics, including family relationships and ethnicity; and on inherited behaviours and lifestyle choices such as language, religion, politics, diet, gender, and even alliance to a favoured football team. There are so many systems of value competing for prominence that each person's identity is unique. Yet, as humans, we feel the need to come together with others who share common values. By forming groups we gain the reassurance of being part of a community, but this requires us to give enhanced significance to those values that help us to bond.

The Greek philosopher Thales was having thoughts of this kind when he is reputed to have said that he thanked the gods for three things: that he was a human and not an animal, a Greek and not a barbarian, and a man and not a woman. He was content to define his identity as being a human, Greek-speaking male. Others have taken a different view. When the inhabitants of Saint-Malo set up their brief republic in 1590–3, the cry was 'not French, not Breton, but Malouin'. For them, belonging to a commercially prosperous city was their strongest claim to identity. Common to both of these examples is that it is by opposition that identity is defined. Without an 'other' to contrast against, it becomes a more tenuous concept. Yet medieval peasant farmers living in the wilds of Finistère would have been able to recognize that their Breton language and Catholic faith were central to their being even though they may never have heard French spoken or have met a non-believer. For them, identity was a given and it was passive. Their successors at the beginning of the nineteenth century were in a very different position. The French language was now being imposed on Breton society, and the power of the Catholic Church was under attack from the French state. This heightened their sense of identity. In other words, as contact with the outside world and its different values grows, so identity becomes an active concept and the energy put into defining it necessarily increases.

Responses of a Peninsular People

Peninsular Armorica is a special place, remote from the continental mainland yet central to a network of maritime connectivity binding the communities of Atlantic Europe. It also commands two major river corridors—the Loire and the Garonne—leading deep inland. Geography has allowed the inhabitants of the peninsula to use the surrounding sea, and the forest and marshes guarding the neck of the promontory, to insulate themselves from external influences if they so wished, or to accept them selectively on their own terms. Contact from across the sea was comparatively easy to control, but the land barrier was long and much more susceptible to determined pressures from continental neighbours. It was for this reason that, from the Roman period, the country began to take on a western and an eastern aspect, corresponding to the Basse-Bretagne and Haute-Bretagne divide we recognize today.

Before that, from the beginning of the Neolithic period to the time of the Roman invasion, it is the coherence and similarity of the culture across the whole peninsula that impresses. The spread of passage graves around the coastal zone in the fifth millennium, and the colonization of the more inland areas, reflected in the distribution of gallery graves that followed, gave peninsular Armorica its recognizable character. This was further enhanced during the Bronze Age, culminating in the remarkable phenomenon of the Armorican axe hoards of the eighth and seventh centuries, which reflect a complex pattern of behaviour and beliefs that is largely restricted to Armorica. The same cultural coherence is even more evident among the Iron Age communities whose stelae, souterrains, and highly decorated pottery set them apart from their neighbours.

The integration of Armorica into the Roman empire imposed Europe-wide systems and values on the people, but below the surface the remoteness of the western part of the peninsula still made itself felt. While Roman urbanization became well rooted in the east (in Rennes, Nantes, and Vannes), elsewhere it failed. The survival of Gallo-Roman place names in the east and their virtual absence in the west may be a further reflection of the limits of Romanization. When the systems of central government began to break down in the later Roman period, peasant uprisings in Armorica hastened the end. The arrival of migrants from Britain and their settlement in some numbers enhanced the separateness of what had now become Brittany.

For the next thousand years the Bretons put up a determined resistance to outside influences, from the Franks and their successors, the Carolingians and the French, and from the Scandinavians, but much energy was spent on internal conflicts like the War of Succession and the causes championed by the aristocracy in pursuit of their own interests. In the confused politics of the time the simple opposition between 'us' and 'the other' became blurred, and there were those who genuinely believed that the future of Brittany lay not in continually opposing France but in reaching accommodation with her. The marriage of Duchess Anne to two successive kings of France and the union which followed in 1532 brought the two countries together at a formal level, but the strict terms setting out the rights of the Breton people gave some assurance that the culture and interests of Brittany would be respected. It was the gradual erosion of those rights over the next 250 years that greatly strengthened the Breton sense of identity and led to the spirited resistance that greeted the idea of the Revolution.

The Chouannerie that gripped large areas of Brittany, a disorganized counter-revolutionary movement, was by no means universally applauded throughout the province. What the Revolution did was to crystallize and to give form to the two Brittanys that had been evident for centuries: the deeply religious Breton-speaking and largely rural-based communities who opposed the Revolution and those who saw the future of the province as a fully integrated part of the new state system of Revolutionary France. The sharpness of the divide was to some extent alleviated by Napoleon's concord with the Pope, formally allowing the churches to open again, but it remained a dominant reality throughout the nineteenth century and was reflected in the creation of the Union Régionaliste Bretonne and the Ligue des Bleus de Bretagne in 1898–9 (p. 406). That said, though politically opposed, both organizations championed Breton culture.

The threat to Breton life and culture from the interventionist activities of the state persisted throughout the nineteenth and well into the twentieth century. The response of the educated class was to research Breton folk culture and to communicate it widely in order to create a nostalgic sense of a present rooted in the distant past, at the same time positioning Brittany firmly within the brotherhood of Atlantic Celticism then being championed in Ireland, Wales, and Scotland. By referring to 'our brothers and cousins' in Wales and Ireland, people like La Villemarqué were distancing the Bretons from the French, stressing their Atlantic identity. Even the sober Renan presented the imagery of the moaning sea as a creative force forging the Breton character. The Breton language, too, was receiving academic attention by lexicographers, while there was continuing pressure for it to be taught in schools.

In parallel with all this a new force, tourism, was beginning to have an impact. Whether they were cultural tourists, like the painters and writers who came in search of inspiration, the curious who hoped to be amused by the people's quaint customs and dress, or the even less demanding for whom sea bathing was purpose enough, the influx of many thousands of foreigners every year created introspection. It made the indigenous population more aware of their own culture by observing the way in which it was valued by outsiders. One manifestation of this was the flood of folkloric postcards available at the turn of the century. While some may have found them patronizing, for others they reinforced the special nature of their identity.

Identity, then, is a flexible concept. As different social pressures on the cultural environment intensify or diminish, so the way we position ourselves changes. In the relatively closed world up to the end of the nineteenth century, when Bretons saw themselves as the oppressed other, identity could be a reasonably stable and clear-cut concept, but after the First World War horizons widened, geopolitical values shifted, and the opportunities for political allegiances became more varied and more confused.

Since the end of that war, regionalist and autonomist movements in Brittany have come and gone with surprising rapidity, differing in their aims and their methods but sharing the desire that Breton should thrive as a living language. But there is now a new optimism, a sense that Breton culture is not just a backward-looking curiosity, nostalgic for a rose-tinted, folksy past, but is valued for its creative contribution to the modern world. Music is playing an increasing part in all this with festivals like the Lorient Inter-Celtic Festival attracting an international audience of over half a million to its annual August gathering. Breton musicians, proud of the Celtic roots of their music, are now performing on the international stage, from the raucous enthusiasm of Tri Yann to the highly original works of Alan Stivell, steeped in the Atlantic tradition, and the more classical piano compositions of Didier Squiben, redolent of the rhythm of the sea. These are confident, assured contributions to world culture. In literature, art, and film, too, Brittany is developing a distinctive voice but shorn of the elitism that so often accompanies these movements. The art exhibitions that are put on free every summer in the chapels of Côtes-d'Armor attract an enthusiastic audience of both visitors and local people, while the bi-monthly magazine *ArMen* presents an easily accessible and well-designed view of a wide range of creative activities together with carefully researched articles on Breton culture in its broader Atlantic context. There is a palpable feeling that Breton culture, and with it Breton identity, is alive and flourishing.

Nor are the roots of that culture neglected. In one small area of Côtes-d'Armor, for example, it is possible to attend a performance of Breton music in the church at Loguivy-Lès-Lannion with the notes of the *bombarde* and the *binioù* reverberating from the roof timbers; to go to the annual sardine festival celebrated at the little fishing port of Locquémeau, where a couple of accordionists striking up a tune will have everyone on their feet dancing a traditional round; or to go to the beach at Saint-Efflam to watch competitors race their two-wheeled horse-drawn vehicles across the sands while the tide is out. The desire of the community to come together to celebrate in their various ways is rooted in tradition. So, too, is the religious faith so evident among the people of Armorica from the time of the menhirs and the megalithic tombs. On the promontory of Le Yaudet, fortified from Iron Age times, on the feast of the Assumption of the Virgin Mary, the priest leads a small procession carrying model ships (which during the year hang in the church) to a rock overlooking the estuary, and there blesses the sea. Placating the gods of the ocean to ensure the safety of sailors is a timeless activity. And then, as All Souls' Day (2 November) approaches, the cemeteries are tidied and swept, and new pots of chrysanthemums are set on the graves. Those who perform the tasks today are following in the tradition of their ancestors, for whom the Celtic festival of Samhain, held on the night of 31 October and into the evening of 1 November, represented the end of the old year and the beginning of the new, a liminal period when the spirits of the dead come briefly back into the world of the living.

It is difficult to resist the conclusion that Bretons are a people in harmony with their past, their heritage contributing creatively to their daily lives. But the constant battle to retain their identity has made them resilient and determined, and it is this that has conditioned their attitude to life.

As the prolific French historian Jules Michelet (1798–1874) wrote in one of the nineteen volumes of his seminal work *Histoire de France* (1835–67), 'The genius of Brittany is a genius of indomitable resistance and of intrepid, obstinate, and often blind opposition.' It is a summation of which every Breton can be proud.

GENEALOGICAL TABLES

Table 1. The Kings of Brittany

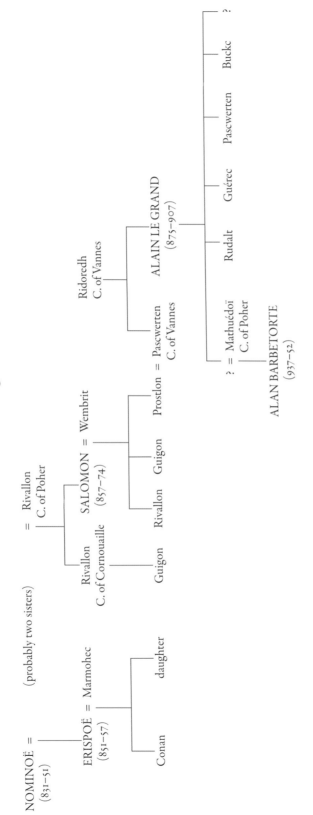

Names in capitals are the Kings with their regnal dates.

Table 2. The Ducal Family: the Descendants of Count Eudes, Brother of ALAIN III (1008–40)

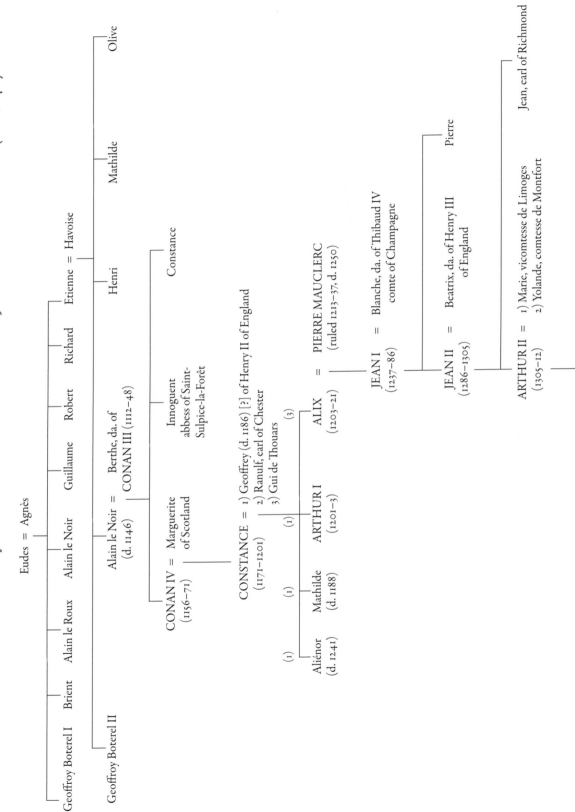

Names in capitals are rulers of the duchy with their regnal dates, unless otherwise stated.

Table 3. The Ducal Family: the Descendants of ARTHUR II

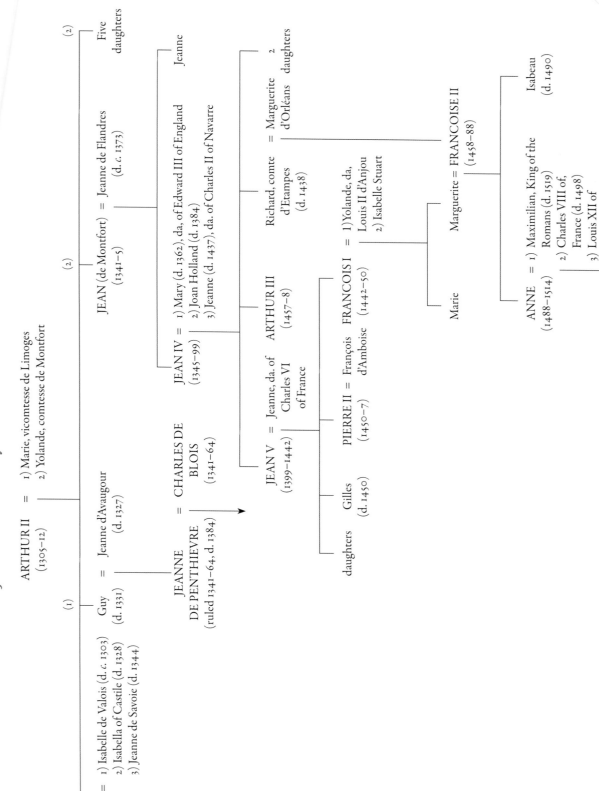

Names in capitals are rulers of the duchy with their regnal dates.

A GUIDE TO FURTHER READING

I N the hope, indeed the expectation, that some of the readers of this book will want to find out more about the subjects explored here, I offer suggestions for Further Reading. Wherever possible I have begun each section with general works which present the broad context and have then gone on to suggest more specific studies for readers who want to delve deeper. Since the majority of publications listed have their own bibliographies, it would be possible, for anyone so inclined, to burrow to the very roots of any issue.

I begin with a selection of general works followed by some notes on journals and series: then follows more specific guidance for each chapter in turn. The greatest difficulty has been to keep the selection within reasonable bounds—to offer an accessible introduction rather than a definitive bibliography. Because of the scope of the book, the suggested reading is an eclectic mix, everything from plate tectonics to postcards. I hope it will open up paths of discovery for all to enjoy.

Some General Works

There are surprisingly few good general books on Brittany apart from a plethora of guidebooks, which tend, these days, to have more pictures than useful text. That said, an excellent place to begin is with P. Galliou and M. Jones, *The Bretons* (Oxford, 1991), a clearly written overview covering the history of Brittany from early prehistory to the present day supported by a carefully chosen bibliography. For readers who, like me, find it helpful to see history expressed spatially in maps, B. Tanguy and M. Lagrée (eds.), *Atlas d'histoire de Bretagne* (Morlaix, 2002), is to be thoroughly recommended. It presents major aspects of the history of the country in seventy-seven maps researched and introduced by experts and is a delight to use. Another useful source is R. Hervé and Y. Poupinot, *Atlas historique de Bretagne* (Nantes, 1995).

The classic study of Breton history is A. le Moyne de La Borderie's *Histoire de Bretagne*, published in six volumes (Paris, 1896–1914). It is, of course, of its time. A more up-to-date treatment is offered in the series *Histoire de la Bretagne*, published by Ouest-France (Rennes, 1979–). These volumes are essential reading and will be detailed below under the chapters to which they are relevant. Another invaluable source is J. Balcon and Y. Le Gallo (eds.), *Histoire culturelle et littéraire de la Bretagne* (3 vols., Paris, 1987), which brings together a range of scholarly essays. Finally, for quick reference the *Dictionnaire du patrimoine breton* (Rennes, 2000), edited by A. Croix and J.-Y. Veillard, is a hugely valuable compilation which has the added benefit of being copiously illustrated.

Much of the more detailed literature is published in specialist journals. The *Annales de Bretagne*, first published in 1886, with its name changed in 1974 to *Annales de Bretagne et des Pays de l'Ouest*, includes papers on all aspects of archaeology and history with more besides. The *Mémoires de la Société d'Histoire et d'Archéologie de Bretagne*, first published in 1920, is equally broad-based. Since 1984 *Revue Archéologique de l'Ouest* has tended to take over the publication of archaeological reports, while a newer journal, *Aremorica*, begun in 2007, focuses on reports of work in the Roman period. Annual journals are also published by learned societies serving each of the departments of Brittany. Another valuable resource is the *Carte archéologique de la Gaule*, a series of very detailed inventories describing all protohistoric and Gallo-Roman sites, with a volume dedicated to each department: P. Galliou, *Le Finistère* (2nd edn, Paris, 2010); P. Galliou *et al.*, *Le Morbihan* (Paris, 2009); C. Bizien-Jaglin, P. Galliou, and H. Kerébel, *Les Côtes-d'Armor* (Paris, 2002); A. Provost and G. Leroux, *L'Ille-et-Vilaine* (Paris, 1980); and M. Provost, *La Loire-Atlantique* (Paris, 1988). These are of great value for the specialist or for a reader wishing to explore in detail the archaeology of a particular locality.

Archaeological excavations often take a long time to be published fully (if they ever are) but Breton researchers have begun to produce attractive and informative summaries for popular consumption. Particularly to be recommended are Y. Menez and S. Hinguant, *Fouilles et découvertes en Bretagne* (Rennes, 2010); Y. Menez, T. Lorho, and E. Chartier-Le Floch, *Archéologie en centre Bretagne* (Spézet, 2015); G. Aubin, C.-T. Le Roux, and C. Marcigny, *Sur le terrain avec les archéologues: trente ans de découvertes dans l'ouest de la France* (Rennes, 2018); and S. Boulud-Gazo and C. Le Pennec, *L'Âge du Bronze dans le Morbihan* (Vannes, 2019). These volumes set a high standard for accessibility. In a class of its own is a stunningly beautiful book on aerial photography by M. Gautier, P. Guigon, and G. Leroux, *Les Moissons du ciel: trente années d'archéologie aérienne au-dessus du Massif armoricain* (Rennes, 2019). It offers a brilliant introduction to both the archaeology of Brittany and the techniques of aerial photography.

Prologue

A most simulating discussion of remote places is provided by E. Ardener's paper '"Remote Areas": Some Theoretical Considerations', *Journal of Ethnographic Theory*, 2/1 (2012), 519–33. The quotation used in the chapter is taken from there. The special quality of islands is explored in P. Rainbird, *The Archaeology of Islands* (Cambridge, 2007). Ernest Renan's emotive piece on Celts can be found, in translation (by W. G. Hutchinson), in *The Poetry of the Celtic Races, and Other Studies by Ernest Renan* (Port Washington, 1970). Renan also wrote a description of his childhood in Tréguer, *Souvenirs d'enfance et de jeunesse*, first published in 1883. An edited and annotated edition prepared by J. Pommier was published in Paris in 1983.

Chapter 1   The Land and the Sea

For readers wanting an introduction to the geography of Brittany two sources can be recommended: P. Flatrès, 'Historical Geography of Western France', in H. D. Clout (ed.), *Themes in the Historical Geography of France* (London, 1977), 301–42, and G. I. Meirion-Jones, *The Vernacular Architecture of Brittany* (Edinburgh, 1982), chapter 2, 'The Physical Landscape of Brittany', and chapter 3, 'The Cultural Landscape'. The standard work, of a rather different era, is M. Le Lannou, *Géographie de la Bretagne* (2 vols., Rennes, 1950). A much briefer but more up-to-date source, with copious maps, is P.-Y. Le Rhun and J.-R. Le Quéau (eds.), *Géographie et aménagement de la Bretagne* (Morlaix, 1994).

The geology of Brittany can be conveniently approached through S. Durand and H. Lardeux (eds.), *Guides géologiques régionaux: Bretagne* (Paris, 1985). Pages 9–26 give a good overview of the geological history of the country; the rest of the book offers a guide to selected regions. A rather more specific but well-illustrated and entertaining book is S. Le Maléfan, *Granites de Bretagne: une pierre, des paysages et des hommes* (Spézet, 2013). The new work on plate tectonics and the relationship between the Armorican plate and Devon and Cornwall is reported in detail in A. H. Dijkstra and C. Hatch, 'Mapping a Hidden Terrane Boundary in the Mantle Lithosphere with Lamprophyres', *Nature Communications*, 9/3770 (2018) (doi: 10.1038/s 41467-018-06253-7).

Sea-level changes during and immediately after the Ice Age are conveniently summed up (by J.-L. Monnier) in P.-R. Giot, J. L'Helgouac'h, and J.-L. Monnier, *Préhistoire de la Bretagne* (Rennes, 1998), chapter 1. The deposition of loëss is discussed by the same author in chapter 2.

Arthur Young, who we will meet again in Chapter 10, described his journey around Brittany in *Travels, during the Years 1787, 1788, 1789: Undertaken More Particularly with a View of Ascertaining the Cultivation, Wealth, Resources, and National Prosperity, of the Kingdom of France* (Bury St Edmunds, 1792). For the background to the visit, see G. E. Mingay, *Arthur Young and his Times* (London, 1975). The state of the Breton landscape in the early modern period is usefully discussed in A. Croix, *La Bretagne aux 16ᵉ et 17ᵉ siècles* (Paris, 1981).

Sailing vessels in use on the Atlantic coast are introduced in B. Cunliffe, *Facing the Ocean: The Atlantic and its Peoples* (Oxford, 2001), chapter 2, and by the same author in *On the Ocean: The Mediterranean and the Atlantic from Prehistory to AD 1500* (Oxford, 2017), chapter 9. Sailing conditions are discussed in S. McGrail, 'Cross-Channel Seamanship and Navigation in the Late First Millennium BC', *Oxford Journal of Archaeology*, 2/3 (1983), 299–337, and in R. Callaghan and C. Scarre, 'Simulating the Western Seaways', *Oxford Journal of Archaeology*, 28/4 (2009), 357–72.

The excavations carried out on the site of Alet at Saint-Servan are conveniently summarized in L. Langouet, *Le Cité d'Alet: de l'agglomération gauloise à l'Île de Saint-Malo* (Saint-Malo, 1996), which has a full bibliography to the detailed excavation reports published in Les Dossiers du Centre Régional d'Archéologie d'Alet. Of these, the more significant are L. Langouët, *Les Fouilles archéologiques du bastion de Solidor, Saint-Malo* (Dossiers du CeRAA, no. F, 1983), and various papers in volumes 2 (1974), 4 (1976), and 6 (1978) of the same publication. The results of the excavation at Le Yaudet are published in three volumes: B. Cunliffe and P. Galliou, *Les Fouilles du Yaudet en Ploulec'h, Côtes-d'Armor*, i, *Le Site: Le Yaudet dans l'histoire et la légende* (Oxford, 2004); ii, *Le Site: de la préhistoire à la fin de l'empire gaulois* (Oxford, 2005); and iii, *Du quatrième siècle apr. J.-C. à aujourd'hui* (Oxford, 2007). A summary of the work appears in B. Cunliffe and P. Galliou, *Le Yaudet en Ploulec'h, Côtes-d'Armor: archéologie d'une agglomération (IIe siècle av. J.C.–XXe siècle apr. J.-C.)* (Rennes, 2015). What little is known of Corbilo is summed up in R. Sanquer, 'Nantes antique', in P. Blois (ed.), *Histoire de Nantes* (Toulouse, 1977), 25–45, and J. Hiernard, 'Corbilo et la route de l'étain', *Bulletin de la Société de l'Ouest et des Musées de Poitiers*, 16 (1982), 497–578. The fortifications at Brest are considered in detail in P. Galliou and J.-M. Simon, *Le Castellum de Brest et la défense de la péninsule armoricaine au cours de l'Antiquité Tardive* (Rennes, 2015). Of the British port sites discussed here, the excavation of Hengistbury Head is published in B. Cunliffe, *Hengistbury Head, Dorset*, i,

The Prehistoric and Roman Settlement, 3500 BC – AD 500 (Oxford, 1987), and the work at Mount Batten, in B. Cunliffe, *Mount Batten, Plymouth: A Prehistoric and Roman Port* (Oxford, 1988).

Chapter 2   Claiming the Land, 6000–2700 BC

The standard textbook for the early prehistoric period in Brittany is P.-R. Giot, J.-L. Monnier, and J. L'Helgouac'h, *Préhistoire de la Bretagne* (2nd edn, Rennes, 1998). For the Neolithic period the most up-to-date survey is C. Scarre, *Landscapes of Neolithic Brittany* (Oxford, 2011). An earlier work, M. Patton, *Statements in Stone: Monuments and Society in Neolithic Brittany* (London, 1993), contains useful insights. These three books cover the archaeological record of the time span explored in this chapter.

For the hunter-gatherers of the Mesolithic period and the overlap with the Neolithic period there are a number of detailed studies, of which the following contain much useful material: Y. Pailler, *Des dernières industries à trapèzes à l'affirmation du Néolithique en Bretagne occidental (5500–3500 av. J.-C.)* (Oxford, 2009); G. Marchand, 'Les Occupations mésolithiques à l'intérieur du Finistère', *Revue Archéologique de l'Ouest*, 22 (2005), 25–84; G. Marchand, 'Le Mésolithique final en Bretagne: une combinaison des faits archéologiques', 66–86, and E. Yven, 'Le Fonctionnement interne des territoires au Mésolithique: approche spatiale de néolithisation', 87–97, both in G. Marchand and A. Tresset (eds.), *Unité et diversité des processus de néolithisation sur la façade atlantique de l'Europe (6ᵉ–4ᵉ millénaires avant J.-C.)* (Paris, 2005); G. Marchand, 'Neolithic Fragrances: Mesolithic–Neolithic Interactions in Western France', in A. Whittle and V. Cummings, *Going Over: The Mesolithic–Neolithic Transition in North-West Europe* (Oxford, 2007), 225–42.

The famous shell middens have generated an extensive literature. The original excavation of Téviec and Hoëdic were reported in M. and S.-J. Péquart, *Téviec: station-nécropole mésolithique du Morbihan* (Paris, 1937), and the same authors' *Hoëdic: deuxième station-nécropole mésolithique du Morbihan* (Antwerp, 1954). Since then there have been a number of interesting studies based on the finds, among them R. J. Schulting, 'Antlers, Bone Pins and Flint Blades: The Mesolithic Cemeteries of Téviec and Hoëdic, Brittany', *Antiquity*, 70 (1996), 335–50, and R. J. Schulting and M. P. Richards, 'Dating Women and Becoming Farmers: New Palaeodietary and AMS Dating Evidence from the Breton Mesolithic Cemeteries of Téviec and Hoëdic', *Journal of Anthropological Archaeology*, 20 (2001), 314–44. The most recent overview of the burials is B. Boulestin, *Les Sépultures mésolithiques de Téviec et Hoedic: révisions bioarchéologiques* (Oxford, 2016). Other useful works include: C. Dupont,

La Malacofaune de sites mésolithiques et néolithiques de la façade atlantique de la France (Oxford, 2006); C. Dupont, 'Les Amas coquilliers mésolithiques de Téviec et d'Hoëdic et le dépôt coquillier néolithique d'Er Yoc'h: de la ressource alimentaire à l'utilisation des coquilles vides', *Melvan*, 4 (2007), 251–64; C. Dupont *et al.*, 'Harvesting the Seashores in Late Mesolithic Northwestern Europe: A View from Brittany', *Journal of World Prehistory*, 22 (2009), 93–111. The remarkable and puzzling pollen evidence for Kerpenhir is fully presented in L. Visset, J. L'Helgouac'h, and J. Bernard, 'La Tourbière submergée de la pointe de Kerpenhir à Locmariaquer (Morbihan): étude environnementale et mise en évidence de deforestation et de pratiques agricoles néolithiques', *Revue Archéologique de l'Ouest*, 13 (1996), 79–87.

A number of papers relevant to an understanding of the Neolithic in northern France are presented in L. Burnez-Lanotte, M. Ilett, and P. Allard (eds.), *Fin des traditions danubiennes dans le Néolithique du bassin parisien et de la Belgique (5100–4700 av. J.C.)* (Paris, 2008). A paper in this volume of direct relevance to Brittany is Y. Pailler *et al.*, 'Le Villeneuve-Saint-Germain dans la péninsule armoricaine: les débuts d'une enquête', 91–111. The impact on Brittany of cultural influences coming from south-western France is considered in G. Marchand, 'La Néolithisation de l'ouest de la France: aires culturelles et transferts techniques dans l'industrie lithique', *Bulletin de la Société Préhistorique Française*, 97 (2000), 377–403. The evidence for extensive links along the Atlantic coasts of France to western Britain are presented in A. Tresset, 'French Connections II: Of Cows and Men', 18–30, and P. Woodman and M. McCarthy, '"Contemplating Some Awful(ly) Interesting Vistas": Importing Cattle and Red Deer into Prehistoric Ireland', 31–9, both in I. Armit *et al.* (eds.), *Neolithic Settlement in Ireland and Western Britain* (Oxford, 2003); and A. Sheridan, 'Neolithic Connections along and across the Irish Sea', in V. Cummings and C. Fowler (eds.), *The Neolithic of the Irish Sea: Materiality and Traditions of Practice* (Oxford, 2004), 9–24. Individual early Neolithic settlements are reported in Cassen *et al.*, 'L'Habitat Villeneuve-Saint-Germain de Haut-Mée (Saint-Étienne-en-Coglès, Ille-et-Vilaine)', *Bulletin de la Société Préhistorique Française*, 95 (1998), 41–75; L. Laporte, 'Another Brick in the Wall: Fifth Millennium BC Earthen-Walled Architecture on the Channel Shores', *Antiquity*, 89 (2015), 800–81; and B. Cunliffe, 'Little Sark Standing Stone (Site L53): 2015–17', in B. Cunliffe and E. Durham, *Sark: A Sacred Island?*, i, *Fieldwork and Excavation, 2004–2017* (Oxford, 2019), 253–77.

Of the early menhirs mentioned here, the Porh Fetan discovery is reported in S. Cassen *et al.*, 'Un dépôt sous-marin de lames polies néolithiques en jadéitite et sillimanite, et un ouvrage de stèles submergé sur la plage dite du Petit Rohu près Saint-Pierre-Quiberon (Morbihan)', *Bulletin de la Société Prehistorique Française*, 107 (2010), 53–84. The Le Douet alignment is summarized in J.-M. Large and E. Mens,

'The Douet Alignment on the Island of Hoëdic (Morbihan): New Insights into Standing Stone Alignments in Brittany', *Oxford Journal of Archaeology*, 28 (2009), 239–54. The Grand Menhir Brisé alignment is described in G. Bailloud *et al.*, *Carnac: les premières architectures de pierre* (Paris, 2009), and in S. Cassen, *Exercice de stèle: une archéologie des pierres dressées. Réflexion autour des menhirs de Carnac* (Paris, 2009).

The question of the origins of the megalithic collective burial tradition is complex and has generated a massive literature. Fortunately, in B. S. Paulsson, *Time and Stone: The Emergence and Development of Megaliths and Megalithic Societies in Europe* (Oxford, 2017), the author brings together the European evidence in a meticulous analysis which concludes by identifying the Morbihan as the possible origin for the phenomenon. There are good descriptions of the long mounds in the books listed in the first paragraph of this section. Other useful sources are J. Lecornec, 'Le Mégalithisme de l'ouest', *Bulletin et Mémoires de la Société Polymathique du Morbihan*, 125 (1999), 9–38, and C.-T. Le Roux (ed.), *Monuments mégalithiques à Locmariaquer (Morbihan): le long tumulus d'Er Grah dans son environnement* (Paris, 2006).

The three general books listed in the first paragraph of this section provide excellent discussions of the passage graves of Brittany. Of those specifically mentioned here, full reports are to be found in J. Le Cornec, *Le Petit Mont, Arzon, Morbihan* (Rennes, 1994); P. R. Giot, *Barnenez, Carn, Guennoc* (Rennes, 1987); C.-T. Le Roux and Y. Lecerf, 'Le Cairn de Ty-Floc'h à Saint-Thois (Fouilles de 1978–1979)', *Bulletin de la Société Archéologique du Finistère*, 108 (1980), 24–49; and C.-T. Le Roux, *Gavrinis* (Paris, 1995). These books are for the specialist. For a reader who simply wants to get a flavour of Breton megaliths, J. Briard, *Mégalithes de Bretagne* (Rennes, 1992), is recommended. It is illustrated with evocative photographs taken by N. Fediaevsky. For those who want to visit some of the megaliths, A. Burl, *Megalithic Brittany* (London, 1985), is an essential companion.

The alignments of Carnac and the associated monuments have generated a massive literature. The best introduction is G. Bailloud *et al.*, *Carnac: les premières architectures de pierre* (Paris, 1995). Excellent shorter guides are also available, including C. Boujot and E. Vigier, *Carnac et environs: architectures mégalithiques* (Paris, 2012), and A.-E. Riskine, *Carnac: l'armée de pierres* (Paris, 1992). The Breton stone alignments are put into a west European context in A. Burl, *From Carnac to Callanish: The Prehistoric Stone Rows and Avenues of Britain, Ireland, and Brittany* (New Haven, 1993). A fascinating insight into how the stones for the alignments were assembled is given in E. Mens, 'Refitting Megaliths in Western France', *Antiquity*, 82 (2008), 25–36. The Er Lannic enclosures and associated finds are considered in P. Grouber, 'Les Coupes-à-socle d'Er Lannic (Arzon, Morbihan)', in S. Cassen, C. Boujot, and J. Vaquero (eds.), *Éléments d'architecture: exploration d'un tertre funéraire à Lannec er

Gadouer (Erdeven, Morbihan) (Chauvigny, 2000), 483–527. The original excavation was reported in Z. Le Rouzic, *Carnac: restaurations faites dans le region. Les Cromlechs de Er-Lannic, commune d'Arzon de 1923 à 1926* (Vannes, 1930). The most accessible general discussion of the later megalithic tombs, the *allées couvertes*, is given in C. Scarre, *The Landscapes of Neolithic Brittany* (Oxford, 2011), chapter 9, with extensive references to individual sites. Speculations about the astronomical significance of the alignments and tombs are offered in A. and A. S. Thom, *Megalithic Remains in Britain and Brittany* (Oxford, 1978).

The networks which bound communities can be traced by plotting the distribution of selected stone types. The dolerite from Séledin is discussed in C.-T. Le Roux, 'Stone Axes of Brittany and the Marches', in T. H. M. Clough and W. A. Cummins, *Stone Axe Studies* (London, 1979), 49–56. This paper also includes other stone sources in Brittany such as fibrolite. The full report of the excavation of the quarry is given in C.-T. Le Roux, *L'Outillage de pierre polie en métadolérite du type A: les ateliers de Plussulien (Côtes-d'Armor)* (Rennes, 1999). The jadeitite axes are considered in S. Cassen and P. Pétrequin, 'La Chronologie des haches polies dites de prestige dans la moitié ouest de la France', *European Journal of Archaeology*, 2 (1999), 7–33, P. Pétrequin *et al.*, 'La Valorisation sociale des longues haches dans l'Europe néolithique', in J. Guilaine (ed.), *Matériaux, productions, circulations du Néolithique à l'Âge du Bronze* (Paris, 2002), 67–98; and P. Pétrequin *et al.*, 'La Circulation des haches carnacéennes en Europe occidentale', in P. Pétrequin *et al.* (eds.), *Jade: Grandes haches alpines du Néolithique européen, Ve et IVe millénaires av. J.-C.* (Dijon, 2013), 1015–45. Variscite sources are discussed in F. Herbant and G. Querré, 'La Parure néolithique en variscite dans le sud de l'Armorique', *Bulletin de la Société Préhistorique Française*, 101 (2004), 497–520, and R. Fabregas Valcarce *et al.*, 'Spain and Portugal: Long Chisels and Perforated Axes. Their Context and Distribution', in Pétrequin *et al.* (eds.), *Jade*, 1008–1135. Grand-Pressigny flint reaching Brittany is fully discussed in E. Ihuel, *La Diffusion du silex du Grand-Pressigny dans le Massif armoricain au Néolithique* (Paris, 2004).

The source and distribution of polished stone rings is explored in several publications: Y. Pailler, *Des dernières industries à trapezes à l'affirmation du Néolithique en Bretagne occidental (5500–3500 av. J.-C.)* (Oxford, 2007); N. Fromont and C. Marcigny, 'Acquisition, transformation et diffusion du schiste du Pissot au Néolithique ancien dans le quart nord-ouest de la France', in L. Burnez-Lanotte, M. Ilett, and P. Alland (eds.), *Fin des traditions danubiennes dans le Néolithique du bassin parisien et de la Belgique (5100–4700 av. J.-C.)* (Paris, 2008); and M. Patton, 'Neolithic Stone Rings from the Channel Islands', *Annual Bulletin of the Société Jersiase*, 25 (1990), 347–52. The spread of farming communities across the Channel to Britain is summed up in an optimistically titled paper by Y. Pailler and A. Sheridan, 'Everything You Always Wanted to Know About . . . la néolithisation de la Grande-Bretagne et de l'Irlande', *Bulletin de la Société Préhistorique Française*, 106 (2009), 25–56.

Chapter 3   The Metal-Rich West, 2700–600 BC

The standard textbook for the archaeology of Bronze Age Brittany is P.-R. Giot, J. Briard, and L. Pape, *Protohistoire de la Bretagne* (Rennes, 1995). All key sites known at the time of its publication are referred to with copious bibliographies. The final stages in the use of megalithic monuments and the introduction of Beakers are usefully summarized in C. Scarre, *Landscapes of Neolithic Brittany* (Oxford, 2011). For an excellent background to the discovery and exploitation of copper, see W. O'Brien, *Prehistoric Copper Mining in Europe, 5500–500 BC* (Oxford, 2015), though Brittany is not specifically treated. An important overview of the circulation of copper alloys throughout Europe is given in C. F. E. Pare, 'Bronze and the Bronze Age', in C. F. E. Pare (ed.), *Metals Make the World Go Round: The Supply and Circulation of Metals in Bronze Age Europe* (Oxford, 2000), 1–38.

The Bell Beaker phenomenon in Europe is extensively treated in the literature. It is a fast-moving area of research and there is no reliable up-to-date overview, but a reader who wishes to get a flavour of the debate will find a number of thoughtful and interesting papers in M. P. Prieto Martínez and L. Salanova (eds.), *The Bell Beaker Transition in Europe* (Oxford, 2015). The most comprehensive work on Bell Beakers in France is L. Salanova, *La Question du Campaniforme en France et dans les îles anglo-normandes: productions, chronologie et rôles d'un standard céramique* (Paris, 2000). The same author's paper 'Le Rôle de la façade atlantique dans la genèse du Campaniforme en Europe', *Bulletin de la Société Préhistorique Française*, 101 (2004), 223–6, specifically relates to the origin of the Breton Beakers. Also relevant to movements along the Atlantic façade is A. A. Rodríguez Casal, 'The Galician Maritime Beaker Complex in the Cultural Framework of the Copper Age of Western Europe', in F. Nicolis (ed.), *Bell Beakers Today: Pottery, People, Culture, Symbols in Prehistoric Europe* (Trento, 2001), 125–37. The practicalities of making the sea journey between north-western Iberia and Brittany are examined in R. Callaghan and C. Scarre, 'Biscay and Beyond? Prehistoric Voyaging between the Two Finistères', *Oxford Journal of Archaeology*, 36 (2017), 355–73. The impact of the Rhine–Seine–Loire corridor on the spread of Beaker culture to Britain is explored in S. Needham, 'Transforming Beaker Culture in North-West Europe: Process of Fusion and Fission', *Proceedings of the Prehistoric Society*, 71 (2005), 171–218.

Beaker metallurgy along the Atlantic façade and the development of a regular tin-bronze is presented in the paper by C. F. E. Pare noted in the first paragraph of this section. For details of the Ross Island copper mines, see W. O'Brien, *Ross Island: Mining, Metal and Society in Early Ireland* (Galway, 2004). The export of the Ross Island copper to Brittany is discussed in H. Gandois *et al.*, 'Early Bronze Age Axe-Ingots from Brittany: Evidence for Connections with South-West Ireland?', *Proceedings of the Royal Irish Academy*, 119C (2019), 1–36. Sources of tin in Brittany are considered in R. D. Penhallurick, *Tin in Antiquity* (London, 1986), 85–94, and C. Mahé-Le Carlier, Y. Lulzac, and P.-R. Giot, 'Étude des déchets de réduction provenant de deux sites d'exploitation d'étain armoricain de l'Âge du Bronze et du Moyen Age', *Revue Archéologique de l'Ouest*, 18 (2001), 45–56. Gold lunulae and other goldwork is discussed in J. Taylor, *Bronze Age Goldwork of the British Isles* (Cambridge, 1980), and G. Eogan, *The Accomplished Arts: Gold and Gold-Working in Britain and Ireland during the Bronze Age (c.2300–650 BC)* (Oxford, 1994). The possibility of a Cornish origin for much of the gold is considered in C. D. Standish *et al.*, 'A Non-Local Source of Irish Chalcolithic and Early Bronze Age Gold', *Proceedings of the Prehistoric Society*, 81 (2015), 149–77.

The Beaker period in Armorica is discussed in detail in J. L'Helgouac'h, 'Le Cadre culturel du Campaniforme armoricain', in Nicolis (ed.), *Bell Beakers Today*, 289–99. The deposit of beakers in the *allée couverte* of Men-ar-Rompet is described in L. Salinova, 'Fabrication et circulation des céramiques Campaniformes', in J. Guilaine (ed.), *Matériaux, productions, circulations du Néolithique à l'Âge du Bronze* (Paris, 2002), 151–66. The imported bronze-handled battle axes from Brittany are described in P.-R. Giot, J. Briard, and L. Pape, *Protohistoire de la Bretagne* (Rennes, 1995), 32–5, while the stone copies of battle axes are treated in P.-R. Giot and J. Cogné, 'Étude pétrographique des haches polies de Bretagne. IV: Les Haches de combat en méta-hornblendite', *Bulletin de la Société Préhistorique Française*, 52 (1955), 401–9.

A useful general paper, now rather dated, which introduces the cross-Channel interactions is J. Briard, 'Relations between Brittany and Great Britain during the Bronze Age', in C. Scarre and F. Healy (eds.), *Trade and Exchange in Prehistoric Europe* (Oxford, 1994), 183–90. The classic study of the round barrows of Brittany is J. Briard, *Les Tumulus d'Armorique* (Paris, 1984), which has been brought up to date in A. Balquet, *Les Tumulus armoricains du Bronze ancien* (Rennes, 2001). Together they provide details of all the excavated barrows. A number of studies of specific categories of material from the burials are available: for bronze daggers, G. Gallay, *Die kupfer- und altbronzezeitlichen Dolche und Stabdolche in Frankreich* (Munich, 1981); for flint arrowheads, C. Nicolas, 'Arrows of Power from Brittany to Denmark (2500–1700 BC)', *Proceedings of the Prehistoric Society*, 83 (2017), 247–87; and for precious cups, S. Needham, 'Encompassing the Sea: "Maritories" and Bronze Age Maritime Interactions', in P. Clark (ed.), *Bronze Age Connections: Cultural Contact in Prehistoric Europe* (Oxford, 2009), 12–37. Evidence for the relationship between the elite burials of Brittany and Wessex is minutely analysed in S. Needham, 'Power Pulses across a Cultural Divide: Cosmologically Driven Acquisitions between Armorica and Wessex', *Proceedings of the Prehistoric Society*, 66 (2000), 151–207. The Langdon Bay and Salcombe finds, usually considered to be shipwrecks, are discussed in S. Needham, D. Parham, and C. Frieman, *Claimed by the Sea: Salcombe, Langdon Bay and Other Marine Finds of the Bronze Age* (York, 2013).

The most accessible overview of Middle Bronze Age hoards from Brittany is P.-R. Giot, J. Briard, and L. Pape, *Protohistoire de la Bretagne* (Rennes, 1995), chapter 3. The material from the hoards is presented in full in J. Briard, *Les Dépôts bretons et l'Âge du Bronze atlantique* (Rennes, 1965). The importance of bronze finds in assessing cross-Channel connections is discussed in B. O'Connor, *Cross-Channel Relations in the Later Bronze Age* (Oxford, 1980). More recent contributions using a full range of archaeological data include C. Marcigny *et al.*, 'Découvertes récentes du l'Âge du Bronze moyen dans le département de la Sarthe (Pays-de-la-Loire)', *Revue Archéologie de l'Ouest*, 19 (2002), 7–13, and C. Marcigny, E. Ghesquière, and I. Kinnes, 'Bronze Age Cross-Channel Relations: The Lower Normandy (France) Example. Ceramic Chronology and First Reflections', in C. Burgess, P. Topping, and F. Lynch (eds.), *Beyond Stonehenge: Essays on the Bronze Age in Honour of Colin Burgess* (Oxford, 2007), 255–67.

The Atlantic Late Bronze Age is a complex study. Summaries can be found in B. Cunliffe, *Facing the Ocean: The Atlantic and its Peoples* (Oxford, 2001), 275–93, and the same author's *Britain Begins* (Oxford, 2013), chapter 8. Two collections of edited specialist papers give some idea of the range of the topic involved: C. Chevillot and A. Coffyn (eds.), *L'Âge du Bronze atlantique* (Beynac, 1991), and S. Oliveira Jorge (ed.), *Existe uma Idade do Bronze Atlantico?* (Lisbon, 1998). An important paper exploring the changing intensity of interaction along the Atlantic is C. Burgess and B. O'Connor, 'Iberia, the Atlantic Bronze Age and the Mediterranean', in S. Celestino, N. Rafel, and X.-L. Armada (eds.), *Contacto cultural entre el Mediterráneo y el Atlántico (siglos XII–VIII ane): la precolonización a debate* (Madrid, 2008), 41–58. Specific to the case of Brittany is D. Brandherm and C. Burgess, 'Carp's-Tongue Problems', in F. Verse *et al.* (eds.), *Durch die Zeiten: Festschrift für Albrecht Jockenhövel zum 65. Geburtstag* (Rahden, 2008), 133–60, and J. Briard, *Les Dépôts bretons et l'Âge du Bronze atlantique* (Rennes, 1965), chapters 10–13. Finds of late Armorican axe hoards are updated in J. Rivallain, *Les Haches à douille armoricaines revisitées* (Rennes, 2012).

There is comparatively little literature yet available on Bronze Age settlements in Brittany, but a useful short account is given in S. Blanchet, 'L'Habitat de l'Âge du Bronze en Bretagne', in S. Boulud-Gazo and C. Le Pennec (eds.), *L'Âge du Bronze dans le Morbihan* (Vannes, 2019), 90–9. It contains brief accounts of recent finds at Caudan, Lenn Sec'h (by M. Levau), Mané à Gurdel (by V. Le Gall and A.-F. Cherel), and Mauron, La Rochette (by J.-Y. Tinevez).

An overview of the Early Iron Age finds in Brittany is given in P.-R. Giot, 'L'Âge du Fer', in P.-R. Giot, J. Briard, and L. Pape, *Protohistoire de la Bretagne* (Rennes, 1995), 203–365. More recent reviews are in P. Galliou, *Les Osismes: peuple de l'occident gaulois* (Spézet, 2014), chapter 4, and P. Galliou, *Les Vénètes d'Armorique* (Spézet, 2017), chapter 4.

Chapter 4 Facing the Expanding World, 600–50 BC

For a broad overview of what was happening in western Europe in the latter part of the first millennium BC, see B. Cunliffe, *Europe between the Oceans, 9000 BC – AD 1000* (London, 2011), chapters 9 and 10. The situation in Gaul is treated in more detail in the same author's *Greeks, Romans and Barbarians: Spheres of Interaction* (London, 1988). The most accessible translation of *Ora Maritima* is Rufus Festus Avienus, *Ora Maritima*, ed. and trans. J. P. Murphy (Chicago, 1977). The tin route across Gaul is discussed in R. Dion, 'Transport de l'étain des Îles Britanniques à Marseille à travers la Gaule préromaine', in Jacques Nazet (ed.), *Actes du 93ᵉ Congrès National des Sociétés Savantes tenu à Tours, 1968* (Paris, 1970), 423–38.

Archaeological evidence for life in Brittany in the Iron Age is most conveniently summarized in P.-R. Giot, 'L'Âge du Fer', in P.-R. Giot, J. Briard, and L. Pape, *Protohistoire de la Bretagne* (Rennes, 1995), 203–365, with a full bibliography. Souterrains are described and discussed in detail in P.-R. Giot and C.-T. Le Roux, *Souterrains armoricains de l'Âge du Fer* (Rennes, 1976). The stelae are introduced in Giot's chapter cited above, 229–51. Since then a systemic survey has been under way by the Patrimoine Archéologique de Bretagne and is being published for each region. The results of the survey are brought together and thoroughly discussed in M.-Y. Daire, *Les Stèles de l'Âge du Fer dans l'ouest de la Gaule* (Saint-Malo, 2005). A small group of decorated stelae are considered in an important paper, M.-Y. Daire and A. Villard, 'Les Stèles de l'Âge du Fer à décors géométrique et curvilignes: état de la question dans l'ouest Armoricain', *Revue Archéologique de l'Ouest*, 13 (1996), 123–56. Breton Iron Age pottery is the subject of F. Schwappach, 'Stempelverzierte Keramik von Armorica', in O.-H. Frey (ed.), *Marburger Beiträge zur Archäologie der Kelten: Festschrift für*

Wolfgang Dehn zum 60. Geburtstag am 6. Juli 1969 (Bonn, 1969), 213–93. The burials are analysed in P.-Y. Milcent, 'L'Âge du Fer en Armorique à travers les ensembles funéraires (IXe–IIIe siècles avant J.-C.)', *Antiquités Nationales*, 25 (1993), 17–50. This paper offers an important reconsideration of the dating of pottery. There has been no recent systematic survey of hill-forts and cliff castles of Brittany, but for the department of Finistère, see P. Maguer, 'Les Enceintes fortifiées de l'Âge du Fer dans le Finistère', *Revue Archéologique de l'Ouest*, 13 (1996), 103–21. Some Breton hill-forts are also described in R. E. M. Wheeler and K. M. Richardson, *Hill-Forts of Northern France* (London, 1957).

The relationship of the Iron Age communities of Brittany to the wider Atlantic community are considered in two papers: B. Cunliffe, 'Social and Economic Contacts between Western France and Britain in the Early and Middle La Tène Period', in J.-P. Daugas *et al.* (eds.), *La Bretagne et l'Europe préhistoriques: mémoire en hommage à Pierre-Roland Giot, Revue Archéologique de l'Ouest*, suppl. 2 (Rennes, 1990), 245–51, and by the same author in 'Brittany and the Atlantic Rim in the Later First Millennium BC', *Oxford Journal of Archaeology*, 19 (2000), 367–86. Work on the port of Mount Batten is detailed in B. Cunliffe, *Mount Batten, Plymouth: A Prehistoric and Roman Port* (Oxford, 1988). The double pyramidal iron ingots from Brittany are reviewed in P.-R. Giot, 'Les Lingots de fer bipyramidaux de Bretagne', *Annales de Bretagne*, 71 (1964), 51–60. The La Tène bronze helmet from Tronoan is thoroughly discussed in U. Schaaff, 'Keltische Eisenhelme aus vorrömischer Zeit', *Jahrbuch des Römisch-Germanischen Zentralmuseums Mainz*, 21 (1974), 149–206, with additional finds listed in E. and F. Schwappach, 'Fragments of the Tronoan Helmet?', *Archaeologia Atlantica*, 2 (1977), 87–93. The journey made by Pytheas around Brittany and Britain is discussed in B. Cunliffe, *The Extraordinary Voyage of Pytheas the Greek* (London, 2001). For tin sources and extraction in Brittany and Britain, see R. D. Penhallurick, *Tin in Antiquity* (London, 1986). The gold coin found on the beach at Lampaul-Ploudalmézeau is illustrated and discussed in Giot, 'L'Âge du Fer', 215–16.

For an overview of the early stage of the Roman occupation of Gaul and the wine trade, see Cunliffe, *Greeks, Romans and Barbarians*, chapters 4 and 5. Evidence for the Roman wine trade is conveniently brought together in A. Tchernia, *Le Vin de l'Italie romaine* (Rome, 1986). Tchernia has given detailed consideration to the wine trade in Gaul in 'Italian Wine in Gaul at the End of the Republic', in P. Garnsey, K. Hopkins, and C. R. Whittaker (eds.), *Trade in the Ancient Economy* (London, 1983), 87–104. See also F. Laubenheimer, *Le Temps des amphores en Gaule: vins, huiles et sauces* (Paris, 1990). For Roman wine amphorae found in Brittany, see P. Galliou, *Les Amphores tardo-républicaines découvertes dans l'ouest de la France et les importations de vins italiens à la fin de l'Âge du Fer* (Brest, 1982), and the same author's 'Days of Wine and Roses? Early Armorica and the Atlantic Wine Trade', in S. Macready and F. H. Thompson (eds.), *Cross-Channel Trade between Gaul and Britain in the Pre-Roman Iron Age* (London, 1984), 24–36. Evidence for trade between Brittany and southern Britain and the port of Hengistbury is outlined in B. Cunliffe, 'Britain, the Veneti and Beyond', *Oxford Journal of Archaeology*, 1 (1982), 39–68, and presented in greater detail in B. Cunliffe and P. de Jersey, *Armorica and Britain: Cross-Channel Relationships in the Late First Millennium BC* (Oxford, 1997). For an assessment of the part played by Alet, see L. Langouet, 'Alet and Cross-Channel Trade', in Macready and Thompson (eds.), *Cross-Channel Trade between Gaul and Britain in the Pre-Roman Iron Age*, 67–77, but see also P. de Jersey, 'The Early Chronology of Alet, and its Implications for Hengistbury Head and Cross-Channel Trade in the Late Iron Age', *Oxford Journal of Archaeology*, 12 (1993), 321–35. The position of Guernsey in cross-Channel trade is assessed in B. Burns, B. Cunliffe, and H. Sebire, *Guernsey: An Island Community of the Atlantic Iron Age* (Oxford, 1996). The results of the excavation of the port of Hengistbury Head can be found in B. Cunliffe, *Hengistbury Head, Dorset*, i, *The Prehistoric and Roman Settlement, 3500 BC – AD 500* (Oxford, 1987).

The opening chapters of P. Galliou, *L'Armorique romaine* (Brest, 2005), reflect on the last days of Armorican independence, the Roman conquest, and the immediate post-conquest period. The situation in the decades leading up to the Roman conquest is best understood through the coinage, issued by the different polities, which is given full consideration in P. de Jersey, *Coinage in Iron Age Armorica* (Oxford, 1994). An earlier, but important, study of the coins of the Coriosolites, dividing them into a chronological series, is K. Gruel, 'Le Trésor de Trébry (Côtes-du-Nord)', *Études de Numismatique Celtique*, 1 (Paris, 1981). Of the large tribal *oppida*, Le Camp d'Artus has been examined by excavations and is reported in R. E. M. Wheeler and K. M. Richardson, *Hill-Forts of Northern France* (London, 1957), 23–38. The large *oppidum* of Poulailler is described and illustrated in the same volume, 113–14, and there is also a brief note on Guégnon, 104. An informative discussion of the *murus gallicus* type of defence, by M. A. Cotton, is to be found in the same volume, 153–216. Reports on the excavation at the defended promontory site at Cap d'Erquy are published in P.-R. Giot, J. Briard, and M. Avery, 'Les Retranchements du Cap d'Erquy: fouilles de 1967 du Fossé Catuélan', *Annales de Bretagne*, 75 (1968), 67–84, and P.-R. Giot and J. Briard, 'Les Retranchements du Cap d'Erquy: fouilles de 1968 au Fossé de Pleine-Garenne', *Annales de Bretagne*, 76 (1969), 21–36.

Julius Caesar's campaigns in Armorica are described by Caesar himself in his *Commentaries on the Gallic War*. There are many good translations. Recommended for the clarity of its language is that by A. and P. Wiseman, *Julius Caesar: The Battle for Gaul* (London, 1980). The tense situation in Gaul following the war, when the conquered tribes were being incorporated into the Roman system, is well described in J. F. Drinkwater, *Roman Gaul: The Three Provinces, 58 BC – AD 260* (London, 1983), chapters 1 and 2. The coin hoards of 30–20 BC are described in P. Galliou, 'Monnaies de la république découvertes ou conservées dans le Finistère', *Archéologie en Bretagne*, 9 (1976), 21–4. A discussion of the large hoards buried about this time on the Channel Islands is offered in P. de Jersey, 'The Island of Jersey: Focus of Resistance or Field of Last Resort?', in A. P. Fitzpatrick and C. Haselgrove (eds.), *Julius Caesar's Battle for Gaul: New Archaeological Perspectives* (Oxford, 2019), 269–85. For a popular account of the massive hoard of nearly seventy thousand coins found in Jersey recently, see R. Miles and R. Mead, *The Jersey Hoard: Le Câtillon II* (Jersey, 2015).

Chapter 5 The Roman Interlude, 50 BC – AD 400

Two books provide a wide-ranging introduction to the reformation of Gaul under the Roman administration: J. F. Drinkwater, *Roman Gaul: The Three Provinces, 58 BC – AD 206* (London, 1983), and G. Woolf, *Becoming Roman: The Origins of Provincial Civilization in Gaul* (Cambridge, 1998). For a more specific work dealing with the early development of urban society, see R. Bedon, *Les Villes des Trois Gaules de César à Néron dans leur contexte historique, territorial et politique* (Paris, 1999).

There are two books devoted to the Roman period in Brittany. The most up to date is P. Galliou, *L'Armorique romaine* (Brest, 2005), but L. Pape, *La Bretagne romaine* (Rennes, 1995), also contains much that is useful. Detailed surveys exist for each of the main tribal regions of Brittany: P. Galliou, *Les Osismes: peuple de l'occident gaulois* (Spézet, 2014); P. Galliou, *Les Vénètes d'Armorique* (Spézet, 2017); and meanwhile (until Galliou has published surveys of the other tribes), G. Guennou, *La Cité des Coriosolites* (Rennes, 1981), and A.-M. Rouanet-Liesenfelt, *La Civilisation des Riedones* (Brest, 1980). The journal *Aremorica: Études sur l'Ouest de la Gaule Romaine*, published annually since 2007, contains reports on matters relating to Brittany in the Roman era. The thoroughness of the bibliography in Galliou's *L'Armorique romaine* makes it possible for the reader to follow up issues raised in this chapter. For that reason suggestions for more detailed reading here will be kept short.

For salt extraction and the garum industry, see P.-L. Gouletquer, *Les Briquetages armoricains: technologie protohistorique du sel en Armorique* (Rennes, 1970); R. Sanquer and P. Galliou, 'Garum, sel et salaisons en Armorique romaine', *Gallia*, 30 (1972), 199–223; and M.-Y. Daire (ed.), *Le Sel gaulois: bouilleurs du sel et ateliers de briquetage à l'Âge du Fer* (Saint-Malo, 1994). The best overview of the wine trade impacting on Brittany is P. Galliou, 'Days of Wine and Roses? Early Armorica and the Atlantic

Wine Trade', in S. Macready and F. H. Thompson (eds.), *Cross-Channel Trade between Gaul and Britain in the Pre-Roman Iron Age* (London, 1984), 24–36. The St Peter Port (Guernsey) wreck is reported in M. Rule and J. Monaghan, *A Gallo-Roman Trading Vessel from Guernsey: The Excavation and Recovery of a Third Century Shipwreck* (St Peter Port, 1993). For the Sept-Îles wreck, see M. L'Hour, 'Un site sous-marin sur la côte de l'Armorique: l'épave antique de Ploumanac'h', *Revue Archéologique de l'Ouest*, 6 (1987), 113–31. On Atlantic navigation, M. Reddé, 'La Navigation au large des côtes atlantiques de la Gaule à l'époque romaine', *Mélanges de l'École Française de Rome: Antiquité*, 91 (1979), 481–9. The use of pottery distribution in tracing trade is explored in M. Fulford, 'Pottery and Britain's Foreign Trade in the Later Roman Period', in D. P. S. Peacock (ed.), *Pottery and Early Commerce* (London, 1977), 35–95. For *céramique à l'éponge*, P. Galliou, M. Fulford, and M. Clement, 'La Diffusion de la céramique "à l'éponge" dans le nord-ouest de l'empire romain', *Gallia*, 38 (1980), 265–78.

Anguipede statues are discussed in J.-Y. Éveillard, 'Les Cavaliers à l'anguipède de l'Armorique: étude comparée', in H. Walter (ed.), *La Sculpture d'époque romaine dans le nord, dans l'est de la Gaule et dans les régions avoisinantes: acquis et problématiques actuelles. Actes du Colloque International, Besançon, 12–14 mars 1998* (Besançon, 2001), 21–34, 263–5. For the carved menhir at Kervadol, see J.-Y. Éveillard, 'Un monument sculpté gallo-roman atypique: la stèle de Kervadol en Plobannalec (Finistère)', *Bulletin de la Société Archéologique Finistère*, 133 (2004), 43–59. The reuse of megalithic monuments in the Iron Age and Roman period is explored in K. R. Dark, 'Roman-Period Activity at Prehistoric Ritual Monuments in Britain and in the Armorican Peninsula', in E. Scott (ed.), *Theoretical Roman Archaeology: First Conference Proceedings* (Aldershot, 1993), 133–46, and J. Lecornec, 'Réutilisation des monuments mégalithiques à l'époque gallo-romaine', in C.-T. Le Roux (ed.), *Du monde des chasseurs à celui des métallurgistes* (Rennes, 2001), 289–94. The development of Locmariaquer as a ritual site associated with a Roman fertility cult is discussed in B. Cunliffe, 'Venus Arising', in H. Roche *et al.* (eds.), *From Megaliths to Metal: Essays in Honour of George Eogan* (Oxford, 2004), 209–14. For the excavation of Le Petit Mont and the Iron Age and Roman ritual deposits therein, J. Lecornec, *Le Petit Mont: Arzon, Morbihan* (Rennes, 1994).

Two distinctive aspects of Roman period culture in Armorica are explored in J. Boislève, F. Labaune-Jean, and C. Dupont, 'Décors peints à incrustations de coquillages en Armorique romaine', *Aremorica*, 5 (2012), 9–32, and L. Langouet *et al.*, 'Les Plaques décorées en schiste de la Bretagne armoricaine sous l'empire romaine', *Revue Archéologique de l'Ouest*, 17 (2000), 215–37.

A useful background to the events of the late third century is presented in J. Drinkwater, *The Gallic Empire: Separation and Continuity in the North-Western Provinces of the Roman Empire, AD 260–274* (Stuttgart, 1987). A collection of specialist papers exploring the issues in detail are brought together in A. King and M. Henig, *The Roman West in the Third Century: Contributions from Archaeology and History* (Oxford, 1981). Of special relevance is the contribution from P. Galliou, 'Western Gaul in the Third Century', 259–86, which reviews much of the Breton evidence with full references. The Carausian episode and the Saxon shore forts are discussed in S. Johnson, *The Roman Forts of the Saxon Shore* (London, 1976), and H. P. G. Williams, *Carausius: A Consideration of the Historical, Archaeological and Numismatic Aspects of his Reign* (Oxford, 2003). Several useful papers relating to the subject are brought together in V. A. Maxfield (ed.), *The Saxon Shore: A Handbook* (Exeter, 1989). For the coastal fortifications constructed in Brittany, see L. Langouet, *La Cité d'Alet: de l'agglomération gauloise à l'Île de Saint-Malo* (Saint-Malo, 1996); B. Cunliffe and P. Galliou, *Les Fouilles du Yaudet en Ploulec'h, Côtes-d'Armor*, ii, *Le Site: de la préhistoire à la fin de l'empire gaulois* (Oxford, 2005); and P. Galliou and J.-M. Simon, *Le Castellum de Brest et la défense de la péninsule armoricaine au cours de l'Antiquité Tardive* (Rennes, 2015). The *Notitia Dignitatum* and the development of the shore defences is conveniently discussed in J. C. Mann, 'The Historical Development of the Saxon Shore', in Maxfield (ed.), *The Saxon Shore*, 1–11, while the continental system is outlined in R. Brulet, 'The Continental *Litus Saxonicum*', in the same volume, 45–77. The question of the peasant revolts was introduced in a now classic paper, E. A. Thompson, 'Peasant Revolts in Late Roman Gaul and Spain', *Past and Present*, 2 (1952), 11–23.

Chapter 6 From Armorica to Brittany, 400–751

The fascinating issue of the end of Roman Armorica and the impact of the British settlement continues to generate a lively debate. The classic work setting the scene is J. Loth, *L'Émigration bretonne en Armorique* (Paris, 1883). Then followed N. K. Chadwick, 'The Colonization of Brittany from Celtic Britain', *Proceedings of the British Academy*, 51 (1965), 235–99; the same author's *Early Brittany* (Cardiff, 1969); and L. Fleuriot's *Les Origines de la Bretagne* (Paris, 1982). These works together present what may be regarded as the traditional view based largely on historical sources and linguistic analysis. In more recent years archaeological evidence has become increasingly relevant to the discussion; see L. Fleuriot and P.-R. Giot, 'Early Brittany', *Antiquity*, 51 (1977), 106–16. In P.-R. Giot, P. Guignon, and B. Merdrignac, *The British Settlement of Brittany: The First Bretons in Armorica* (Stroud, 2003), the authors offer a range of views on aspects of the settlement of Brittany from the fifth to the eighth century. A. Chédeville and H. Guillotel, *La Bretagne des saints et des rois, VIᵉ–Xᵉ siècle* (Rennes, 1984), presents an essentially historical approach covering an extended time span. Traditional views on the nature and duration of the settlement of Armorica from Britain have, more recently, come under scrutiny in G. Le Duc, 'The Colonisation of Brittany from Britain: New Approaches and Questions', in R. Black *et al.* (eds.), *Celtic Connections: Proceedings of the Tenth International Congress of Celtic Studies*, i, *Language, Literature, History, Culture* (East Linton, 1999), 133–53. A more profound and closely argued critique is provided in C. Brett, 'Soldiers, Saints and States? The Breton Migrations Revisited', *Cambrian Medieval Celtic Studies*, 61 (2011), 1–56, which clears away many of the old circular arguments and opens up the debate once more.

One of the issues that Brett set out to question was the long-held suggestion that Roman troops from Britain began to arrive in Armorica from the late third century as a bow-wave to the main migration. Some evidence for this was offered in P. Galliou, 'The Defence of Armorica in the Later Roman Empire', in W. S. Hanson and L. J. G. Keppie (eds.), *Roman Frontier Studies: Papers Presented to the 12th International Congress of Roman Frontier Studies* (Oxford, 1980), 398–411. It was further developed in S. Kerneis, *Les Celtiques: servitude et grandeur des auxiliaires bretons dans l'empire romain* (Clermont-Ferrand, 1998), and was accepted in B. Merdrignac, *D'une Bretagne à l'autre: les migrations bretonnes entre histoire et légendes* (Rennes, 2012). The material evidence has now been critically re-examined in P. Galliou, 'The Late Roman Military Migration: A Historiographical Myth' (forthcoming).

The question of the Bagaudic rebellions in Armorica, raised in E. A. Thompson, 'Peasant Revolts in Late Roman Gaul and Spain', *Past and Present*, 2 (1952), 11–23, was considered again by the same author in *Saint Germanus of Auxerre and the End of Roman Britain* (Woodbridge, 1984), 71–7, and, in a broader context, in J. F. Drinkwater, 'The Bacaudae of Fifth-Century Gaul', in J. F. Drinkwater and H. Elton (eds.), *Fifth-Century Gaul: A Crisis of Identity?* (Cambridge, 1992), 208–17. Gildas as a source is considered in M. Lapidge and D. Dumville (eds.), *Gildas: New Approaches* (Woodbridge, 1984).

For early place names, see B. Tanguy, 'Les Paroisses primitives en Plou: et leur saints éponymes', *Bulletin de la Société Archéologique du Finistère*, 109 (1981), 121–55, and the same author's 'La Limite linguistique dans la péninsule armoricaine à l'époque de l'émigration bretonne (IVe–Ve siècle) d'après les données toponymiques', *Annales de Bretagne*, 87 (1980), 229–62. For an introduction to the Breton languages, L. Fleuriot, *Les Origines de la Bretagne* (Paris, 1982), chapter 4, and F. Falc'hun, *Perspectives nouvelles sur l'histoire de la langue bretonne* (3rd edn, Paris, 1981). The question of the saints who sailed from Britain to Brittany is introduced in E. G. Bowen, *Saints, Seaways and Settlements in the Celtic Lands* (2nd edn, Cardiff, 1977), and is considered in detail in the context of Brittany in B. Merdrignac, 'The Saints and the Second British Migration', in P.-R. Giot, P. Guigon, and B. Merdrignac, *The British Settlement* of *Brittany* (Stroud, 2003), 119–54. See also the same author's *Les Vies de saints bretons durant le haut Moyen Âge: la culture, les croyances en Bretagne (VIIe–XIIe siècle)* (Rennes, 1993). For the later development of the Breton language, F. Broudic, *Histoire de la langue bretonne* (Rennes, 1999).

An excellent introduction to the Franks is presented in E. James, *The Franks* (Oxford, 1988). P. Lasko, *The Kingdom of the Franks: North-West Europe before Charlemagne* (London, 1971), offers a shorter but copiously illustrated account. The classic work covering the whole of western Europe at this time is J. M. Wallace-Hadrill, *The Barbarian West, 400–1000* (3rd edn, London, 1985).

Aspects of daily life can be gathered from excavation reports. The work on the farmstead on Île Guennoc is reported in P.-R. Giot, 'Ennez Guennoc ou Geignog, un ancien microsme celtique', in Olivier Guyotjeannin (ed.), *Mélanges d'archéologie et d'histoire médiévale en l'honneur du doyen Michel de Boüard* (Paris, 1982), 170–90. The agricultural settlement which developed within the earthen defences of Le Yaudet is discussed in detail in B. Cunliffe and P. Galliou, *Les Fouilles du Yaudet en Ploulec'h, Côtes-d'Armor*, iii, *Du quatrième siècle apr. J.-C. à aujourd'hui* (Oxford, 2007). For the early Christian community on Île Lavret, see P.-R. Giot, 'St Badoc and the Isle of Lavret, Brittany', in S. M. Pearce (ed.), *The Early Church in Western Britain and Ireland: Studies Presented to C. A. Ralegh Radford* (Oxford, 1982), 197–210. Work on the monastery at Landévennec is described in A. Bardel, 'L'Abbaye Saint-Guénolé de Landévennec', *Archéologie Médievale* (1991), 51–101, and a number of interesting papers relating to the monastery are to be found in M. Coumert and Y. Tranvouez (eds.), *Landévennec, les Vikings et la Bretagne: en hommage à Jean-Christophe Cassard* (Brest, 2015). Inscriptions on standing stones are brought together in a fully illustrated corpus, W. Davies *et al.*, *The Inscriptions of Early Medieval Brittany* (Aberystwyth, 2000).

The use of the Atlantic seaways by travellers and traders is thoroughly surveyed in J. Wooding, *Communications and Commerce along the Atlantic Sea Lanes, AD 400–800* (Oxford, 1996). The evidence for Mediterranean goods being traded along the Atlantic coast of Iberia is presented in P. Reynold, *Hispania and the Roman Mediterranean, AD 100–700* (London, 2010). A more detailed assessment of trade along the Atlantic, based on the distribution of imported pottery, is given in E. Campbell, *Continental and Mediterranean Imports to Atlantic Britain and Ireland, AD 400–800* (York, 2007), and in its international context in M. Duggan, *Links to Late Antiquity: Ceramic Exchange and Contacts on the Atlantic Seaboard in the 5th to 7th Centuries AD* (Oxford, 2018). Imported pottery is found in Brittany at Le Yaudet: see B. Cunliffe and P. Galliou, *Les Fouilles du Yaudet en Ploulec'h, Côtes-d'Armor*, iii, *Du quatrième siècle apr. J.-C. à aujourd'hui*, 38 and 86–8; Île Lavret, P.-R. Giot and G. Querre, 'Le Tesson d'amphore B2 de l'Île Lavret (Bréhat, Côtes-du-Nord) et le problème des importations', *Revue*

Archéologique de l'Ouest, 2 (1985), 95–100; and Guisseny, P.-R. Giot, 'Les Sites "proto-historiques" des dunes de Guisseny (Finistère)', *Annales de Bretagne*, 80 (1973), 105–27.

Chapter 7 Conflicting Identities, 751–1148

General introductions to the development of Europe in this period can be found in R. Collins, *Early Medieval Europe, 300–1000* (London, 1999), and J.-P. Poly and E. Bournazel, *La Mutation féodale, X^e–XIIe siècles* (Paris, 1980). Two books, A. Chédeville and H. Guillotel, *Le Bretagne des saints et des rois, V^e–Xe siècle* (Rennes, 1984), and A. Chédeville and N.-Y. Tonnerre, *La Bretagne féodale, XIe–XIIIe siècle* (Rennes, 1987), provide the essential detailed background to this chapter. For Brittany at the time of the kings, see also J.-C. Cassard, *Les Bretons de Nominoë* (Brasport, 1990).

Among the many books on Charlemagne and the Carolingian period, R. McKitterick, *Charlemagne: The Formations of a European Identity* (Cambridge, 2008), R. Collins, *Charlemagne* (London, 1998), and R. Matthias, *Charlemagne* (Newhaven 2005), all provide accessible overviews. The subject of Brittany during the Carolingian period is fully treated in J. H. M. Smith, *Province and Empire: Brittany and the Carolingians* (Cambridge, 1992). Other useful accounts include B. Merdrignac, 'Brittany in the Carolingian Orbit', in P.-R. Giot, P. Guigon, and B. Merdrignac, *The British Settlement of Brittany* (Stroud, 2003), chapter 6, and J. M. H. Smith, '"The Archbishopric" of Dol and the Ecclesiastical Polities of Ninth-Century Brittany', in S. Mews (ed.), *Religion and National Identity*, Studies in Church History, 18 (Cambridge, 1982), 59–70. Among other sites mentioned in the chapter, aspects of the abbey of Landévennec in the Carolingian period are discussed in several papers in M. Coumert and Y. Tranvouez (eds.), *Landévennec, les Vikings et la Bretagne: en hommage à Jean-Christophe Cassard* (Brest, 2015), 21–100. The foundation of the abbey of Redon is considered in Merdrignac, 'Brittany in the Carolingian Orbit', 176–9.

There are many good books covering the activities of the Vikings in Europe, among them P. Sawyer (ed.), *The Oxford Illustrated History of the Vikings* (Oxford, 1997), which includes a chapter by J. L. Nelson, 'The Frankish Empire', 19–47; J. Graham-Campbell *et al.* (eds.), *Cultural Atlas of the Viking World* (Oxford, 1994); and G. Jones, *A History of the Vikings* (Oxford, 1984). The Viking impact on Brittany is presented in detail in N. S. Price, *The Vikings in Brittany* (London, 1989), and J.-C. Cassard, *Le Siècle des Vikings en Bretagne* (Paris, 1996). In an essay, N. S. Price, 'Viking Brittany: Revisiting the Colony that Failed', in A. Reynolds and L. Webster (eds.), *Early Medieval Art and Archaeology in the Northern World* (Leiden, 2013), 731–42, the author reviews more recent scholarship and discoveries. The impact of the Viking attacks is further explored in H. Guillotel, 'L'Exode du clergé breton devant les invasions scandinaves', *Mémoires de la Société d'Histoire et d'Archéologie de Bretagne*, 59 (1982), 269–315. Details of the Viking ship burial on Île de Groix are given in M. Müller-Wille, 'Das Schiffsgrab von der Ile de Groix (Bretagne): ein Exkurs zum Bootkammergrab von Haithabu', *Berichte über die Ausgrabungen in Haithabu*, 12 (1978), 48–84. The date of the fortified site at Péran is considered in J.-P. Nicolardot, 'Éléments de datation du Camp de Péran, Plédran (Côtes-du-Nord)', in X. Barral i Altet (ed.), *Bretagne, Pays de Loire, Touraine, Poitou, à l'époque mérovingienne* (Paris, 1987), 73–8. The earthworks at Trans-la-Forêt are presented in J.-Y. Hamel-Simon *et al.*, 'Fouille d'un retranchement d'Alain Barbetorte datable de 939: le camp des Haies à Trans (Ille et Vilaine)', *Dossiers du Centre Régional Archéologique d'Alet*, 7 (1979), 47–74.

An incomparable account of life in the early medieval countryside, based on the rich collection of charters housed in the abbey at Redon, is given in W. Davies, *Small Worlds: The Village Community in Early Medieval Brittany* (Berkeley, 1998). It focuses on the economy and organization of the village community, placing it in the broader social context. In a follow-up study by G. Astill and W. Davies, *A Breton Landscape* (London, 1997), using both documentary research and fieldwork, the *longue durée* development of four communes in the Oust-Vilaine watershed is explored. Another interesting account of landscape development, this time in the Trégor, is J.-Y. Tinevez, *Archéologie et peuplement dans le Trégor occidental* (Rennes, 1988).

Early medieval fortifications abound in Brittany, especially mottes. There are three published regional surveys: M. Brand'Honneur, *Les Mottes médiévales en Ille-et-Vilaine* (Rennes, 1990); S. Hinguant, *Les Mottes médiévales des Côtes-d'Armor* (Rennes, 1994); and P. Kernevez, *Les Fortifications médiévales du Finistère: mottes, enceintes et châteaux* (Rennes, 1997). Also of interest is C. Amiot, 'Le Château d'Aubigné et les châteaux à motte avec construction de pierre en Bretagne', *Bulletin de la Société Archéologique d'Ille-et-Vilaine*, 96 (1994), 38–88.

The revival of monasteries in Europe is discussed in H. Leyser, *Hermits and the New Monasticism: A Study of Religious Communities in Western Europe, 1000–1150* (London, 1984). For an earlier study, more specific to Brittany, see L. Raison and R. Niderst, 'Le Mouvement érémetique dans l'ouest de la France à fin du XIe et au début du XIIe siècle', *Annales de Bretagne*, 55 (1948), 1–46. A useful review of early church architecture is offered in P. Guigon, *L'Architecture pré-romane en Bretagne: le premier art roman* (Rennes, 1993). Guigon's paper 'La Crypte de Lanmeur (Finistere)', *Revue Archéologique de l'Ouest*, 14 (1997), 175–86, is a detailed study of an unusual monument. M. Déceneux, *La Bretagne romane* (Rennes, 1998), provides an attractive and well-illustrated account of the development of Romanesque architecture.

The fascinating subject of the Breton elite who accompanied William the Conqueror to Britain in 1066 and were given estates is discussed at some length in M. Jones, 'Notes sur quelques familles bretonnes en Angleterre après la conquête normande', originally published in 1981 but reprinted in M. Jones, *The Creation of Brittany: A Late Medieval State* (London, 1988), 69–93. The subject is further explored in K. S. B. Keats-Rohan, 'The Bretons and Normans of England, 1066–1154: The Family, the Fiefs and the Feudal Monarchy', *Nottingham Medieval Studies*, 36 (1992), 42–78.

The question of the wandering Bretons and the transmission of Breton traditions is variously treated in L. Fleuriot and A.-P. Segalan (eds.), *Histoire littéraire et culturelle de la Bretagne*, i, *Héritage celtique et captation française* (Paris, 1987); P. Simms-Williams, 'Did Itinerant Breton *Conteurs* Transmit the *Matière de Bretagne*?', *Romania*, 461/2 (1998), 72–111; and R. S. Loomis (ed.), *Arthurian Literature in the Middle Ages: A Collaborative History* (Oxford, 1959). See also further reading for Chapter 11.

Chapter 8 Our Nation of Brittany, 1148–1532

This chapter spans a long and complex period of European history generating a vast literature, so here we must be highly selective. The two essential books which cover the period in Brittany are A. Chédeville and H. Guillotel, *La Bretagne feudale, XIᵉ–XIIIᵉ siècle* (Rennes, 1987), and J.-P. Leguay and H. Martin, *Fastes et malheurs de la Bretagne ducale, 1213–1532* (2nd edn, Rennes, 1997). These two volumes provide the central narrative and are fully referenced. To these should be added M. Jones, *Ducal Brittany, 1364–1399: Relations with England and France during the Reign of Duke John IV* (Oxford, 1970), and a collection of papers by Michael Jones published in various journals and helpfully brought together in *The Creation of Brittany: A Late Medieval State* (London, 1988). Essential reading is P. Tourault, *La Bretonne et la France du XVᵉ siècle à nos jours* (Paris, 2018), which in part I deals with the period 1458–1532.

The Angevin empire is a popular subject. Among the more accessible general works are J. Gillingham, *The Angevin Empire* (London, 1984), and M. Aurell, *The Plantagenet Empire, 1154–1224* (London, 2007). For Brittany in this period, see J. Le Patourel, 'Henri II Plantagenêt et la Bretagne', *Mémoires de la Société d'Histoire et d'Archéologie de Bretagne*, 58 (1981), 99–116, and J. A. Everard, *Brittany and the Angevins: Province and Empire, 1158–1203* (Cambridge, 2006). The Capetian rule in France is discussed in E. M. Hallam, *Capetian France, 937–1328* (London, 1983). The use of Brittany as a pawn in the English–French conflict is carefully analysed in Y. Hillion, 'La Bretagne et la rivalité Capétiens–Plantagenêts', *Annales de Bretagne*, 92 (1985), 111–44. The best account of the colourful character Pierre Mauclerc is in S. Painter, *The Scourge of the*

Clergy: Peter of Dreux, Duke of Brittany (Oxford, 1937). The short essay by M. Jones, 'The Duchy of Brittany in the Middle Ages', in M. Jones, *The Creation of Brittany* (London, 1988), 1–12, puts this fascinating period into perspective.

The War of Succession is described in M. Jones, 'The Breton Civil War', in Jones, *The Creation of Brittany*, 197–218. The same author's 'Edward III's Captains in Brittany', in W. M. Ormrod (ed.), *England in the Fourteenth Century* (Woodbridge, 1986), 99–118, adds detail. The Froissart *Chronicles* are available in a version edited by G. T. Diller (Geneva, 1972). An assessment of the chronicles is given in P. Ainsworth, 'Froissart, Jean', in G. Dunphy (ed.), *Encyclopaedia of the Medieval Chronicle* (Leiden, 2010), 642–5. The development of the rules of chivalry in the Middle Ages is described in M. H. Keen, *Chivalry* (New Haven, 2005). A useful overview of the Hundred Years War between France and Britain is D. Seward's *The Hundred Years War* (London, 2003). For the hyperactive Bertrand de Guesclin, see R. Vernier, *The Flower of Chivalry: Bertrand de Guesclin and the Hundred Years War* (Woodbridge, 2003). The Combat of the Thirty is considered in S. Muhlberger, 'The Combat of the Thirty against Thirty', in L. J. A. Villalon and D. J. Kagay (eds.), *The Hundred Years War (Part II): Different Vistas* (Leiden, 2008), 289–94.

For the fourteenth and fifteenth centuries in Brittany, the works cited in the first paragraphs provide the essential background to the history of the period. To these should be added: J. Kerhervé, *L'État breton aux 14e et 15e siècles: les ducs, l'argent et les hommes* (Paris, 1987); the same author's edited volume *Noblesses de Bretagne du Moyen Âge à nos jours* (Rennes, 1999); and M. Nassiet, *Noblesse et pauvreté: la petite noblesse en Bretagne, XVe–XVIIIe siècle* (Rennes, 1993). Henry Tudor (Henry VII) and his ambivalent relations to Brittany and France can be followed in T. Penn, *Winter King: Henry VII and the Dawn of Tudor England* (London, 2011). Anne, duchess of Brittany, has received much attention. Recent studies include G. Minois, *Anne de Bretagne* (Paris, 1999); D. Le Fur, *Anne de Bretagne* (Paris, 2000); and H. Pigaillem, *Anne de Bretagne: épouse de Charles VIII et de Louis XIII* (Paris, 2008). G.-M. Tanguy, *Sur les pas de Anne de Bretagne* (Rennes, 2003), offers a well-illustrated popular account.

The most comprehensive account of the maritime commercial relations of medieval Brittany is H. Touchard's *Le Commerce maritime breton à la fin du Moyen Âge* (Paris, 1967). The same author's 'La Consommation et l'approvisionnement en vin de la Bretagne médiévale', *Mémoires de la Société d'Histoire et d'Archéologie de Bretagne*, 40 (1960), 29–76, has further detail. The Bordeaux wine trade is discussed in M. James, *Studies in the Medieval Wine Trade* (Oxford, 1971), and in more detail in J. Barnard, *Navires et gens de mer à Bordeaux vers 1400* (vol. i) and *vers 1550* (vol. ii) (Paris, 1968); also J.-C. Cassard, 'Les Marins bretons à Bordeaux au début du XIVe siècle', *Annales de Bretagne*, 86 (1979), 378–97. Trade through Nantes is assessed in P. Bois (ed.), *Histoire de Nantes* (Toulouse, 1977), and C. Decours, *Le Port de Nantes à 3000 ans* (Nantes, 2006).

The growing awareness of Breton identity is the theme of M. Jones, '"Mon pais et ma nation": Breton Identity in the Fourteenth Century', in M. Jones, *The Creation of Brittany* (London, 1988), 283–307.

The deeply religious life of the Bretons is probably best appreciated by reading A. Le Braz, *Au pays des pardons* (Rennes, 1894). The elaborate stone and wood carving used to elaborate churches, calvaries, and ossuaries began in the period covered by this chapter and continued in the later sixteenth and seventeenth centuries. Three well-illustrated sources are Y. Pelletier, *Les Enclos paroissiaux de Bretagne* (Rennes, 1986); A. Vircondelet (with photography by R. Gain), *Les Enclos bretons: chefs-d'œuvre de l'art populaire* (Paris, 2003); and E. Royer, *Nouveau guide des calvaires bretons* (Rennes, 1985). For Ankou, see E. Badone, 'Death Omens in a Breton Memorate', *Folklore*, 98 (1987), 99–104. A. Le Braz, *La Légende de la mort chez les Bretons armoricains* (Paris, 1893), provides a much fuller account of the context. The *danse macabre* painted on the walls of the chapel of Kermaria-an-Iskuit is discussed in T. Lévy, 'La Chapelle Kermaria-an-Isquist: les peintures murales', *Congrès Archéologique de France, 173e session: Monuments des Côtes-d'Armor* (Paris, 2015), 303–11.

Although the subject of architecture has not featured in this chapter, there is a rich literature relevant to the period. Two books cover the homes of the elite: A. Salamagne, J. Kerhervé, and G. Davet (eds.), *Châteaux et modes de vie aux temps des ducs de Bretagne, XIIIe–XVIe siècle* (Rennes, 2012), and G. Meirion-Jones (ed.), *La Demeure seigneuriale dans l'espace Plantagenêt: salles, chambres et tours* (Rennes, 2013). For more humble buildings, see N.-Y. Tonnerre (ed.), *La Maison paysanne: 2500 ans d'habitat rural en Bretagne* (Spézet, 2008), and G. Meirion-Jones, *The Vernacular Architecture of Brittany* (Edinburgh, 1982).

Chapter 9   Four Rebellions and a Revolution, 1532–1802

The nearly three centuries covered by this chapter was an action-packed time in Brittany as it was in the rest of Europe. The first part of the period is covered in A. Croix, *L'Âge d'or de la Bretagne, 1532–1675* (Rennes, 1993), the second part in J. Quéniart, *La Bretagne au XVIIIe siècle, 1675–1789* (Rennes, 2004). A. Croix's *La Bretagne aux 16e et 17e siècles: la vie, la mort, la foi*, in two volumes (Paris, 1981), offers a more detailed consideration. Another important study, extending to the late eighteenth century, is J. B. Collins, *Classes, Estates, and Order in Early Modern Brittany* (Cambridge, 1994). The question of Breton resistance to France is fully considered in P. Tourault, *La Bretagne et la France du XVᵉ siècle à nos jours* (Paris, 2018).

The end of Breton independence and the union with France is discussed in D. Le Page and M. Nassiet, *L'Union de la Bretagne à la France* (Morlaix, 2003). The Breton economy in the 'golden age' is most conveniently approached through A. Croix, *L'Âge d'or de la Bretagne*, and J. B. Collins, *Classes, Estates, and Order in Early Modern Brittany*, chapter 1. Additional works of direct relevance include: R. Leprohon, *Vie et mort des Bretons sous Louis XIV* (Brest, 1984); J. B. Collins, 'The Role of Atlantic France in the Baltic Trade: Dutch Traders and Polish Grain at Nantes, 1625–1675', *Journal of European Economic History*, 2 (1984), 231–80; the same author's 'Les Impôts et le commerce du vin en Bretagne au XVIIIe siècle', in A. Dierkens (ed.), *Actes du 107e Congrès National des Sociétés Savantes* (Brest, 1982), 155–68; J. Tanguy, 'L'Essor de la Bretagne aux XVIe et XVIIe siècles', in *Histoire de la Bretagne et des pays celtiques*, iii, *La Bretagne province (1532–1789)* (Morlaix, 1968); and the same author's 'La Production et le commerce des toiles "Bretagne" du 16e au 18e siècle', in *Actes du 91e Congrès National des Sociétés Savantes* (Brest, 1966), 105–41.

For Saint-Malo, see S. and J. Beaulieu, *Saint-Malo et l'histoire* (Châteaubourg, 1993). R. Cook (ed.), *The Voyages of Jacques Cartier* (Toronto, 1993), and Y. Jacob, *Jacques Cartier* (Saint-Malo, 2000), cover the opening up of Canada by the French. Further French colonial expansion is the subject of P. Boucher, *The Shaping of the French Colonial Empire: A Bio-Bibliography of the Careers of Richelieu, Fouquet and Colbert* (New York, 1985), and E. M. Greenwald, *Marc-Antoine Caillot and the Company of the Indies in Louisiana: Trade in the French Atlantic World* (Baton Rouge, 2016). For the port of Lorient, L. Chaumeil, 'Abrégé d'histoire de Lorient de la fondation (1666) à nos jours (1939)', *Annales de Bretagne*, 46 (1939), 66–87. Richelieu's amazing life is well described in J.-V. Blanchard, *Eminence: Cardinal Richelieu and the Rise of France* (New York, 2011).

The migration of craftsmen to Britain can be followed up in J. Allan, 'Breton Woodworkers in the Immigrant Communities of Southwest England, 1500–1550', *Post-Medieval Archaeology*, 48 (2014), 320–56. The Dallam family of organ makers is discussed in S. Bicknell, *The History of the English Organ* (Cambridge, 1996), chapter 6.

The intricacies of the Wars of Religion are explored in M. P. Holt, *The French Wars of Religion, 1562–1629* (Cambridge, 2005). For the Thirty Years War, which put so much economic pressure on France, see G. Parker, *The Thirty Years War* (London, 1984), and P. H. Wilson, *Europe's Tragedy: A History of the Thirty Years War* (London, 2009). Also M. P. Gutmann, 'The Economic and Social Consequences of the Thirty Years War', *Past and Present*, 39 (1968), 44–61. Social structure in Brittany is thoroughly covered in J. P. Collins, *Classes, Estates and Order in Early Modern Brittany* (Cambridge, 1994), with a discussion of the burden of taxation in chapter 6 and the problem of social order in chapter 7.

The Franco-Dutch War and the other activities of Louis XIV which so destabilized the French economy are dealt with in J. A. Lynn, *The Wars of Louis XIV, 1667–1714* (London, 1996). His impact on Brittany is discussed in J.-Y. Barzic, *Les Bretons et Louis XIV* (Fouesnant, 2018). V. Cronin's *Louis XIV* (London, 1996) is a highly readable account of the king's life. The revolt of the Bonnets Rouges is described in A. de La Borderie, *La Révolte du papier timbré advenue en Bretagne en 1675* (Saint-Brieuc, 1884; new edn, Bécherel, 2019), and, more recently, Y. Garlan and C. Nières, *Les Révoltes bretonnes de 1675* (Paris, 1975), and A. Puillandre, *Sébastien Le Balp: Bonnets Rouges et papier timbré* (Spézet, 1996). For a detailed analysis together with contemporary accounts, see J. Lemoine, 'La Révolte dite du papier timbré; ou, Des Bonnets Rouges en Bretagne en 1675', spread through three volumes of *Annales de Bretagne*, 12 (1894), 13 (1895), and 14 (1896). J. Bérenger, 'La Révolte des Bonnets Rouges et l'opinion internationale', *Annales de Bretagne*, 82 (1975), 443–58, puts the event in its contemporary context. A short popular account of the revolt is given in A. Croix, 'La Révolte des Bonnets Rouges: de l'histoire à la mémoire', *ArMen*, 131 (Nov.–Dec. 2002), 2–11.

The revolt of the nobles, or the Pontcallec Conspiracy, is placed in its broad historical context in J. Meyer, *La Noblesse bretonne au XVIIIe siècle* (Paris, 1995), and is explained in detail in A. Tanguy, 'La Conspiration de Pontcallec: un complot séparatiste sous la Régence', *ArMen*, 147 (July–Aug. 2008), 10–19. The Seven Years War, involving most of the European nations, is discussed in F. A. J. Szabo, *The Seven Years War in Europe, 1756–1763* (London, 2008), and in D. Baugh, *The Global Seven Years War, 1754–1763* (London, 2011). For the significance of the British navy during this period, see N. A. H. Rodger, *Command of the Ocean: A Naval History of Britain, 1649–1815* (London, 2006), and, for balance, J. R. Dull, *The French Navy and the Seven Years War* (Lincoln, Nebr., 2015). The Belle-Île incident is discussed in M. Taylor, *L'Invasion et l'occupation de Belle-Isle par les Anglais, 1761–1763* (Belle-Île, 2016). The naval battle in Quiberon Bay is described in G. Marcus, *Quiberon Bay: The Campaign in Home Waters, 1759* (London, 1960). La Chalotais and his conflict with the duc d'Aiguillon is put into its historical context, together with transcripts of contemporary documents, in J. Rothney (ed.), *The Brittany Affair and the Crisis of the Ancien Régime* (Oxford, 1969).

There are so many books on the French Revolution that selection is invidious, but any list must include W. Doyle (ed.), *The Oxford History of the French Revolution* (Oxford, 1989), and J. D. Popkin, *A Short History of the French Revolution* (5th edn, Oxford, 2019). For the revolutionary period in Brittany, A. du Chatellier, *Histoire de la Révolution en Bretagne* (Morvan, 1977), and D. Sutherland, *The Chouans: The Social*

Origin of Popular Counter-Revolution in Upper Brittany, 1770–1796 (Oxford, 1982). And finally, for light relief, Honoré de Balzac's novel *Les Chouans*, first published in 1829, offers a vivid impression of the insurrection and social turmoil of the early Revolutionary years.

Chapter 10   Ourselves As Others See Us, 1789–1900

One of the most readable and informative accounts of the Napoleonic period is V. Cronin's *Napoleon* (London, 1971). Napoleon's negotiations with the Pope leading to the Concordat are described in chapter 14. An excellent discussion of the Breton reaction to the Revolution is to be found in P. Tourault's *La Bretagne et la France du XVᵉ siècle à nos jours* (Paris, 2018), 223–80. Bertrand Barère's report to the Comité de Salut Public on the importance of the French language was published as *Rapport et projet de décret, présentés au nom du Comité de Salut Public: sur les idiomes étrangers, et l'enseignement de la langue française (8 pluviose an II)* (1794), Convention Nationale, Imprimerie Nationale. For discussions on the subject, see two papers by D. Bernard: 'Deux écrits de propaganda en langue bretonne', *Annales de Bretagne*, 21 (1911), 605–13, and 'La Révolution française et la langue bretonne', *Annales de Bretagne*, 28 (1912), 287–331. These matters and many others relating to Breton identity are explored in Maryon McDonald's broadly based study *'We Are Not French!': Language, Culture and Identity in Brittany* (London, 1989), which is strongly to be recommended. Irénée Carré's paper on education is published as 'De la manière d'enseigner les premiers éléments du français dans les écoles de la Basse-Bretagne', *Revue Pédagogique*, 12 (1888), 217–36.

One of the earliest British travellers to write engagingly about the Bretons was Arthur Young, who published his observations in *Travels, during the Years 1787, 1788, 1789: Undertaken More Particularly with a View of Ascertaining the Cultivation, Wealth, Resources, and National Prosperity, of the Kingdom of France* (Bury St Edmunds, 1792). The journey and the author are put into context by G. E. Mingay in his *Arthur Young and his Times* (London, 1975). The huge outpouring of observations and reminiscences by nineteenth-century travel writers, of widely varying abilities, are discussed with patient care in J.-Y. Le Disez, *Étrange Bretagne: récits de voyageurs britanniques en Bretagne (1830–1900)* (Rennes, 2002). One of the earliest, and arguably the most entertaining, was T. A. Trollope's *A Summer in Brittany* (2 vols., London, 1840). The account of a trip made by the Celtic scholar Thomas Price in 1829 was finally published as 'A Tour through Brittany in the Year 1829', in *The Literary Remains of the Rev. Thomas Price, Carnhuanawc*, i (London, 1854). For a review of his visit, see P.

Morgan, 'Thomas Price Carnhuanawc (1787–1848) et les Bretons', in *Parcours: Pays de Galles-Bretagne* (Brest, 1995), 5–13. The illustrator Randolph Caldecott, who travelled with Henry Blackburn, is treated to a biography: H. Blackburn, *Randolph Caldecott: A Personal Memoir of his Early Art Career with One Hundred and Seventy-Two Illustrations* (London, 1896). Many of Caldecott's delightful drawings appear in H. Blackburn and R. Caldecott, *Breton Folk* (London, 1884). Jephson's expedition is described in J. M. Jephson, *Narrative of a Walking Tour in Brittany, Accompanied by Notes of a Photographic Expedition by L. Reeve* (London, 1859).

Aspects of mass tourism in Brittany are the subject of N. Richard and Y. Pallier (eds.), *Cent ans de tourisme en Bretagne, 1840–1940* (Rennes, 1996). Among the many interesting contributions is M. Angelier, 'Trains et bains de mer', 31–9, reflecting on the importance of the coming of the railway to tourism. On this, see also R. an Hir, *By Road, Rails and Waves: Brittany's Transport System through the Centuries* (Lesneven, 1990).

The British archaeologists who visited Brittany early in the nineteenth century have left accounts of their researches. These include: A. Logan, 'Account of a Visit to the Monument Usually Considered as Druidical at Carnac in Brittany', *Archaeologia*, 22 (1829), 191–7, and J. B. Deane, 'Remarks on Certain Celtic Monuments of Locmariaker, in Brittany', *Archaeologia*, 25 (1834), 230–4. The visit of W. C. Lukis and Sir Henry Dryden generated a significant pictorial record of the megalithic monuments of Brittany, which remains unpublished. The expedition and its products are discussed in R. J. C. Atkinson's 'Lukis, Dryden and the Carnac Megaliths', in J. V. S. Megaw (ed.), *To Illustrate the Monuments: Essays on Archaeology Presented to Stuart Piggott* (London, 1976), 111–24. The little guidebook produced by Lukis is entitled *A Guide to the Principal Chambered Barrows and Other Prehistoric Monuments in the Islands of the Morbihan, the Communes of Locmariaker, Carnac, Plouharnel, and Erdeven; and the Peninsulas of Quiberon and Rhuis, Brittany* (Ripon, 1875). James Miln's two contributions are *Excavations at Carnac (Brittany): A Record of Archaeological Researches in the Bossenno and the Mont Saint Michel* (Edinburgh, 1877), and *Excavations at Carnac: A Record of Archaeological Researches in the Alignments of Kermario* (Edinburgh, 1881). Augustus Lane-Fox (later known as Pitt-Rivers) did not publish his observations and collections from Brittany, but for the man, see M. W. Thompson, *General Pitt Rivers: Evolution and Archaeology in the Nineteenth Century* (Bradford-on-Avon, 1977), and M. Bowden, *Pitt Rivers: The Life and Archaeological Work of Lieutenant-General Augustus Lane Fox Pitt Rivers* (Cambridge, 1991).

The foreign painters who flocked to Brittany in the second half of the nineteenth century were numerous, as indeed are the publications about them. For more general works, see D. Delouche (ed.), *Artistes étrangers à Pont-Aven, Concarneau et autres lieux de Bretagne* (Rennes, 1989); J. Duroc, *Camaret, cité d'artistes* (Fougères, 1988); *Peintres américains en Bretagne, 1864–1914* (Pont-Aven, 1995); *Artistes finlandais en Bretagne* (Pont Aven, 1999); S. Courtade and E. Chapuis (eds.), *La Bretagne: vue par les peintres* (Lausanne, 1987); and Groupement Touristique de Cornouaille, *La Route des peintres en Cornouaille, 1850–1950* (Briec-de-l'Odet, 1997). For some of the specific painters mentioned in the chapter: B. Thompson, *Gauguin* (London, 1987); B. Denvir, *Paul Gauguin: The Search for Paradise. Letters from Brittany to the South Seas* (London, 1992); D. Delouche, *Eugène Boudin et la Bretagne* (Quimper, 2000); and C. Boyle-Turner, *Paul Sérusier: peintre de la Bretagne* (Lausanne, 1988).

It was almost compulsory for aspiring French writers of the nineteenth century, seeking inspiration, to expose themselves to Brittany and the Bretons. Balzac, Stendhal, Flaubert, Zola, and Maupassant all made visits and incorporated their impressions, observations, and prejudices into their literary works. Flaubert made an extended journey described in Madame Le Herpeux's 'Flaubert et son voyage en Bretagne', *Annales de Bretagne*, 47 (1940), 1–152. His detailed description of the places visited was later published in *Over Strand and Field: A Record of Travel through Brittany* (1881); a translation by Gerard Hopkins is available (2016). Maupassant also made some brief jottings about Brittany which were published in 1884 as 'En Bretagne', available in English translation as Guy de Maupassant, *To the Sun*, ed. and trans. J. Wilson (London, 2008), 105–20. Pierre Loti's famous *Pêcheur d'Islande* (Paris, 1886) has inspired a tourist industry in Paimpol, where the novel was set, a theme carefully analysed in F. Chappé, 'De l'usage touristique d'un mythe: Paimpol et l'Islande', in N. Richard and Y. Pallier, *Cent ans de tourisme en Bretagne, 1840–1940* (Rennes, 1996), 82–91.

Chapter 11   Creating Identities

The search for Breton identity is explored in a number of works: C. Ford, *Creating the Nation in Provincial France: Religion and Political Identity in Brittany* (New Jersey, 1999); R. Le Coadic, *L'Identité bretonne* (Rennes, 1998); J.-Y. Guiomar, *Le Bretonisme: les historiens bretons au XIXe siècle* (Mayenne, 1987); B. Tanguy, *Aux origines du nationalisme breton* (2 vols., Paris, 1977), and the same author's 'Des celtomanes aux bretonistes: les idées et les hommes', in J. Balcon and Y. Le Gallo (eds.), *Histoire littéraire et culturelle de la Bretagne II* (Paris, 1987), 293–334.

An excellent introduction to the British antiquarian tradition is provided in S. Piggott, *Ancient Britons and the Antiquarian Imagination: Ideas from the Renaissance to the Regency* (London, 1989), and T. D. Kendrick, *British Antiquity* (London, 1950). For Geoffrey of Monmouth's *History of the Kings of Britain*, Lewis Thorpe's translation is recommended (Harmondsworth, 1966). It has the advantage of a comprehensive introduction by the translator. The sources used by Geoffrey are discussed in S. Piggott, 'The Sources of Geoffrey of Monmouth', *Antiquity*, 15 (1941), 269–86, 305–19.

The literature on King Arthur is endless and of varied value. One of the most useful basic sources is N. J. Lacy (ed.), *The Arthurian Encyclopedia* (London, 1986), which contains sound, balanced contributions. T. Jones, 'The Early Evolution of the Legend of Arthur', *Nottingham Medieval Studies*, 8 (1964), 3–23, introduces some of the complexity of the transmission. Other important contributions are: R. S. Loomis (ed.), *Arthurian Literature in the Middle Ages* (Oxford, 1959); A. Lupack, *The Oxford Guide to Arthurian Literature and Legend* (Oxford, 2007); and O. J. Padel, 'The Nature of Arthur', *Cambridge Medieval Celtic Studies*, 27 (1994), 1–31. For Marie de France, see *The Lais of Marie de France*, ed. and trans. G. S. Burgess and K. Busby (Harmondsworth, 1986). Also R. H. Bloch, *The Anonymous Marie de France* (Chicago, 2003). For Chrétien de Troyes, J. Frappier, *Chrétien de Troyes: The Man and his Work* (Athens, Ohio, 1982). For Wace, C. Foulon, 'Wace', in Loomis (ed.), *Arthurian Literature in the Middle Ages*, 94–103. Also of interest is J. Kerhervé, 'Aux origines d'un sentiment national: les chroniqueurs bretons de la fin du Moyen Âge', *Bulletin de la Société Archéologique du Finistère*, 108 (1980), 165–206.

The Celts are a very popular subject. B. Cunliffe, *The Ancient Celts* (2nd edn, Oxford, 2018), offers a review of the archaeological evidence. The way in which the Celtic topos has been used to create identities is discussed at length in M. Chapman, *The Celts: The Construction of a Myth* (Basingstoke, 1992), and more briefly in S. James, *The Atlantic Celts: Ancient People or Modern Invention?* (London, 1999). The two fathers of Celtic studies are well covered in the literature. R. A. Gunter, *Life and Letters of Edward Lhuyd* (Early Science at Oxford, 14; Oxford, 1945), is the standard source. Other biographies include F. Emery, *Edward Lhuyd, FRS, 1660–1709* (Cardiff, 1971). The contribution of Paul-Yves Pezron is assessed in P. T. J. Morgan, 'The Abbé Pezron and the Celts', *Transactions of the Honourable Society of Cymmrodorion* (1965), 286–95. The creative life of William Stukeley and his obsession with Druids is attractively presented in S. Piggott, *William Stukeley: An Eighteenth-Century Antiquary* (2nd edn, London, 1985). Jacques Cambray's main contribution was his *Monumens celtiques; ou, Recherches sur le culte des pierres, précédées d'une notice sur les Celtes et sur les Druides, et suivis d'étymologies celtiques* (Paris, 1805), and his emotive account of Finistère in *Voyage dans le Finistère; ou, État de ce département en 1794 et 1795* (Paris, 1799). The impact of the Académie Celtique is discussed in N. Belmont and J. Chamarat, 'L'Academie Celtique', in *Hier pour demain: arts, traditions et patrimoine. Catalogue d'exposition du Grand-Palais, 13 juin – 1er septembre 1980* (Paris, 1980), 54–77, and is placed in a broader context in J.-Y. Guiomar, 'La Révolution française et les origines celtiques de la France', *Annales Historiques de la Révolution Française*, 287 (1992), 63–85. The importance of the Académie Celtique to the study of folklore is empha-sized in H. Senn, 'Folklore Beginnings in France: The Académie Celtique, 1804–1813', *Journal of the Folklore Institute*, 18 (1981), 23–33. See also M. Ozouf, 'L'Invention de l'ethnographie française: le questionnaire de l'Académie Celtique', *Annales. Histoire, Sciences Sociales*, 36 (1981), 210–30.

The context for the Celtic Romantic movement is the subject of P. Sims-Williams, 'The Visionary Celt: The Construction of Ethnic Preconceptions', *Cambridge Medieval Celtic Studies*, 11 (1986), 71–96. James Macpherson's Ossian created an exten-sive literature. For a nineteenth-century view, T. B. Saunders, *The Life and Letters of James Macpherson: Containing a Particular Account of his Famous Quarrel with Dr Johnson and a Sketch of the Origin and the Influence of the Ossianic Poems* (London, 1895). For more recent assessments, F. J. Stafford, *The Sublime Savage: A Study of James Macpherson and the Poems of Ossian* (Edinburgh, 1989); T. M. Curley, *Samuel Johnson: The Ossian Fraud and the Celtic Revival in Great Britain* (Cambridge, 2009); D. S. Thomson, *The Gaelic Sources of Macpherson's Ossian* (Edinburgh, 1952). The remarkable enthusiasm for Ossian in Europe is described in H. Gaskill, *The Reception of Ossian in Europe* (London, 2002). For anyone who might happen to want to read the poems the most convenient text is James Macpherson, *The Poems of Ossian and Related Works*, ed. H. Gaskill (Edinburgh, 1996). For Edward Williams (Iolo Morganwg) there are two authoritative recent assessments: G. H. Jenkins (ed.), *A Rattleskull Genius: The Many Faces of Iolo Morganwg* (Cardiff, 2005), and M. Löffler, *The Literary and Historical Legacy of Iolo Morganwg, 1826–1926* (Cardiff, 2007).

A very helpful introduction to the study of Breton oral tradition is M.-A. Constantine's *Breton Ballads* (Aberystwyth, 1996). The most useful source for Émile Souvestre is a collection of scholarly papers brought together in B. Plötner-Le Lay and N. Blanchard (eds.), *Émile Souvestre, écrivain breton porté par l'utopie sociale: Actes du Colloque de Morlaix, 3–4 février 2006* (Brest, 2006). A full biography of La Villemarqué was published by Francis Gourvil in his *Théodore-Claude-Henri Hersart de La Villemarqué (1815–1895) et le Barzaz-Breiz (1839–1845–1867): origines, éditions, sources, critiques, influence* (Rennes, 1960). The encounter with Prosper Mérimée is discussed by the same author in '"Voleur" sans le savoir: Prosper Mérimée et "Gwenc'hlan" en 1835', *Nouvelle Revue de Bretagne*, 2 (1949), 104–15, 211–22, 299–306. See also M.-A. Constantine, 'Prophecy and Pastiche in the Breton Ballads: Groac'h Ahès and Gwenc'hlan', *Cambrian Medieval Celtic Studies*, 30 (1995), 87–121. New evidence from La Villemarqué's notebooks is presented in D. Laurent, *Aux sources du Barzaz-Breiz: la mémoire d'un peuple* (Douarnenez, 1989). F.-M. Luzel's critique of La Villemarqué was published as *De l'authenticité des chants du Barzaz-Breiz de M. de*

La Villemarqué (Saint-Brieuc, 1872). For Luzel, see P. Batany, *Luzel: poète et folkloriste breton, 1821–1895* (Rennes, 1941). Selected stories from Luzel's *Contes populaires de Basse-Bretagne* (1874) are presented in translation in D. Bryce (ed.), *Celtic Folk-Tales from Armorica* (Felinfach, 1992). Anatole Le Braz's creative life is summed up in J. Jigourel, *Anatole Le Braz, sa vie, son œuvre: biography* (Le Faouët, 1996). Two of his more popular works were translated into English by F. M. Gostling and published as *The Land of Pardons* (London, 1906) and *The Night of Fires* (London, 1912).

The activities of the Union Régionaliste Bretonne are brought together in *Breton Association and Breton Regionalistic Union: Reports, Official Reports, Memories. Congress of the 150th Birthday in Rennes, 1993* (Rennes, 1994).

A useful introduction to postcards is A. Ripert and C. Frère, *La Carte postale, son histoire, sa fonction sociale* (Lyon, 1983). For a specific example of how postcards were used to illuminate aspects of Breton culture, L. Langouët and J. Briard, *Meilleurs souvenirs mégalithiques de Bretagne: archéologie et cartes postales anciennes* (Rennes, 1993). One familiar figure on early Breton postcards was the bard Théodore Botrel, friend of Émile Hamonic. For a brief biography, L. McKernan, 'Théodore Botrel, the Bard of Brittany (1868–1925)', *Picture Postcard Monthly* (July 1994), 19–20. The use of postcards to depict Bretons as interesting curiosities is nicely brought out in J. Éveillard and P. Huchet, *Une Bretagne si étrange, 1900–1920* (Rennes, 1999).

ILLUSTRATION SOURCES

0.1 Author.

Chapter 1 opener and 1.7: Author; **1.1** PlanetObserver/Science Photo Library; **1.2** After G. I. Meirion-Jones, *The Vernacular Architecture of Brittany* (Edinburgh, 1982) fig.6; **1.3** Phoenix Mapping; **1.4** Author using data from A. H. Dijkstra and C. Hatch, 'Mapping a hidden terraine boundary in the mantle lithosphere with lamprophyres', *Nature Communications* (2018) 9. 3770; **1.5** After P.-R. Giot et al., *Préhistoire de la Bretagne* (Rennes 1998), 74; **1.6** After H Sebire and J. Renouf, 'Sea change: new evidence for Mesolithic and Early Neolithic presence in the Channel Islands with particular reference to Guernsey and the rising Holocene sea' *Oxford Journal of Archaeology* 29 (2010), fig. 7; **1.8** Author: after N. Chadwick, *Early Brittany* (Cardiff, 1969), fig. 1 with modifications and additions; **1.9** Yannick Derennes; **1.10** Stanislas Fautre/ ASK Images/Alamy Stock Photo; **1.11** The Celtic Coin Index, School of Archaeology, University of Oxford; **1.12** Author; **1.13** Author using multiple sources; **1.14** Hemis/ Alamy Stock Photo; **1.15** (top) Author, after B. Cunliffe and P. Galliou, *Les Fouilles du Yaudet en Ploulec'h, Côtes-d'Armor* Vol. 2 (Oxford, 2005), fig. 1; (bottom) Author, after B. Cunliffe and P. Galliou (op. cit.), fig. 175; **1.16** Ian R. Cartwright; **1.17** Author, using multiple sources; **1.18** © Historic England Archive; **1.19** Author, after B. Cunliffe, *Mount Batten, Plymouth. A Prehistoric and Roman Port* (Oxford, 1988), figs. 1 and 2; **1.20** After G. I. Meirion-Jones, *The Vernacular Architecture of Brittany* (Edinburgh, 1982), fig. 11.

Chapter 2 opener and 2.19: © Marc SCHAFFNER-Morbihan Tourisme; **2.1** After C. Scarre, *Landscapes of Neolithic Brittany* (Oxford, 2011), fig. 3.3 with additions; **2.2** After R. J. Schulting, 'Antler, bone pins and flat blades. Mesolithic cemeteries in Brittany' *Antiquity* 70 (1990), fig. 1; **2.3 (top)** From M. Péquart and S.-J. Péquart, *Hoëdic*

Deuxième station-nécropole mésolithique du Morbihan (Antwerp, 1954); **2.3 (bottom)** From M. Péquart and S.-J. Péquart, *Téviec. Station-Nécropole mésolithique du Morbihan* (Paris, 1937); **2.4** Author, multiple sources; **2.5** After S. Cassen et al., 'L'habitat Ville-neuve-Saint-Germain du Haut-Mée (Saint-Etienne-en-Coglès, Ille-et-Vilaine)' *Bulletin de la Société Préhistorique Française* 95 (1998), figs. 5 and 6; **2.6** From G. Bailloud, C. Boujot et al., *Carnac, Les premières architectures de pierre*, CNRS (Paris, 1995), 113; **2.7** Jean-Marc Large, photo by Patrice Birocheau; **2.8** Maurice Gautier; **2.9** Multiple sources; **2.10** After G. Bailloud et al. (op. cit.), 89; **2.11** Hemis/Alamy Stock Photo; **2.12** After C. Scarre, *Landscapes of Neolithic Brittany* (Oxford, 2011), fig. 2.7; **2.13** After J. Lecornec, *Le Petit Mont, Arzon, Morbihan* (Rennes, 1994), fig. 8; **2.14** Thibault Poriel; **2.15** After P.-R. Giot, *Barnenez, Cairn, Guennoc* Vol. II (Rennes, 1987), figs. B2 and B3; **2.16** After C.-T. Le Roux, *Gavrinis et les Îles du Morbihan* (Paris, 1985), fig 13; **2.17** Robert Estall Photo Agency/Alamy Stock Photo; **2.18** Maurice Gautier; **2.20** After Z. Le Rouzic, *Carnac. Restaurations faites dans la région: Les cromlechs de Er-Lannic, commune d'Arzon de 1923 à 1926* (Vannes, 1930), Planche I; **2.21** After C. Scarre (op. cit.), fig. 2.7; **2.22** After J. L'Helgouac'h, *Les Sépultures mégalithiques en Armorique* (Rennes, 1965), fig. 84; **2.23** Author; **2.24** With courtesy of the CReAAH (Centre de Recherche en Archéologie, Archéosciences, Histoire) Joint Research Unit, archives of the Archéosciences laboratory, Rennes. Rights reserved; **2.25** Philip De Jersey; **2.26** From J. L'Helgouac'h, *Locmariaquer*, Éditions Jean-Paul Gisserot (Luçon, 1994), 24; **2.27** Hemis/Alamy Stock Photo; **2.28** After C.-T. Le Roux, 'Stone Axes of Brittany and the Marches' in T. H. McK Clough and W. A. Cummins (eds.), *Stone Axe Studies* (London, 1979), fig. 3; **2.29** © Clichés musées de Vannes; **2.30** After E. Ihuel, *La Diffusion du Silex du Grand-Pressigny dans la Massif Armoricain au Néolithique* (Paris, 2004), fig. 30; **2.31** After A. Sheridan, 'Neolithic connections along and across the Irish Sea' in V. Cummings and C. Fowler (eds.), *The Neolithic of the Irish Sea* (Oxford, 2004), fig. 2.2; and after A. Sheridan, 'French Connections I: Spreading the marmites thinly' in I. Armit et al. (eds.), *Neolithic Settlement in Ireland and Western Brittany* (Oxford, 2003), fig. 28.

Chapter 3 opener and 3.15: © Clichés musées de Vannes; **3.1** Author incorporating B. Cunliffe, *Facing the Ocean* (Oxford, 2001), fig. 6.5; **3.2** After P.-R. Giot et al., *Protohistoire de la Bretagne* (Rennes, 1995), 51; **3.3** After J. Briard, *Les Depôts Breton et l'Âge du Bronze Atlantique* (Rennes, 1965), figs. 2, 3 and 4; **3.4** © RMN-Grand Palais (musée d'Archéologie nationale)/Gérard Blot; **3.5** Service régional de l'archéologie de Bretagne, photo by Hervé Paitier/INRAP; **3.6** From P.-R. Giot et al., *Protohistoire de la Bretagne* (Rennes, 1995), 33; **3.7** After C.-T. Le Roux, 'Stone Axes of Brittany and the Marches' in T. H. McK Clough and W. A. Cummings (eds.), *Stone Axe Studies* (London, 1979), fig. 4; **3.8** After P.-R. Giot, Barnenez, Carn, Guennoc, Vol 2 (Rennes, 1987) C2'; **3.9** After J. Briard, *Les Tumulus d'Armorique* (Paris, 1984), fig. 4; **3.10** From P.-R. Giot et al., *Protohistoire de la Bretagne* (Rennes, 1995), 71; **3.11** From P.-R. Giot et al. (op. cit.), 89; **3.12** Maurice Gautier; **3.13** From P.-R. Giot et al. (op. cit.), 104; **3.14** After J. Briard, *Les Depôts Breton et l'Âge du Bronze Atlantique* (Rennes, 1965), figs. 22 and 391; **3.16** After J. Waddell, 'Celts, Celticization and the Irish Bronze Age' in J. Waddell and E. Twohig (eds.), *Ireland in the Bronze Age* (Dublin, 1995), fig. 60; **3.17** After K. Cleary and C. Gibson, 'Connectivity in Atlantic Europe during the Bronze Age (2800-800 B.C.)' in B. Cunliffe and J. T. Koch (eds.), *Exploring Celtic Origins* (Oxford, 2019), fig. 4.19; **3.18** After D. Brandherm and C. Burgess, 'Carp's-tongue problems' in *Durch die Zeiten* (Rahden, 2008), figs. 3 and 5; **3.19** © Clichés musées de Vannes; **3.20** After J. Briard (op. cit.), fig. 105 updated by J. Rivallain, Les Haches à Douille Revisitées (Rennes, 2012), fig. 79a; **3.21** © Clichés musées de Vannes; **3.22** © Clichés musées de Vannes.

Chapter 4 opener and 4.6: Heritage Image Partnership Ltd/Alamy Stock Photo; **4.1** After B. Cunliffe, *The Ancient Celts* (Oxford, 2018), map 29, with modifications; **4.2** From U. Schaaff, 'Eisenhelme aus vorrömischer Zeit' *Jahrb. Röm.-Germ.* Zentralmuseum, Mainz 21 (1974), abb. 26 and 27; **4.3** After P.-R. Giot et al., *Protohistoire de la Bretagne* (Rennes, 1995), 284; **4.4** After P.-R. Giot et al. (op. cit.), 285; **4.5** After M.-Y. Daire and A. Villard, 'Les stèles de l'âge du Fer à décors géométrique et curvilignes. État de la question dans l'Ouest Armoricain' *Revue Archéologique de l'Ouest* 13 (1996), fig. 11; **4.7** Heritage Image Partnership Ltd/Alamy Stock Photo; **4.8** Redrawn from M.-Y. Daire and A. Villard (op. cit.), fig 2; **4.9** Various sources including P. de Chatellier, *La Poterie aux époques préhistorique et gauloise en Armorique* (Rennes, 1897), Planche 14; **4.10** Redrawn from various sources from B. Cunliffe, 'Brittany and the Atlantic rim in the late first millennium B.C.' *Oxford Journal of Archaeology* 19 (2000), fig. 7; **4.11** After B. Cunliffe, *Iron Age Communities in Britain* (London, 2005), fig. 17.28 with additions; **4.12** Musée Saint-Raymond, Toulouse, photo by Jean-François Peiré; **4.13** Author; **4.14** Author; **4.15** After P. de Jersey, *Coinage in Iron Age Armorica* (Oxford, 1994), fig. 34; **4.16** © Clichés musées de Vannes; **4.17** After P. de Jersey (op. cit.), fig. 63; **4.18** Images from N. V. L. Rybot, *Armorican Art*, Société Jersiaise (St Helier, 1952) passim; **4.19** Maurice Gautier; **4.20** Redrawn after R. E. M. Wheeler and K. M. Richardson, *Hillforts of Northern France* (Oxford, 1957), pl. II; **4.21** Ian R Cartwright; **4.22** After B. Cunliffe, *Facing the Ocean* (Oxford, 2001), fig. 9.19.

Chapter 5 opener and 5.5: Author; **5.1** After B. Cunliffe, *Greeks, Romans and Barbarians: Spheres of Interaction* (London, 1988), fig. 49; **5.2** After J.-Y. Éveillard, *Les Voies Romaines en Bretagne* (Morlaix, 2016), 41 with additional details added; **5.3** After A. Provost et al., *L'Aqueduc de Vorgium/Carhaix (Finistère). Contribution à l'étude des aqueducs antique* (Paris, 2013); **5.4** Service régionale des affaires culturelles de Bretagne, photo by Michael Batt; **5.6** After P. Galliou and M. Jones, *The Bretons* (Oxford, 1991), fig. 16; **5.7** After P. Galliou, *L'Armorique Romaine* (Brest, 2005) fig. 58; **5.8** Collection et cliché Musée départemental breton, Quimper. © Musée départemental breton/ Serge Goarin; **5.9** After E. Ars, 'Le figurines gallo-romanes en terre cuite du Morbihan' *Bulletin de la Société Polymathique du Morbihan* 123 (1997), 45; **5.10** Redrawn from J. Lecornec, *Le Petit Mont, Arzon, Morbihan* (Rennes, 1994), figs. 63 and 66; **5.11** After B. Cunliffe, 'Venus arising' in H. Roche et al. (eds.), *From Megaliths to Metal* (Oxford, 2004), fig. 24.4; **5.12** Distributional information from J. Boislève et al., 'Décors peints à incrustations de coquillages en Armorique romaine' *Aremorica* 5 (2012), fig. 4, and L. Langouet and L. Quesnel, 'Les plaques décorées en schiste de la Bretagne armoricaine sous l'Empire romaine' *Revue Archéologique de l'Ouest* 17 (2000), fig. 1; **5.13** J. Boislève et F. Labaune-Jean, Inrap; **5.14** Coll. Musée de Dinan – Ville de Dinan; **5.15** Author, various sources; **5.16** Distributional information from P. Galliou, 'Western Gaul in the Third Century' in A. King and M. Henig (eds.), *The Roman West in the Third Century*. Contribution from *Archaeology and History* (Oxford, 1981), figs. 18.3 and 18.5; **5.17** Bibliothèque nationale de France; **5.18** Patrick André; **5.19** After B. Cunliffe and P. Galliou, *Les Fouilles du Yaudet en Ploulec'h, Côtes-d'Armor.* Vol. 2, fig. 266; **5.20** Author, multiple sources; **5.21** The Bodleian Libraries, The University of Oxford. Ms. Canon. Misc.378, fol 163r.

Chapter 6 opener and 6.14: Author; **6.1** From B. Cunliffe and P. Galliou, 'Bretons and Britons: some new evidence from Le Yaudet' *Archaeological Journal* 157 (2000), illus. 5; **6.2** Distributional information from B. Tanguy and M. Lagrée (eds.), *Atlas d'Histoire de Bretagne* (Morlaix, 2002), maps 23 and 24; and from P. Galliou and M. Jones, *The Bretons* (Oxford, 1991), fig. 18; **6.3** After E. Jones, *The Francs* (Oxford 1988), figs. 6 and 7; **6.4** After E. Jones (op. cit.), fig. 10; **6.5** After E. Jones (op. cit.), fig. 11; **6.6** Photo © Leonard de Selva/Bridgeman Images; **6.7** After P.-R. Giot, 'Ennez Guennoc ou Geignog, un ancien microcosme celtique' in *Mélanges d'archéologie et d'histoire médiévales en l'honneur du Doyen Michael de Boüard* (Paris, 1982), fig. 3; **6.8** After B. Cunliffe and P. Galliou, 'Bretons and Britons: some new evidence from Le Yaudet' *Archeological Journal* 157 (2000), illus. 3 and 6; **6.9** Author; **6.10** Author; **6.11** After P.-R. Giot, 'L'établissement et le cimetière de l'île Lavret près Bréhat' *Actes des VIe Journées nationales de l'Association française d'Archéologie mérovingienne*, Rennes, 1984 (Paris, 1987), 63;

6.12 After E. G. Bowen, *Saints, Seaways and Settlements* (Cardiff, 1977), fig. 45; **6.13** De Agostini/Albert Ceola/agefotostock; **6.15** (left) Jean-Jacques Czerniak; (right) from W. Davies et al., *The Inscriptions of Early Medieval Brittany* (Aberystwyth, 2000), fig. C 1.2; **6.16** After E. Campbell, *Continental and Mediterranean Imports to Atlantic Britain and Ireland, A.D. 400-800* (York, 2007), figs. 83 and 84; **6.17** After B. Tanguy and M. Lagrée (eds.), *Atlas d'Histoire de Bretagne* (Morlaix, 2002), map 25.

Chapter 7 opener and 7.2: Bibliothèque municipale de Boulogne-sur-Mer; **7.1** After A. Chédeville and H. Guillotel, *La Bretagne des saints et des rois Ve-Xe siècle* (Rennes, 1984), 209; **7.3** After R. Pérennec and A. Bardel, 'Landévennec, un monastère carolingien à la pointe de la Bretagne' in M. Coumert and Y. Tranvouez (eds.), *Landévennec, les Vikings et la Bretagne* (Brest, 2015), fig. 19; **7.4** Réalisation R. Gestin d'après A. Bardel et R. Pérennec, cl. A. Bardel; **7.5** After B. Tanguy and M. Lagrée (eds.) (op. cit.), map 26; **7.6** After J. Graham-Campbell et al. (eds.), *Cultural Atlas of the Viking World* (Oxford, 1994), 146; **7.7** Bibliothèque nationale de France/Bridgeman Images; **7.8** After J. Haywood, *The Historical Atlas of the Celtic World* (London, 2001), 69; **7.9** Maurice Gautier; **7.10** After N. S. Price, *The Vikings in Brittany* (London, 1989), fig. 31; **7.11** Catherine BIZIEN-JAGLIN. 2007; **7.12** After L. Langouet, *La Cité d'Alet* (Saint-Malo, 1996), fig. 96; **7.13** After B. Tanguy and M. Lagrée (eds.), *Atlas d'Histoire de Bretagne* (Morlaix, 2002), map 29; **7.14** Patrick KERNEVEZ, 1987; **7.15** (top) DeAgostini Picture Library/© Photo Scala, Florence; (bottom) Bridgeman Images.

Chapter 8 opener and 8.12: Bibliothèque nationale de France; **8.1** After A. Mackay and D. Ditchburn (eds.), *Atlas of Medieval Europe* (London, 1997), 70; **8.2** After M. Jones, *The Creation of Brittany* (London, 1988), 198; **8.3** MT 30307. Gift of Julien Chapée, 1924. © Lyon, Textile Arts Museum/musée des Tissus – Pierre Verrier; **8.4** Bibliothèque nationale de France; **8.5** BEGNE Bernard - Région Bretagne; **8.6** Purchase of 1834 by the Fondation Calvet © Fondation Calvet; **8.7** Maurice Gautier; **8.8** Hemis/Alamy Stock Photo; **8.9** Bibliothèque nationale de France; **8.10** National Museum of Wales; **8.11** After M. Jones, *The Creation of Brittany* (London, 1988), 16 (fig. 1); **8.13** Maurice Gautier; **8.14** Christophe Boisvieux/Alamy Stock Photo; **8.15** iStock.com/Guy-ozenne; **8.16** (left) Musée de Morlaix; (right) Margaret Herdman; **8.17** Hervé Champollion/akg-images.

Chapter 9 opener and 9.3: John Bentley/Alamy Stock Photo; **9.1** After B. Tanguy and M. Lagrée (eds.), *Atlas d'Histoire de Bretagne* (Morlaix, 2002), map 50; **9.2** After B. Tanguy and M. Lagrée (eds.) (op. cit.), map 47; **9.4** Stuart Black/Alamy Stock Photo; **9.5** After B. Tanguy and M. Lagrée (op. cit.), map 42; **9.6** (top) Photo © Leonard de

Selva/Bridgeman Images; (bottom) Bibliothèque nationale de France; **9.7** Collections Musée de Bretagne et Ecomusée du Pays de Rennes; **9.8** Hemis/Alamy Stock Photo; **9.9** After B. Tanguy and M. Lagrée (op. cit.), map 52; **9.10** mauritius images GmbH/ Alamy Stock Photo; **9.11** Distributions after J. Allan, 'Breton woodworkers in the immigrant communities of south-west England, 1500-1550' *Post-Medieval Archaeology 48* (2014), fig. 1; **9.12** John P. Allan; **9.13** © Région Bretagne, Service de l'Inventaire du patrimoine culturel, Bernard Bègne; **9.14** Collections Musée de Bretagne et Eco-musée du Pays de Rennes; **9.15** Special Collections, Princeton University Library; **9.16** Ackles29/Wikimedia Commons (CC BY-SA 3.0); **9.17** After R. Natkiel and A. Preston, *The Weidenfeld Atlas of Maritime History* (London, 1986), 76; **9.18** Margaret Herdman; **9.19** Bibliothèque nationale de France; **9.20** After B. Tanguy and M. Lagrée (eds.) (op. cit.), map 58; **9.21** Coll. Bibliothèque municipale de Dinan.

Chapter 10 opener and 10.7: Collection et cliché Musée départemental breton, Quimper. © Musée départemental breton/Serge Goarin; **10.1** After B. Tanguy and H. Lagrée (eds.) (op. cit.), map 55; **10.2** National Trust Images © Egremont Collection; **10.3** The Bodleian Libraries, The University of Oxford, 40.1071 (v.1), from T. A. Trol-lope, *A Summer in Brittany* (London, 1840), title page; **10.4** British Library, from T. A. Trollope (op. cit.); **10.5** Author's collection: from H. Blackburn, *Breton Folk* (London, 1884), illustrations by R. Caldecott, iv; **10.6** Author's collection: from H. Blackburn (op. cit.), opp. p. 62; **10.8** Author's collection: from A. Logan, 'Account of a visit to the monument usually considered as Druidical, at Carnac in Brittany' *Archaeologia* 22 (1829), fig. 1; **10.9** Courtesy of Guernsey Museums & Galleries (States of Guern-sey); **10.10** Author's collection: from J. Miln, *Fouilles faites à Carnac*, Morbihan (Paris, 1877), 244; **10.11** Burrell Collection/Bridgeman Images; **10.12** Courtesy National Gal-lery of Art, Washington; Collection of Mr. and Mrs. Paul Mellon; **10.13** Private collec-tion/Bridgeman Images; **10.14** National Galleries of Scotland, Edinburgh/Bridgeman Images; **10.15** Bibliothèque municipale de Rouen (Cote: Flaubert E2 p12); **10.16** After C. Drezen, 'Par les champs et par les grèves' in N. Richard and Y. Pallier, *Cent ans de tourism en Bretagne 1840-1940* (Rennes, 1996), 18; **10.17** Coll. Musée de la carte postale – Baud (56); **10.18** Author.

Chapter 11 opener and 11.7: Private collection/© Archives Charmet/Bridgeman Images; **11.1** © British Library Board. All Rights Reserved/Bridgeman Images; **11.2** © Ashmolean Museum/Mary Evans Picture Library; **11.3** The Bodleian Libraries, The University of Oxford, Gough Gen.Top.129(1), title page; **11.4** The Bodleian Librar-ies, The University of Oxford, MS.Eng. Misc.c.323, fol.1r(colour); **11.5** Bibliothèque nationale de France; **11.6** Collection bibliothèque municipale de Lyon; **11.8** Statens

Museum fur Kunst, Denmark; **11.9** Bibliothèque nationale de France; **11.10** Musée de Morlaix; **11.11** Jean-François du Cosquer; **11.12** Supplied by Llyfrgell Genedlaethol Cymru/The National Library of Wales; **11.13** Coll. Musée de la carte postale – Baud (56); **11.14** Author's collection; **11.15** Author's collection; **11.16** Author's collection.

Table 1 After A. Chédeville and H. Guillotel, *La Bretagne des saints et des rois Ve-Xe siècle* (Rennes, 1984), pp. 232, 356; **Table 2** After P. Galliou and M. Jones, *The Bretons* (Oxford, 1991), p. 191; **Table 3** After P. Galliou and M. Jones (op. cit.), p. 219.

The publisher apologizes for any errors or omissions in the above list. If contacted, they will be pleased to rectify these at the earliest opportunity.

Picture Research by Sandra Assersohn.

INDEX